Black Women's Intellectual Traditions

BLACK WOMEN'S INTELLECTUAL TRADITIONS

Speaking Their Minds

Edited by

Kristin Waters and Carol B. Conaway

University of Vermont Press
Burlington, Vermont

PUBLISHED BY UNIVERSITY PRESS OF NEW ENGLAND
HANOVER AND LONDON

University of Vermont Press
Published by University Press of New England,
One Court Street, Lebanon, NH 03766
www.upne.com
© 2007 by University of Vermont Press
Printed in the United States of America

5   4   3   2

Library of Congress Cataloging-in-Publication Data

Black women's intellectual traditions : speaking their minds /
edited by Kristin Waters and Carol B. Conaway.
p.   cm.
Includes bibliographical references and index.
ISBN-13: 978–1–58465–633–3 (cloth : alk. paper)
ISBN-10: 1–58465–633–6 (cloth : alk. paper)
ISBN-13: 978–1–58465–634–0 (pbk. : alk. paper)
ISBN-10: 1–58465–634–4 (pbk. : alk. paper)
1. African American women—Intellectual life—19th century.
2. African American women—Biography. 3. African American intellectuals—Biography.
4. African American women—Political activity—History—19th century.
5. African Americans—Politics and government—19th century.
6. African American philosophy. 7. Feminism—United States—History—
19th century. I. Waters, Kristin. II. Conaway, Carol B.
E185.86 .B5445
305.48'896073009034—dc22   2006035257

Chapter 1 has been reprinted in its entirety from "Introduction" in *Maria W. Stewart: America's First Black Woman Political Writer*, edited and introduced by Marilyn Richardson (Bloomington: Indiana University Press, 1987).

(Continued on page 463)

Dedicated to our mothers,

Shirley Barnard Waters and Aunita Napper Conaway

CONTENTS

ACKNOWLEDGMENTS

This collection of writings honors and acknowledges the nineteenth-century black women who courageously gave voice to their views against all efforts to silence them, and the twentieth- and twenty-first-century women whose works are collected here, who bring these ideas to voice again.

We would like to acknowledge and thank the University of New Hampshire and the Dean of the College of Liberal Arts, Marilyn Hoskin, as well as Thomas McNamara and Steve Bostic of the Worcester State College Foundation Board for supporting this research. We would also like to thank the UNH Center for the Humanities and its director, Burt Feintuch, for Carol Conaway's Faculty Fellowship Award. A special note of thanks goes to Mara Witzling and Linda Blum, coordinators of the UNH Women's Studies Program, and to Larry Prelli, chair of the UNH Department of Communication, for their sound counsel and support.

The careful comments of our reviewers, Lewis R. Gordon, Gertrude Gonzalez de Allen, and Charles Mills, helped to shape this volume. The Caribbean Philosophical Association has provided a comfortable space for discourse about Africana philosophy for many people who otherwise might find few places for discourse in this vital field.

We are extremely grateful to Diane Bell, Ann Bookman, Marla Brettschneider, Cynthia Enloe, Debbie Fisher, Julie Frechette, Rick Friedman, SunHee Gertz, Lewis and Jane Gordon, Marlene Karas, Ken Marshall, Dan Shartin, and Karen Turner for their astute criticisms, ongoing intellectual conversations, friendship, and generosity. Our editor, Ellen Wicklum of University Press of New England, has provided welcome encouragement throughout the project.

We are grateful to Don Vescio for his crucial technological assistance. We appreciate the clerical assistance of Samantha D'Ortona, Lu Houde, and Melanie Wilcox. For keeping body and soul together, we thank Doris Worcester and Jane Anable.

Kris would like to thank Carol, who has been an enduring friend, teacher, and stalwart editor. She honors her children, Jiaqi and Colin, for their sustaining presence and is very grateful for the quiet support provided by Ed O'Reilly. The care and encouragement of her parents, George and Shirley Waters, are very much appreciated. Her sister, Nancy Waters, never fails to provide friendship and support.

Carol extends special thanks to Suzanne V. Armstrong for her wisdom and encouragement, to Cicely Stetson for her proofreading, cheerleading, wisdom, and unending support that were always available and generously given, and to Kristin for her support, generosity, encouragement, and friendship at every stage in the development of this project.

Finally, Carol would like to acknowledge the memory of her parents, Carl and Aunita Napper Conaway, and grandparents, the Reverend Robert O. and Bertha Scott Napper, and Carl and Ada Taylor Conaway who, despite enduring horrible racism, led lives of accomplishment and distinction. Out of the ashes of slavery and degradation, a young child was expected to be the hope of her family. Their enormous sacrifices, devotion, and unending inspiration and faith in her inspired her to walk in their footsteps.

Black Women's Intellectual Traditions

Introduction

CAROL B. CONAWAY AND KRISTIN WATERS

> I ask no monument, proud and high,
> To arrest the gaze of passer-by,
> All that my yearning spirit craves,
> Is bury me not in a land of slaves.
> —Frances E. W. Harper, "Bury Me in a Freeland"

Far from being buried in a land of slaves, Frances E. W. Harper was buried in Eden. As editors, we discovered in preparing this anthology that Harper is buried in Eden Cemetery, just outside Philadelphia, the oldest black-owned cemetery in the United States. When we stumbled across this small fact, we were momentarily stunned. Many members of the national black intellectual and cultural elite, including William Still, "Father of the Underground Railroad," and contralto Marian Anderson join Harper there. But also buried in Eden cemetery are Carol's maternal grandparents, Reverend Robert Oliver Napper and Bertha Scott Napper, and when we learned that Harper shared the same burial place, we were deeply moved at the symbolic significance of this coincidence. Her biographer, Frances Smith Foster, calls Harper "the best known and best loved poet of her time," and I. Garland Press called her "the journalistic mother . . . of so many brilliant young women" writers.[1] And yet how many of us, like Carol, might have walked past Harper's grave and not known her legacy? This anthology is a step toward reclaiming the legacies of Harper and other nineteenth-century black women whose lives we otherwise might have "walked past" without knowing and appreciating their remarkable contributions to the traditions of black thought.

Black women's intellectual traditions in North America span almost four centuries. Their voices range as far and as deep as the more well-rehearsed contemporary ones, but one may have to listen especially carefully to hear them. These traditions have been transmitted orally and in writing, through religious teachings, speeches and texts, domestic arts and everyday activities. From before the formation of the nation, poetry and song conveyed beliefs about power and resistance, as well as particular notions of community and spirituality, family and labor. As literary critic Barbara Christian observed in 1990, "My folk . . . have always been a race for theory—though more in the form of the hieroglyph, a written figure which is both sensual and abstract, both beautiful and communicative."[2]

As Christian notes, theory comes in many forms. The complex traditions of black feminism emerge from the essays of Maria W. Stewart, Frederick Douglass, and Anna Julia Cooper, the preaching of Sojourner Truth, the lectures of Ida B. Wells, the novels of Frances E. W. Harper and Pauline Hopkins, and many other sources. Some work comes in the form of the hieroglyph; much of it benefits from interpretation and amplification. As with all social, political, and literary theory, interpretative works such as the ones in this volume can expose systematic thought—trace the outlines, uncover the formal structures and themes, develop and build upon the original material until a body of work emerges that carries force and power in contemporary argument.

The novels of Toni Morrison and Alice Walker are well known, but they rarely are seen as connected to a long history of ideas. Why have black feminist theories been so obscured? In her landmark book, *Black Feminist Thought: Knowledge, Consciousness, and the Politics of Empowerment*, sociologist Patricia Hill Collins details the ways that dominant epistemologies and power structures erase subordinate ones. Using economic, political, and ideological means, power works hegemonically to deny credibility to the theoretical productions of black women, or even to deny that such theories exist. She writes:

> The shadow obscuring this complex Black women's intellectual tradition is neither accidental nor benign. Suppressing the knowledge produced by any oppressed group makes it easier for dominant groups to rule because the seeming absence of dissent suggests that subordinate groups willingly collaborate in their own victimization. Maintaining the victimization of

Black women and our ideas not only in the United States, but in Africa, the Caribbean, South America, Europe and other places where Black women now live, has been critical in maintaining social inequalities.[3]

In the past, restrictions on and obstacles to literacy, public speaking, publishing, writing, and reading meant that women's voices often were not heard. Even now, the gatekeepers deny their work entrance to the canon, the hate-mongers ridicule them, and the elite ignores them. As Dale Spender argues, how can we begin to gain access to power when each succeeding generation must spend its time "rediscovering" the works of the past?[4]

That black women's theoretical traditions often are unrecognized diminishes their effectiveness as instruments of contemporary political power. A parent, community leader, or politician need only allude to a well-established concept of liberalism or conservatism to have the intellectual weight of the centuries favor her or his argument. Yet when black women speak, if they are heard at all, their thoughtful assertions often are viewed as issuing from nowhere, lacking theoretical substance, disconnected from long-standing systems of classic Western thought. Thus, not only is there theoretical value to affirming black feminist intellectual production, but there are also serious implications for activism and political power.

This collection of essays joins a growing body of work that serves as a corrective to the prevailing view that no long-standing black women's intellectual traditions exist. We use the plural, "traditions," quite consciously, because the thoughts and expressions of black women follow a variety of different threads, for example, the more radical activism of Ida B. Wells and the more mainstream writings of Anna Julia Cooper. Black feminism is not a single unified body of thought, although there are common themes. By following these threads into the present, this book demonstrates a continuum of black women's ideas that moves alongside, or in opposition to, the white discourses of feminism, liberalism, socialism, conservatism, and so on.

Since the intellectual productions of women, and especially black women, often have been *silenced*, making these theorists heard and recognized is of central importance. Self-generated and authentic "voices" constitute a powerful means of reclaiming the territory of black women's intellectual production. Do not walk past these intellects and activists. Listen carefully to their voices and the voices of those who elucidate and amplify their work, bringing their legacies into the present. Christian proposes "reading and studying the history and literature of black women, a history that had been totally ignored, a contemporary literature bursting with originality, passion, insight and beauty."[5] The essays in this volume reveal the intellectual stature of these black foremothers and their far-reaching contributions.

Part I: Maria W. Stewart

Widely recognized as one of the first women in the United States to speak publicly to an audience of men and women, black and white, Maria W. Stewart is someone whose work is radical, even revolutionary. She wrote for abolitionist William Lloyd Garrison's prominent journal, *The Liberator,* and lectured at the African American Meeting House in Boston in the 1830s. Slave rebellions were common in the 1820s, and in his *Appeal to the Coloured Citizens of the World,* David Walker advocated various forms of rebellion and resistance.[6] Walker was a friend of Stewart's, and after his demise she carried on his message, expanding it to address issues of gender, virtue, women's historical accomplishments, and sexism in the black community.

This anthology opens with the meticulous historical work of Marilyn Richardson, the scholar who produced the first major biographical study of Stewart and who carefully researched and reproduced Stewart's original texts to make her work widely available. Richardson's chapter puts Stewart's life into historical context and reveals her political thought and activism in detail.

The next chapter focuses on the practice of women organizing to develop their intellectual capabilities and to unite in Christian love to uplift the race. Lena Ampadu argues that Stewart followed what has been called a "sublimated path" to ministry, since religious preaching was not an occupation open to women. (These themes are picked up in Carla Peterson's chapter on Truth in part II and Karen Baker-Fletcher's on Cooper in part IV.) Stewart develops a form of religious abolitionism, and according to Ampadu her essays should be recognized as original contributions to the black sermonic tradition.

Ebony Utley further develops this theme and addresses Stewart's reinvention of herself through her rhetoric as a way of making an effective and persuasive political argument. It follows that the sermonic tradition is not just about preaching the words of God; it is about using a particular form of address to create the maximum political effect within the most acceptable rhetorical or social norms. Even within this framework, Stewart pushes the conventions to extremes, showing innovation and daring in both the form and content of her work.

Dianne Bartlow's chapter concludes the section by making the links between Stewart's innovations and second-wave black feminism. She connects Stewart's work with that of Patricia Hill Collins, Barbara Christian, Beverly Guy-Sheftall, Margaret Anderson, Katie Cannon, Paula Giddings, Jacqueline Grant, and Cheryl Townsend Gilkes. Bartlow fulfills the promise made by this book to weave the past into the present by following the threads developed by Stewart into contemporary discourse.

The elusive Stewart emerges as someone better known and understood. She can be seen to stand squarely in the camp of radical politics, carefully traversing the dangerous terrain of limited speech for women and blacks with a message of uplift but also of treasonous rebellion. As someone whose work is beginning to command its own canon of interpretation, her sophisticated analysis is emerging as the founding voice of black feminist theory. This section represents the first collection of essays about her work gathered in one volume.

Part II: Incidents in the Lives

Hazel Carby's reputation was sealed with *Reconstructing Womanhood: The Emergence of the Afro-American Woman Novelist*, published in 1987.[7] In the selection from her book reprinted here, Carby attends to the complicated, coercive, and often brutal ways in which whites treated black women. The culture of oppression made it much more difficult to develop empowering ideas about what it meant to be a black woman with limited control over sexuality and motherhood. Yet, women like the world traveler Nancy Prince and the former slave Linda Brent manage to address issues of sexuality and motherhood in ways that defy conventional morality and reclaim dignity for black women, as Carby reveals.

Michele Garfield traces the activities of a group of free black women in a Philadelphia literary society. Within the broader goal of promoting racial uplift, these societies had two purposes: first, to create a rigorous program of intellectual improvement that included reading, presenting essays, and subjecting each other's work to criticism, and second, finding ways to express opposition to slavery. In the first case, they "pushed education beyond the rudiments of literacy and encouraged blacks to embrace the vision of a black intelligentsia." In the second case, their goals remind us that in the 1830s, and even today, "the world of black female activism is 'hidden in plain view.'"

The third chapter in part II tackles the difficult subject of the great feminist abolitionist Sojourner Truth, an icon whose primary representations in her time were through the voices of the white women who wrote her "autobiographies." Carla Peterson, one of the foremost interpreters of Truth's work, argues that Truth nonetheless managed to recraft herself as "a sign possessing historical agency," as "a sign unto this nation," to use Truth's phrase, in defiance of the efforts of others to control her symbolic meaning in the context of her national fame. Truth used oratory, her portrayal in photographs, and other modes of presentation including speech styles that drew on African culture to assess the state of the nation—the United States—and call it to account. As such, she is a "doer of the word," to use the title phrase from Peterson's acclaimed book.

Part III: Harper, Hopkins and Shadd Cary

The next two chapters focus on the work of Frances Ellen Watkins Harper, one the most prolific black American writers of the nineteenth century. Classically educated, Harper was a poet, essayist, novelist, and social activist, one of the best-known black women of her time. Both she and Pauline Hopkins recognized the potential political power of fiction. In her essay on the novelists, Vanessa Diana uncovers a literary device of twinning used to amplify the figurative elements of fiction in ways that dramatize political messages for the reader. Both novelists use the conventional form of the sentimental novel to explore "the family tree" and marriage in ways that reveal patterns of resistance to the dominant social norms. Through their fiction, they create concepts of citizenship and nationhood that critique existing society and create models of a more egalitarian future.

Valerie Palmer-Mehta shifts the focus from Harper's fiction to two of her major addresses: one, "We Are All Bound Up Together" from the beginning of her career as an activist, delivered at the eleventh National Women's Rights Convention in 1866, and the other, "Women's Political Future," presented more than twenty-five years later at the Chicago World's Fair in 1893. This essay explores themes such as experiential epistemologies, essentialism, activism, and the ways in which racism in the white feminist movement, then and today, often forces black women to prioritize racism above sexism.

In the final chapter of this section, Carol Conaway addresses the strong tradition and savvy understanding among African Americans regarding the use of newspapers as a major conveyance of information, ideology, and subversive text. She develops distinctions between separatists and integrationists, nativists and emigrationists to explore black-generated theories about how to solve the race problems in North America. Shadd Cary became a prominent journalist, starting a newspaper to further her views. In keeping with her philosophy, she moved to Canada, where she worked to shape the beliefs of a newly free black collectivity.

Part IV: Anna Julia Cooper

After slavery, the dialogue about race underwent a radical transformation. Verbal formulations moved away from the rhetoric of violence and revolution found in Stewart's work. Anna Julia Cooper, a graduate of Oberlin College who was to go on to earn a Ph.D. from the Sorbonne, like Harper, was a classically educated intellectual who was a model and an advocate of racial uplift, an educator and essayist of prominent national stature. Mary Helen Washington accomplished for Anna Julia Cooper what Marilyn Richardson has done for Maria W. Stewart: Through extensive research, advocacy and publication, she reclaimed Cooper as an activist intellectual and put her back in the limelight after decades of obscurity. The biographical tenor of this selection is augmented by the revelations about Cooper's treatment by a white establishment intent on discrediting black accomplishment, and it provides a morality tale about how race politics function today.

In her book *A Singing Something: Womanist Reflections on Anna Julia Cooper*, theologian and scholar Karen Baker-Fletcher argues that Cooper has developed a distinctive black womanist theology.[8] In the selections from the book reprinted here in chapter 12, Baker-Fletcher addresses Cooper's place alongside Harper and others who proclaim this post-bellum period to be "the Woman's Era," and who develop a distinctive theory of women's, especially black women's, special role as educators, as moral leaders, as knowledge-producers, and as religious guides.

Janice Fernheimer argues that several decades after slavery ended, many whites still had a hard time recognizing that blacks were indeed fully human, much less capable of advanced intellectual thought. Fernheimer shows how Cooper's rhetorical sophistication enables her to work within the familiar vocabularies such as those set forth by Ralph Waldo Emerson to argue against popular ideas, including Social Darwinism.

Part V: Leadership, Activism, and the Genius of Ida B. Wells

Olga Idriss Davis picks up the theme of "voice" central to Cooper's work and follows it into the praxis of Ida B. Wells, who "challenged the master narrative of lynching by employing a liberatory discourse" that appealed to black women's political consciousness. Positing "voice" as a "rhetorical strategy of otherness," she connects Wells's work with slave narratives and ways of creating a womanist culture of resistance.

Melina Abdullah argues that because leadership standards most commonly are evaluated against white and masculinist models, the more subtle and subversive leadership styles of black women go almost unnoticed. Abdullah uncovers several features of black women's leadership by investigating the anti-lynching activism of Ida B. Wells and the black women's club movements, demonstrating their strengths.

Joy James develops the concept of "shadowboxing" to describe the covert status of black women's intellectual production. Yet, in her treatment of Wells, she uncovers a model of radical black feminism that has little of the genteel qualities of other post-Reconstruction writers such as Anna Julia Cooper. Wells uses her voice, in speeches and newspaper editorials, to reveal the ugly truth that the rule of law did not apply to African Americans and that whites were free, through lynching, to murder blacks brutally as a spectacle for the delight of white families across the South. The analogue for this might be the racist legal system of today that disproportionately incarcerates African Americans; only now, instead of the spectacle of lynching as entertainment for whites, the scope of black segregation and incarceration is more hidden, with only selected media images feeding the prevailing racist ideologies.

Part VI: Creating Black Feminist Theory

Kristin Waters' chapter focuses on the themes that unify black feminist thought and provide coherence to the disparate writings by nineteenth-century black women. For example, while white Christianity is often a force of oppression for blacks, black forms of Christianity provide spiritual succor and moral ammunition against racial violence. Addressing the gendered conception of ethics, the multiplicity of oppressions, control of sexuality and reproduction, and of knowledge and education, Waters identifies and chronicles an impressive continuum of thought that takes its place alongside standard social and political theories, one which provides a consistent critique of the revered canon.

The next chapter is Patricia Hill Collins' now classic opening chapter of her book, *Black Feminist Thought: Knowledge, Consciousness, and the Politics of Empowerment.* Collins uses Maria W. Stewart as the paradigm example of a black feminist whose work needs to be recovered from obscurity. She identifies Stewart as one who "urged Black women to forge self-definitions of self-reliance and independence," and lay "a vital analytical foundation for a distinctive standpoint on self, community, and society and, in doing so, created a Black women's intellectual tradition."[9] Collins develops the themes of exploitation of black women's labor, the political dimensions of oppression, and the controlling images of black women. Using these themes, Collins develops the dual notions of activism and thought that unite to form a distinct black feminist theory.

On the practical side, these essays propose concrete ways of directing academic research to bring about a more objective understanding of black feminism. As Evelyn M. Simien shows in the final chapter, social science research methodologies, including large-scale polls and studies, often are designed in ways that force black women respondents to choose between race and gender identities. These studies fail to capture the multiple consciousness that is a signature feature of black feminism.

To do justice to black women of the past, present, and future, contemporary research must be designed in ways that allow sensitive exploration into the particular conditions faced by many black women historically and the multifaceted ideas that emerge from these conditions. These essays reveal the intellectual legacy that black activists have known in their hearts but lacked access to because of the dearth of published scholarly research. They lay the groundwork for recognizing a tradition of black feminist theory that extends over several centuries.

Notes

We wish to thank Valerie Palmer-Mehta and Daniel Shartin for assistance with the introduction.

1. Frances Smith Foster, ed., *A Brighter Day Coming: A Frances Ellen Watkins Harper Reader* (New York: The Feminist Press at the City University of New York, 1990), 5.

2. Barbara Christian, "A Race for Theory," in *The Black Feminist Reader*, ed. Joy James and T. Denean Sharpley-Whiting (Malden, Mass.: Blackwell, 2000), 12.

3. Patricia Hill Collins, *Black Feminist Thought: Knowledge, Consciouness, and the Politics of Empowerment*, 2nd ed. (New York: Routledge, 2000), 3.

4. Dale Spender, *Women of Ideas and What Men Have Done to Them* (London: Routledge and Kegan Paul, 1982).

5. Christian, "A Race for Theory," 11.

6. Peter P. Hinks, ed., *David Walker's Appeal to the Coloured Citizens of the World* (University Park: Pennsylvania State University Press, 2000).

7. Hazel V. Carby, *Reconstructing Womanhood: The Emergence of the Afro-American Woman Novelist* (New York: Oxford University Press, 1987).

8. Karen Baker-Fletcher, *A Singing Something: Womanist Reflections on Anna Julia Cooper* (New York: Crossroad Press, 1994).

9. Collins, *Black Feminist Thought*, 5.

Part I

Maria W. Stewart

Black Feminism in Public Places

Chapter 1

Maria W. Stewart

America's First Black Woman Political Writer

MARILYN RICHARDSON

In Boston, Massachusetts, on August 10, 1826, little more than a month after the July 4 deaths of both John Adams and Thomas Jefferson, Maria Miller and James W. Stewart stood before the Rev. Thomas Paul and exchanged their marriage vows.[1] The bride, a young woman of twenty-three, and "one of the most beautiful and loveliest of women," had been born in Hartford, Connecticut, in 1803. She was orphaned at the age of five, and was soon, by her account, "bound out in a clergyman's family," where she remained until the age of fifteen. After that, it appears that she supported herself through employment as a domestic servant. During those years of servitude, she struggled to gather isolated fragments of an education when and where she could, attending Sabbath school classes which offered the rudiments of literacy along with religious instruction.[2]

The groom, "a tolerably stout well built man; a light, bright mulatto," was some years his wife's senior.[3] He had served in the War of 1812 on three different ships, including the *Guerriere* under Stephen Decatur, and had been captured and held for a time as a prisoner of war. An independent businessman, he worked as a shipping agent engaged in outfitting whaling and fishing vessels from offices at 83 Broad Street.[4] While the couple were to have no children of their own, James Stewart entered into the marriage, his first, acknowledging one, possibly two, illegitimate daughters.[5]

The officiating clergyman, Rev. Thomas Paul (1773–1831), was the founding minister of Boston's African Baptist Church, a spiritual, intellectual, and political focal point of the black community. A dignified, urbane, and attractive man, known as an exuberant and cultivated speaker, Paul was a leading figure in the movement for Independent Negro Baptist churches in the United States. His church, on Belknap Street on the north side of Beacon Hill, was located in the African Meeting House, where Stewart was to give one of her early speeches. Founded in 1805, the building housed as well an independent black school. It was in this building, in the early 1830s, that the first meetings of the New England Abolitionist Society would be held.

Following their union, Maria Miller Stewart adopted at her husband's request his middle initial, "W," as part of her own signature.[6] As they were joined in marriage, Maria Miller and James W. Stewart, in their choice of locale and officiant for their wedding ceremony, suggested a sympathy for black social and political causes.

The newlyweds settled in as members of Boston's small black middle class. Between 1820 and 1830, the city's black population increased by 185 individuals to a total of 1,875 members, 3 percent of a total population of 61,392.[7] The City Directory for 1826 lists blacks employed in a variety of occupations. They worked as waiters, coachmen, sailors, barbers and hairdressers, dealers in new and used clothing, tailors, wood sawyers, musicians, and teamsters, among other jobs. The great majority of men, however, are listed simply as laborers. Black women are listed as cooks, launderesses, and proprietors of boarding houses. There are two ministers in the directory; no physicians or attorneys. The largest concentration of black families lived on the lower North slope of Beacon Hill in an area known to the larger community as Nigger Hill.[8] In a community where economic opportunity for most blacks was restricted by attitude and custom if not strictly by law, many of the better-off black Bostonians were not content to enjoy their relative security and prosperity without regard to the situation of the vast majority of their fellow blacks, both North and South. Such men and women were aware of the extent of the domestic and international political unrest which characterized the decade of the 1820s. Black publications such as *Freedom's Journal* kept them abreast of, in the words of its editors, "whatever concerns us as a people . . . interwoven with all the principal news of the day."[9] They followed with interest the news of liberation struggles in Greece and Poland, and saw in the unification of Haiti, as well as in slave uprisings in the West Indies and the

Denmark Vesey plot in Charleston, South Carolina, a few years earlier, harbingers and incentives for anti-slavery ferment in America.[10]

The year of the Stewarts' marriage saw the founding of the Massachusetts General Colored Association, an organization dedicated to the betterment of local conditions and to agitation for the abolition of slavery. Among its most active and outspoken members was a tall, slender, dark-skinned, southern-born man, the son of a free black mother and a slave father. David Walker (1785–1830) kept a clothing shop on Brattle Street in Boston. Although his business prospered, Walker, due to his personal generosity, lived close to the financial edge. His home, close by the African Meeting House, was well known as a refuge for those in need; "His hands were always open to contribute to the wants of the fugitive," wrote Henry Highland Garnet, who described him further as "emphatically a self-made man, . . . [who] spent all his leisure moments in the cultivation of his mind."[11] David Walker's influence on Maria Stewart was to prove profound and enduring.

A voracious reader and spirited writer, Boston agent for *Freedom's Journal* and one of its contributors, Walker, in 1829, published the first edition of *Walker's Appeal, In Four Articles; Together With A Preamble, To The Coloured Citizens Of The World, But In Particular, And Very Expressly, To Those Of The United States Of America.* "This little book," declared Garnet, "produced more commotion amongst slaveholders than any volume of its size that was ever issued from an American press."[12]

Walker's incendiary manifesto was divided into four sections: "Our Wretchedness in Consequence of Slavery"; "Our Wretchedness in Consequence of Ignorance"; "Our Wretchedness in Consequence of the Preachers of the Religion of Jesus Christ"; and "Our Wretchedness in Consequence of the Colonizing Scheme." He denounced American slavery as the most vicious form of bondage known to history. A deeply religious man, whose writing is filled with biblical references and theological reflections, he found slavery in America all the more odious because it was supported by a supposedly Christian populace. He argued at length against the Jeffersonian principles of white supremacy expounded in *Notes on Virginia*, which served to maintain all blacks, slave or free, in the status of inferior human beings. By way of rebuttal, he presented historical evidence of the achievements of "the sons of Africa or of Ham, among whom learning originated."[13]

Education, Walker contended, would go far toward enabling blacks to take the initiative for reversing their fortunes in this country. Such initiative might well, however, because of white intransigence, take a violent turn. "They want us for their slaves," he wrote, "and think nothing of murdering us to subject us to that wretched condition—therefore, if there is an *attempt* made by us, kill or be killed."[14]

Walker's business was apparently what was known as a "slop shop" where bartenders sold the gear they regularly took from sailors in exchange for drinks. Proprietors of such shops would in turn sell the gear to ship's pursers or to seamen preparing for another voyage. Historian Charles Wiltse suggests that Walker would:

> undoubtedly "plant" the pamphlet in the ample pockets of the jackets and trousers he sold to sailors bound for Southern ports. There, he was confident, the garments would again be bartered for drink, and again fall into the hands of Negro dealers who would know what to do with them. Walker probably also had more certain contacts among Negro seamen and with pursers and stewards sympathetic to his cause.[15]

And who among his Boston colleagues would be better situated to help further such a scheme than James W. Stewart, ship's outfitter? This collusion, which must for the moment remain speculation based on Stewart's position as the only black man of his profession listed in the Boston Directory of the time, could have lasted for only a few months, however, for by December, Stewart had taken to his bed with an illness severe enough to prompt him to draw up his last will and testament. On 17 December 1829, he died.[16]

Left a widow after barely three years of marriage, Maria Stewart found herself, in the depths of her grief, deceived and victimized by a group of white businessmen intent on profiting from her husband's death. As the result of a series of legal maneuvers so blatant and shameless that even the presiding judge found them hard to stomach—at one point a mystery woman was put forth as a competing widow—Stewart, after more than two years of litigation, ended up effectively stripped of what should have amounted to a substantial inheritance.[17]

Such abuses were not, by Walker's account, uncommon in the Boston of that day. In the first section of his *Appeal*, he described Stewart's circumstances with uncanny prescience. "In this very city," he wrote, "when a man of color dies, if he owned any real estate it most generally falls into the hands of some white person. The wife and children of the deceased may weep and lament if they please, but the estate will be kept snug enough by its white possessor."[18]

A year after her husband's death, Stewart suffered the further loss of her political and intellectual mentor as well. A high price had been put on Walker's head. According to Garnet, a group of men in Georgia offered ten thousand dollars to anyone who would capture him alive; one thousand dead.[19] Walker's friends and family urged him to cross into Canada. He chose to stand his ground, declaring that although somebody must die in the cause, "it is not in me to falter if I can promote the work of emancipation." "He was soon," Garnet wrote of Walker's mysterious death in 1830, "laid in the grave." "It was the opinion of many," he continued, "that he was hurried out of life by the means of poison, but whether this was the case or not, the writer is not prepared to affirm."[20] The cause of Walker's death was investigated and debated without resolution by his contemporaries and remains a mystery to this day.[21]

"For several years," Stewart wrote, "my heart was in continual sorrow." Her anguish at her husband's death, which she described in one of her published religious meditations, led her to reassess the place of religion in her life. Although she had been previously affiliated with the First African Baptist Church, it appears that Stewart underwent a conversion or "born again" experience which deepened her religious commitment. Her belief became both more personal and more central to her daily life, leading to what anthropologist Paul Radin in his discussion of black conversion experiences refers to as a "new individuation, [and] inward reintegration," whereby she gave herself over to a secular ministry of political and religious witness.[22]

With her conversion there came to Stewart the understanding that her new allegiance to the will of God would place her in conflict with many of the ways of the world, making her a "warrior" and even a potential martyr for "the cause of oppressed Africa." Nonetheless, moved by "holy indignation," she began to write and to speak out publicly against tyranny, victimization, and injustice as she felt them affecting her life, her community, and her nation. "In 1831 [I] made a public profession of my faith in Christ," she declared in the document which stands as the first political manifesto written by a black American woman, and pronounced herself willing to place her faith at the service of social activism, as a "strong advocate for the cause of God and for the cause of freedom."[23]

From the start, her religious vision and her socio-political agenda were intrinsically bound together, defined one by the other.

> From the moment I experienced the change I felt a strong desire . . . to devote the remainder of my days to piety and virtue and now possess that

spirit of independence that, were I called upon, I would willingly sacrifice my life for the cause of God and my brethren. All the nations of the earth are crying out for liberty and equality. Away, away with tyranny and oppression! And shall Afric's sons be silent any longer?[24]

An opponent not only of slavery, but also of political and economic exploitation, she invoked both the Bible and the Constitution of the United States as documents proclaiming the universal birthright to justice and freedom. Resistance to oppression was, for Stewart, the highest form of obedience to God.

Religion and social justice are so closely allied in her analysis that, to her mind, one could not be properly served without a clear commitment to the other. The centrality of her faith in both her public and private lives is apparent in her speeches and essays, but most strongly expressed in a volume of religious meditations published in 1832.[25] An avid student of both the Old and New Testaments, Stewart appears to have practiced a doctrinal eclecticism, over the years affiliating herself at various times with Methodist, Baptist, and Episcopal congregations. Throughout her work, her faith in divine immanence in human affairs is set against a pragmatic political perspective which enables her to examine the plight of blacks North and South in a broad historical context. Her earliest work set forth those dynamic elements of her ideology which continued to shape her social gospel over the ensuing years: the inestimable value of education; the historical inevitability of black liberation, through violent means if necessary; the need for black unity and collective action; and the special responsibilities of women.

Stewart's initial political arguments grew out of a black protest and abolitionist tradition independent of the later white and integrated organizations which went on to advance the cause of New England abolitionism. Her work carried forward themes prevalent in the progressive black political climate of the day, and sounded in such publications as the aforementioned *Freedom's Journal*, a black newspaper founded in 1827 by Samuel Cornish and John B. Russwurm. "We wish to plead our own cause," they wrote in their inaugural issue, "too long have others spoken for us." They went on to extoll the importance of education, economic independence, and political activism against slavery and discrimination, all causes championed by both Walker and Stewart.

As did Walker, whose son born following his father's death was given the middle name of Garrison, Stewart affiliated herself with white activists who did not at first share her unqualified militance. When, in the fall of 1831, Stewart went to call on William Lloyd Garrison at the offices of his recently established abolitionist newspaper, *The Liberator,* she brought with her a completed manuscript statement of her challenge to the black community to "Sue for your rights and privileges. Know the reason that you cannot attain them." In this essay, published a mere two months after Nat Turner's insurrection, Stewart leveled a warning to whites that "our souls are fired with the same love of liberty and independence with which your souls are fired, . . . we are not afraid of them that kill the body and after that can do no more." At the time, Garrison was still hedging on the matter of his admiration for the late Walker's firebrand call to black self-defense.

Arriving at the *Liberator* office at No. 11 Merchant's Hall, Stewart entered a large room with "dingy walls; the small windows besmattered with printer's ink; the press standing in one corner . . . the bed of the editor and publisher on the floor."[26] There Garrison and his colleague Isaac Knapp struggled with meager material resources to publish the weekly journal which was to become a major voice and chronicle of the anti-slavery movement. As they announced in their first issue, they had "formed their copartnership with a determination to print the paper as long as they [could] subsist upon bread and water . . . The friends of the cause [might] therefore take courage; its enemies [might] surrender at discretion."[27] Around and about there stalked a friendly cat who kept the journalists company and "protected them from the depredations of mice." That day, as author and editor discussed the extraordinary document which was her pioneering statement of her religious, abolitionist, and feminist views, there began a friendship and professional affiliation which would see much of what Stewart was to write published first in *The Liberator* and later, by Garrison and Knapp, as pamphlets and volumes for sale in the anti-slavery cause. Ironically, Stewart's essays, calling for the liberation of all human potential, black and white, male and female, were, for the sake of editorial propriety according to the conventions of the day, relegated to the paper's "Ladies' Department."

In a letter to Stewart written almost fifty years later, Garrison recalled his first meeting with the young writer. Commenting that he had been impressed by her "intelligence and excellence of character," he remembered her as well as a young matron "in the flush and promise of ripening womanhood, with a graceful form and a pleasing countenance." "Soon after I started the publication of *The Liberator,*" he wrote:

you made yourself known to me by coming into my office and putting into my hands, for criticism and friendly advice, a manuscript embodying your devotional thoughts and aspirations, and also various essays pertaining to the condition of that class with which you were complexionally identified . . . You will recollect, if not the surprise, at least the satisfaction I expressed on examining what you had written . . . I not only gave you words of encouragement, but in my printing office put your manuscript into type, an edition of which was struck off in tract form.[28]

Thus appeared the 1831 edition of the pamphlet, *Religion And The Pure Principles Of Morality, The Sure Foundation On Which We Must Build*. In that essay, composed in the wake of Walker's untimely death, Stewart declared herself at the outset prepared to face the possibility of similar consequences for her outspoken militant activism. "Many will suffer for pleading the cause of oppressed Africa," she wrote, "and I shall glory in being one of her martyrs." She was able to sustain such equilibrium through her faith that "[God] is able to take me to himself, as he did the most noble, fearless, and undaunted David Walker."[29]

Further evidence of Walker's influence is apparent in Stewart's assumptions about her audience. As did he, whether she was writing or speaking, she addressed herself squarely to black audiences. In discussing the heated response to Walker's *Appeal*, Garnet comments that he had many enemies, "not a few of whom were his brethren . . . They said that he went too far, and was making trouble."[30] Stewart likewise was determined to speak her mind despite the possibility that her caustic frankness in dissecting causes and proposing severe cures for problems within the black community might alienate some in her black audience and reinforce racist stereotypes in the minds of whites. She trusted the inherent strength and potential of the black community to absorb the trauma of naming the sources of disorder and disunity as prerequisite to finding solutions for complex problems, many imposed by outside forces controlling black life in a manner at once irrational and calculating.

Remarkable in the number and range of issues she chose to address, Stewart saw strengths and weaknesses in both black and white life. She urged her audiences to adopt certain habits of mind and character which she felt helped to keep whites strong and powerful, while warning them to resist the worldly temptations which she saw as eroding will and ambition in her community. She asked her people to prove black virtue equal to any white standard, while challenging in turn her sisters and brothers to transcend what she recognized as the hypocrisy of many of those professed standards.

Not that Stewart was indifferent to white opinion. Her eager encouragement to blacks to prove that "Though black your skins as shades of night/Your hearts are pure, your souls are white," shows her as more than merely vulnerable to the racist iconography of the day. She was at times an early advocate of the position that whites, shown irrefutable evidence of black worthiness, refinement, virtue, and ability, would be awakened to the inherent equality of the races and, spontaneously perhaps, be moved to repent of ever having degraded a people in whom "nothing is wanting . . . but opportunity," and welcome them into the mainstream of American life. Blind though it might be to political reality, that attitude, based on the seductive optimism of belief in the innate goodness and rationality of human nature, in the nineteenth-century doctrine of social perfectionism, and in the promise of a prize—acceptance—to be won through hard work and clean living, has long persisted as one thread in the weave of black social thought.

Stewart was clearly stung by the atmosphere of casual racial insult which was tolerated in the Boston of her day. Blacks lived in segregated housing in a few crowded areas of the city. They were restricted to special sections on public transportation, in lecture halls, and in places of entertainment. They were, as Prince Hall, a founder of the black Masonic movement, had complained sometime earlier, subjected to "daily insults met in the streets," some of which occasionally led to fisticuffs, and were not safe in some parts of the city.[31] Morale and self-esteem among young people, even of the black middle class, were low as a consequence of inferior schools and limited opportunities beyond school. "Look at our young men," Stewart wrote, "—smart, active and energetic, with souls filled with ambitious fire; . . . They can be nothing but the humblest laborers, on account of their dark complexion."[32] She described men in their middle years whose "every cent [went] to buy their wood and pay their rent," while their wives "toil[ed] beyond their strength to help support their families."[33] Declaring that their lot in life was the result of "prejudice, ignorance and poverty," Maria Stewart felt herself called by God to unite her people in acting to change such conditions.[34]

Her sense of having an urgent, divinely inspired mission to the black community allowed Stewart to quickly find her true voice, one full of assurance, spirit, energy, creative imagination, and fervor. As with Walker, much of the force of Stewart's message was borne by a rhetorical power that appealed to the ear as well as to the intellect. Not only did she master the Afro-American idiom of thundering exhortation uniting spiritual and secular concerns, she was able early on to exercise that skill with equal success on the printed page and at the podium. Her command of such sophisticated techniques as the implied call-and-response cadence set in motion by sequential rhetorical questions; of anaphora, parataxis, and the shaping of imperative and periodic sentences; along with the powerful and affecting rhythms of her discourse, all show Stewart to be a predecessor to Sojourner Truth, Frederick Douglass, Henry Highland Garnet, Frances Harper, and other black nineteenth-century masters of language deployed to change society.

"I have borrowed much of my language from the holy Bible," she wrote, "During the years of childhood and youth, it was the book that I mostly studied." Her technique of interpolating into her text biblical passages, or paraphrases and restatements of such passages, was one common with preachers and religious writers of her day. Her years as a domestic servant in a clergyman's family might well have exposed her to certain of her employer's "tools of the trade."[35] Such compendia as the 1818 American edition of Hugh Gaston's *A Scripture Account of the Faith and Practice of Christians Consisting of an Extensive Collection of Pertinent Texts of Scripture Given At Large Upon the Various Articles of Revealed Religion . . .*, were much relied upon by religious orators to concoct an elegant blend of their own language and the emphatic support and justification of scriptural quotation.[36] Stewart demonstrated a sure and resourceful hand at the creative and subtle command of this technique.

In particular, much of the language and many of the themes and images throughout her political essays and lectures are drawn from the Old Testament book of the prophet Jeremiah and from his Book of Lamentations, a spiritual descent she was quick to claim as she drew parallels between the plight of insufficiently pious black Bostonians and those biblical peoples who had turned away from the will of God. "When I see the greater part of our community following the vain bubbles of life," she wrote, "I really think we are in as wretched and miserable a state as was the house of Israel in the days of Jeremiah."[37] She drew as well upon the prophets Isaiah and Ezekiel, and displayed a comfortable knowledge of the historical books, including Judges and Esther. Among the Gospels, she favored that of Matthew. She quoted widely from the various books of Epistles, and was especially drawn to the prophetical Book of Revelation.

In her unsparing examination of her personal behavior and that of her community, Stewart wrestled with the perennial conundrum of a supposedly just and merciful God's ostensible willingness to tolerate the continued, undeserved suffering of the innocent. Her search for justification of such divine wrath led her to adopt at times a severe, excoriating, and denunciatory style. It appears that it did not sit well with many in her audience, a number of whom were no doubt still struggling with the propriety of encouraging a woman who had appropriated the patriarchal voice of the language of the King James Bible to publicly express her views from a speaker's platform.

Her gender would indeed underscore what some must have considered the unpalatable nature of her message. Walker, citing armed struggles for liberty around the globe, could dramatically bemoan the failure of manhood among American blacks as a spur to inciting rebellion. It was much less likely that accusations of cowardice, ignorance, and lack of ambition hurled by a woman would rally Stewart's listeners, male or female, to the barricades of social activism. Still, she clearly asked nothing of others that she did not expect of herself.

Stewart's God was given to direct intervention in the affairs of nations and individuals, against the wicked and on behalf of the downtrodden, but according to his own timetable. By that standard, black Americans, although standing in need of grace and repentance, were, nonetheless, clearly in the ascendant. Whites, mired in the moral decay of maintaining a slave society, were clearly living on borrowed time. There is in Stewart's fervor a sense that if the black community could only be goaded into a frenzy of urgent spiritual purification, they might call forth the moment of retribution against decadent America.

In this she was in the line of those orators perpetuating what Sacvan Bercovitch, building on Perry Miller's influential work, describes as "the persistence of the Puritan Jeremiad throughout the eighteenth and nineteenth centuries," down through the years to "Martin Luther King, descendant of slaves, denouncing segregation as a violation of the American dream."[38] In her "political sermons" presented in secular forums, even as she denounced the many ways in which her people continued to fall from grace, Stewart announced and elaborated upon a celebratory vision of redemptive progress toward independence of body and spirit.

Wilson Moses, in his astute discussion of the "Black Jeremiad," extending the boundaries of the Miller-Bercovitch discourse, uses the term to describe "the constant warnings issued by blacks to whites, concerning the judgment that was to come for the sin of slavery."[39] Such warnings, delivered to whites on the inevitable outcome of their blindness to the workings of divine justice, though not as central as Moses might have it, were an integral part of Stewart's message, as they were of Walker's. Such detailed descriptions, indeed promises, of the slaveholders' impending doom were intended as much to hearten and edify the oppressed as to warn the oppressor.

Although she found fault with blacks for doing less than she felt they should on their own behalf, Stewart never lost sight of the reality that the primary cause of black oppression and suffering lay with the larger white society and for this group she envisioned, as did Walker, a divine punishment that might well take the form of a violent black uprising. The American Revolution was a model from which she felt blacks as well as whites were entitled to draw inspiration. Her use of graphic battle imagery is such that in many of her most compelling declarations, Stewart speaks as a writer under siege. Her denunciation of the colonization movement, a scheme to send free blacks to Africa and emancipate others on condition that they too go, provides a good example of her technique of invoking black historic and collective entitlement to American liberty and justice, in combination with her personal statement of willingness to risk physical confrontation if need be. "And now," she wrote, "that we have enriched their soil and filled their coffers . . . they would drive us to a strange land. But before I go, the bayonet shall pierce me through."[40]

Able to draw freely on an extensive knowledge of Old and New Testament writings to buttress her arguments—in her "Farewell Address" she cited or quoted (in order of appearance) Psalms, Matthew, Isaiah, Romans, Luke, Philomen, Ezekiel, Revelation, Judges, Esther, Ephesians, and Proverbs—it was to the Book of Revelation of the Prophet John the Divine that she unfailingly returned as to a *cantus firmus* to sustain all of her melismatic flights.[41]

The Book of Revelation, with its emphasis on the written word, on didactic prophecy, and on the cataclysmic destruction of the forces of evil, was the source of much of Stewart's spiritual self-definition. In it she found justification for what secular authorities might well have considered inciting to riot. The forces of rebellion and destruction, she argued, would act as the instruments of God's punishment of a slave-holding society. Human virtue and heavenly justice join forces in her apocalyptic vision of a day when

> many powerful sons and daughters of Africa will shortly arise, who will put down vice and immorality among us, and declare ... that they will have their rights; and if refused, I am afraid that they will spread horror and devastation around. I believe that the oppression of injured Africa has come up before the majesty of Heaven.[42]

This at the very period of which Tocqueville was moved to observe: "If ever America undergoes great revolutions, they will be brought about by the presence of the black race on the soil of the United States; that is to say, they will owe their origin, not to the equality, but to the inequality of condition."[43]

A passage from the Psalms served as Stewart's recurrent statement of the unity of black America's historic past and its spiritual destiny. "Ethiopia shall soon stretch out her hands unto God" became the touchstone biblical passage for generations of religious social activists.[44] Not the first black speaker to cite what was considered an aptly prophetic verse, she perpetuated its use as a rallying cry in joining the black past and present, religious and secular. In calling on blacks to claim their civil and human rights, Stewart evoked an African past of pride and accomplishment. In citing as she did in her Masonic Hall speech the African continent as a seat of learning and discovery, she spoke to a people who had lost their ties to an ancient collective identity, who no longer had a source of mutual history from which they could draw paradigms for the present moment. Both her religion and her understanding of history carried Stewart back to African roots which would, she felt, if properly understood, demonstrate to her audience that the assertion of their rights was in fact the reclaiming of an ancient prerogative.

Her religious faith and Walker's political analyses provided a theoretical foundation upon which Stewart constructed a model of struggle for social justice. She drew from Walker's impassioned manifesto an ethic of resistance to physical and political oppression, as well as a synthesis of commitment to religion, education, and community organization intended to promote the welfare and survival, both physical and cultural, of blacks in America. She moved beyond Walker's influence, however, in insisting upon the right of women to take their place in the front ranks of black moral and political leadership.

Maria Stewart took up a life of public political activism at a time when it was considered highly inappropriate for a woman to put herself forward in such a way. She defended herself with an appeal to biblical precedent and by defining herself as a passive instrument in God's hands.

> The spirit of God came before me and I spake before many . . . reflecting on what I had said, I felt ashamed . . . A something said within my breast, "press forward, I will be with thee." And my heart made this reply, "Lord, if thou wilt be with me, then I will speak for thee as long as I live."[45]

With such disclaimers, Stewart attempted a balance between the protective claims of passivity to divine will that early female preachers used to deflect denominational censure, and the active role she urged her sisters to take with her in assuming greater responsibility for their lives and their communities.[46] As her confidence and determination grew, so too her resistance to the assumptions and arguments put forth to silence women. Turning again to the Bible, she refuted the most frequently cited injunction against female activism by placing Paul's admonitions to women to remain silent in religious affairs and to take their cues from their husbands in other matters, against the demands of the black woman's social and historical context.[47] "Did St. Paul but know of our wrongs and deprivations," she argued, "I presume he would make no objection to our pleading in public for our rights." Ultimately, Stewart claimed full entitlement to speak and to act by way of what she called a "spiritual interrogation."[48]

> "Who shall go forward, and take off the reproach that is cast upon the people of color?" asked a voice from within, "Shall it be a woman?" And my heart made this reply—"If it is thy will, be it even so, Lord Jesus!"[49]

From the earliest formulation of her views in the 1831 essay *Religion And The Pure Principles Of Morality,* Stewart singled out the women in her audience by citing what she considered their special responsibilities within the black community. "Ye daughters of Africa, awake! . . . Arise! . . . distinguish yourselves," she exhorted, "Show forth to the world that ye are endowed with noble and exalted faculties." These faculties included the ability to achieve intellectual distinction, the cultivation of refined sensibilities such that young men would "fall in love with their virtues," and the capacity as mothers to "create in the minds of your little girls and boys a thirst for knowledge, the love of virtue." In this she was generally in accord with the nineteenth-century American ideal of True Womanhood whereby a woman was measured in terms of her "piety, purity, submissiveness and domesticity."[50]

Early on, when Stewart encouraged women to devote themselves to the advancement of opportunities for their children, she followed the conventional pattern of favoring male offspring over female and of seeing in young men the hope for the future of the race. By the time she delivered her "Farewell Address to Her Friends in the City of Boston," however, she had moved to a position of squarely urging black women to strike out on their own, pursuing education as a means of fulfilling their individual and collective destinies.

Her emphasis on black women's formal education was not rooted solely in images of feminine cultural refinement; it was a matter of the greatest political urgency. For Stewart, the pursuit of literacy was a sacred quest at this period when laws passed in the South made it a crime to teach slaves to read or write.[51] Hers is the earliest recorded call to black women to take up what would become one of the great traditions in their social and political history, their pioneering work as teachers, founders of schools, and innovators in many areas of black education. Freedom, literacy, and religion were, as Loewenberg and Bogin remark in their study of nineteenth-century black women, "a trinity of interlacing values." The achievement of literacy was, for blacks slave or free, "a move toward freedom of mind and spirit."[52]

While testifying to first-hand knowledge through "bitter experience . . . that continual hard labor [as a domestic servant] deadens the energies of the soul, and benumbs the faculties of the mind," Stewart asked her sisters for the sake of their own families to "strive to excel in good housewifery, knowing that prudence and economy are the road to wealth," a position consistent with the conservative traditional sphere of influence alloted to women. However, in almost the same breath, she boldly redefined black women's domestic situation—as homemakers and as employees— as a status to be transcended. "How long," she asked, with incisive eloquence, "shall the fair daughters of Africa be compelled to bury their minds and talents beneath a load of iron pots and kettles?" Calling on women to pool their economic resources, Stewart conjured the vision of a time not far off when they "might be able to lay the corner stone for the building of a High School, that the higher branches of knowledge might be enjoyed by us."[53]

Stewart's call for such an institution built by and for black women came

at a time when black Boston's political and intellectual life, male-oriented
and male-dominated, reflected assumptions of male primacy in such matters. A group of young men formed the Juvenile Colored Association of
Boston (also known as the Garrison Independent League) in the fall of
1831 as a group dedicated to social and cultural advancement with membership restricted to "young men 10 to 20 years old of decent, sober and
industrious habits."[54] Over the course of many months in late 1831, readers of *The Liberator* followed the attempt to establish a college for young
black men in New Haven, Connecticut. The plan, which met with vigorous opposition from many of that city's most influential white citizens, a
number of whom proposed establishing the school in West Africa, was
eventually dropped.[55] That same year saw the founding of Boston's Afric-
American Female Society, an organization whose goals were perhaps
somewhat more modest than Stewart might have wished, but which nevertheless proclaimed the spirit of union and mutual concern she advocated. In the face of such concerted opposition to the development of
educational opportunities for black young men, it was a bold move indeed for Stewart to take a principled public stand for the independent
higher education of black women.

In the Boston of Stewart's day, black women were subject to a domestic double standard. They were admonished by church and society to consider the home their proper sphere, to look up to men, to demonstrate an
appropriate subservience, all of which suggested a life of protected dependency. As the annual Boston Directory listings show, however, the
reality was that many black women had to contribute financially to keep
their households afloat. They were most often laundresses, cleaning women,
and domestic servants. Many black households took in boarders to sup-
plement the family income. Furthermore, no matter how hardworking or
virtuous they might be, black women were, as Stewart related, by white
definition considered subject to sexual compromise. The pillars of the
temple of True Womanhood were upheld, as historian Barbara Welter suc-
cinctly points out, by the American woman's "frail white hand."[56]

Stewart's "Farewell Address" was delivered in late 1833, the year in
which Prudence Crandall was harassed, arrested, and ultimately forced to
close her Canterbury, Connecticut, school because she had enrolled a young
black woman as a student. The speech contains Stewart's fullest discussion of the right of women to aspire to the highest positions of responsibility and authority in both religious and public spheres.

> What if I am a woman; is not the God of ancient times the God of these modern days? Did he not raise up Deborah, to be a mother, and a judge in Israel? Did not Queen Esther save the lives of the Jews? And Mary Magdalene first declare the resurrection of Christ from the dead?

Drawing on both the Old and New Testaments, Stewart placed herself in the line of women activists given divine sanction. "If such women as are here described have once existed, be no longer astonished...that God...should raise up your own females."

In the secular realm, she cited classical role models: "Among the Greeks, women delivered the oracles; the respect the Romans paid to the Sybils is well known...The predictions of the Egyptian women obtained much credit at Rome."

It is, however, in the example of certain women from the late Middle Ages and the Renaissance that Stewart found her strongest personal justification. The "young lady of Bologne" who pronounced a funeral oration in Latin at the age of twenty-three, went on to become a Doctor of Laws, and "taught the law" publicly, "to a prodigious concourse of scholars from all nations," was clearly an heroic figure in Stewart's personal pantheon. By the fifteenth century, she told her audience, in what must have been a virtuoso display of learning laid at the feet of a skeptical crowd, one could see "women preaching and mixing themselves in controversies. Women occupying the chairs of Philosophy and Justice; women haranguing in Latin before the Pope; women writing in Greek and studying in Hebrew."

Her summary statement of the unity of the religious and feminist vision connecting her with these heroines of the past posits a striking recapitulation of the sequential roles she saw herself as playing: "The religious spirit which has animated women in all ages...has made them by turns martyrs, apostles, warriors," she wrote, "and concluded in making them divines and scholars."

In her farewell statement, Stewart, who as a fire-and-brimstone practitioner of the "Black Jeremiad" had regularly bemoaned sinfulness and predicted doom, rose at moments to a serene lyricism. Her idealized vision of what her life and the lives of black women might be, based on the ultimate union of religious faith and intellectual discipline, was stated as an explicit challenge first to the women in her audience and then to the men.

> Why cannot a religious spirit animate us now? Why cannot we become divines and scholars...What if such women as are here described should

rise among our sable race? And it is not impossible . . . Brilliant wit will shine from whence it will.

To credit the source of her citations, Stewart referred her audience to a volume she identified only as "Sketches of the Fair Sex." This hook, the full title of which is *Woman, Sketches Of The History, Genius, Disposition, Accomplishments, Employments, Customs And Importance Of The Fair Sex In All Parts Of The World Interspersed With Many Singular And Entertaining Anecdotes By A Friend Of The Sex*, was published by one John Adams (1750–1814) in London in 1790.[57] It was known to Stewart in an 1807 American edition from which she excerpted passages on the Medieval and Renaissance women quoted above. This compendium of fact (Laws and Customs Respecting the Roman Women), fancy (Of the First Woman, And Her Antediluvian Descendants), and eccentric inquiry (A Comparison Between The Mahometans and Dutch, With Regard To Their Women), was a volume likely to open new horizons for a reader such as Stewart. Adams's evocation of an international sisterhood, diverse, influential, and equally valid in the contexts of their cultural relativity, would provide an array of potential role models hardly available to most black women in slave-holding America.

The women Stewart approvingly spoke of early in her career—wives and mothers who exercised influence upon their husbands and through them perhaps in some way upon the world beyond the home—are replaced in her later work by examples of biblical and historical figures who wield genuine power and authority.

Moving through Adams's wide-ranging roster of women prominent in a variety of times and places, East and West, Stewart was most clearly drawn not to accounts of women who occupied high positions and enjoyed power through social status alone, but those who gained respect and renown through their mastery of such intellectual disciplines as law, theology, and the arts. Aspiration to such achievements, she believed, would be the key to the successful survival, indeed the triumph, of black women in white America.

It is clear that Stewart's public career exacted a high personal cost. From the start she faced a series of poignant contradictions: could she be both "African" and American? Both female and independent? Both a woman and a prophet? Piety was considered one of the prime virtues of True Womanhood; church work was thought to be compatible with submissive domesticity, an area in which women might "labor without the apprehension of detracting from the charms of feminine delicacy."[58]

When in mourning and distress, however, Stewart turned to religion, and she found there the same imperative that had communicated itself to Denmark Vesey, Gabriel Prosser, and her contemporaries David Walker and Nat Turner.[59] By perceiving her mission as in that line of militant spiritual descent, she veered sharply from the prescribed sphere of women's religious activity. In that regard, her willingness to embrace armed struggle would put her at philosophical odds with her colleague and publisher, Garrison. Although her later affiliation in New York with *The North Star*, later called *Frederick Douglass' Paper*, would find her in more ideologically compatible company, she was, in the early 1830s, in a real sense alone in unexplored territory, a woman placed by God—as she saw it—on an ethical and societal frontier.[60] She could fulfill her calling only by behaving in a manner almost exactly opposite what she had once considered the ideal of black womanhood.

Stewart was removed from the sphere of the home by the death of her husband, leaving her once again, as had the earlier death of her parents, thrown upon her own resources. Widowhood allowed her an intermediary position in the community in that she could move about in the world more freely than she could have had she never married, and still maintain her respectability. It left her legitimately free of the demands of domesticity as well. She had, after all, shown herself willing to assume the traditional female role, but was deprived by fate of the opportunity to continue in that life.

As the author of a political pamphlet, she moved into the proscribed realm of masculine authority. The authoritative word, written or spoken, was a long-standing male prerogative, not easily relinquished. If in the beginning was the word, it was the patriarchal word of a God who created Eve as Adam's helpmeet. Stewart, distinct from the vast majority of black women of her day, was a reader, a writer, and a student of texts. We know that she read the Bible, *The Liberator* and other periodicals, and the works of Walker and Adams with an inquiring and critical sensibility, and that she was a published writer before she was a public speaker.[61]

Convinced of a calling she could not refuse, Stewart was thrust into the public role not only of teacher—an acceptable position for a woman—but of prophet. Her claim that God communicated with her directly could only be regarded with uneasy suspicion by the organized black church. In order to obey God, she had to act in contradiction to the secular identity to which she had once aspired, that of a traditionally refined and accomplished woman, by her own definition "a chaste keeper at home, . . . possessing a meek and quiet spirit." Orphan, widow, solitary visionary, a woman who could claim to have "traveled a good bit in my day," she was both an independent and an isolated figure in the world.[62] Her calling was not merely reformist, it was subversive, and she herself was the first to encounter its transformative character by its challenge to her own identity.

Her lecture to the Afric-American Female Intelligence Society, which opened with the full-fledged conjuring of an apocalyptic vision and concluded with homely advice to wives and mothers, shows Stewart speaking in first one and then the other of the two voices of her antiphonal mode, in an attempt to reconcile the insistent dialogue between the exigencies of divine will and those of historical necessity. To this group she spoke as a woman prophet among women, to an audience whose lives closely paralleled her own, and whose approval would be crucial to her sense of appropriate behavior. Such approval, she makes clear, was far from unanimous.

She understood the censure of the world as the inevitable response to her behavior, and seemed to believe that her secular self was subject to the inevitable workings of cause and effect whereby a woman behaving in an unacceptable manner would be chastened in a worldly context, even as she understood that she enjoyed a special dispensation superseding those temporal standards. Stewart's descriptions of harsh and censorious responses to her outspokenness are supported by a letter written almost two decades later by the black historian William C. Nell to Garrison. "In the perilous years of 33–35," he recalled, "a colored woman—Mrs. Maria W. Stewart—fired with a holy zeal to speak her sentiments on the improvement of colored Americans, encountered an opposition even from her Boston circle of friends, that would have dampened the ardor of most women."[63]

The uncharacteristic serenity of tone in much of her "Farewell Address" suggests that Stewart had embraced a decision to, in effect, annihilate her public persona. She addressed her audience in the language of one dying into a new life, with such remarks as, "Farewell. In a few short years from now, we shall meet in those upper regions where parting will be no more." She proclaimed a spiritual testament advocating the pursuit of godliness and peace, the cultivation of intellect and morality, and finally, thinking herself to be a prophet distinctly without honor in that land, bade farewell to Boston.

In New York, Stewart continued her political activities. She joined women's organizations, attended the Women's Anti-Slavery Convention of 1837, and was an active participant in a black women s literary society.[64] While it appears that she did not pursue a public speaking career there, according to the advertisements for the 1879 edition of her work, she did lecture in New York.[65] The volume of her collected work, *Productions of Mrs. Maria W. Stewart*," which appeared the year after her departure from Boston, was advertised for sale with the major anti-slavery and human rights writings of the abolitionist movement.[66] Within a year of its appearance other women, black and white, following the dictates of mind and conscience, began to emerge from the shadows and, taking the path she had opened, walked up the steps to the podiums of churches and meeting halls throughout the land to proclaim the social gospel of liberation and justice for all.

Notes

1. Their marriage certificate, on file at the Registry of Marriages, Boston, Massachusetts, reads, "James W. Stewart & Maria Miller (people of color) married by the Rev. Thomas Paul 10 August, 1826."

2. John Wesley Cromwell, in "The First Negro Churches in the District of Columbia," *Journal of Negro History* 7, no. 1, (January 1922), describes such classes at which "the Bible was the book from which morals and religion were taught, and Webster's blue-back speller was the constant companion of [those who] were learning to read the word of God" (89).

3. Pension Claim file No. 35165, War of 1812, Claim of Widow for Service Pension, National Archives, Washington, D.C. The claim form for Maria Stewart's widow's pension gives his age as "about 30" at the time of his enlistment in the navy during the War of 1812. His death certificate gives his age as fifty at his death in 1829.

4. Stewart's business was at a choice location in a newly built-up commercial area near India Wharf, not far from the Custom-house, developed under the auspices of the Broad Street Association. See Walter Muir Whitehill, *Boston: A Topographical History* (Cambridge: Belknap Press, Harvard University, 1959), 86. It is not certain that this "light, bright mulatto" was recognized in the business community as a person of color. While he is listed at his business address in the Boston City Directory prior to his marriage, it is only after his marriage that he is listed in the "colored" section of the directory.

5. James W. Stewart's Will, Appendix A, in *Maria W. Stewart: America's First Black Woman Political Writer,* ed. Marilyn Richardson (Bloomington: Indiana University Press, 1987).

6. According to the pension claim form, "the W. as middle letter in her name

was inserted at the instance [sic] of her said husband . . . and that sometimes he was called Steward by mistake."

7. John Daniels, *In Freedom's Birthplace* (Boston and new York: 1914; Houghton Mifflin Co., repr., New York: Arno Press and the New York Times, 1969), 457. This census figure should be considered unreliable in that the most destitute blacks, residents of poorhouses, were not counted, nor were fugitive slaves, of course. Many black seamen were omitted as well. See James Oliver Horton, *Black Activism in Boston 1830–1860* (Ph.D. dissertation, Brandeis University, 1973), 16.

8. Horton, *Black Activism,* 16.

9. *Freedom's Journal* 1, no. 1 March 16, 1827): 1.

10. See Herbert Aptheker, *One Continual Cry: David Walker's Appeal to the Colored Citizens of the World 1829–1830, Its Setting and Its Meaning* (New York: Humanities Press, 1965), 28–37, for a discussion of the "watershed" decade of black anti-slavery agitation and organization from 1820 to 1830.

11. Henry Highland Garnet, *Walker's Appeal with a Brief Sketch of His Life* (New York: J.H. Tobitt, 1848), vi.

12. Ibid.

13. David Walker, *Walker's Appeal in Fourth Articles Together with a Preamble . . .* (Boston: Published by David Walker, 1830), 2nd ed., with corrections, 22.

14. Ibid., 29.

15. Charles M. Wiltse, ed., *David Walker's Appeal* (New York: Hill and Wang, 1965), viii–ix. Wiltse describes Walker's shop as "near the wharves." In fact, Brattle Street was closer to the center of Boston than to the waterfront, but not at such a remove as to render his speculation implausible.

16. Stewart's death certificate, filed at Boston City Hall, gives heart disease as the cause of his death.

17. Document submitted as James W. Stewart's Will, Appendix A. Also Probate Court Records, Boston Municipal Court, Boston, Massachusetts. This is a curious and tangled case indeed. It appears from the numerous documents on file that two separate actions in probate went forward simultaneously, one by the white businessmen claiming possession of Stewart's will, and one by Maria Stewart who later said she had no knowledge of such a will and who at the same time filed for relief as the widow of the intestate deceased. What is certain is that Stewart emerged from her encounter with the courts virtually penniless.

18. Walker, *Walker's Appeal,* 12.

21. Garnet, *Walker's Appeal,* vii.

20. Ibid.

21. Aptheker considers the mystery of Walker's death in *One Continual Cry,* citing Garrison's sons who claim in their biography of their father that it was of natural causes. On the other hand, Garnet, who had interviewed Walker's widow, was unable to resolve the question to his satisfaction. "Until other and more conclusive evidence appears," writes Aptheker, "—which is quite unlikely—the modern historian can only conclude that deep mystery surrounds the manner of David Walker's death in his 44th year" (52–53).

22. Clinton H. Johnson, ed., *God Struck Me Dead: Religious Conversion Experiences and Autobiographies of Ex-Slaves* (Philadelphia: Pilgrim Press, 1969), vii-xiii. Although Stewart was never a slave, Radin's discussion touches upon many of the psychological phenomena that she reports in connection with her conversion.

23. Marilyn, Richardson, ed., *Maria W. Stewart: America's First Black Woman Political Writer*, (Bloomington: Indiana University Press, 1987), 29.

24. Ibid.

25. Maria W. Stewart, *Meditations from the Pen of Mrs. Maria W. Stewart* (Boston: Garrison and Knapp, 1832).

26. Wendell Phillips Garrison, *William Lloyd Garrison: The Story of His Life Told by His Children* (New York: Century Press, 1885), 220–221. In its crucial early years *The Liberator*, although published and edited by whites, was sustained by a predominantly black readership. In April 1843, for instance, whites comprised only one-quarter of the 2,300 subscribers. Benjamin Quarles, *Black Abolitionists* (London: Oxford University Press, 1969), 20.

27. Wendell Phillips Garrison, *Garrison*, 221.

28. William Lloyd Garrison, letter to Maria W. Stewart in *Maria W. Stewart, America's First Black Woman Political Writer*, (Bloomington: Indiana University Press, 1987), 89.

29. Maria W. Stewart, *Religion and the Pure Principles of Morality, the Sure Foundation on which We Must Build* in *Maria W. Stewart: America's First Black Woman Political Writer*, ed. Marilyn Richardson (Bloomington: Indiana University Press, 1987).

30. Garnet, *Walker's Appeal*, vii.

31. James Oliver Horton and Lois E. Horton, *Black Bostonians* (New York: Holmes and Meier, 1979), 67–68.

32. Maria W. Stewart, "Lecture Delivered at the Franklin Hall," in *Maria W. Stewart: America's First Black Woman Political Writer*, ed. Marilyn Richardson (Bloomington: Indiana University Press, 1987), 49.

33. Ibid.

34. Ibid.

35. Maria W. Stewart, *Meditations from the Pen of Mrs. Maria W. Stewart* (Boston: Garrison and Knapp, 1832).

36. Hugh Gaston, A Scripture Account of the Faith and Practice of Christians..., (1843). (Frederickston, Maryland; Philadelphia: D. Hogan, 1820). Gaston, a British clergyman, died in 1766.

37. Maria W. Stewart, "Religion and the Pure Principles of Morality," in *Maria W. Stewart: America's First Black Woman Political Writer*, ed. Marilyn Richardson (Bloomington: Indiana University Press, 1987), 32.

38. Sacvan Bercovitch, *The American Jeremiad* (Madison: University of Wisconsin Press, 1978), 11. Bercovitch's discussion of the "litany of hope" at the heart of the American jeremiad—as opposed to Perry Miller's "concept of ambiguity" in such tests—illuminates most effectively certain of Stewart's rhetorical strategies.

39. Wilson Jeremiah Moses, *Black Messiahs and Uncle Toms: Social and Literary Ma-*

nipulations of a Religious Myth (University Park: Pennsylvania State University Press, 1982), 30–49.

40. Maria W. Stewart, "An Address Delivered at the African Masonic Hall," in *Maria W. Stewart: America's First Black Woman Political Writer,* ed. Marilyn Richardson (Bloomington: Indiana University Press, 1987), 64.

41. Maria W. Stewart, "Mrs. Stewart's Farewell Address to Her Friends in the City of Boston," in *Maria W. Stewart: America's First Black Woman Political Writer,* ed. Marilyn Richardson (Bloomington: Indiana University Press, 1987), 65–74.

42. Stewart, "Address," 63.

43. Alexis De Tocqueville, *Democracy in America,* ed., Phillips Bradley, (New York: Vintage Books, Random House, 1945), vol. II, 270. *Marie, ou l'esclavage aux Etats-Unis* (Paris: Ch. Gosselin, 1835), a work of fiction by G. Beaumont, Tocqueville's traveling companion and fellow writer, is even more to the point in its sustained look at the situation of blacks in the North and South. See Bradley, 398, for a description of this novel in which a young Frenchman falls in love with a woman of mixed blood, but is not allowed to marry her until "he has seen with his own eyes the true position of Negroes in America."

44. Psalms 68:31.

45. Stewart, "Mrs. Stewart's," 67.

46. See William L. Andrews, *Sisters of the Spirit: Three Black Women's Autobiographies of the Nineteenth Century* (Bloomington: Indiana University Press, 1986), 14, for a discussion of the ways in which black women asserting the right to preach in the early nineteenth century "chose to step outside their appointed sphere and seek a new way of defining themselves vis-à-vis the people of God and the people of the world."

47. 1 Corinthians 14:34, 35.

48. Stewart, "Mrs. Stewart's," 68.

49. Stewart, "Lecture," 45.

50. Barbara Welter, *Dimity Convictions: The American Woman in the Nineteenth Century* (Athens: Ohio University Press, 1976), ch. 2, "The Cult of True Womanhood," 21.

51. Eugene D. Genovese, in *Roll, Jordan, Roll: The World the Slaves Made* (New York: Pantheon, 1974), comments in his chapter on "Reading, Writing, and Prospects," that "the estimate by W. E. B. DuBois that, despite prohibitions and negative public opinion, about 5 percent of the slaves had learned to read by 1860 is entirely plausible and may even be too low" (563).

52. Bert James Loewenberg and Ruth Bogin, eds., *Black Women in Nineteenth-Century American Life: Their Words, Their Thoughts, Their Feelings* (University Park: Pennsylvania State University Press, 1976), 282.

53. Stewart, "Lecture," 47; Stewart, *Religion,* 37.

54. *The Liberator,* January 5, 1833.

55. *The Liberator,* September 24, 1831, and subsequent issues.

56. Welter, *Dimity,* 21.

57. John Adams, *Women, Sketches of the History, Genius, Disposition, Accomplishments,*

Employments, Customs and Importance of the Fair Sex . . . (London: G. Kearsley, No. 46 Fleet Street, 1790).

58. Welter, *Dimity*, 21.

59. See Eugene D. Genovese, *From Rebellion to Revolution: Afro-American Slave Revolts in the Making of the New World* (New York: Vintage Books, 1981), in particular the chapter, "Slave Revolts in Hemispheric Perspective," 1–50, for discussion of the Prosser, Vesey, and Turner revolts, and the influence of religion in their motivation.

60. I am grateful to Dorothy Sterling for pointing out that Maria W. Steward [sic] is mentioned in *The North Star* of April 12, 1850, as a member of the committee of arrangements organized to plan a fair for the benefit of the paper.

61. Not that Stewart was the first black woman in America to know to draw on such intellectual resources. Two outstanding early examples merit mention. Lucy Terry (1730–1822) in 1746 witnessed the Indian raid that inspired her later poem, "Bar's Fight," the earliest surviving work in verse by a black American. She later successfully defended herself before the United State Supreme Court against a challenge to her property rights with a dazzling display of legal knowledge. The presiding justice, Samuel Chase, commented that she had "made a better argument than he had heard from any lawyer at the Vermont Bar." On an earlier occasion, she had appeared before the trustees of Williams College; for three hours, citing "an abundance of law and Gospel, chapter and verse," she argued against the refusal to admit her son, Caesar, on account of his race. The trustees were unmoved. See Sidney Kaplan, *The Black Presence in the Era of the American Revolution 1770–1800* (Greenwich: The New York Graphic Society, 1973), 210–11. Phillis Wheatley (1754?–1784), much of whose poetry Stewart saw reprinted in *The Liberator* between February and December of 1832, was steeped in the study of the Bible, the Greek and Roman classics, and the work of Alexander Pope when she flourished as a poet in late eighteenth-century Boston. Her 1773 volume, *Poems on Various Subjects Religious and Moral,* is thought to be the first book published by a black woman residing in America. (The first edition was printed in England.) No doubt there were others who left less conspicuous records of their achievement.

62. Stewart, *Religion*, 36.

63. William C. Nell, letter to William Lloyd Garrison in *The Liberator,* March 5, 1852, in *Maria W. Stewart: America's First Black Woman Political Writer,* ed. Marilyn Richardson (Bloomington: Indiana University Press, 1987), 90.

64. *Proceedings of the Anti-Slavery Convention Of American Women Held in the City of New York, May 9th, 10th, 11th, and 12th 1837* (New York: William S. Dorr 1837).

65. Since the 1879 edition of *Meditations* contains no new speeches or essays, it is possible that she drew on some of the earlier material for New York lectures.

66. The title page reads: *Productions of Mrs. Maria W. Stewart, Presented To The First African Baptist Church & Society, Of The City Of Boston,* Boston: Published By Friends Of Freedom And Virtue, 1835.

Chapter 2

Maria W. Stewart and the Rhetoric of Black Preaching

Perspectives on Womanism and Black Nationalism

LENA AMPADU

Maria W. Miller Stewart gained her public speaking voice invoking moral suasion and displaying a profound faith in God. In this chapter, I provide a close textual analysis of her rhetoric to show that her speeches resemble sermons, and contribute to the Black sermonic tradition. The chapter also will ground Stewart's texts in womanist theory and inscribe a place for her in a rhetorical tradition historically dominated by men. As an outspoken advocate for women, she produced a sustained body of political and religious rhetoric directed specifically at liberating women, although her discourse was not always aimed exclusively at women. I will argue, as well, that Stewart overcame limitations of race and gender to set historical precedents in promoting Black nationalist thought, an important component of religious rhetoric usually categorized as masculine. Her place in history as one of the first woman to address mixed-race or gender audiences has been assured.

The Rhetoric of Black Preaching

The term "rhetoric" has taken on a wide range of meanings. Some see it as a tool to make truth and justice prevail; others see it as an art to deceive.[1] A classical definition offered by Aristotle regards it as "an ability, in each [particular] case to see the available means of persuasion."[2] Cicero emphasized its importance in training clergy and statesmen, and Quintilian, a teacher of rhetoric in Spain, asserted that the rhetor must be a good and moral man.[3] Agreeing with Quintilian, Richard Weaver expressed rhetoric's concern with ethics when he observed, "As rhetoric confronts us with choices involving values, the rhetorician is a preacher to us, noble if he/she tries to direct our passion toward noble ends and base if he uses our passion to confuse and degrade us."[4]

Rhetoric, as discussed here, is considered ethically based and implies choices for both the speaker and the audience. The Black preacher as rhetorician develops strategies for creating an effect in an audience to which the audience can respond freely. The rhetoric of Black preaching refers to the ways that the preachers skillfully employ language to appeal to and influence their listeners. This rhetoric, based on a tradition handed down orally and forged in the African experience in America, commonly manifests itself in the sermons of the Black Methodist, Baptist, or Pentecostal preachers. These sermons contain real dialogue in which the preacher calls the people into his discourse, while the people respond by uttering aloud that they are in full accord with the call issued.[5] Everything in the sermon is directed toward the point of emotional climax and catharsis. Congregants act as co-makers of the sermon by shouting "Amen" and "preach it" to show agreement, while the calls of "well!" tend to urge the preacher on.[6] Many of these sermons are of the chanted variety with a highly rigid rhythmic style, this rhythmic form having been developed most fully, though not exclusively, by the Black preacher.[7]

Stewart as Womanist and Contributor to the Black Preaching Tradition: An Analysis of Her Major Speeches

The nineteenth-century pulpit, dominated by men, produced such revered figures as Prince Hall, Absalom Jones, and Richard Allen. Women were not officially sanctioned as preachers until the 1830s, when Jarena Lee preached in the African Methodist Episcopal (A.M.E.) Church, while Zilpha Elaw, with roots in Methodism, and Julia Foote from the African Methodist Episcopal Zion (A.M.E.Z.) Church, preached to those of various denominations.[8] However, most women who had a spiritual calling were never given the opportunity to occupy the pulpit set aside for men. Furthermore, women like Jarena Lee were denied the right and privilege of ordination. These women followed what authors Lincoln and Mamiya have labeled a "sublimated path" to the ministry.[9] These authors contend that since women like Stewart, Tubman, and Truth could not become preachers, they practiced their faith through religious abolitionism. They also claim that the "unordained black woman has long been preacher-spiritual leader."[10] To illustrate this claim, Judith Weidman used Sojourner Truth as an example of one who resorted to the traditional style of a Black preacher.[11] Indeed, Truth, who claimed to have been charged to travel the country spreading the gospel, delivered messages emphasizing the primacy of the word in African-American communities. Women such as Maria Stewart entered the public sphere primarily as workers, especially as domestics and seamstresses.[12] Within this public sphere, Black women routinely experienced insults and indignities, unlike anything experienced by their white brothers and sisters. This unprotected space, nevertheless, allowed black women to achieve economic independence as well as the physical freedom and geographic mobility to participate in the public sphere as evangelists. Stewart spread the word evangelizing in much the same manner as a preacher, using the word to critique racism and oppression prevalent during that era. In fact, one of her earliest speeches was believed to have been delivered from the pulpit of the African Meeting House, where Boston's African Baptist Church was located.[13] My analysis of several of her speeches places them in the same rhetorical vein as that of a Black preacher.

This analysis argues that in her speeches Maria Stewart paralleled the stylistic and thematic features of Black religious oratory, contributing to the rhetorical tradition of the Black preacher. Integral to her messages were features that sustain the tradition of African-American preaching: the blending of hymns into her text, use of varied sentence structure and a style evoking a call-response, use of apocalyptic discourse, and of the Black jeremiad—a rhetorical device warning whites of the devastating consequences of their continued participation in slavery.[14] Moreover, she employed themes common in nineteenth-century oratory that have emerged as salient in Black preacher rhetoric: black nationalism and liberation in their spiritual, physical, or intellectual forms. One of the most common techniques upon which Black preachers rely is citing religious text and using religious testimonial, both of which Stewart used abundantly in her oratory.

Stewart's political-religious rhetoric espoused women's rights long before the women's movement gained popularity in the larger society a decade later. The concept of womanism, first proposed by Alice Walker in 1988, is crucial to understanding Stewart's stance advocating women's equality.[15] Multiple dimensions of Walker's definition are especially relevant to analyzing Stewart's rhetoric: her love of her fellow sisters, as well as of the entire community; her enthusiasm for spiritual matters; and her courage to speak out against social injustice. A variant ideology that revises Walker's definition is Africana womanism, defined by Hudson-Weems as centering on the survival of the family.[16] The application of the concept of womanism or extensions of it can be seen in some of the ideas common in Stewart's speeches.

Many of the techniques of Black preaching rhetoric, having evolved from the male-dominated pulpit, did not allow women to draw heavily upon the experiences of women as examples in their sermons. Countering this patriarchal practice by citing numerous exemplary women in her speeches, Stewart began a feminist tradition long before the women's movement had its beginnings. Consistent with this womanist dimension of Stewart's strategy is a contemporary construction of the type of woman-centered model by womanist theologian Rev. Dr. Ann Farrar Lightner Fuller, who underscores the womanist conceptions integral to her scriptural analyses:[17]

> Because I am Woman, when I study a certain passage, I generally find myself looking for ways to bring out the female aspect of the text. I look for the female interpretation, the womanist side of the story, digging deep enough, without destroying the meaning of the text so as to unveil what God wants and needs women to learn from the Word. It is, however, very important that women preachers and writers be diligent in their explication of this female angle because most often, readily and naturally, men would see the "male" elements in the text.[18]

The rhetorical predecessor to speakers such as Sojourner Truth, Ida Wells Barnett, and Frances E. W. Harper, Stewart used a similar provocative sermonic style attributed to Sojourner Truth.[19] In her widely acclaimed, "Arn't I a Woman?" speech, when Truth used the examples of herself as mother and Mary and Martha as women active in Christian service, she participated in this tradition celebrating women.[20] Likewise, Stewart, in her "Farewell Address," used an array of examples of women, including one of the same examples of Mary that Truth uses. She also compared herself to Deborah, a powerful Old Testament prophet who balanced the

traditional role of mother with one requiring her to give advice and counsel outside the home: "What if I am a woman; is not the God of ancient
times the God of these modern Days? Did he not raise up Deborah, to
be a mother, and a judge in Israel?" (68).

Stewart not only abundantly used illustrations drawn from women's
experiences, but at times, she addressed an audience composed predominantly of women. In Stewart's "Address Before the Afric-American Female Intelligence Society," she urged the women to free themselves by developing their intellectual capabilities and by uniting in Christian love to
uplift themselves, their families, and ultimately the race. She proclaimed:

> We might become a highly respectable people; respectable we now con-
> sider ourselves, but we might become a highly distinguished and intelli-
> gent people. And how? In convincing the world, by our own efforts, how-
> ever feeble, that nothing is wanting on our part but opportunity. Without
> these efforts, we shall never be a people, nor our descendants after us. (53)

In delivering this message emphasizing the well-being and survival of
family, Stewart can best be described as adhering to the principles of
Africana womanism. Addressing Black audience members attending her
"Franklin Hall" speech, she exhorted them to raise their sons and daughters from servitude to overcome ignorance and poverty (48). By striving
for higher educational opportunities, these members of the laboring class
would be able to empower themselves intellectually and economically.

Realizing the pivotal role of women within the family, she called for
women to work for racial uplift and liberation through spiritual means.
Near the close of the speech to the Female Intelligence Society, she issued a plea to the women based, in part, on biblical scripture:

> O woman, woman! Upon you I call; for upon your exertions almost en-
> tirely depends whether the rising generation shall be any thing more than
> we have been or not. O woman, woman! Your example is powerful, your
> influence great; it extends over your husbands and your children, and
> throughout the circle of your acquaintance. Then let me exhort you to
> cultivate among yourselves a spirit of Christian love and unity, having
> charity one for another, without which all our goodness is as sounding
> brass, and a tinkling cymbal [I Corinthians 13:1]. And, O, my God, I be-
> seech thee to grant that the nations of the earth may hiss at us no longer!
> O suffer them not to laugh us to scorn forever! (55)

Her words encouraged women to gain freedom in the ways that her
mentor David Walker had advocated. Influenced by Walker's revolution-

ary, religious rhetoric, Stewart echoed his call for African Americans in this country to become intellectually capable through learning. In an impassioned appeal to "the daughters of Africa," Stewart implored Black women to display their intellectual abilities to the world (30). Support for the idea of freedom through intellectual advancement later was articulated in Frederick Douglass's realization that "the pathway from slavery to freedom" would be hastened through his becoming literate; thus, Stewart anticipated his emphasis on the significance of literacy as a tool for liberation.

As a female speaker, Stewart was concerned to prove herself a virtuous woman of "high moral character."[21] To gain acceptance as a public speaker, she explained to her audience that she was doing the work of God. She assured her audience that the only motive that has prompted her to raise her voice is "to promote the cause of Christ and the good of souls" (50). In the tradition of a preacher, she testified as to what God had done for her and as to her "chosen" status:

> Be not offended because I tell you the truth; for I believe that God has fired my soul with a holy zeal for his cause. It was God alone who inspired my heart to publish the meditations thereof; and it was done with pure motives of love to your souls, in the hope that Christians might examine themselves, and sinners become pricked in their hearts. (52)

As one committed to a womanist ideology, Stewart, who emphasized moral fortitude and righteous living, made clear her mission: to encourage her audience to repent. To gain their attention and confidence, she had to convince them that her motives were based in truth, love, and righteousness. She continued her attempts at audience identification by reminding them that she was as human as they were: "Ah, my friends, I am speaking as one who expects to give account at the bar of God; I am speaking as a dying mortal to dying mortals" (52). In typical preacherly fashion, she impressed upon her audience that they are humans who will one day die. She tried to induce them to repent so that they would be able to give an account of themselves before their Maker.

In her introduction, Stewart set herself up "in the tradition of the Black preacher who identifies himself as one chosen by God to herald a fiery end of time that will come unless his listeners repent."[22] She warned her audience that the day will be a "great day of joy and rejoicing to the humbler followers of Christ, but a day of terror and dismay to hypocrites and unbelievers" (51). Echoing David Walker in his use of this rhetorical element, Stewart began with an apocalyptic message to impress upon them the need to act urgently, to repent and alter their positions in society. She kept the thought of the impending doom, that day of "fire and storm," uppermost in their minds (51).

To further emphasize this apocalyptic message, she incorporated the text of the stanza of a hymn written by Isaac Watts, one of the most popular hymn writers with Blacks, especially with Black Baptists, who "blackened or Africanized" these hymns by singing them in the lined style.[23] This uniquely African style of singing employs a call-response method in which a deacon or preacher intones a line or couplet that the congregation echoes in response. The fire-and-brimstone message in this hymn forecasts the day that Christ will come—the apocalypse. The hymn's text is as follows:

> High on a cloud our
> God shall come
> Bright thrones, prepare his way
> Thunder and darkness, fire and storm
> Lead on the dreadful day. (51)

When Stewart, who had a long association with the Black Baptists, included this Watts hymn, she was participating in a technique significant to the tradition of the Black preacher: incorporating text from a hymn in a sermon, text that is sometimes recited or sung. Directly traceable to Africa, where music, religion, and life holistically unite, the combination of music and preaching survives today in the Black sermon. Reciting hymn stanzas in her oratory was a recurring feature of Stewart's speeches, a technique also used by one of the pioneer women evangelists in the A.M.E. Church, Jarena Lee. Dr. Patricia Outlaw, an ordained itinerant elder and associate minister in the A.M.E. Church supports the idea of wedding music and text in the sermon.[24] She maintains that "in the same way that Jesus used parables to relate heavenly experiences to the people using everyday language, the Black minister presents these songs as a way of establishing rapport with the audience using the familiar."[25] This technique further allows the speaker to enliven the message for the audience. The hymn, a form of enargeia, vividly portrays the second coming of Christ, contrasting light and dark images. Mentioned in conjunction with bright thrones preparing the way, the cloud portrays brightness, while thunder, darkness, fire, and storm, all images of nature associated with the wrath of God, evoke gloom.

No clues exist as to whether Stewart sang these words or whether she recited them. As part of her oratory, the words probably were recited with a dramatic appeal that helped to touch and stir the emotions of her audience. Such "emotional and highly charged" language comprises the sacred style integral to the Black church.[26]

This dramatic appeal remains a key feature of Black oratory, especially of Black preaching style.[27] Because of the rhythm, imagery, and musicality that contribute to this attribute of Black preaching rhetoric, James Weldon Johnson compared the Black folk preachers to musical instruments by labeling them "God's Trombones." Johnson believed that "the old-time Negro preacher of parts was above all an orator, and in good measure as an orator. He knew the secret of oratory, that at the bottom it is a progression of rhythmic words more than it is anything else."[28] Like those old-time preachers, Stewart achieved dramatic appeal through her "command of such sophisticated techniques as the implied call-response set in motion by sequential rhetorical questions, of anaphora, parataxis, and the shaping of imperative and periodic sentences, along with the powerful and affecting rhythms of her discourse" (14).

Through conjecture, one can hear her audience energetically respond to her series of rhetorical questions:

> And why is it, my friends, that we are despised above all the nations upon the earth? Is it merely because our skins are tinged with a sable hue? . . . What then is it? . . . Shall we be a hissing and a reproach among the nations of the earth any longer? Shall they laugh us to scorn forever? (53)

She motivated her audience to examine themselves introspectively and to ponder the reasons that peoples around the globe viewed Blacks with contempt and disdain. By using such loaded words as "reproach" and "hissing," she conveyed a negative tone. A particularly effective strategy she used was the onomatopoeic "hissing," which vivified and emphasized her audience's sense of sound, heightening the audience's ability to remember what had been said.

In similar fashion, anaphoric language set forth rhythmic phrases that could engage the audience deeply in the message, making it more memorable for them. Her use of anaphora made her purpose striking when she told her audience of having been chosen to deliver God's word:

> *It is the word of God,* though men and devils may oppose it. *It is the word of God;* and little did I think that any of the professed followers of Christ would have frowned upon me, and discouraged and hindered its progress. (52)

In this passage, she launched an indirect attack on those who stood as obstacles to the dissemination of the word of God, an attack standing in direct relationship to her opening statement, "The frowns of the world shall never discourage me" (50). Using irony in the anaphoric passage mentioned above, she scorned the professed Christians who would have "frowned" upon her and "discouraged" the advancement of her ministry.

To further reach her audience with a sense of rhythmic appeal, she skillfully interwove various types of sentences into her oratory. One such device that contributed to the dramatic effect is the imperative sentence, which helped to establish a commanding voice with the audience. To win the respect of her audience, she could command gently, as in her statement, "Be not offended because I tell you the truth" (52), or she could command more assertively, as in her statement, "But I beseech you to deal with gentleness and godly sincerity towards me" (54). Her choice of "beseech" illustrates this more authoritative use of language, since it means "beg or implore." A common biblical verb, "beseech" helped to strengthen the public voice Stewart used to establish rapport with the audience.

Continuing this varied sentence structure, she combined paratactic and periodic sentences, creating different responses in her audience. On the one hand, she runs a sentence without clearly ordering relationships for the audience:

> Christians have too long slumbered and slept; sinners stumbled into hell, and still are stumbling, for the want of Christian exertion; and the devil is going about like a roaring lion, seeking whom he may devour. (51–52)

By employing the running style, she made the audience responsible for clearly establishing the relationship between and among the various ideas. Perhaps she did not have time to order these ideas; the ideas are simply presented through a succession of dependent clauses in normal order, with subject preceding verb. On the other hand, she ordered other sentences using periodic style, thus telling her audience that she was one who could control her language. This ability to masterfully guide language was exemplified in the following sentence: "Oh it is because that we and our fathers have dealt treacherously with one another, and because many of us now possess that envious and malicious disposition, that we had rather die than see each other rise an inch above a beggar?" (54). She gave her audience reasons, which she placed in the subordinate structures and then concluded. By deemphasizing the reasons, she emphasized the major point of her sentence: to stress the consequences that the negative actions of the audience members and their fathers had on the audience members.

Maria Stewart and Black Nationalism

Many historical accounts have traced the beginnings of Black nationalism to the *Appeal in Four Articles, Together with a Preamble to the Coloured Citizens of the World, but in Particular and Very Expressly to Those of the United States of America*, a fiery rhetorical tract written by David Walker in 1829, demanding equitable treatment of Blacks in American society. Walker's document, as illustrated in the title, specifically addressed Blacks in America and throughout the world. It exemplifies key aspects of Black preacher rhetoric: Its authorship and audience are both black.[29] Like her mentor David Walker, Stewart directed many of her speeches using black nationalist themes to black audiences. Black nationalism has been defined as "the belief among African-Americans that they constitute a nation, due to their common history, common destiny, and unbridgeable distinctiveness."[30] Viewed by Wilson Moses as a religious movement, Black nationalism as a component of that common history helped to establish the nationality of blacks.[31] Historians and other scholars often have gravitated to the ideas of male figures, those of Marcus Garvey, Henry Highland Garnet, and Martin Delany, as central to examining nineteenth-century black nationalism to the exclusion of women's ideas.[32] When Stewart embraced nationalist thought in her religious speeches, she continued to break the traditional mold by participating in a political discourse mostly associated with men.

In her "Address to the Afric-American Intelligence Society," Maria Stewart, who clearly regarded her people as a "nation," compared them to the Greeks, Poles, and Haitians, who had unified themselves, and had raised their esteem among the nations of the world. She pointed with pride to the spirit celebrating the future independent nation of Haiti:

> Look at the French in the late revolution! No traitors among them, to expose their plans to the crowned heads of Europe! "Liberty or Death!" was their cry. And the Haytians, though they have not yet been acknowledged as a nation, yet their firmness of character, and independence of spirit have been greatly admired, and high [sic] applauded. Look at the Poles, a feeble people! They rose against three hundred thousand mighty men in Russia; and though they did not gain the conquest, yet they obtained the name of gallant Poles. (53–54)

It is significant that she included Haiti as one of the nations since, as part of the African diaspora, it served as a source of pride and emulation for African Blacks in America; its status as an autonomous majority Black nation was unprecedented. This advancement of race pride has been identified by Dexter Gordon as one of the primary elements of Black nationalism.[33]

Although Stewart maintained the rights of Blacks to resist their expulsion to "a strange land," she nevertheless espoused nationalistic thought. Her brand of nationalism, written in response to arguments of racial inequality, promoted not only race pride and uplift, but other important elements of nationalism such as unity, group consciousness, and self-determination. Contemporary nationalist Molefi Asante, countering Wilson Moses' arguments that true nationalism is tied to the creation of a nation-state, labeled this variety of nationalistic thought as "systematic nationalism," one not dependent upon land acquisition, often considered the ultimate stage of nationalism.[34] Stewart's statement advocating her nationalistic views proposed in the "Address Delivered Before to Afric-American Female Intelligence Society of America," insisted on the need for self-determination and unity by pointing to the audacious efforts exhibited among many nations around the globe:

> It is useless for us any longer to sit with our hands folded, reproaching the whites; for that will never elevate us. All the nations of the earth have distinguished themselves, and have shown forth a noble and gallant spirit. Look at the suffering Greeks! Their proud souls revolted at the idea of serving a tyrannical nation, who were no better than themselves, and perhaps not so good. They made a mighty effort and arose; their souls were knit together in the holy bonds of love and union; they were united, and came off victorious. (53)

Stewart's nationalism became more evident as she castigated the audience for their acquiescence to the oppressed condition of the race. She began with a direct query to try to understand the reasons for the methods used to discourage unity among those of her race. The series of questions created a sense of urgency:

> And why is it, my friends, that we are despised above all the nations upon the earth? Is it merely because our skins are tinged with a sable hue? No, nor will I ever believe that it is. What then is it? Oh, it is because that we and our fathers have dealt treacherously with one another, and because many of us now possess that envious and malicious disposition, that we had

rather die than see each other rise an inch above a beggar. No gentle methods are used to promote love and friendship among us, but much is done to destroy it. Shall we be a hissing and a reproach among the nations of the earth any longer? (53–54)

Infused with David Walker's passionate rhetoric, Stewart's speech contains a direct echo of a segment of his *Appeal*, intended to make Black citizens aware of their degraded state, incite them to voice their discontent with their lowly status, and to fight to ameliorate their oppressed condition. As an advocate of African-American nationalism, she joined the ranks of most of the best-known and most literate African-American clergy who revealed elements of nationalism in their rhetoric and of the nationalists who struggled "to awaken blacks to a bitter consciousness of degradation" in order to help them establish a Black identity antithetical to the one constructed by the white supremacist discourse prevalent during that era.[35]

To further her nationalist stance, Stewart incorporated into her speech the nineteenth-century rallying cry, popular with Black preachers and other leaders, "who from the late eighteenth century to the present day have never tired of explicating it."[36] This verse, "Ethiopia shall stretch forth her hand unto him," is based on the verse of the psalmist, "Princes shall come out of Egypt; Ethiopia shall soon stretch forth her hands unto God" (Psalms 68:31). Usually this phrase implied that God had some great destiny in mind for Blacks as they looked for guidance and support from Him. Nineteenth-century Methodist minister Prince Hall and African Methodist Episcopal Zion minister Peter Williams both invoked this rhetorical device in their sermons. Twentieth-century African Orthodox Church minister and founder Marcus Garvey also commonly invoked this image in his oratory. By placing a variation of the Ethiopian allusion in an African context, Garvey used it to motivate the men in his audience to join his movement by stating, "I see Ethiopia stretching forth her hands unto God and methinks I see the Angel of God taking up the Standard of the Red, the Black, and the Green, and saying Men of the Negro Race, Men of Ethiopia, follow me."[37] When Stewart used this phrase, she contributed to a lineage of African Americans who have used this strategy to create a sense of Black pride drawn from a verse in a common nineteenth-century text, the Bible. This African-centered rhetorical strategy can be compared to the outcry popularized in the South African Apartheid struggle *"Amandala!"* recited with raised, clenched fists at the conclusion of a political speech. Translated as, "power!" it signifies national pride and collective advancement and determination.

As a nationalist, Stewart spoke not only with Black pride and unity, but with a militant "Zionist" rhetoric that Wilson Moses calls the "Black jeremiad," citing definitions such as a "response to some present tragedy and a warning of greater tribulations to come." Another author described it as "a mode of discourse that urges people to change their sinful ways so as to avert or avoid threatened changes; it also forecasts great misery."[38] According to Moses, the Black jeremiad is used to describe the constant warnings from Blacks to whites for the sins of their participation in slavery.[39] Blacks' adaptation of the jeremiadic tradition exhibited itself in their use of this rhetorical device to reveal themselves as a chosen people. Furthermore, it showed "a clever ability to play on the belief that America as a whole was a chosen nation with a covenantal duty to deal justly with the blacks."[40] In short, the Black jeremiad, overly concerned with impending doom, was directed mostly at a white audience, forecasting God's punishment for those who had disobeyed natural and divine law. Absalom Jones and Richard Allen pointed at the divine retribution that might take place.

In invoking the Black jeremiad, Stewart was most influenced by her political and intellectual mentor, David Walker. In his incendiary *Appeal*, he wrote, "The whites want slaves and want us for their slaves, but some of them will curse the day they ever saw us. As true as the sun ever shone, in its meridian splendor, my color will root some of them out of the very face of the earth."[41]

Stewart's use of the Black jeremiad paralleled Walker's. In her "Address at the Masonic Hall," she compared America to Babylon:

> She is indeed a seller of slaves and the souls of men; she has made the Africans drunk with the wine of her fornication . . . God will surely raise up those among us who will plead the cause of virtue and the pure principles of morality more eloquently than I am able to do . . . They will have their rights; and if I refused, I am afraid they will spread horror and destruction. (63)

Stewart issued a direct threat to Americans that if they did not change their ways America (white Americans) would be destroyed, perhaps by a Black revolt. Considering the audience she addressed (Black men), she appealed to them to fight to ameliorate their condition and the condition of other oppressed Blacks.[42]

As revealed in her "Address Delivered Before the Afric-American Female Intelligence Society of America," she continued to act in the tradition of Black preachers, militant ones who consider themselves soldiers engaged in a holy battle for Christ. Unashamedly, she proclaimed that she was one who had "enlisted in the holy warfare" (52). Moreover, with Jesus as her captain, she was willing to fight, even to die "in defence of God and his laws" (52). Joining the ranks of slave preacher Nat Turner, whom Gayroud Wilmore called a "general in the Lord's army," she no doubt would have fought as vehemently for her religious beliefs as Turner did for freedom.[43] Used abundantly in African-American hymns and folk songs, from which many Black preachers draw their sermonic texts, the image of the Christian soldier prevalent in the well-known spiritual, "We are Climbing Jacob's Ladder," represents this martial role in the emphatic line: "We are climbing Jacob's ladder . . . soldiers of the cross."

Maria Stewart's role as a female pioneer in establishing rhetorical traditions of nineteenth-century oratory has been established firmly through her ground-breaking speeches to audiences of both sexes. To overcome the constraints that she faced as a woman daring to gain a public voice, she assumed a religious stance that emphasized her profound and abiding faith in God and acknowledged him as the source of her authority to speak. Through the ideologies of womanism and Black nationalism, she encouraged the building of community and its liberation through the empowerment of women and men, as well as the rejection of racial degradation as a significant step in the formation of Black identity.

Viewing herself as a prophet chosen by God, she grounded her discourse in the rhetorical traditions of her African-American heritage. Her passionate, moving oratory contained many of the rhetorical features of what traditionally was considered a male-dominated sphere: the Black preaching tradition. Rhetorical strategies evoking audience participation, themes of special significance to the African community, rhetorical forms that helped to instill African-American pride or that originated in Africa—these were the most salient rhetorical features from this spiritual tradition.

Although Stewart eventually was forced to abandon her public speaking career because of the conservative, sexist views towards women, she left an enduring legacy. As one who dared to speak out publicly from the confines of race and sex, she offered her people hope and inspiration, while challenging them to advance both spiritually and intellectually.

Notes

1. Erika Lindemann, *A Rhetoric for Writing Teachers* (New York: Oxford University Press, 1987), 40.

2. Aristotle, *On Rhetoric: A Theory of Civic Discourse*, trans. George A. Kennedy (New York: Oxford University Press, 1991), 36.

3. Lindemann, *A Rhetoric*, 40.

4. Richard M. Weaver, *Language Is Sermonic* (Baton Rouge: Louisiana State Press, 1985), 224.

5. Henry Mitchell, *Black Preaching* (New York: J. P. Lippincott Co., 1971), 96–97.

6. C. Eric Lincoln and Lawrence H. Mamiya, *The Black Church in the African American Experience* (Durham: Duke University Press, 1990), 175.

7. Bruce A. Rosenberg, *The Art of the American Folk Preacher* (New York: Oxford University Press, 1970).

8. William Andrews, *Sisters of the Spirit: Three Black Women's Autobiographies of the Nineteenth Century* (Bloomington: Indiana University Press, 1986), 4–8.

9. Lincoln and Mamiya, *The Black Church*, 281–82.

10. Ibid.

11. Judith Weidman, *Women Ministers* (New York: Harper and Row, 1985), 73.

12. Carla Peterson, *"Doers of the Word": African-American Women Speakers and Writers in the North (1830–1880)* (New York: Oxford University Press, 1995), 16.

13. Marilyn Richardson, ed., *Maria W. Stewart: America's First Black Woman Political Writer* (Bloomington: Indiana University Press, 1987), 3–4. All further quotations from Richardson's edition of Stewart's essays will be noted in the text with page number references in parentheses following the quotations.

14. Wilson Jeremiah Moses, *Black Messiahs and Uncle Toms: Social and Literary Manipulations of Religious Myth* (University Park: Pennsylvania State University Press, 1982), 31.

15. Alice Walker, *In Search of Our Mothers' Gardens: Womanist Prose* (New York: Harcourt Brace Jovanovich, 1983), xi–xii. "1. Womanism from womanish . . . Usually referring to outrageous, audacious, courageous, or *willful* behavior . . . 2. . . . a woman who loves other women, sexually and/or nonsexually . . . Committed to survival and wholeness of entire people, male and female . . . 3. Loves music . . . Loves the Spirit . . . Loves struggle . . . 4. Womanist is to feminist as purple is to lavender."

16. Clenora Hudson-Weems, "Africana Womanism: An Historical, Global Perspective for Women of African Descent," in *Call and Response: The Riverside Anthology of the African American Literary Tradition*, ed. Patricia Liggins Hill et al. (Boston: Houghton Mifflin, 1998), 1814–15. Grounded in African culture, the term "Africana womanism," coined in the 1980s, offers an alternative to Black feminism. It emphasizes both ethnicity and gender, as well as family centeredness.

17. Womanist theology is an important religious movement whose name was derived from Walker's "womanism." See key texts, e.g., Katie G. Cannon,

Katie's Canon: Womanism and the Soul of the Black Community (New York: Continuum, 1995); Delores Williams, *Sisters in the Wilderness: The Challenge of Womanist God-Talk* (Maryknoll, N.Y.: Orbis Books, 1993).

18. Ann Farrar Lightner Fuller, "Oral Tradition—Women in Religion: Recount Extualizing the Sermon to Tell Her Story," in *Religion and Society, Black Creativity and the State of the Race,* ed. Rose U. Mezu (Randallstown, Black Academy Press, 1999), 63.

19. A thorough discussion of the contradictory representations of Sojourner Truth's delivery of her women's right's speech at the Akron, Ohio, convention is in Nell Irvin Painter, *Sojourner Truth: A Life, A Symbol.* (New York: W.W. Norton, 1996). Painter maintains that Frances Gage's version of the speech is probably less than authentic.

20. Sojourner Truth, "Speech Delivered to the Woman's Rights Convention, Akron, Ohio," in *With Pen and Voice: A Critical Anthology of Nineteenth-Century African-American Women,* ed. Shirley Wilson Logan (Carbondale: Southern Illinois University Press, 1995), 24–27. Logan includes two versions of Truth's speech in her anthology.

21. Lillian O'Connor, *Pioneer Women Orators* (New York: Columbia University Press, 1954), 137.

22. Houston Baker, *Long Black Song* (Charlottesville: University of Virginia Press, 1972), 51.

23. Lincoln and Mamiya, *The Black Church,* 355.

24. Rev. Dr. Patricia Ann Outlaw, Associate Minister in the A.M.E. Church and Associate Professor of Theology, Samford University, Birmingham, Alabama, telephone and e-mail interview, June 2004.

25. Outlaw interview.

26. Geneva Smitherman, *Talking that Talk: Language, Culture, and Education in African America* (New York: Routledge, 2000), 63.

27. Sonya Haynes Stone, "The Black Preacher as Teacher" (Ph.D. dissertation, Northwestern University, 1976), 83.

28. James Weldon Johnson, *God's Trombones* (New York: Penguin Books, 1976), 49.

29. Stone, "The Black Preacher," 79.

30. Wilson Jeremiah Moses, *The Ways of Ethiopia: Studies in African American Life and Letters,* 1st ed. (Ames: Iowa State University Press, 1990), 160.

31. Ibid., 113.

32. Peterson, *"Doers of the Word,"* 4.

33. Dexter B. Gordon, *Black Identity: Rhetoric, Ideology, and Nineteenth-Century Black Nationalism* (Carbondale: Southern Illinois University Press, 2003), 90.

34. Molefi Kete Asante, "Systematic Nationalism: A Legitimate Strategy for National Selfhood," *Journal of Black Studies* 9 (1978): 124.

35. Moses, *Ways of Ethiopia,* 159; Gordon, *Black Identity,* 174.

36. Moses, *Ways of Ethiopia,* 159.

37. Marcus Garvey, "Speech Delivered at Liberty Hall, New York City,

During Second International Convention of Negroes, August 1921," in *Black Writers of America*, ed. Richard Barksdale and Keneth Kinnamon (New York: Macmillan, 1972), 569.

38. Moses, *Ways of Ethiopia*, 31; Barry Brummett, *Contemporary Apocalyptic Rhetoric* (New York: Praeger, 1991), 17.

39. Moses, *Ways of Ethiopia*, 31.

40. Ibid.

41. David Walker, *Appeal* in *Black Writers of America*, ed. R. Barksdale and K. Kinnamon, (New York: Harper and Row, 1985), 152.

42. Stewart probably produced much of her oratory for the benefit of whites, although much of it was directed to Black audiences, as Wilson Moses suggests. See Moses, *Black Messiahs and Uncle Toms*, 37.

43. Gayraud Wilmore, *Black Religion and Black Radicalism* (New York: Doubleday, 1972), 47.

Chapter 3

A Woman Made of Words

The Rhetorical Invention of Maria W. Stewart

EBONY A. UTLEY

On September 21, 1832, Maria W. Stewart delivered a lecture at Franklin Hall, located at number 16 Franklin Street in Boston. On that Friday she "did what no American-born woman, black or white, before her is recorded as having done. She mounted a lecture platform and raised a political argument before a racially mixed, 'promiscuous' audience, that is, one composed of both men and women."[1] In 1832, it was unprecedented for a black woman to publicly decry the evils of racial oppression and to condemn blacks and whites alike for their declension from religion and the pure principles of God. Nonetheless, when Stewart spoke she was competent, fearless, and unwaveringly committed to disseminating her prophetic message. Stewart's extant texts are irreplaceable artifacts heralding the rhetorical and political prowess of the first black woman and the third American-born woman to address a promiscuous crowd.[2]

This rhetorical analysis of Stewart's public discourse considers how her attention to audience advances her intrepid political agenda. I argue that Stewart's inclusion of white *and* black, male *and* female audience members adds clarity to the complexity of her vision of racial and gender parity and participates in a tradition of black public dual audience construction commonly referred to as the antebellum black jeremiad.[3] After historicizing the black jeremiad, I will consider how personal and political events in Stewart's life prefigured a unique black female articulation of the jeremiad.

The jeremiad persists as a significant rhetorical form because it emphasizes American exceptionality. Contemporary scholarship on American public address and culture must account for the perennial belief that the United States of America was and is a nation chosen by God. As Stewart's jeremiads call attention to the life experiences of a black woman living in America, she highlights the disparities and hypocrisy of a country under divine guidance. Beyond that, however, she also offers hope—as long as Americans perceive their fates as intertwined. Stewart's message of racial and gendered interdependence as a revised premise for American exceptionality contributes to the bedrock of black feminist calls for social justice.

This chapter first explores the nature of the black jeremiad. It then considers invisible audiences or the readers constructed by Stewart, the writer of a political pamphlet—"Religion and the Pure Principles of Morality, the Sure Foundation on which We Must Build." The final section focuses on Stewart, the orator. Through an analysis of the utterances or specific speech acts of Stewart's public address, I explore how Stewart re-invented herself and her rhetoric to adjust to hostile physical audiences resistant to a black woman advancing a political argument.

Black Jeremiad

Jeremiads or lamentations prophesying righteous retribution as a result of sin are named for the prophet Jeremiah, who urged Israel, God's chosen people, to turn from their wicked ways and restore their covenant with God. In America, the jeremiad was appropriated primarily as antebellum discourse spurred by the Puritans' belief that they were God's chosen people. Constructing themselves as the new Israel escaping the corrupt European (Egyptian) society, Puritan ministers monitored sins and preached repentance in order to ensure God's promise of greatness. Victory over the British in the Revolutionary War further confirmed for many Americans that their republic was indeed a nation chosen by God. However, for blacks who described American slavery as more horrific than the Israelites' under the Egyptians, the major victory remained on the horizon.

Black jeremiads consistently emphasized three core themes: being chosen by God, declension, and restoration, but in his book *Black Messiahs and Uncle Toms*, Wilson Moses uses the specific term black jeremiad "to describe the constant warnings issued by blacks to whites, concerning the judgment that was to come for the sin of slavery."[4] In the black jeremiad, blacks situate themselves as a chosen people within a chosen nation, singled out by God to urge whites to turn from their hypocrisy and abandon the slavocracy. Whites, however, were the ostensible but not the only audience of the jeremiad. Stewart's biographer Marilyn Richardson notes that the jeremiadic tradition was "intended as much to hearten and edify the oppressed as to warn the oppressor" (17). "Despite" what David Howard-Pitney calls "its dark surface tones, the American jeremiad was filled with underlying optimism about America's fate and mission." Wilson concurs that the jeremiads' fervent language constituted "warnings of evils to be avoided, not prescriptions for revolution."[5]

Thus, the black jeremiad was a carefully crafted discourse that served multiple purposes. On the one hand, it callously warned whites while it affirmed the black commitment to "the principles of egalitarian liberalism and to the Anglo-Christian code of values."[6] On the other, it provided a verbal outlet for black frustration, affirmed black humanity (slaves were not considered human), buffered the black psyche by convincing blacks that "God permitted but did not will slavery," and finally predicted an end to the peculiar institution.[7] Howard-Pitney confirms the duality of black jeremiadic discourse in his book *The Afro-American Jeremiad.* "The Afro-American jeremiad tradition then characteristically addresses *two* American chosen peoples—black and white—whose millennial destinies, while distinct, are also inextricably entwined."[8] Both black and white audiences of the jeremiad were accountable to God and thus had important social work to do.

Clothing shopkeeper and militant abolitionist journalist David Walker articulated the responsibilities of both races in his 1829 "incendiary manifesto," *Walker's Appeal, In Four Articles; Together With A Preamble, To The Coloured Citizens Of The World, But In Particular, And Very Expressly, To Those Of The United States Of America.* Born free in 1785 yet stifled by the oppression of the South, Walker vowed to avenge the degradation of African slaves when he left his North Carolina homeland for Boston. His most infamous effort was the *Appeal.* Peter Hinks, editor of a 2000 edition of the *Appeal,* describes it as "one of the nineteenth century's most incisive and vivid indictments of American racism and the insidious undermining it wrought on the black psyche."[9] When Walker wrote directly to blacks, as the title implies, he urged them to support each other and to strive for an existence beyond subservience. He expressed his motive clearly: "to awaken in the breasts of my afflicted, degraded and slumbering brethren, a spirit of inquiry and investigation respecting our miseries and wretchedness in this *Republican Land of Liberty!!!!!!*"[10]

Walker's invectives to "Christian Americans" that upbraid their racism and hypocrisy were just as powerful. Walker admonished Christian Americans who "chain and handcuff us [blacks] . . . like brutes, and go into the house of the God of justice to return him thanks for having aided them in their infernal cruelties inflicted upon us."[11] Mimicking the biblical prophet Jeremiah, Walker decried the destruction of a sinful society: "O Americans! Americans!! I call God—I call angels—I call men, to witness, that your destruction *is at hand*, and will be speedily consummated unless you REPENT."[12] Walker's vehement rhetorical style and appeal to black and white audiences inspired many generations of African Americans, including his friend Maria Stewart. Stewart's jeremiads borrow from Walker's language and are indebted to his passionate expressions. Nonetheless, her attention to the particularities of the female experience endows her jeremiads with a uniqueness of their own.

Personal and Political Context

A review of pertinent personal and political events will contextualize Stewart's entrance into the public sphere. Born in 1803 in Hartford, Connecticut, Stewart was bound out to a clergyman and his family after she was orphaned at the age of five. Between the ages of fifteen and twenty, she left the family, worked as a domestic, and attended Sabbath schools. When Stewart (then Maria Miller) was twenty-three, she and James W. Stewart were married in Boston. The couple joined Boston's small free black population. The majority of Bostonian blacks lived in a segregated portion of town called Nigger Hill. Transportation, lecture halls, and places of entertainment were segregated. Education for blacks was substandard. Although the Stewarts' community consisted of free blacks, they were still acutely aware of the liberation struggles of blacks elsewhere in America and abroad. *Freedom's Journal*, the first black newspaper in the United States, kept black Bostonians abreast of the struggles in Greece, Poland, Haiti, and the West Indies as well as of incidents such as the Denmark Vesey plot in Charleston, South Carolina (4).[13] In 1826, the Massachusetts General Colored Association was founded. It was "dedi-

cated to the betterment of local conditions and to agitation for the abolition of slavery" (5). It was also one of the first black organizations to
have an international political agenda.[14] One of the organization's prominent members was David Walker. The maelstrom left in the wake of his
Appeal resulted in a thousand dollar bounty on a dead Walker's head and
his mysterious death in 1830. He died of either natural causes due to consumption or murder due to poisoning. Neither account has been ir-
refutably affirmed.

The impact on Maria Stewart of Walker's death and of her husband's
death less than a year before Walker's should not be underestimated. Racist
practices stripped Stewart of her inheritance and as an uneducated child-
less widow, her livelihood was threatened. Her experiences as poor domestic, middle-class wife, and teetering on the precipice of poor again
widow familiarized her with the experiences of a range of women. Not
only did this personal anguish influence Stewart's religious recommit-
ment, but the absence of male benefactors effectively removed all practical prohibitions from her entrance to the public sphere. In other words,
no one could accuse her of leaving her husband to embark on a public
career. Further reverberations of political events profoundly influenced
her public discourse. The dire social conditions of free and enslaved black
people, American Colonization Society agitation for emigrating free blacks
to Africa, and Nat Turner's 1831 Southampton, Virginia, slave rebellion,
his subsequent trial, and hanging all propelled Stewart into the public
sphere.

Stewart: A Woman of the Written Word

Stewart's entrance into political public life did not begin with public address but with the October 1831 publication of her pamphlet, "Religion
and the Pure Principles of Morality, the Sure Foundation on Which
We Must Build," published by Garrison and Knapp, editors of the *Liberator*. In 1835, after Stewart left Boston, the Friends of Freedom and Virtue
published *Productions from the Pen of Mrs. Maria W. Stewart*. This publication
includes "Religion and the Pure Principles of Morality," as well as essays,
meditations, and speeches written by Stewart while living and lecturing
in Boston from 1831 to 1833.[15] Since "Religion and the Pure Principles of
Morality" marked her entrance into the public realm, I begin by analyzing her written words. I believe Stewart was extremely cognizant of the

pamphlet's ability to appeal to unexpected or unintended readers. My goal is to illuminate the seamless transitions between her jeremiadic appeals to black women, white women, black men, and white men.

Early in the text, Stewart appeals to the "daughters of her people."

> O, ye daughters of Africa, awake! Awake! Arise! No longer sleep nor slumber, but distinguish yourselves. Show forth to the world that ye are endowed with noble and exalted faculties. O, ye daughters of Africa! What have you done to immortalize your names beyond the grave? What examples have ye set before the rising generation? What foundation have ye laid for generations yet unborn? (30)

Emphasis on daughters of Africa as mothers of the rising generation reveals Stewart's persistent faith in black women as the foundation of black people's improved future. As we will continue to see, Stewart often models the behavior she would like to see in her people, particularly in black women. The act of writing "Religion and the Pure Principles of Morality" exemplifies the temerity with which Stewart hoped to inspire in further generations. Stewart speaks to, for, and with the daughters of her people. As she delivers her prophetic lament, she asks nothing more of her audience than she asks of herself. In the tradition of the jeremiad, she exhorts, "But *we* have a great work to do. Never, no, never, will the chains of slavery and ignorance burst, till *we* become united as one, and cultivate among ourselves the pure principles of piety, morality, and virtue"(30; italics added).

As she continues to exalt black mothers' responsibility for raising virtuous children, Stewart employs an example of American (white) mothers who expand their familial responsibilities to include social ones. "The good women of Wethersfield, Conn[ecticut] toiled in the blazing sun, year after year . . . and procured enough money to erect them a house of worship." Stewart queries, "shall we not imitate their examples, as far as they are worthy of imitation?" (37). This aside about white women serves as a reproach. Black women's intimate experience with Christian white women's hypocrisy, their familiarity with difficult labor, their true closeness to God, and yet their inability to distinguish themselves should have shamed them. Stewart acknowledges that not all white ladies' behavior is worthy of imitation, but the work done to uplift their communities is. Moreover, this same aside about white women that motivates black women also carries a message for white women. This passage ingeniously unites Americans with daughters of Africa through the sacrifice of labor. Hav-

ing toiled for their reward, American women finally share a commonality
with the daughters of Africa. Just as black women should have felt shamed
at the American women's progress in spite of their hypocrisy, white
women with their newfound appreciation for the rewards of labor should
feel ashamed of their exploitation of black women's labor. Despite the
shame, as is characteristic of the jeremiad, there is room in this brief excerpt for optimism—namely the redemption of black and white women.
Black women must toil for their spiritual and social uplift. White women
must learn to appreciate rather than exploit black women's physical toil.

The justification for interpreting this passage as an aside to American
women is Stewart's subsequent chastisement of the gentlemen in America
who shook the shackles of Great Britain yet refused to loose the shackles
of "Afric's sons." Characteristic of Stewart's discourse thus far, before she
addresses American gentlemen, she asks why Afric's sons have not shared
the white fervor for freedom. Part of her message is reproach for black
men who would not rather die than be slaves. Part of her reproach is directed toward white men who have so destroyed the black male spirit that
it never occurs to them to prefer death over slavery. Stewart's reproach increases in specificity:

> Oh, America, America, foul and indelible is thy stain! Dark and dismal is
> the cloud that hangs over thee, for thy cruel wrongs and injuries to the
> fallen sons of Africa. The blood of her murdered ones cries to heaven for
> vengeance against thee. Thou art almost become drunken with the blood
> of her slain; thou has enriched thyself through her toils and labors; and
> now thou refuseth to make even a small return. And thou hast caused the
> daughters of Africa to commit whoredoms and fornications; but upon
> thee be their curse. (39)

As Stewart's jeremiad describes American declension, she clearly distinguishes between the fallen sons of Africa's "cruel wrongs and injuries"
and the daughters of Africa's "whoredoms and fornications," all of whose
injuries were no fault of their own. This passage increases the male and
female children of Africa's indignation toward whites as well as increases
their anticipation for retribution and redemption from God. Also, her persistent use of Africa unites them as a people with a shared nation. Shirley
Logan, scholar of black women's discourse, explains Stewart's connection
to Africa as an attempt "to reclaim an honorable African past that would
place her black auditors in a superior rather than inferior relationship
with Anglo-Americans."[16]

In the following passage, Stewart argues that Africans in America are like Americans. She confirms that they are a distinct people within a chosen people:

> but we will tell you that our souls are fired with the same love of liberty and independence with which your souls are fired. We will tell you that too much of your blood flows in our veins, too much of your color in our skins, for us not to possess your spirits. (40)

When Stewart prompts her black audience to look to whites as examples, she emphasizes self-help as the fundamental solution to their problems. Scapegoating whites and begging desperately for white assistance are absent from her prompt. Instead, she challenges her people to return to God in order to release themselves from physical and intellectual bondage. Returning to God, taking pride in their race, suing for rights, and possessing the spirit of independence were characteristics of both black and white Americans. Implicit in this commonality, however, is a traditional jeremiadic threat. Her people may rise up violently as a result of their protracted mistreatment and as a result of the same love of liberty in their souls that inspired the American Revolution. The fervor increases as her argument gains momentum: "AND WE CLAIM OUR RIGHTS. We will tell you that we are not afraid of them that kill the body, and after that can do no more; but we will tell you whom we do fear. We fear Him who is able, after He hath killed, to destroy both soul and body in hell forever" (40). By closing her argument with an unmistakable invective against whites in the explicit and recognizable form of the jeremiad, Stewart ingeniously tempers her rhetoric by referring to the power of God. Even as she preaches militancy uncharacteristic of a woman, she embodies the prophetic lament of a prophetess sent by God who had no choice but to be a voice for those who would be lost.

Although powerful, the printed pamphlet "Religion and the Pure Principles of Morality" lacked embodiment and thus was less threatening than physically speaking in public. In her essay, "In Praise of Eloquent Diversity: Gender and Rhetoric as Public Persuasion," Celeste Condit asserts that writing hides the body. Because audiences cannot see the writer, they may misinterpret the gender of the author. To be more specific, these audiences may excuse a women for her masculinist rhetoric because they cannot see her. Condit writes, "In writing, biological sex may be made relevant, but in public speaking it is hard to make it irrelevant."[17] Such is the case with Maria Stewart.

It was unusual and for many contemporaries inappropriate for Stewart to write as vehemently as she did, but because she was writing, her gender was less of an immediate hindrance. In fact, I argue that her lack of embodiment as well as that of her audience permitted her expansion of the audience. Nonetheless, Stewart was rhetorically conscious of her engagement in a patriarchal practice. Her public addresses offer empirical evidence that the choices she made were grounded in an awareness of her audience and an awareness of how her audience perceived her as a black woman. In discussing the following four public addresses given in Boston between 1832 and 1833, I focus on how Stewart's utterances constantly adjust to the demands of the audience.

Stewart: A Woman of the Spoken Word

Lecture Delivered at the Franklin Hall

In her "Lecture Delivered at the Franklin Hall" on September 21, 1832, Stewart commences the first political argument presented by a black woman to an audience of blacks and whites, men and women: "Why sit ye here and die?" Immediately, she asks her audience to make a decision. To blacks in the audiences, she is perhaps asking why they remain idle and suffer injustice unto death. To whites in the audience, she may, in a traditional jeremiad, be asking why they persist in their maltreatment of blacks and speed God's judgment and consequently their own deaths. After this initial rhetorical question, she clarifies her audience by directly addressing the black attendees. "Come let us plead our cause before the whites: if they save us alive, we shall live—and if they kill us, we shall but die" (45). At this juncture, all of her audience members should feel uncomfortable. When Stewart asserts that blacks have no choice but to act, she simultaneously warns the white members of her audience to get ready for the action of a group of people who are not afraid to die.

Characteristic of her pamphlet, Stewart is always already in touch with her audience and their wariness of her femaleness. She adjusts by expanding the issue so that it becomes a matter of who, male or female, should be the representative for people of color. She poses two questions. "Methinks I heard a spiritual interrogation—'Who shall go forward, and take off the reproach that is cast upon the people of color? Shall it be a woman?' And my heart made this reply—'If it is thy will, be it even so,

Lord Jesus!'" (45). Neither the religious reference nor the use of herself as a model is an unexpected defense for Stewart.

Stewart's call for action demands more than the imitation of herself; it demands an imitation of white virtue. She implies that if "the American free people of color" were more moral and educated then "the whites would be compelled to say unloose those fetters! Though black your skins as shades of night your hearts are pure, your souls are white." The repetition of this line as well as "I am a true born American; your blood flows in my veins, and your spirit fires my breast" assume more meaning in the presence of a white audience because Stewart uses her strategy of imitation to craft identification between whites and blacks (46). She enhances this identification by referring to blacks as Americans. In "Religion and the Pure Principles of Morality," the word "American" refers to whites only.[18] By contrast, this public speech strengthens the association between the races. Responding to the claim that blacks were lazy and idle, Stewart says to her white audience, "I acknowledge, with extreme sorrow, that there are some who never were and never will be serviceable to society. And have you not a similar class among yourselves?" (47). After issuing a clever identification strategy among lazy and idle blacks and whites, she shifts back to her more positive examples of imitation. Stewart concludes the address with references to the pilgrims, Washington, and Lafayette as exemplars that blacks should emulate in order to secure their rights and privileges (49).

Similar to the conclusion of the pamphlet, the conclusion of her public address speaks directly to a white audience, but there are several noticeable and strategic distinctions at the close of "Lecture Delivered at the Franklin Hall." For the first time, Stewart asserts dependency and places women in a subordinate position to men. She continues to use herself as a model. She describes herself as one of the wretched women of her wretched race and makes a noticeable shift in her rhetoric: "It is upon you that woman depends; she can do but little besides using her influence; and it is for her sake and yours that I have come forward and made myself a hissing and a reproach among the people; for I am also one of the wretched and miserable daughters of the descendants of fallen Africa" (48). Never in the pamphlet or earlier in this speech has Stewart suggested that women were less capable of the self-help she demanded from men. In fact, there are several explicit examples in the pamphlet where she calls women to act for themselves and the futurity of the races (30, 35, 37–39).

This modification in her position on women is not an ideological shift for Stewart, but a conscious adjustment to the expectation that she be apologetic for leaving her place at home and presenting her unwomanly argument before the public. Reverting to the burgeoning ideology of domesticity allowed Stewart to suggest that she was only a lowly woman with a motherly concern for her people. This choice is not a weakness but an acute awareness of the tropes available to her as a woman. In the same way that she uses religion and domesticity as justification, Stewart looks for and finds other means of increasingly secular justification for her entrance into the Boston lecture circuit.

Address Delivered Before The Afric-American Female Intelligence Society of America

In "Address Delivered Before The Afric-American Female Intelligence Society of America," given in the spring of 1832, Stewart focuses her entire message on womanhood.[19] Speaking to an audience primarily of black women, she addresses them intimately. "I am not your enemy, but a friend both to you and to your children. Suffer me, then, to express my sentiments but this once, however severe they may appear to be, and then hereafter let me sink into oblivion, and let my name die in forgetfulness" (52). Then she begins to speak not so much to an audience of friends, but of family.

> It appears to me that there are no people under the heavens so unkind and so unfeeling towards their own, as are the descendants of fallen Africa. I have been something of a traveller in my day; and the general cry among the people is, 'Our own color are our greatest opposers;' and even the whites say that we are greater enemies towards each other, than they are towards us. (53)

This familial warning about internal divisions among her people is consistent with her rhetoric and appropriate for an intimate address. Such a discussion of internal strife is absent from her first message to a mixed audience. Only in the presence of family can one speak in love about their greatest flaws. Otherwise, a severe reproach, like the one that follows, would lead to public embarrassment.

> And why is it, my friends, that we are despised above all the nations upon the earth? Is it merely because our skins are tinged with a sable hue? No, nor will I ever believe that it is. What then is it? Oh, it is because many of

us now possess that envious and malicious disposition, that we had rather
die than see each other rise an inch above a beggar. (54)

Knowing that Stewart often used herself as a model, one could also assume that these persistent references to internal strife might have paralleled conflicts between Stewart and some of the black women in her
audience.

In a final call for redemption, Stewart concludes with "O woman,
woman! Upon you I call; for upon your exertions almost entirely depends whether the rising generation shall be anything more than we have
been or not. O woman, woman! Your example is powerful, your influence
great. . ." (55). In stark contrast to her September 1832 speech, Stewart
ends with an exhortation about the powers of women, particularly black
women. This is another example of Stewart's acute ability was to align her
rhetoric with her audience.

Address Delivered at the African Masonic Hall

Stewart has no introduction for the "Address Delivered at the African
Masonic Hall" given on February 27, 1833, but she does immediately unify
her intended audience of black folk with the phrase, "African rights and
liberty is a subject that ought to fire the breast of every free man of color
in the United States." The gender distinction refers to men because in this
address Stewart makes a conscious choice to construct an audience of men.

Stewart reproaches her male audience for contributing to their wretched
state. She suggests blacks are spurned not because of race, but because they
let themselves "be considered as dastards, cowards, mean, faint hearted
wretches." (57). She urges men to come forward in the strength of God
to be useful and active in the community as she is "for they [whites] admire a noble and patriotic spirit in others; and should they not admire it
in us?" (57). She laments that there are no men of the modern day who
are speaking in defense of blacks. "Talk, without effort, is nothing; you
are abundantly capable, gentlemen, of making yourselves men of distinction; and this gross neglect, on your part, causes my blood to boil within
me"(58). She exclaims that if men had turned to "mental and moral improvement" she might have stayed at home (60).

Similar to her address to the Afric-American Female Intelligence Society of America, Stewart speaks intimately to her people. She directs this
message to black males whose inactivity forced a woman to step up to the

podium and do the work that they should have been preparing themselves to do. Stewart uses every possible persuasion, including risking her justification to speak, to goad black men into action. These arguments would be incomplete, of course, without her reminder that blacks must critique each other in love.

> The reason why our distinguished men have not made themselves more influential, is because they fear that the strong current of opposition through which they must pass would cause their downfall and prove their overthrow. And what gives rise to this opposition? Envy. And what has envy amounted to? Nothing. (62)

Central to every political argument Stewart has made thus far, internal division is a hindrance to emancipation because, as she concludes in the speech, commitment to "African rights and liberty is a subject that ought to fire the breast of every free man of color in the United States."

Mrs. Stewart's Farewell Address to Her Friends in the City of Boston

"Mrs. Stewart's Farewell Address to Her Friends in the City of Boston," given on September 21, 1833, is her most aggressive speech. Addressed to a crowded mixed audience, Stewart speaks defiantly and defensively. She commences with the woman question: "What if I am a woman[?]" She mentions biblical heroines: Deborah, Esther, Mary Magdalene, and the Samarian woman at the well. She asserts that the God of these women is her God, and that St. Paul would have changed his mind about women speaking in public if he knew of "our wrongs and deprivations" (68). Her second rhetorical query is also powerful. "Again; why the Almighty hath imparted unto me the power of speaking thus, I cannot tell" (68). With this line, she reminds her audience that she did not call herself; God called her.

Then to defend her right to speak, Stewart reaches beyond God's authority to secular texts. She challenges her audience to read up to page 51 in "Sketches of the Fair Sex," a text about women's influence throughout the ages around the world. She mentions fifteenth-century women martyrs, apostles, warriors, divines, and scholars (68–69). She also tells a story of a thirteenth-century woman of letters in Latin and law. By using these examples of learned women, Stewart defends herself as a learned woman. She uses herself as model to suggest that when her people become educated, they also will be competent enough to petition for their rights even in the face of opposition.

For I find it is no use for me as an individual to try to make myself useful among my color in this city. It was contempt for my moral and religious opinions in private that drove me thus before a public. Had experience more plainly shown me that it was the nature of man to crush his
fellow, I should not have thought it so hard. Wherefore, my respected
friends, let us no longer talk of prejudice, till prejudice becomes extinct
at home. Let us no longer talk of opposition, till we cease to oppose our
own. For while these evils exist, to talk is like giving breath to the air, and
labor to the wind. (70–71)

Stewart points out that their rejection of her is a rejection of the efforts
of their women, a rejection of their freedom, and a reminder of their self-
indulgence, prejudice, and malice amongst each other.

Upon her official exit from the public arena, Stewart thanks her friends,
urges the members of the church to keep struggling, and reminds the un-
converted that hell is hot (72–73). "The bitterness of my soul has de-
parted from those who endeavored to discourage and hinder me in my
Christian progress; and I can now forgive my enemies, bless those who
have hated me, and cheerfully pray for those who have despitefully used
and persecuted me" (74). Concluding in this way, Stewart reminded her
audiences that they were not just rejecting her, but they were rejecting
God and very possibly an emancipated future. This final messianic message placed her audience in the declension stage of the jeremiad. The
prophecy would remain unfulfilled as long as they rejected messages and
messengers like her.

Conclusion

In order to understand fully the decisions that Stewart made and the risks
that she took in disseminating her discourse, we must pay particular attention to her audiences. Benefiting from the invisible author and reader
characteristics of the written word, Stewart unabashedly addressed multiple
audiences at once. When in public, she contended with the fact that, as
her farewell address implied, audiences often were hostile toward the embodiment of a black woman. Thus Stewart constantly made adjustments.
Her 1832 address to a mixed audience offered a humbled image of herself.
In her address to other black women, she asked for permission to be sincere and severe. She became more daring and perhaps more frustrated in
her early 1833 direct chastisement of the men who would criticize her. For

the farewell speech, her sense of urgency was at its peak. She knew that she had to leave the lecture circuit in light of public reproach. She knew that she had to leave Boston altogether, and if anything were to be salvaged from her attempts, she would have to make explicit claims that her gender had nothing to do with the prophetic message she was bringing from God. It is this desperation that forced Stewart to make unambiguous claims about the right of a woman to speak in public. Without the exigence, she might have been content to skirt the issue with a reliance on domesticity and deliverance from the divine. This sense of urgency drove Stewart's career and the publication of her second edition of essays, speeches, and meditations in 1879. She made sure to leave her texts because she wanted her message, God's message, to reach as many audiences as possible.[20] And it has.

Stewart's contribution to black feminist discourse extends beyond the fact of her being the first black woman to address a promiscuous crowd. Her prescient commitment to publishing her work, including her speeches, left extant texts for audiences more diverse than Stewart ever could have imagined. Her expansion of the jeremiad to include races as well as genders models the inclusivity and coalition building that are the foundations of black feminist thought. Furthermore, her inclusion of multiple audiences demonstrates an awareness of the complexity of articulating a black political agenda.

Stewart was one of the earliest orators to understand that ameliorating the black condition demanded participation from multiple audiences. Her uncompromising message of self-help reiterated that there would be no freedom for blacks or whites until all Americans lived up to their divine calling as virtuous Americans. This inclusion of blacks and whites both male and female allowed her to project a rhetorical vision of parity under God that modeled the society in which she wanted to live.

Notes

1. Marilyn Richardson, ed., *Maria W. Stewart: America's First Black Woman Political Writer* (Bloomington: Indiana University Press, 1987), xiii. All further quotations from Richardson's edition of Stewart's essays will be noted in the text with page number references in parenthesis following the quotations.

2. Richardson's claim that Stewart was the first American-born woman to raise a political argument is disputable. Miss Priscilla Mason of Philadelphia presented a salutatory oration that justified (to a promiscuous audience) a

woman's right to speak in public. This epideictic oration may or may not be considered a political argument, but it is the earliest extant speech given by an American woman; it was published in 1794. Deborah Sampson Gannett was the second American-born woman to address a promiscuous crowd. Her lectures about posing as a man in the Revolutionary War were given in New England in 1802. Karlyn Kohrs Campbell, "Gender and Genre: Loci of Invention and Contradiction in the Earliest Speeches by U.S. Women," *Quarterly Journal of Speech* 81 (1995): 479–95.

3. Throughout this essay I am purposefully using black and white as indeterminate racial signifiers. Although Stewart never refers to the sons and daughters of Africa as black, using the alternative term African American confounds the distinction she makes between the children of Africa and Americans (whites).

4. Wilson Jeremiah Moses, *Black Messiahs and Uncle Toms: Social and Literary Manipulations of a Religious Myth* (University Park: Pennsylvania State University Press, 1993), 30–31.

5. David Howard-Pitney, *The Afro-American Jeremiad* (Philadelphia: Temple University Press, 1990), 7; Moses, *Black Messiahs*, 32.

6. Moses, *Black Messiahs*, 38.

7. Shirley Wilson Logan, *We Are Coming: The Persuasive Discourse of Nineteenth-Century Black Women* (Carbondale: Southern Illinois University Press, 1999), 40.

8. Howard-Pitney, *Afro-American Jeremiad*, 15.

9. Peter P. Hinks, ed., *David Walker's Appeal to the Coloured Citizens of the World* (University Park: Pennsylvania State University Press, 2000), xiv.

10. Ibid., 5.

11. Ibid., 45.

12. Ibid.

13. Ibid., xxiii–xxiv.

14. Ibid., xxiv.

15. My citations refer to the reprinted collection in Richardson. Richardson does not include the meditations originally published as a pamphlet by Garrison and Knapp in 1832. I am not concerned with the meditations in this paper because of their limited political content, but they can be found in their entirety, as well as the complete texts of her speeches from the original edition of *Productions from the Pen of Mrs. Maria W. Stewart*, in Henry Louis Gates, ed., *Spiritual Narratives* (New York: Oxford University Press, 1988).

16. Logan, *We Are Coming*, 40.

17. Celeste M. Condit, "In Praise of Eloquent Diversity: Gender and Rhetoric as Public Persuasion," *Women's Studies in Communication* 20 (1997): 110–11.

18. Earlier, I quote "Religion and the Pure Principles of Morality" where Stewart makes reference to black and white souls sharing the same blood and spirit, but only in this address does she explicitly refer to blacks as Americans.

19. Although "An Address Delivered Before The Afric-American Female Intelligence Society of America" appeared in the *Liberator* in April 1832, which would be before "Lecture Delivered at the Franklin Hall" in September 1832,

Stewart reversed the order in *Productions,* and I present the lectures in the order she published them.

20. Upon receiving a pension from her late husband's service in the War of 1812, Stewart published *Meditations from the Pen of Mrs. Maria W. Stewart.* The following preface reaffirms her commitment to spread the Word. "The author believes that God's time has come for the work to be recognized among His people; for God seeth not as man seeth, but uses such instruments as He sees proper to bring about His most wise and glorious purposes. That God's blessing may accompany this work, and that souls may be brought to the knowledge of the truth as it is in Jesus, is the prayer of the unworthy author" (87).

Chapter 4

"No Throw-away Woman"

Maria W. Stewart as a Forerunner
of Black Feminist Thought

R. DIANNE BARTLOW

Men of eminence have mostly risen from obscurity; nor will I, although a female
of a darker hue, and far more obscure than they, bend my head or hang my
harp upon willows; for though poor, I will virtuous prove.
—Maria W. Stewart.[1]

African-American women have a rich legacy of independence steeped
in the ability to lead and to forge new ground, often making "a way
out of no way."[2] Our efforts throughout history have not simply duplicated the feats of Black men or White women but rather reflect African-
American women's "distinct concerns, values, and the role they have played
as both" women and African Americans.[3] In *When and Where I Enter: The Impact of Black Women on Race and Sex in America*, Paula Giddings asserts that Black
women have been able "to understand the relationship between racism and
sexism because they had to strive against both. In doing so," she adds,
African-American women "became the linchpin between two of the most
important social reform movements in American history: the struggle for
Black rights and women's rights. In the course of defying the imposed
limitations on race and sex, they loosened the chains around both."[4]

The acknowledgment of African-American women's contributions to
end racist practices and to uphold feminist principles by-and-large has

been grossly underestimated. In discussing the way in which race, rap, gender, and the public sphere can be theorized, Gwendolyn Pough argues that "we can no longer simply say that the women were present. We need to articulate fuller accounts of their voices and works." She suggests the "need to extend our interrogations and discussions in ways that validate not only the presence of women in the Black public sphere but women's roles in shaping that sphere."[5] Maria Miller Stewart is among the African-American foremothers whose contributions to "Black women's expressive culture, Black struggles for liberation, and feminist thought and struggle" impacted what these struggles "would (and could) eventually become."[6] This chapter argues that Maria Miller Stewart advanced women's rights in the nineteenth century by creating an intellectual tradition that foregrounded Black feminist thought, and by proposing visions for liberal and cultural feminisms through the lens of African-American women's experiences.

Sociologist Margaret Anderson observes that Stewart has been "rarely recognized in the histories of feminism," and yet Stewart's "exhortations to women domestic workers and day laborers to improve their minds and talents, which she saw thwarted by women's servitude, are clear and passionate feminist ideals."[7] In *Black Feminist Thought: Knowledge, Consciousness, and the Politics of Empowerment*, sociologist Patricia Hill Collins suggests that "[d]espite Maria Stewart's intellectual prowess, the ideas of this extraordinary woman come to us only in scattered fragments that not only suggest her brilliance but speak tellingly of the fate of countless Black women intellectuals."[8] Collins suggests that what has been revealed in the "painstaking process of collecting the ideas and actions of "thrown away" Black women like Maria Stewart is the discovery that "Black women intellectuals have laid an analytical foundation for a distinctive standpoint on self, community, and society and, in doing so, created a Black women's intellectual tradition" (Collins, 5).

For Stewart, that intellectual tradition was infused with the urgent need to speak out against the horrors of prejudice, ignorance, and poverty, and she communicated a theory for civil and women's rights in the nineteenth century through her commanding oratory and "chastening tongue."[9] Giddings suggests that although Stewart's public career was short-lived, she nonetheless "articulated the precepts upon which the future activism of Black women would be based."[10] The late literary and feminist critic Barbara Christian argued that "people of color have always theorized," implying that making theory is for us a way "to survive with such spiritedness the assault on our bodies, social institutions, countries, our very humanity." Christian adds, "My folk, in other words have always been a race for theory—though more in the form of the hieroglyph, a written figure which is both sensual and abstract, both beautiful and communicative."[11] Maria Stewart produced theory as a way to survive because she witnessed the horrors of slavery and the assault on Black people's bodies through forced servitude.

Collins argues that "[a]t the core of Black feminist thought lie theories created by African American women which clarify a Black women's standpoint—in essence, an interpretation of Black women's experiences and ideas by those who participate in them." Collins notes that "African-American women not commonly certified as intellectuals by academic institutions have long functioned as intellectuals by representing the interests of Black women as a group and fostering Black feminist thought" (Collins, 15). In reclaiming the Black women's intellectual tradition, Collins claims that we must tap into "so-called nontraditional sources":

> Reclaiming the Black women's intellectual tradition involves examining the everyday ideas of Black women not previously considered intellectuals. The ideas we share with one another as mothers in extended families, as othermothers in Black communities, as members of Black churches, and as teachers to the Black community's children have formed one pivotal area where African-American women have hammered out a Black women's standpoint. (Collins, 15)

Part of the project of reclaiming the theories and ideas of Black women intellectuals like Stewart, "involves discovering, reinterpreting, and, in many cases, analyzing for the first time the works of U.S. Black women thinkers who were so extraordinary that they did manage to have their ideas preserved," according to Collins. She notes that "[i]n some cases this process involves locating unrecognized and unheralded works, scattered and long out of print."[12] Fortunately, Maria Stewart left extant copies of her public addresses and written work that laid center the interlocking dimension of race, class, and gender in African-American women's lives.[13] Her work focused on a number of issues that were important to black women in her day and are still relevant for us now.

In *Words of Fire: An Anthology of African-American Feminist Thought*, Beverly Guy-Sheftall notes that Stewart spoke of the plight of the "daughters of Africa," and urged Black women "to develop their intellects, become teachers, combine family and work outside the home, oppose subservience to men, and participate fully in all aspects of community building."[14] Another lofty goal "was the unusual call for Black women to build schools for themselves," according to Guy-Sheftall. Oberlin College was the first university to admit women, in 1833, albeit primarily women of the upper class. Despite her subordinate position, and being denied an opportunity to be educated in institutions of higher learning, Stewart nonetheless encouraged her sisters to aspire to being fully educated. Historically, educational institutions have disenfranchised African Americans. Collins argues that "[p]ast practices such as denying literacy to slaves and relegating Black women to under-funded, segregated Southern schools worked to ensure that a quality education for Black women remained the exception rather than the rule" (6). Stewart criticized the systematic denial of education to Blacks and she actively resisted discrimination by urging her sisters to build their own schools. This was part of the radical/liberal feminist and intellectual tradition that Stewart developed. It was a philosophy that was informed by the classical liberal perspective that philosopher Rosemarie Putnam Tong explains was one that envisioned the ideal state as protecting civil liberties. Property and voting rights in addition to freedom of speech, religion, and association were among these liberties. Tong observes that "instead of interfering with the free market," the classical liberal framework provided "all individuals with an equal opportunity to determine their own accumulations within the market."[15] Moreover, Stewart's philosophy embraced the liberal feminist framework that Anderson suggests "assumes that the inequality of women stems both from the denial of equal rights and from women's learned reluctance to exercise their rights" (Anderson, 362–63). Stewart's standpoint was radical in calling attention to the link between race and gender in women's experiences (Anderson, 380).

In her speech on September 21, 1832, delivered at Franklin Hall in Boston, Stewart argued that with education, Blacks could have some measure of influence in society, thereby reducing prejudice:

> Yet, after all, methinks there are no chains so galling as those that bind the soul, and exclude it from the vast field of useful and scientific knowledge. O, had I received the advantages of an early education, my ideas would, ere now, have expanded far and wide; but alas! I possess nothing but moral capability—no teachings but the teachings of the Holy Spirit.
> Yet, after all, methinks were the American free people of color to turn their attention more assiduously to moral worth and intellectual im-

provement, this would be the result: prejudice would gradually diminish, and the whites would be compelled to say, unloose those fetters![16]

Stewart was creating a critical social theory in ways described by Collins, who points out "[a]s an historically oppressed group, U.S. Black women have produced social thought designed to oppose oppression" and that "[s]ocial theories emerging from and/or on behalf of U.S. Black women and other historically oppressed groups aim to find ways to escape from, survive in, and/or oppose prevailing social and economic injustice."[17] Moreover, Collins explains that "in the United States . . . African-American social and political thought analyzes institutional racism, not to help it work more efficiently, but to resist it."[18] That resistance is a tenet of the Black feminist thought in which Stewart engaged.

As alluded to earlier in this essay, Stewart saw the path to liberation thwarted by Black women and Black people's forced servitude, which she spiritedly resisted in her oratory. She forcefully contested the "happy slave" image, debunking existing stereotypes and suggesting instead that Black females would prefer death ultimately over a life of servitude (Stewart, 31–32) In advancing women's rights, Stewart argued that Black females ought to be given the opportunity to live their lives in freedom and on their own terms: "Let our girls possess whatever amiable qualities of soul they may; . . . let their natural taste and ingenuity be what they may; . . . it is impossible for scarce an individual of them to rise above the condition of servants" (Stewart, 30). Stewart questions the "cruel and unfeeling distinction" of servitude in the lives of Black females and asks if the distinction is made "merely because God made our complexion to vary?" (Stewart, 30–31). Stewart suggests it is to society's shame that a such a dominant view of Black females holds, since "few white persons of either sex, who are calculated for anything else, are willing to spend their lives" to "bury their talents in performing mean, servile labor" (Stewart, 31). She suggests this is the "horrible idea" she must "entertain": living "a life of servitude, that if" she "conceived of their [sic] being no possibility of . . . rising above the condition of servant," she "would gladly hail death as a welcome messenger" (Stewart, 31).

Stewart's fiery words bring to mind a similar assessment made by Alice Walker in her book *In Search of Our Mother's Gardens: Womanist Prose* detailing the strain our foremothers endured in being forced to accept that their talents would be unused and unwanted:

Did you have a genius of a great-great grandmother who died under some ignorant and depraved white overseer's lash? Or was she required to bake biscuits for a lazy backwater tramp, when she cried out in her soul to paint watercolors of sunsets, or the rain falling on the green and peaceful pasturelands? Or was her body broken and forced to bear children (who were more often than often sold away from her)—eight, ten, fifteen, twenty children—when her one joy was the thought of modeling heroic figures of rebellion, in stone or clay?[19]

Long before Walker's time, Stewart adopted a radical/liberal feminist platform that argued that forced servitude impinged on the rights of African Americans. She suggested that it was a "horrible idea indeed! to possess noble souls aspiring after high and honorable acquirements, yet confined to the chains of ignorance and poverty to lives of continual drudgery and toil." Moreover, she reasoned that she had not known "of any who have enriched themselves by spending their lives as house-domestics, washing windows, shaking carpets, brushing boots, or tending gentlemen's tables" (Stewart, 31).

In laying bare her admonishment of prejudice, she called upon the women in the audience of the New England Anti-Slavery Society, particularly White women business owners, to take a stand and employ young Black girls in various positions: "I have asked several individuals of my sex, who transact business for themselves, if providing our girls were to give them the most satisfactory references, they would not be willing to grant them an equal opportunity with others? Their reply has been—for their own part, they had no objection; but it was not the custom, were they to take them into their employ, they would be in danger of losing the public patronage" (Stewart, 30).

Stewart argued that the response of White women business owners illumined the "powerful force of prejudice" (Stewart, 30). Moreover, she asked these same women; the "fairer sisters whose hands are never soiled, whose nerves and muscles are never strained," to "go learn by experience!" (Stewart, 32). Stewart was suggesting that White women be cognizant of their own white privilege and be mindful of the Black woman's experience:

Had we had the opportunity that you have had, to improve our moral and mental faculties, what would have hindered our intellects from being as bright, and our manners from being as dignified as yours? Had it been our lot to have been nursed in the lap of affluence and ease, and to have basked beneath the smiles and sunshine of fortune, should we not have naturally supposed that we were never made to toil? (Stewart, 32)

Stewart called attention to the way in which the intersection of race, class, and gender in Black women's lives rendered them all but invisible: "Owing to the disadvantages under which we labor, there are many flowers among us that are . . . born to bloom unseen and waste their fragrance on the desert air" (Stewart, 32).

She was attempting to lay the groundwork for a radical form of liberal feminism that could have been inclusive of all women. But it was a model of feminism that her White sisters could not see and that was overshadowed by their own racist and classist experience. In her discussion of early liberal feminism, Margaret Anderson draws upon Ellen DuBois' work in *Feminism and Suffrage* in assertaining that "White women who worked in the abolition movement gained an understanding from African American women of the concept of institutional power and adopted the political conviction of natural rights for all individuals, regardless of race or sex," and yet "[e]arly White feminists did not develop an understanding that took account of the historical specificity of the African American experience in the United States, nor did they ever make the kind of analysis that could adequately account for class and other cultural differences among women" (Anderson, 366). Anderson notes that, "as a result, the liberal tradition of feminism that was established by the leaders of the women's rights movements such as Elizabeth Cady Stanton (1815–1902) and Susan B. Anthony (1820–1906) began and continued with an inadequate comprehension of race and class issues in women's experience" (Anderson, 366). In short, liberal feminism was premised on White privilege. In great part, as Anderson points out, the weakness of liberal feminism lies in its inability to explain "how White women's and White men's experience is also conditioned by racism" (Anderson, 374). She notes that while "[l]iberal feminism sees race as barrier to individual freedom . . . it does not see that the position of White women is structurally tied to that of women of color" (Anderson, 374).

The difficulty of Stewart's successfully enabling her "fairer sisters" to see their connection to women of color can be seen in the roots of liberal feminism. In drawing upon Alice Rossi's work in *The Feminist Papers*, Anderson suggests that those roots are tied to the Age of Enlightenment:

> The origins of contemporary liberal feminism reach back to the seventeenth- and eighteenth-century Age of Enlightenment in western Europe (also known as the Age of Reason). This period fostered an array of political, social and intellectual movements, most of them characterized by

the explicit faith in the capacity of human reason to generate social reform. As the setting for the early philosophies of feminism, the Age of
Enlightenment is noted for its libertarian ideals, its pleas for humanitarian reform, and its conviction that "reason shall set us free."[20]

The philosophy of the period provided the theme for major changes in
Western social organization (including the French and American revolutions), and it set the stage for the eventual development of social-scientific
thought and the emergence of sociology as an academic field. The historical context of early feminist thought is found in conditions that inspired
more general appeals to social reform through the application of human
reason. This period provides the historical arena for the emergence of
contemporary liberal feminism. (Anderson, 359)

While liberal feminism has its roots in the intellectual movement of the
Enlightenment, women and the working class largely were left out of the Age
of Reason because the ideology it espoused was premised on the thought
of bourgeois White men. Anderson points out that "[d]uring this same
period in the United States, most African American women and men
were still enslaved, and, although slavery was one of the concerns of the
men of the Enlightenment, histories of feminist thought rarely look to
the thoughts of African American women, slave or free, as an origin for
early feminist work" (Anderson, 360).

Stewart was attempting to call attention to the connection between
White and Black women from the standpoint of the Black woman's experience. Her call shows that she was developing a strain of feminist
thought outside of Enlightenment thinking that White women had difficulty envisioning, but that nevertheless could have moved liberal feminism in new and uncharted directions. Stewart was arguing for liberty of
choice, and the means to economic parity for women, both of which are
ideals promoted within the liberal feminist platform. What Stewart was
advocating and what white women could not see, was that Black women
ought to be included and in fact had a rightful place within this liberal
feminist framework. Anderson draws upon Cheryl Townsend Gilkes"
essay, "Together and in Harness: Women's Traditions in the Sanctified
Church," in ascertaining that "[t]o exclude women such as Stewart and
the many other African American thinkers and activists of this early period from the history of feminist thought is to take White European and
American philosophers as creating the history of feminism and to see African American women's feminist ideas only as secondary or as a reaction
to White thought" (Anderson, 360–61).

Beyond the unspoken White privilege shared among her fairer sisters, Stewart also noted how racism against Blacks pervaded popular newspapers of the day. Collins explains that Stewart "challenged African-American women to reject the negative images of Black womanhood so prominent in her times, pointing out that racial and sexual oppression were the fundamental causes of Black women's poverty" (Collins, 3). In one speech, Stewart disputed a piece in the *Liberator* newspaper that asserted Blacks were lazy and idle:

> Take us generally as a people, we are neither lazy or idle; and considering how little we have to excite or stimulate us, I am most astonished that there are so many industrious and ambitious ones to be found; although I acknowledge, with extreme sorrow, that there are some who never were and never will be serviceable to society. And have you not a similar class among yourselves?
>
> Again, it was asserted that we were "a ragged set, crying for liberty." I reply to it, the whites have so long and so loudly proclaimed the theme of equal rights and privileges, that our souls have caught the flame also, ragged as we are. As far as our merit deserves, we feel a common desire to rise above the condition of servants and drudges. I have learnt, by bitter experience, that continual hard labor deadens the energies of the soul, and benumbs the faculties of the mind; the ideas become confined, the mind barren, and, like the scorching sands of Arabia, produces nothing; or like the uncultivated soil, brings forth thorns and thistles. (Stewart, 31)

In *Black Womanist Ethics*, Katie Cannon suggests that Black men and women were viewed as inferior beings in an elaborate hierarchy as "a species between animal and human."[21] Her discussion of the context surrounding Black women's moral situation during the period from 1619 to 1900 helps us to see why Stewart felt an urgent need to challenge racial ideology that denigrated Blacks: "White colonists, caught in the obsessive duality of understanding the slave as property rather than a person, concurred with racist ideology that proclaimed Blacks as lazy, cunning, lewd, impure, naturally inferior, full of animality and matriarchal proclivities, incapable of life's higher thoughts and emotion, and thus incapable of equality with whites."[22] Paula Giddings notes that "although Stewart had a rudimentary education, her rhetoric often demonstrated knowledge of ancient history."[23] In her final lecture, Stewart drew upon history to rationalize the elevation of women in both the public and private spheres and even upon the mystical power that she implied gave women the right to speak on their own behalf:

Among the Greeks, women delivered oracles. The respect the Romans paid to the Sybils is well known. The Jews had their prophetesses. The prediction of the Egyptian women obtained much credit at Rome, even unto the emperors. And in most barbarous nations all things that have the appearance of being supernatural, the mysteries of religion, the secrets of physic, and the rights of magic, were in the possession of women.

If such women as are here described have once existed, be no longer astonished, then, my brethern and friends, that God at this eventful period should raise up your own females to strive by their own example, both in public and private, to assist those who are endeavoring to stop the strong current of prejudice that flows so profusely against us at present. No longer ridicule their efforts, it will be counted for sin. For God makes use of feeble means sometimes to bring about his most exalted purposes ...

What if such women as are here described should rise among our sable race? And it is not impossible, for it is not the color of the skin that makes the man or the woman, but the principle formed in the soul.[24]

The exalted purpose that Stewart professed is a tenet of feminism; the right of women to exercise voice whether in private or public particularly in naming the sources of our own oppression. In the early nineteenth century, it was not customary for women to speak in public on issues like civil rights, and especially feminism, according to Giddings.[25] The limits constraining the public activities of Philadelphia's white women in the nineteenth century further illuminates Giddings contention. White women were considered either "public women" or "women of the street" when they assumed performative roles outside the home, according to Susan Davis. In *Parades and Power: Street Theatre in Nineteenth-Century Philadelphia*, Davis suggests that "women who mounted the speaker's platform in the cause of abolitionism or feminism, were not only vilified for their ideas, but also attacked for daring to manifest them in public, a move critics interpreted as a betrayal of their gender's nature."[26] Thus, operating from a multiple-consciousness informed by gender, race, and class, Maria Stewart's purpose was to exercise voice in advocating against slavery and for women's rights. Her mission illuminates a central precept that would guide the future of Black women's activism. "Her ideas reflected both the fundamentals of the Victorian ethic and criticism of its inherent biases," according to Giddings. "Out of that mix emerged a distinct ethos which underlined Black women's activism for generations to come."[27] It was an ethos that revealed the contradiction of what it meant to be an African-American woman. Collins suggests that African-American women have questioned the "ideologies of womanhood and Black women's devalued status," particularly in relation to the inherent biases of the Victorian ethic (Collins, 12). She asks, "If women are allegedly passive and fragile, then why are Black women treated as 'mules' and assigned heavy cleaning chores?" (Collins, 12). This question was a central one posed by Maria Stewart's public platform in her quest for Black women's equality.

Like Giddings and Collins, Beverly Guy-Sheftall helps to explain the contradiction between the White woman's imagined fragility and the Black woman's capacity for hard labor. Guy-Sheftall suggests that the feminist discourse of Maria Stewart, among other African-American women, was "impacted by other discourses, particularly the Victorian 'cult of true womanhood,' which dictated that women embrace values such as piety, chastity, domesticity, and submissiveness," (28) noting that, "women who embraced these values might be labeled 'cultural feminists' because they did not reject altogether the gender prescriptions of their times. Though they espoused greater independence for women, they also insisted that enlightened wifehood and motherhood were appropriate as-pirations" (Guy-Sheftall, 24). In *Feminist Thought*, Rosemarie Tong suggests that "cultural" or "gender" feminists believe that "women are essentially connected" and valorize "the traits and behaviors traditionally associated with women." She also points out that "cultural feminists praise women's capacities for sharing, nurturing, giving, sympathizing, emphasizing, and especially, connection." Moreover, explains Tong, "in cultural feminists' estimation, relationships with family members and friends are so impor-tant to women that they view separation from others as the quintessen-tial harm."[28]

Stewart's essay, "Religion And The Principles Of Morality, The Sure Foundation On Which We Must Build," espouses the responsibilities the daughters of Africa should have to their families and especially children. The piece is evidence of her contribution to early cultural feminist thought particularly around what she terms women's "domestic concerns," and building high schools for children, all of which she considered an honor for women:

> The American ladies have the honor conferred on them, that by prudence and economy in their domestic concerns, and their unwearied attention in forming the minds of and manners of their children, they laid the foundation of their becoming what they are now. The good women of Wethersfield, Conn., toiled in blazing sun, year after year, weeding onions,

then sold the seed and procured enough money to erect them a house of worship. And shall we not imitate their examples, as far as they are worthy of imitation? Why can we not do something to distinguish ourselves, and contribute some of our hard earnings that would reflect honor upon our memories, and cause our children to arise and call us blessed? Shall it any longer be said of the daughters of Africa, they have no ambition, they have no force? By no means. Let every female heart become united, and let us raise a fund ourselves, and at the end of one year and a half, we might be able to lay the corner stone for the building of a High School, that the higher branches of knowledge might be enjoyed by us; and God would raise us up, and enough to aid us in our laudable designs. Let each one strive to excel in good housewifery, knowing that prudence and economy are the road to wealth. Let us not say we know this, or we know that, and practise nothing; but let us practise what we do know. (Stewart, 28)

Giddings argues the key issues that Black women during Stewart's time saw no contradiction between were "domesticity and political action." Giddings adds that this is the reason that "Stewart could talk about dependence on men and excelling in good housewifery, and at the same time make an unmistakably feminist appeal to Black women."[29] Certainly, encouraging Black women to make a practice of using their minds to help the young, and to invest in their own economy as a way to build wealth, are distinct ways in which she laid the ground for Black feminist thought. Stewart promoted the idea of women's independence from a Black women's standpoint and she provided a framework for a distinct cultural and radical/liberal feminist vision.

In addition to using the trajectory of domesticity and political action as a guide for her feminist activism, Stewart drew upon "the teaching of the Holy Spirit." In her essay "Biblical Theodicy and Black Women's Spiritual Autobiography," Clarice Martin suggests that "Stewart closely interwove the concerns of both religion and social justice in her analysis."[30] Invoking the "teachings of the Holy Spirit" was central to her activism on behalf of social justice and the development of Black feminist thought, and it was a step in devising a critical social theory for Black women. Collins points out that the social theories expressed by Black women reflect their "efforts to come to terms with lived experiences within intersecting oppressions of race, class, gender, sexuality, ethnicity, nation, and religion."[31] Part of Stewart's lived experience relied heavily on her religious bearings as a source of empowerment to speak and write. In *White*

Women's Christ and Black Women's Jesus: Feminist Christology and Womanist Response, Jacqueline Grant writes that "[t]heological investigation into the experiences of Christian Black women reveals that Black women considered the Bible to be a major source for religious validation in their lives." Grant adds that "[t]hough Black women's relationship with God preceded their introduction to the Bible, this Bible gave some content to their God-consciousness," so that "God's revelation as witnessed in the Bible and as read and heard [happened] in the context of their experience."[32]

Stewart's experience showed her how religion could be used not only as a source of empowerment if not entitlement to speak in public, but also as an oppressive devise to discriminate against women, a power that she sought to challenge. Stewart saw that the latter splintered the connection cultural feminism prizes. Cheryl Townsend Gilkes' discussion of gendered views in religion is useful in contextualizing this dilemma:

> Taking seriously the social fact of gendered antagonism in religion means always addressing the pattern and the processes that women and men construct as they go about the routine of doing sacred work. Black women and men share a religious life but often disagree about how that life should be organized and the relative importance of women's roles to that life. Black men and women agree on the necessity of opposing racial oppression, but they often disagree over the degree to which the patriarchy that is normative in the dominant society should be reproduced in their lives.[33]

The patriarchy that was normative is evidenced in women's public speech. Drawing upon the work of Paula Giddings, Townsend Gilkes suggests that "As early as the 1830s, black women orators refuted biblical arguments demanding their silence as public speakers," and instead employed a "moral agency" premised on "their being black and female" that "suffused black women with a tenacious feminism."[34] Maria Stewart stood at the vanguard:

> What if I am a woman; is not the God of ancient times the god of these modern days? Did he not raise up Deborah to be a mother and a judge in Israel? Did not Queen Esther save the lives of the Jews? And Mary Magdalene first declare the resurrection of Christ from the dead? Come, said the woman of Samaria, and see a man that hath told me all things that ever I did; is not this the Christ? St. Paul declared that it was a shame for a woman to speak in public, yet our great High Priest and Advocate did not condemn the woman for a more notorious offense than this; neither

will he condemn this worthless worm . . . Did St. Paul but know of our wrongs and deprivations, I presume he would make no objection to our pleading in public for our rights.[35]

Guy-Sheftall explains that "in 1833, after a short career on the lecture circuit," Stewart "delivered a farewell speech to the black community, particularly ministers, in which she expressed resentment about its negative responses to her defiance of gender conventions" (Guy-Sheftall, 25). In her farewell lecture in Boston on September 21, Stewart boldly stated the reasons for her departure:[36]

> I am about to leave you, perhaps never more to return; for I find no use for me, as an individual, to try to make myself useful among my color in this city. It was contempt for my moral and religious opinions in private that drove me thus before a public. Had experience more plainly shown me that it was the nature of man to crush his fellow, I should not have thought it so hard. Wherefore, my respected friends, let us no longer talk of prejudice til prejudice becomes extinct at home. Let us no longer talk of opposition til we cease to oppose our own.[37]

Gilkes provides further contextualization regarding Black women's calling to speak in public that uncovers the agony Stewart must have felt. She suggests that while men may have viewed women's sharing the pulpit as a threat to male superiority, Black women have viewed their involvement in church, and furthering its aims, as part of their duty:

> Through it all, black women have remained committed to an institution that exists largely because of their extraordinary investments of time, talent, and economic resources.
>
> Black women have a sense of their own importance in their churches and communities that is perhaps unmatched in the sense of self-importance felt by women in other racial-ethnic communities in the United States. When describing, analyzing, and criticizing the black church, almost every eye tends to be turned toward the pulpits, pastors, and their convocations and conflicts. Unfortunately, while black women's story may be larger and perhaps more important, the perceptions and realities of their importance have been the source of criticism, deviant images, and stereotypes. Black women know how radically dependent their churches and communities are on their presence and actions for both organizational integrity and effective mobilization. When blocked from the most visible leadership positions, women find ways to make their voices heard and their power felt in alternative spaces of their own creation, spaces that often give them limited access to the sacred platform. While such access

affirmed their importance, that affirmation was essentially tokenism. I
have concluded that black women are fundamentally correct in their self-
assessment: "If it wasn't for the women," the black community would not
have had the churches and other organizations that have fostered the psychic and material survival of individuals and that have mobilized the constituencies that have produced change and progress. At every level of social interaction and cultural production women are present, and at the
same time they are conscious of the way the dominant white society dis-
respects and rejects their presence.[38]

And yet while many African-American women experienced sexism and
discrimination in the dominant white society and within many Black communities during Stewart's time, as a mode of survival, redemption was key
for them. Grant suggests that for many Black Christian women, "The
understanding of God as creator, sustainer, comforter, and liberator took
on life as they agonized over their pain, and celebrated the hope that as
God delivered the Israelites, they would be delivered as well."[39] It was this
understanding that fostered the Black woman's intellectual tradition produced by Stewart and the framework she forged for a radical form of liberal and cultural feminism, which could have encompassed inclusiveness
for all women. Collins argues that "examining the ideas and actions" of
women like Stewart "reveals a world in which behavior is a statement of
philosophy and in which a vibrant, both/and scholar/activist tradition
remains intact" (Collins, 15–16). Stewart's activism on behalf of women's
rights and humanity reveals she is no "throw-away woman," but in fact
she is a testament to the genius that resides in all of us against the most
inconceivable odds. Her work gives us a legacy upon which we must continue to build unabatedly.

Notes

1. Maria W. Stewart, "What If I Am A Woman?" from "Mrs. Stewart's
Farewell Address to Her Friends in the City of Boston. Delivered September 21,
1833, Productions of Mrs. Maria W. Stewart" (Boston: W. Lloyd Garrison and
Knapp, 1832), 76–79. As quoted in Gerda Lerner, ed., *Black Women in White America: A Documentary History* (New York: Vintage Books, 1992), 566.

2. Darlene Clark Hine, Wilma King, and Linda Reed, eds., *"We Specialize in the
Wholly Impossible": A Reader in Black Women's History* (Brooklyn: Carlson Publishing,
1995), xii, xiv.

3. Paula Giddings, *When and Where I Enter: The Impact of Black Women on Race and
Sex in America* (New York: Bantam Books, 1999), 6.

4. Ibid., 6–7.

5. Gwendolyn D. Pough, *Check It While I Wreck It: Black Womanhood, Hip Hop Culture and the Public Sphere* (Boston: Northeastern University Press, 2004), 37.

6. Ibid., 48.

7. Margaret Anderson, *Thinking About Women: Sociological Perspectives on Sex and Gender* (Boston: Allyn and Bacon, 2003), 3. Hereafter cited in text.

8. Patricia Hill Collins, *Black Feminist Thought: Knowledge, Consciousness, and the Politics of Empowerment* (New York: Routledge, 1991), 4 Hereafter cited in text.

9. Giddings, *When and Where I Enter*, 50.

10. Ibid.

11. Barbara Christian, "The Race for Theory," in *Making Face, Making Soul: Haciendo Caras*, ed. Gloria Anzaldua (San Francisco: Aunt Lute Books, 1990), 336.

12. Patricia Hill Collins, "The Politics of Black Feminist Thought," in *Feminist Theory Reader: Local and Global Perspectives*, ed. Carole R. McCann and Seung-Kyung Kim (New York: Routledge, 2003), 329.

13. Ibid. Also, see Giddings, *When and Where I Enter*, 50.

14. Beverly Guy-Sheftall, ed., *Words of Fire: An Anthology of African-American Feminist Thought* (New York: New Press, 1995), 25. Hereafter cited in text.

15. Rosemarie Putnam Tong, *Feminist Thought*, 2nd ed. (Boulder: Westview, 1998), 11.

16. Maria Stewart, "Lecture Delivered at the Franklin Hall, Boston, September 21, 1832." As quoted in *Words of Fire*, 30–31. Hereafter cited in text.

17. Collins, "Politics of Black Feminist Thought," 325.

18. Ibid.

19. Alice Walker, *In Search of Our Mothers' Gardens: Womanist Prose* (San Diego: Harcourt Brace, 1983), 233.

20. Anderson, *Thinking About Women*, 359.

21. Katie G. Cannon, *Black Womanist Ethics* (Atlanta: Scholars Press, 1988), 41.

22. Ibid.

23. Giddings, *When and Where I Enter*, 50.

24. Maria W. Stewart, "What If I Am A Woman?" 564–65.

25. Giddings, *When and Where I Enter*, 49.

26. Susan Davis, *Parades and Power: Street Theatre in Nineteenth-Century Philadelphia* (Berkeley: University of California Press, 1988), 41.

27. Giddings, *When and Where I Enter*, 50.

28. Tong, *Feminist Thought*, 296–97.

29. Giddings, *When, and Where I Enter*, 52.

30. Clarice J. Martin, "Biblical Theodicy and Black Women's Spiritual Autobiography," in *A Troubling In My Soul: Womanist Perspectives on Evil and Suffering*, ed. Emile M. Townes (Maryknoll, N.Y.: Orbis Books, 1993), 26.

31. Collins, "Politics of Black Feminist Thought," 326.

32. Jacquelyn Grant, *White Women's Christ and Black Women's Jesus: Feminist Christiology and Womanist Response* (Atlanta: Scholars Press, 1989), 211.

33. Cheryl Townsend Gilkes, *If It Wasn't For the Women: Black Women's Experience and Womanist Culture in Church and Community* (Maryknoll: Orbis Books, 2001), 6–7.

34. Ibid., 109.

35. Stewart, "What If I Am A Woman?"

36. Gilkes, *If it Wasn't For the Women*, 563.

37. Ibid., 565–566.

38. Ibid., 7.

39. Grant, *White Women's Christ and Black Women's Jesus*, 211.

Part II

Incidents in the Lives
Free Women and Slaves

Chapter 5

"Hear My Voice, Ye Careless Daughters"

Narratives of Slave and Free Women before Emancipation

HAZEL V. CARBY

A survey of the general terrain of images and stereotypes produced by antebellum sexual ideologies is a necessary but only preliminary contribution to understanding how the ideology of true womanhood influenced and, to a large extent, determined the shape of the public voice of black women writers. What remains to be considered is how an ideology that excluded black women from the category "women" affected the ways in which they wrote and addressed an audience. The relevance of this question extends beyond the writing of slave narratives, and I will first examine texts written by free black women living in the North before turning to a slave narrative, Harriet Jacobs's *Incidents in the Life of a Slave Girl*.

In 1850, Nancy Prince published in Boston her *Life and Travels*. A free woman, Nancy Prince declared that her object in writing was not "a vain desire to appear before the public"; on the contrary, her book was the product of her labor by which she hoped to sustain herself. In other words, Prince regarded her writing as her work. The publication of her *Life and Travels* was the occasion for an assertion of Prince's intention to retain and maintain her independence:

> The Almighty God our heavenly father has designed that we eat our bread by the sweat of our brow; that all-wise and holy Being has designed and requires of us that we be diligent, using the means, that with his bless-

ing we may not be burdensome, believing we shall be directed and go through.[1]

But this statement was double-edged: it was at once an assertion of her present condition and a comment on her history which was retold in the main body of the text. Prince's assertion appealed to the values of the "Protestant ethic," while the opening pages of her text were an apt demonstration of economic racial discrimination; however hard the young Nancy and her family labored in the North, the fruits of that society were not granted to them. At fourteen years old, Nancy replaced a sick friend in service and "thought herself fortunate" to be with a religious family, as she herself had received religious instruction and had been taught "right from wrong" by her grandfather. Prince recounted the details of her arduous duties and cruel treatment and then interrogated the hypocritical religion of her employers:

> Hard labor and unkindness were too much for me; in three months, my health and strength were gone. I often looked at my employers, and thought to myself, is this your religion? I did not wonder that the girl who had lived there previous to myself, went home to die. They had family prayers, morning and evening. Oh! yes, they were sanctimonious! I was a poor stranger, but fourteen years of age, imposed upon by these good people. (11–12)

After seven years of "anxiety and toil," Prince married and went to live in Russia, where her husband was employed and where there was "no prejudice against color" (20–23). Prince established her international perspective in a section which detailed life in Russia and then condemned the racism which permeated the United States, North and South. In a direct address to her audience, which Prince considered to be primarily a Northern readership, she described how, upon her return to her own country, "the weight of prejudice . . . again oppressed [her]," even while she retained her belief in ultimate justice:

> God has in all ages of the world punished every nation and people for their sins. The sins of my beloved country are not hid from his notice; his all-seeing eye sees and knows the secrets of all hearts; the angels that kept not their first estate but left their own habitations, he hath reserved in everlasting chains unto the great day. (43)

By extending the logic of religious conviction, Prince revealed the hypocrisy at the heart of American society. Her thinly veiled threat of revenge gained additional power from her earlier, obviously sympathetic response to those she had witnessed rebelling against the injustices of Russian society.

The dignity and power of Prince's narrative was gained from her position at once inside and outside the society she wished to condemn. Her narrative voice was given strength through her presentation of herself as a true practitioner of Christian principles who was able to comment on the hypocritical attitudes and forms of behavior that she saw practiced throughout the country. Prince used her knowledge of other societies to compare and contrast with her own. Somewhat ironically, she commented that she "may not see as clearly as some" because of the weight of oppression, but, of course, this rhetorical device revealed exactly how appropriate a witness and how effective a narrator of racist practices she was (42). Prince made clear her double position inside U.S. society as a citizen and outside it as an outcast because of her color; her final narrative position, however, was above "this world's tumultuous noise," at the side of the ultimate judge (89).

In her narrative, one action in particular used, but also questioned, a fundamental attribute of true womanhood: the possession of sexual purity. Having discovered that her eldest sister had been "deluded away" into a brothel and become a prostitute, Prince responded: "[t]o have heard of her death, would not have been so painful to me, as we loved each other very much" (12). This statement was in accord with conventional expectations of the importance of sexual purity; death was easier to accept than loss of virtue. However, Prince did not continue to follow the conventional pattern of regarding her sister as "lost" forever but searched for, found, and rescued her. Far from seizing the narrative opportunity to condemn her sister, Prince claimed her "soul as precious" and revealed the contradiction of a sexual ideology that led her sister to feel she was neither "fit to live, nor fit to die." Returning her sister to the bosom of a family Prince declared not shame but a sense of "victory" (13–16). As author, Prince used the structure of spiritual autobiography not to conform to a conventional representation of experience but to begin to question the limits of those conventions as they contradicted aspects of her own experience. *A Narrative of the Life and Travels of Mrs. Nancy Prince. Written by Herself* is an early example of a black woman who attempted to use a conventional narrative form, spiritual autobiography, in unconventional ways.[2] Princes's adoption of a public voice assumed and asserted the authority of her experience.

The conviction that writing was work was attested to by another free black woman, Harriet Wilson, in her narrative *Our Nig; or, Sketches from the Life of a Free Black* (1859).[3] A comparison of Wilson's motives for writing with those of Prince is fruitful. Wilson stated in her preface:

> In offering to the public the following pages, the writer confesses her inability to minister to the refined and cultivated, the pleasure supplied by abler pens. It is not for such these crude narrations appear. Deserted by kindred, disabled by failing health, I am forced to some experiment which shall aid me in maintaining myself and my child without extinguishing this feeble life.

Prince established that her book was the product of her labor, and Wilson appealed to her audience to buy her narrative as a product of her labor so that she and her son could survive. But, unlike Prince, Wilson sought her patronage not from a white Northern audience but from her "colored brethren." Wilson attempted to gain authority for her public voice through a narrative that shared its experience with a black community which she addressed as if it were autonomous from the white community in which it was situated.

In his introduction to Wilson's text, Henry Louis Gates, Jr., calls it the first novel by a black writer because of its use of the plot conventions of sentimental novels (xiii). But the use of these particular conventions can be found not only in the novel but also in many slave narratives. I would argue that *Our Nig* can be most usefully regarded as an allegory of a slave narrative, a "slave" narrative set in the "free" North. The first indication of the possibility of an allegorical reading occurs in the subtitle, "Sketches from the Life of a Free Black, in a Two-Story White House, North. Showing That Slavery's Shadows Fall Even There." Wilson used her voice as a black woman addressing a black audience to condemn racism in the North and criticize abolitionists. This placed Wilson in a position similar to that of Prince, both inside and outside the society subject to critique. Whereas Prince gained narrative dignity and power from her experience of other countries, her outcast status, and her "true" religious principles, Wilson's narrative authority derived from an assertion of independence from the patronage of the white community. Her narrative was written apart from any links to the abolitionist movement, and her direct appeal to the black community marginalized a white readership.

The "two-story white house" can be interpreted initially as the equivalent of the Southern plantation, in which the protagonist, Frado, was held in virtual slavery. Scenes of punishment and brutality, whippings, and beatings were evoked, as in a conventional slave narrative, to document the relentless suffering and persecution to which the slave was subject. The Northern house, like its Southern counterpart, was the sovereign territory of a tyrant, ruled by a mistress whom Wilson described as being "imbued with *southern principles*" (preface). Mrs. Bellmont, the white mistress, was described as having power over the whole family—husband, sons, daughters, and Frado—and was symbolic of the power of the South. The domestic realm, within which Wilson represented Mrs. Bellmont as the ultimate power, was the terrain of struggle over the treatment of Frado in which debates about the position and future of blacks in the United States are re-created. Sensitivity and compassion were to be found in some members of the family, including Mr. Bellmont and one of his sons, but their protests were ignored; the power of the mistress, like the power of the South, was never effectively challenged. The actions of Mrs. Bellmont determine and structure the overall pattern of her slave's life in the house; a house which increasingly resembles the nation, as the resolve of Mrs. Bellmont's opponents to improve Frado's conditions disintegrated at the slightest possibility of conflict. Mr. Bellmont was portrayed as preferring to leave the house to the tyrannical rages of his wife, hiding until the recurring ruptures receded and Frado had again been punished. In a close resemblance to the position of many abolitionists, Mr. Bellmont and his son offered sympathy and loud protestations but were unwilling to assert the moral superiority of their position by fighting the mistress, the South, and imposing an alternative social order. Both men merely dressed Frado's wounds and turned their backs when battles were renewed. The two-story house was an allegory for the divided nation in which the object of controversy and subject of oppression was *Our Nig.* Like Prince, Wilson gained her narrative authority from adapting literary conventions to more adequately conform to a narrative representation and re-creation of black experience. It is important to identify the source of many of these conventions in the sentimental novel and also to recognize that Wilson's particular use of sentimental conventions derives from the sentimental novel via slave narratives to produce a unique allegorical form. That *Our Nig* did not conform to the parameters of contemporary domestic fiction can be attributed to this cultural blend.

The issue of conformity to conventions has been linked to questions concerning the authenticity of slave narratives by historians, particularly in the case of Harriet Jacobs's narrative, *Incidents in the Life of a Slave Girl* (1861).[4] Arguing, convincingly, that historians need to recognize both the "uniqueness" and the "representativeness" of the slave narrative, John Blassingame, in *The Slave Community*, concluded that Jacobs's narrative is inauthentic because it does not conform to the guidelines of representativeness.[5] Blassingame questioned the narrative's orderly framework and the use of providential encounters and continued:

> the story is too melodramatic: miscegenation and cruelty, outraged virtue, unrequited love, and planter licentiousness appear on practically every page. The virtuous Harriet sympathizes with her wretched mistress who has to look on all of the mulattoes fathered by her husband, she refuses to bow to the lascivious demands of her master, bears two children for another white man, and then runs away and hides in a garret in her grandmother's cabin for seven years until she is able to escape to New York . . . In the end, all live happily ever after.[6]

With regard to internal evidence and the question of the authority of the public voice, the critique that Blassingame offers focuses heavily, though perhaps unconsciously, on the protagonist, Linda Brent, as conventional heroine.

In comparing slave narratives to each other, historians and literary critics have relied on a set of unquestioned assumptions that interrelate the quest for freedom and literacy with the establishment of manhood in the gaining of the published, and therefore public, voice. The great strength of these autobiographies, Blassingame states, is that, unlike other important sources, they embody the slaves' own perception of their experiences. Yet it is taken for granted that this experience, which is both unique and representative, is also male:

> If historians seek to provide some understanding of the past experiences of slaves, then the autobiography must be their point of departure; in the autobiography, more clearly than in any other source, we learn what went on in the minds of *black men*. It gives us a window to the "inside half" of the slave's life which never appears in the commentaries of "outsiders." Autobiographers are generally so preoccupied with conflict, those things blocking their hopes and dreams, that their works give a freshness and vitality to history which is often missing in other sources.[7]

The criteria for judgment that Blassingame advances here leave no room for a consideration of the specificity and uniqueness of the black female experience. An analogy can be made between Blassingame's criticism of

Incidents as melodrama and the frequency with which issues of miscegenation, unrequited love, outraged virtue, and planter licentiousness are found foregrounded in diaries by Southern white women, while absent or in the background of the records of their planter husbands. Identifying such a difference should lead us to question and consider the significance of these issues in the lives of women as opposed to men, not to the conclusion that the diaries by women are not credible because they deviate from the conventions of male-authored texts. Any assumption of the representativeness of patriarchal experience does not allow for, or even regard as necessary, a gender-specific form of analysis. Indeed, the criteria chosen by Blassingame as the basis for his dismissal of the narrative credibility of Jacobs's narrative are, ideologically, the indicators of a uniquely female perspective.

Jean Fagan Yellin, a literary historian, critic, and biographer of Jacobs, has (from external evidence) established the authenticity of Jacobs's narrative.[8] Jacobs wrote under the pseudonym Linda Brent. *Incidents in the Life of a Slave Girl* was first published in Boston in 1861, under the editorship of Lydia Maria Child, and a year later it appeared in a British edition.[9] In the discussion that follows, the author will be referred to as Jacobs, but, to preserve narrative continuity, the pseudonym Linda Brent will be used in the analysis of the text and protagonist.

Incidents in the Life of a Slave Girl is the most sophisticated, sustained narrative dissection of the conventions of true womanhood by a black author before emancipation. It will be the object of the following analysis to demonstrate that Jacobs used the material circumstances of her life to critique conventional standards of female behavior and to question their relevance and applicability to the experience of black women. Prior to a close examination of the text itself, it is necessary to document briefly the conditions under which Jacobs wrote her autobiography and gained her public voice.

At the time of writing, Jacobs worked as a domestic servant for and lived with Nathaniel P. Willis and his second wife, the Mr. and Mrs. Bruce of the text. Unlike either his first or second wife, Nathaniel Willis was proslavery. Against Jacobs's wishes but to protect her from the fugitive slave law, the second Mrs. Willis persuaded her husband that Jacobs should be purchased from her owners and manumitted by the family. Because of her suspicions of Nathaniel Willis, Jacobs did not want him to be aware that she was writing of her life in slavery; the need for secrecy and the demands of her domestic duties as nurse to the Willis children forced Jacobs to write at night.[10] Jacobs recognized that the conditions under which she lived and wrote were very different from those under which other female authors were able to write and under which her audience, "the women of the North," lived. In her preface, Linda Brent stated:

> Since I have been at the North, it has been necessary for me to work diligently for my own support, and the education of my children. This has not left me much leisure to make up for the loss of early opportunities to improve myself; and it has compelled me to write these pages at irregular intervals, whenever I could snatch an hour from Household duties. (xiii)

Unlike her white female audience or contemporary authors, Jacobs had neither the advantages of formal education nor contemplative leisure. She contrasted both her past life as a slave and her present condition, in which the selling of her labor was a prime necessity, with the social circumstances of her readership. Jacobs thus established the context within which we should understand her choice of epigram, from Isaiah (32:2): "Rise up, ye women that are at ease! Hear my voice, Ye careless daughters! Give ear unto my speech" (iv). Jacobs had achieved her freedom from slavery, but she was still bound to labor for the existence of herself and her children.

The closing pages of *Incidents* contrasted the "happy endings" of the conventional domestic novel with the present condition of the narrator, Linda Brent: "Reader, my story ends with freedom; not in the usual way with marriage. . . . We are as free from the power of slaveholders as are the white people of the north; and though that, according to my ideas, is not saying a great deal, it is a vast improvement in my condition" (207). Contrary to Blassingame's interpretation, *Incidents* does not conform to the conventional happy ending of the sentimental novel. Linda Brent, in the closing pages of her narrative, was still bound to a white mistress.

Jacobs's position as a domestic servant contrasted with the lives of the white women who surrounded and befriended her. Mrs. Willis, though she was instrumental in gaining her manumission, had the power to buy her and remained her employer, her mistress. Jacobs's letters to Amy Post, although to a friend, revealed her consciousness of their different positions in relation to conventional moral codes. Desiring a female friend who would write some prefatory remarks to her narrative, Jacobs consulted Post, but the occasion led her to indicate that the inclusion of her sexual history in her narrative made her "shrink from asking the sacrifice from one so good and pure as yourself."[11] It was as if Jacobs feared that her own history would contaminate the reputation of her white friend. Lydia Maria Child, who became Jacobs's editor, and Harriet Beecher Stowe, with whom Jacobs had an unfortunate brush, were both described by her as "satellite[s] of so great magnitude."[12] This hierarchy in Jacobs's relations with white women was magnified through the lens of conventional ideas of true womanhood when they appeared in print together, for Jacobs's sexuality was compromised in the very decision to print her story and gain her public voice. As she wrote to Post, after Post had agreed to endorse her story, "Woman can whisper her cruel wrongs into the ear of a very dear friend much easier than she can record them for the world to read."[13] Jacobs had children but no husband and no home of her own. In order to be able to represent herself in conventional terms as a "true" woman, Jacobs should have had a husband to give meaning to her existence as a woman. Any power or influence a woman could exercise was limited to the boundaries of the home. Linda Brent, in the concluding chapter of her narrative, recognized that this particular definition of a woman's sphere did not exist for her, and this factor ensured her dependence on a mistress. She stated, "I do not sit with my children in a home of my own. I still long for a hearthstone of my own, however humble. I wish it for my children's sake far more than my own" (207).

The ideological definition of the womanhood and motherhood of Linda Brent (and Jacobs) remained ambivalent as Linda Brent (and Jacobs) were excluded from the domain of the home, the sphere within which womanhood and motherhood were defined. Without a "woman's sphere," both were rendered meaningless. Nevertheless, the narrative of Linda Brent's life stands as an exposition of her womanhood and motherhood contradicting and transforming an ideology that could not take account of her experience. The structure of Jacobs's narrative embodied the process through which the meaning of Linda Brent's and Jacobs's motherhood and womanhood were revealed. Jacobs, as author, confronted an ideology that denied her very existence as a black woman and as a mother, and, therefore, she had to formulate a set of meanings that implicitly and fundamentally questioned the basis of true womanhood. *Incidents* demystified a convention that appeared as the obvious, common-sense rules of behavior and revealed the concept of true womanhood to be an ideology, not a lived set of social relations as she exposed its inherent contradictions and inapplicability to her life.[14]

Jacobs rejected a patronizing offer by Harriet Beecher Stowe to incorporate her life story into the writing of *The Key to Uncle Tom's Cabin.* This incorporation would have meant that her history would have been circumscribed by the bounds of convention, and Jacobs responded that "it needed no romance." The suggestion that Stowe might write, and control, the story of Jacobs's life raised issues far greater than those which concerned the artistic and aesthetic merit of her narrative; Jacobs "felt denigrated as a mother, betrayed as a woman, and threatened as a writer by Stowe's action."[15] Jacobs knew that to gain her own public voice, as a writer, implicated her very existence as a mother and a woman; the three could not be separated. She also knew from experience, as did Prince and Wilson, that the white people of the North were not completely free from the power of the slaveholders, or from their racism. To be bound to the conventions of true womanhood was to be bound to a racist, ideological system.

Many slave authors changed the names of people and places in their narratives to protect those still subject to slavery. However, Jacobs's need for secrecy in the act of writing and her fear of scorn if discovered meant that her pseudonym, Linda Brent, functioned as a mechanism of self-protection. The creation of Linda Brent as a fictional narrator allowed Jacobs to manipulate a series of conventions that were not only literary in their effects but which also threatened the meaning of Jacobs's social existence. The construction of the history of Linda Brent was the terrain through which Jacobs had to journey in order to reconstruct the meaning of her own life as woman and mother. The journey provided an alternative path to the cult of true womanhood and challenged the readers of *Incidents* to interrogate the social and ideological structures in which they were implicated and to examine their own racism. Jacobs denied that she wrote to "excite sympathy" for her own "sufferings" but claimed that she wanted to "arouse the women of the North to a realizing sense of the condition of two millions of women at the South, still in bondage, suffering what I suffered, and most of them far worse" (xiv). Jacobs established that hers was the voice of a representative black female slave, and in a contemporary interpretation this appeal is defined as being an appeal to the sisterhood of all women:

> Seen from this angle of vision, Jacobs' book—reaching across the gulf
> separating black women from white, slave from free, poor from rich,

reaching across the chasm separating "bad" women from "good"—represents an attempt to establish an American sisterhood and to activate that sisterhood in the public arena.[16]

However, these bonds of sisterhood are not easily or superficially evoked. "Sisterhood" between white and black women was realized rarely in the text of *Incidents*. Jacobs's appeal was to a potential rather than an actual bonding between white and black women. The use of the word *incidents* in the title of her narrative directs the reader to be aware of a consciously chosen selection of events in Jacobs's life.[17] Many of the relationships portrayed between Linda Brent and white women involve cruelty and betrayal and place white female readers in the position of having to realize their implication in the oppression of black women, prior to any actual realization of the bonds of "sisterhood."

The narrative was framed by Linda Brent's relationships to white mistresses. The relationship to Mrs. Willis with which the narrative concluded has already been discussed. The opening chapter, "Childhood," described Linda's early disillusion with a mistress whom she loved and trusted. Linda's early childhood was happy, and only on the death of her mother did Linda learn that she was a slave. *Sister* and *sisterhood* were made ambiguous terms for relationships which had dubious consequences for black women. Early in the text Linda referred to her mother and her mother's mistress as "foster sisters" because they were both fed at the breast of Linda's grandmother. This intimate "sisterhood" as babes was interrupted by the intervention of the starkly contrasting hierarchy of their social relationship. Linda's grandmother, the readers were told, had to wean her own daughter at three months old in order to provide sufficient food for her mistress's daughter. Although they played together as children, Linda's mother's slave status was reasserted when she had to become "a most faithful servant" to her "foster sister." At the side of the deathbed of Linda's mother, her mistress promised her that "her children [would] never suffer for anything" in the future. Linda described her subsequent childhood with this mistress as "happy," without "toilsome or disagreeable duties." A diligent slave, Linda felt "proud to labor for her as much as my young years would permit," and she maintained a heart "as free from care as that of any free born white child" (4–5).

Unlike Kate Drumgold in *A Slave Girl's Story*, Linda Brent did not attempt to replace this mistress as surrogate mother. The phrase carefully chosen by Jacobs was "almost like a mother." The juxtaposition of the concepts of a carefree childhood with laboring registered an experience alien to that of the readership. This gentle disturbance to middle-class ideas of childhood moved toward a climactic shock at the death of the mistress, when Linda was bequeathed to the daughter of her mistress's sister. Linda and her community of friends had been convinced that she would be freed, but, with bitterness, Linda recalled the years of faithful servitude of her mother and her mistress's promise to her mother. In a passage that used a narrative strategy similar to that used by Prince in her *Life and Travels,* Jacobs's narrator indicted the behavior of her mistress according to conventional moral codes. Linda Brent reasserted the religious doctrine espoused by her mistress to condemn her action and reveal the hypocrisy of her beliefs: "My mistress had taught me the precepts of God's word: 'Thou shall love thy neighbor as thyself.' 'Whatsoever ye would that men should do unto you, do ye even so unto them.' But I was her slave, and I suppose she did not recognize me as her neighbor" (6). The disparity between "almost a mother" and the lack of recognition as "neighbor" highlighted the intensity of Jacobs's sense of betrayal. Having taught her slave to read and spell, this mistress had contributed to the ability of Jacobs to tell her tale, but the story Jacobs told condemned the mistress, for it was her "act of injustice" that initiated the suffering in Linda Brent's life.

Because of the hierarchical nature of their social, as opposed to emotional, relationships, white mistresses in the text were placed in positions of power and influence over the course of the lives of slave women, an influence that was still being exerted at the close of the narrative after Linda's emancipation. Linda did not recount the actions of her mistress as if they were only an individual instance of betrayal but placed them within a history of acts of betrayal toward three generations of women in her family: herself, her mother, and her grandmother. Each served as faithful servant, each trusted to the honor of her mistress, and each was betrayed. The reconstruction of these acts through time and over generations was an attempt to assert their representative status within a historical perspective of dishonesty and hypocrisy.

The polarization between the lives of white sisters and black sisters was a recurring motif. The material differences in their lives that determined their futures and overwhelmed either biological relation or emotional attachment were continually stressed in the text. Linda Brent told the reader:

I once saw two beautiful children playing together. One was a fair white child; the other was her slave, and also her sister. When I saw them embracing each other, and heard their joyous laughter, I turned sadly away from the lovely sight. I foresaw the inevitable blight that would fall on the little slave's heart. I knew how soon her laughter would be changed to sighs. The fair child grew up to be a still fairer woman. From childhood to womanhood her pathway was blooming with flowers . . . How had those years dealt with her slave sister, the little playmate of her childhood? She was also very beautiful; but the flowers and sunshine of love were not for her. She drank the cup of sin, and shame, and misery, whereof her persecuted race are compelled to drink. (28–29)

Any feminist history that seeks to establish the sisterhood of white and black women as allies in the struggle against the oppression of all women must also reveal the complexity of the social and economic differences between women. Feminist historiography and literary criticism also need to define the ways in which racist practices are gender-specific and sexual exploitation racialized. The dialectical nature of this process is reconstructed in the "incidents" that Jacobs reconstructed between the slave woman and her mistress.

Linda Brent described her second mistress, Mrs. Flint, in ways that utilized the conventions of an antebellum ideal of womanhood while exposing them as contradictory: "Mrs. Flint, like many southern women, was totally deficient in energy. She had not strength to superintend her household affairs; but her nerves were so strong, that she could sit in her easy chair and see a woman whipped, till the blood trickled from every stroke of the lash" (10). Mrs. Flint forced Linda Brent to walk barefoot through the snow because the "creaking" of her new shoes "grated harshly on her refined nerves" (17). In these and other passages the conventional figure of the plantation mistress is ironically undermined. The qualities of delicacy of constitution and heightened sensitivity, attributes of the Southern lady, appear as a corrupt and superficial veneer that covers an underlying strength and power in cruelty and brutality.

Linda Brent realized that because of Dr. Flint's overt sexual advances and intentions she represented an actual as well as potential threat to the dignity and pride of Mrs. Flint. Jacobs demonstrated the slave's capacity to analyze the grief and pain of her mistress; the slave, however, waited in vain for a reciprocal display of kindness or sympathy. The sisterhood of the two abused women could not be established, for Mrs. Flint, who "pitied herself as a martyr . . . was incapable of feeling for the condition of shame and misery in which her unfortunate, helpless slave was placed" (32).

In an attempt to appeal directly to the compassion of her white Northern readers, Jacobs contrasted the material conditions of black female slaves with their own lives:

> O, you happy free women, contrast your New Year's day with that of the poor bond-woman! With you it is a pleasant season, and the light of the day is blessed . . . Children bring their little offerings, and raise their rosy lips for a caress. They are your own, and no hand but that of death can take them from you. But to the slave mother New Year's day comes laden with peculiar sorrows. She sits on a cold cabin floor, watching the children who may all be torn from her the next morning; and often does she wish that she and they might die before the day dawns. (14)

Linda Brent was a demonstration of the consequences for motherhood of the social and economic relations of the institution of slavery. Jacobs recognized that plantation mistresses were subject to forms of patriarchal abuse and exploitation, but because they gave birth to the heirs of property they were also awarded a degree of patriarchal protection. Slave women gave birth to the capital of the South and were therefore, in Linda Brent's words, "considered of no value, unless they continually increase their owner's stock" (49). Upon this hierarchical differential in power relations an ideology was built which ensured that two opposing concepts of motherhood and womanhood were maintained. As Linda Brent argued, "that which commands admiration in the white woman only hastens the degradation of the female slave" (27). If a slave woman attempted to preserve her sexual autonomy, the economic system of slavery was threatened: "[I]t [was] deemed a crime in her to wish to be virtuous" (29).

The barriers to the establishment of the bonding of sisterhood were built in the space between the different economic, political, and social positions that black women and white women occupied in the social formation of slavery. Their hierarchical relationship was determined through a racial, not gendered, categorization. The ideology of true womanhood was as racialized a concept in relation to white women as it was in its exclusion of black womanhood. Ultimately, it was this racial factor that defined the source of power of white women over their slaves, for, in a position of dependence on the patriarchal system herself, the white mistress identified her interests with the maintenance of the status quo. Linda Brent concluded:

No matter whether the slave girl be as black as ebony or as fair as her mistress. In either case, there is no shadow of law to protect her from insult, from violence, or even from death; all these are inflicted by friends who bear the shape of men. The mistress, who ought to protect the helpless victim, has no other feelings towards her but those of jealousy and rage. (26–27)

Jacobs thus identified that mistresses confirmed their own social position at the expense of denying the humanity of their slaves particularly when they were insecure in their own relation to patriarchal power: "I knew that the young wives of slaveholders often thought their authority and importance would be best established and maintained by cruelty" (94).

The Northern women who formed Jacobs's audience were implicated in the preservation of this oppression in two ways. In a passage that directly addressed the reader, Linda Brent accused Northerners of allowing themselves to be used as "bloodhounds" to hunt fugitives and return them to slavery (34–35). More subtly, Linda Brent also illustrated how Northerners were not immune to the effects of the slave system or to the influence of being able to wield a racist power when she described how, "when northerners go to the south to reside, they prove very apt scholars. They soon imbibe the sentiments and disposition of their neighbors, and generally go beyond their teachers. Of the two, they are proverbially the hardest masters" (44). *Incidents* also documented the numerous acts of racist oppression that Linda Brent had to suffer while in the Northern states. A major motive for her escape from the South was her determination to protect her daughter, Ellen, from the sexual exploitation she herself had experienced. However, Ellen was subject to sexual harassment in the household in which she lived and worked as a servant in New York, which made Linda Brent question the nature and extent of her freedom in the "free" states of the North. Described as being in a position of "servitude to the Anglo-Saxon race," Linda Brent urged the whole black community to defy the racism of Northerners, so that "eventually we shall cease to be trampled underfoot by our oppressors" (180–82).

This spirit of defiance characterized Jacobs's representations of all Linda Brent's encounters with her master. Conventional feminine qualities of submission and passivity were replaced by an active resistance. Although Flint had "power and law on his side," she "had a determined will," and "there was might in each." Her strength and resourcefulness to resist were not adopted from a reservoir of masculine attributes but were shown to have their source in her "woman's pride, and a mother's love for [her] children" (87). Thus, Jacobs developed an alternative set of definitions of womanhood and motherhood in the text, which remained in tension with the cult of true womanhood.

The slave became the object of the jealousy and spite of her mistress; Jacobs wrote that Mrs. Flint even vented her anger on Linda Brent's grandmother for offering Linda and her children protective shelter: "She would not even speak to her in the street. This wounded my grandmother's feelings, for she could not retain ill will against the woman who she had nourished with her milk when a babe" (91). In an effective adaptation of convention it was Linda Brent's grandmother who was portrayed as a woman of genuine sensitivity. The two women were polarized: the grandmother exuded a "natural" warmth, but Mrs. Flint, as Jacobs's choice of name emphasized, displayed an unnatural, cold, and hard heart. For the grandmother, the act of nurturing gave rise to sustained feelings of intimacy; Mrs. Flint's rejection of this mothering relationship implied that she was an unnatural woman. Linda Brent stated that she was "indebted" to her grandmother for all her comforts, "spiritual or temporal" (9). It was the grandmother's labor that fed and clothed her when Mrs. Flint neglected her slave's material needs, and it was the grandmother who stood as the source of a strong moral code in the midst of an immoral system. In a considerable number of ways, Jacobs's figure of the grandmother embodied aspects of a true womanhood; she was represented as being pure and pious, a fountainhead of physical and spiritual sustenance for Linda, her whole family, and the wider black community. However, the quality of conventional womanhood that the grandmother did not possess was submissiveness, and Linda Brent was portrayed as having inherited her spirit. Her love for her grandmother was seen to be tempered by fear; she had been brought up to regard her with a respect that bordered on awe, and at the moment when Linda Brent needed the advice of another woman most desperately she feared to confide in her grandmother, who she knew would condemn her. Out of the moment of her most intense isolation Jacobs made her narrator forge her own rules of behavior and conduct of which even her grandmother would disapprove.

Dr. Flint was characterized by Jacobs as the epitome of corrupt white male power. He was a figure that was carefully dissected to reveal a lack of the conventional qualities of a gentleman. His lack of honor was established early in the text when he defrauded Linda Brent's grandmother.

Presented as a representative slaveholder, Dr. Flint embodied the evil licentiousness that was the ultimate threat to virtue and purity. He whispered foul suggestions into Linda's ears when she was still an innocent girl and used his power to deny her the experience of romance, preventing her from marrying her first, true love. In the chapter entitled "The Lover," a free-born black carpenter was described as possessing the qualities that were absent in Dr. Flint. Honor was posed against dishonor, respect for Linda's virtue against disrespect and insult. The lover Jacobs described as both "intelligent and religious," while Dr. Flint appeared as an animal watching a young girl as his prey. The "base proposals of a white man" were contrasted with the "honorable addresses of a respectable colored man" (40–41). But, despite the fact that Dr. Flint was the embodiment of the corruption of the slave system, as his prey Linda Brent was not corrupted by him, and her struggle was an aggressive refusal to be sexually used and compromised or to succumb to the will of the master.

Instead, hoping to gain a degree of protection from Dr. Flint, Linda Brent decided to become the lover of a white "gentleman," a Mr. Sands. She thought that in his fury Dr. Flint would sell her to her newly acquired lover and that it would be easier in the future to obtain her freedom from her lover than from her master. Linda's reasoning was shown to be motivated by consideration not only for her own welfare but also for improving the chances of survival for any children she might bear. From her experience she knew that Dr. Flint sold his offspring from slave women and hoped that if her children were fathered by Sands he could buy them and secure their future.

The struggle of Linda Brent to retain some control over her sexuality climaxed in a confession of her loss of virtue. It was at this point in the narrative that Jacobs most directly confronted conventional morality. In order to retain narrative authority and to preserve a public voice acceptable to an antebellum readership, Jacobs carefully negotiated the tension between satisfying moral expectations and challenging an ideology that would condemn her as immoral. Jacobs's confession was at once both conventional and unconventional in form and tone. The narrator declared in a direct address to her readers that the remembrance of this period in her "unhappy life" filled her with "sorrow and shame" and made no reference to sexual satisfaction, love, or passion, as such feelings were not meant to be experienced or encouraged outside of marriage and were rarely figured to exist within it.[18] Yet Jacobs refused to follow convention in significant ways. In contrast to the expected pattern of a confessional passage, which called for the unconditional acceptance of the judgment of readers, Linda Brent's act of sexual defiance was described as one of "deliberate calculation": the slave actively chose one fate as opposed to another. Jacobs attempted to deflect any judgmental response of moral condemnation through consistent narrative reminders to the reader that the material conditions of a slave woman's life were different from theirs. Readers were the "happy women" who had been "free to choose the objects of [their] affection." Jacobs, through Linda Brent, claimed the same right in her attempt to assert some control over the conditions of her existence: "It seems less degrading to give one's self, than to submit to compulsion. There is something akin to freedom in having a lover who has no control over you, except that which he gains by kindness and attachment" (55). Jacobs argued that the practice of conventional principles of morality was rendered impossible by the condition of the slave. Her own decision to take a lover was not described as immoral or amoral but as outside conventional ethical boundaries. In a key passage for understanding the extent to which Jacobs challenged ideologies of female sexuality, Linda Brent reflected, "in looking back, calmly, on the events of my life, I feel that the slave woman ought not to be judged by the same standard as others" (56). Within the series of "incidents" that Jacobs represented, this decision was pivotal to the structure of the text and to the development of an alternative discourse of womanhood. Previous events focused on the disruption to a normative journey through childhood, girlhood, and romantic youth; following incidents established the unconventional definitions of womanhood and motherhood that Jacobs, herself, tried to determine.

Linda Brent's decision as a slave, to survive through an act that resulted in her loss of virtue, placed her outside the parameters of the conventional heroine. Barbara Welter has described how heroines who were guilty of a loss of purity, in novels or magazines, were destined for death or madness.[19] According to the doctrine of true womanhood, death itself was preferable to a loss of innocence; Linda Brent not only survived in her "impure" state, but she also used her "illicit" liaison as an attempt to secure a future for herself and her children. Jacobs's narrative was unique in its subversion of a major narrative code of sentimental fiction: death, as preferable to loss of purity, was replaced by "Death is better than slavery" (63). *Incidents* entered the field of women's literature and history transforming and transcending the central paradigm of death versus virtue. The consequences of the loss of innocence, Linda Brent's (and Jacobs's) children, rather than being presented as the fruits of her shame, were her links to life and the motivating force of an additional determination to be free.

Linda Brent's second child was a girl, and the birth caused her to reflect on her daughter's possible future as a slave: "When they told me my new-born babe was a girl, my heart was heavier than it had ever been before. Slavery is terrible for men; but it is far more terrible for women. Superadded to the burden common to all, they have wrongs, and sufferings, and mortifications peculiarly their own" (79). The narrative that Jacobs wrote was assertively gender-specific and resonated against the dominant forms of the male slave narrative. But the sexual exploitation that Linda Brent confronted and feared for her daughter was, at the same moment, racially specific, disrupting conventional expectations of the attributes of a heroine. Death became the price that Linda Brent was prepared to pay to free her daughter from slavery: "I knew the doom that awaited my fair baby in slavery, and I determined to save her from it, or perish in the attempt." The slave mother made this vow by the graves of her parents, in the "burying-ground of the slaves," where "the prisoners rest together; they hear not the voice of the oppressor; the servant is free from his master" (92). Jacobs added the voice of her narrator to a history of slave rebels but at the same time completed a unique act. The transition from death as preferable to slavery to the stark polarity of freedom or death was made at this narrative moment. "As I passed the wreck of the old meeting house, where, before Nat Turner's time, the slaves had been allowed to meet for worship, I seemed to hear my father's voice come from it, bidding me not to tarry till I reached freedom or the grave" (93). Freedom replaced and transcended purity. Linda Brent's loss of innocence was a gain; she realized the necessity of struggling for the freedom of her children even more than for herself. Thus, the slave woman's motherhood was situated by Jacobs as the source of courage and determination.[20]

In order to save her children, Linda Brent apparently had to desert them. To precipitate a crisis and persuade Dr. Flint that he should sell the children to their father, Sands, Linda escaped and hid. The children were sold and returned to their great-grandmother's house to live, where, unknown to them, their mother was in hiding. However, Linda Brent's hopes for emancipation for her children were shattered when her daughter,

Ellen, was "given" as a waiting maid to Sand's relatives in New York. After years in hiding, Linda escaped to New York and found employment. Her daughter was neglected, inadequately fed and clothed, and when Benjamin, her son, was finally sent north to join her, Linda realized that in order to protect her children she must own herself, freeing them all from the series of white people's broken promises that had framed her life.

Having obtained Ellen's freedom, Linda Brent confided her sexual history to her daughter as the one person whose forgiveness she desired. As opposed to the earlier confession, which was directly addressed to readers, Jacobs portrays Linda as in need of the unmediated judgment of Ellen. Ellen refused to condemn her mother and told her that she had been aware of her sexual relations with Sands, rejected her father as meaning nothing to her, and reserved her love for Linda. The motherhood that Jacobs defined and shaped in her narrative was vindicated through her own daughter, excluding the need for any approval from the readership. Jacobs bound the meaning and interpretation of her womanhood and motherhood to the internal structure of the text, making external validation unnecessary and unwarranted. Judgment was to be passed on the institution of slavery, not on deviations from conventions of true womanhood.

Jacobs gained her public voice and access to a sympathetic audience through the production of a slave narrative, a cultural form of expression supported and encouraged by the abolitionist movement. She primarily addressed the white Northern women whom she urged to advocate the abolition of the system of slavery. However, Jacobs's narrative problematized assumptions that dominated abolitionist literature in general and male slave narratives in particular, assumptions that linked slave women to illicit sexuality. Jacobs's attempt to develop a framework in which to discuss the social, political, and economic consequences of black womanhood prefigured the concerns of black women intellectuals after emancipation. For these intellectuals the progress of the race would be intimately tied to and measured by the progress of the black woman.

Black women writers would continue to adopt and adapt dominant literary conventions and to challenge racist sexual ideologies. Like Prince, Wilson, and Jacobs, they would explore a variety of narrative forms in the attempt to establish a public presence and continue to find ways to invent black heroines who could transcend their negative comparison to the figure of the white heroine. The consequences of being a slave woman did not end with the abolition of slavery as an institution but haunted the texts of black women throughout the nineteenth century and into the twentieth. The transition from slave to free woman did not liberate the black heroine or the black woman from the political and ideological limits imposed on her sexuality.

Notes

1. Nancy Prince, *A Narrative of the Life and Travels of Mrs. Nancy Prince. Written by Herself* (Boston: by the author, 1850), preface. Page numbers will be given parenthetically in the text.

2. See the recent edition of *The Life and Religious Experience of Jarena Lee; Memoirs of the Life, Religious Experience, Ministerial Travels and Labors of Mrs. Zilpha Elaw;* and *A Brand Plucked from the Fire: An Autobiographical Sketch by Mrs. Julia A. J. Foote,* in *Sisters of the Spirit: Three Black Women's Autobiographies of the Nineteenth Century,* ed. William L. Andrews (Bloomington: Indiana University Press, 1986).

3. Harriet E. Wilson, *Our Nig; or, Sketches from the Life of a Free Black, in a Two-Story White House, North. Showing That Slavery's Shadows Fall Even There,* introduction by Henry Louis Gates, Jr. (Boston: by the author, 1859; reprint, New York: Random House, 1983). References are to the 1983 edition; page numbers will be given parenthetically in the text.

4. Harriet Jacobs [Linda Brent], *Incidents in the Life of a Slave Girl, Written by Herself,* ed. L. Maria Child, (Boston: for the author, 1861). A paperback edition with an introduction by Walter Teller was published in New York by Harcourt Brace Jovanovich in 1973; the pages cited in parentheses are in this edition.

5. John Blassingame, "Critical Essay on Sources," in *The Slave Community: Plantation Life in the Antebellum South,* 2nd ed. (New York: Oxford University Press, 1979), 367–82.

6. Ibid., 373.

7. Ibid., 367 (emphasis added).

8. This evidence has focused on the discovery of a collection of Jacob's letters to Amy Post held in the Post family papers at the University of Rochester library. See Dorothy Sterling, ed., *We Are Your Sisters: Black Women in the Nineteenth Century* (New York: W.W. Norton, 1984); and Jean Yellin, "Written by Herself: Harriet Jacobs' Slave Narrative," *American Literature* 53 (November 1981): 479–86; "Texts and Contexts of Harriet Jacobs' Incidents in the Life of a Slave Girl: Written by Herself," in *The Slave's Narrative,* ed. Charles T. Davis and Henry Louis Gates, Jr. (New York: Oxford University Press, 1985), 262–82; and her introduction to a new annotated edition of *Incidents in the Life of a Slave Girl* (Cambridge, Mass.: Harvard University Press, 1987). Yellin also has verified details of Jacob's life in Edenton, North Carolina, and is preparing to write her biography.

9. Harriet Jacobs [Linda Brent], *The Deeper Wrong: Or, Incidents in the Life of a Slave Girl, Written by Herself,* ed. L. Maria Child (London: W. Tweedie, 1862).

10. For Jacobs on Willis, see Yellin, "Texts and Contexts," 265, 279n.

11. Jacobs to Post, May 18 and June 18 (1857?), cited in Yellin, "Written by Herself," 485–86.

12. Jacobs to Post, October 8 (1860?), in ibid., 483.

13. Jacobs to Post, June 21 (1857?), cited in Yellin, Texts and Contexts," 269.

14. I am grateful to Jean Yellin for reading an earlier draft of this chapter and helping me clarify my ideas. Yellin argues that "Jacobs' narrator dramatizes the failure of her efforts to adhere to the sexual patterns she had been taught to endorse . . . and tentatively reaches toward an alternative moral code" (Texts and Contexts," 270–71). I am arguing that this alternative is the development of a discourse of black womanhood and that, far from being tentative, this movement away from the ideology of true womanhood is assertive.

15. Yellin, "Written by Herself," 482.

16. Yellin, "Texts and Contexts," 276.

17. See the discussion of incidents in relation to plot in Nina Baym, *Novels, Readers and Reviewers: Responses to Fiction in Antebellum America* (Ithaca: Cornell University Press, 1984), 75–79.

18. Nina Baym's observations on morality in novels and reviews of novels are enlightening in any consideration of the extent to which writers could challenge convention. See *Novels, Readers and Reviewers*, 173–89, where she makes the argument that female sexuality was consistently policed by reviewers: "Two basic Victorian assumptions about female character—that women do not experience sexual desire and that they are naturally suited to monogamous marriage where they are the servants of their husbands, their children, and society at large—are here exposed as cultural constrictions whose maintenance requires constant surveillance, even to the supervision of novel reading" (183).

19. Barbara Welter, *Dimity Convictions: The American Woman in the Nineteenth Century* (Colombus: Ohio University Press, 1976), 23.

20. Jacobs intended that this note of rebellion be repeated in her final chapter, which was about John Brown, but at the suggestion of Lydia Maria Child, the chapter was dropped. Had it been retained, it would have strengthened this interpretation of the importance of the linking of freedom and death.

Chapter 6

Literary Societies

The Work of Self-Improvement and Racial Uplift

MICHELLE N. GARFIELD

> You have talents—only cultivate them; you have minds—enrich them;
> you have a desire after knowledge—encourage it.
> —Beatrice, *The Liberator*, July 7, 1832

During the early nineteenth century, three events facilitated the rise of the black intellectual and literary movement. In 1827, *Freedom's Journal* was published as the first black newspaper in the United States. Printed in New York City, it employed subscription agents in Boston and Philadelphia as well. In 1829, David Walker of Boston, a free-born black, published his essay, *Appeal to the Coloured Citizens of the World, But in Particular, and Very Expressly, to Those of the United States of America.* And in 1831, Maria Stewart, a black female activist and orator, wrote a tract, *Religion and the Pure Principles of Morality, the Sure Foundation on Which We Must Build*, which was printed by William Lloyd Garrison. These three events were not necessarily the beginning of a black intellectual tradition; to claim this would deny the extant writings and letters of earlier periods. But these three texts articulated an intellectualism that was owned by blacks. In the first edition of the *Freedom's Journal*, the editors state, "We wish to plead our own cause. Too long have others spoken for us."[1] Maria Stewart also urged "if no one will promote and respect us, let us promote and respect ourselves."[2] They pushed black education beyond the rudiments of literacy, which had dominated previous discussions. Blacks were encouraged to take on the intellectual challenge of mental improvement and to embrace a vision of a black intelligentsia.

Under the editorial leadership of Samuel Cornish and John Browne Russworm, *Freedom's Journal* provided a forum for blacks to discuss issues of racial concern across the country, and specifically within the northern states. The paper sold in the United States, Canada, England, and Haiti. The widespread readership of the newspaper, its anti-slavery mission, and its political nature forged the beginnings of a black nationalist tradition. Women were among the contributors to as well as readers of the paper, which reported regularly on the efforts of female literary, anti-slavery, and moral reform societies.

David Walker's essay, commonly referred to as "Walker's Appeal," was perhaps the most electrifying racial publication of its time.[3] Published in Boston in 1829, this seventy-six-page pamphlet called for an immediate end to slavery. Walker indicted white Americans for their avarice and injustice in their dealings with blacks. And yet he claimed that America was the home of blacks, perhaps more so than whites. The most controversial components of Walker's argument revolved around his analysis of the military potential of the Southern slave population. He argued that in areas where there were substantial numbers of blacks, they could overturn their oppressors by sheer physical force. He reflected on the possibility that blacks would "meet death with glory" in battle against their oppression. These statements were considered incendiary, and the discovery of copies of "Walker's Appeal" in southern states created an uproar. In three states, the governor called special legislative sessions to discuss the pamphlet. Several southern mayors asked the mayor of Boston to imprison Walker and burn the pamphlet. But Walker's words rang in the hearts of many blacks, even if they thought his proposal too militant. The call to racial uplift and racial responsibility was gaining ground within black communities. Walker called upon blacks to take not only physical, but intellectual responsibility for themselves. He wanted them to refute racist arguments regarding the inferiority of their race. It has been alleged that "Walker's Appeal" inspired Nat Turner's rebellion in 1831.[4] It is likely that the literate Turner read Walker and was motivated to take up arms, but it is also clear that Maria Stewart read Walker and was inspired to take up her pen.

In her 1831 pamphlet, *Religion and the Pure Principles of Morality*, Stewart called Walker "noble, fearless and undaunted" (40). Like Walker, she admonished blacks to take responsibility for their lives and future generations, but Stewart's text was unique in that she often spoke directly to black women. She called upon black women to cast off excuses and to take their place as contributors to society: "O, ye daughters of Africa, awake! Awake! Arise! No longer sleep nor slumber, but distinguish yourselves. Show forth to the world that ye are endowed with noble and exalted faculties" (30). Stewart went on to encourage black women to take responsibility for the education of their children. Acknowledging that black children had limited educational opportunities, particularly beyond the basic skills, she challenged black women to raise the funds to build their own high school (37). Stewart thus articulated a challenge for Racial Motherhood. Her words were laced with a vision of a better future for the race, one in which black women played crucial roles. Stewart was a religious writer and speaker. In her tract, she used scripture to define the ways in which God would aid the efforts of industrious black women. While "Walker's Appeal" spoke in terms of urgency and immediacy, Stewart called upon blacks, and women in particular, to work diligently and faithfully. Her vision was not one of instant results, but of committed action toward a common goal of intellectual uplift. Her basic theme was one of education and knowledge. "Oh then, turn your attention to knowledge and improvement; for knowledge is power" (41).[5]

The concept that "knowledge is power" for blacks was one of the most important ideas developed in the 1830s. It would define the decade by its literary and intellectual activity. No longer satisfied with only basic skills, blacks began to see themselves as producers and contributors to the literary arena. They took possession of their intellectual future and began to carve it out of their own experiences, strengths, and hopes. *Freedom's Journal*, as well as Walker's and Stewart's writings, laid a foundation for a black intellectualism that was proprietary and self-defined.

Throughout the late 1820s and early 1830s, racial violence was on the rise and free blacks struggled to maintain the freedoms that they had enjoyed in times past. David Walker's publication in 1829, and the 1831 rebellion led by Nat Turner in Southampton County, Virginia, reminded Americans that slavery was a contested institution. It was not simply a subject for political debate, but had the potential to bring about armed conflict and bloodshed. The frustration and impatience that were found in Walker's work were redirected by Maria Stewart as she called blacks to constructive service for their race. These writings, along with the publication of *Freedom's Journal*, were among the first black literary efforts to articulate a social, political, and intellectual agenda for blacks both free and slave. The literary societies of the 1830s benefited from these initiatives. By linking intellectualism and education to the uplift of the race and the emancipation of the enslaved, these writers helped establish the wide-ranging significance of organizations such as literary, debating, and reading societies. As free blacks struggled to maintain their place in society, Maria Stewart admonished them, "knowledge is power." These three publishing events formed the roots of a black intellectualism that was no longer isolated and individualized. They articulated a vision of freedom and equality for blacks across the United States and throughout the world. The black nationalist ideas that matured during the remainder of the nineteenth century were born in the early efforts of Cornish and Russworm, Walker and Stewart.

The work of racial uplift was multifaceted during the early decades of the nineteenth century. There was no discrete formula that dictated what black activists should do to end slavery, racism, and inequality. Therefore they did not leave a linear history of activism. Their story is one of multiple organizations and diverse strategies. The historical record, particularly as documented in black and abolitionist newspapers, advertised a virtual jumble of meetings, organizations, constitutions, fairs, publications, and editorials. But in the midst of this cacophony of activity, blacks were concerned primarily about the struggle to uplift the race. In literary organizations, the elite created an avenue through which they could both attack injustice and further their intellectual interests. At these mental *feasts*, black women became aware of the influence that the pen could wield for traditionally powerless groups.

In September 1831, a group of free black women in Philadelphia gathered to found the Female Literary Association. At this time, there were approximately two million slaves in the United States. A vast majority of these were enslaved in the South and thus subject to strict laws that governed their behavior. Prohibitions against teaching slaves to read or write were intended to keep them ignorant and isolated. Literacy historically had been considered a tool, but many Southerners considered it a weapon in the hands of the slave population. They feared a slave's ability to read items that might prove incendiary, such as newspapers or the Bible. Therefore, they attempted to keep them in the shadows of ignorance and illiteracy. But slaves realized that literacy was a valuable skill that was well guarded and well regarded by whites, and they worked by subtlety and subterfuge to learn how to read, and sometimes how to write.

Free women in the North who established the literary organizations of the 1830s were literate and relatively well educated. They were often active in other organizations that called upon their literary talents and skills. While gaining an education was not a crime for them, it was not always easy. There were a variety of options for basic education, but they fell along a continuum in terms of quality and affordability. Among those establishing literary societies, there was an assumption of basic literacy that was not only tied to their status as free women, but to their standing as women of economic means and social resources. These women proved that literacy was an important skill in itself and that it could become a political weapon if utilized in particular ways.

The establishment of reading societies during the 1830s introduced a new figure, the black female writer. This is not to say that black women were not writing prior to 1830; Phillis Wheatley proved that a black woman of talent could gain success and notoriety as a poet during the late eighteenth century.[6] Certainly there were scores of other black women who were engaged in their own literary pursuits. Still, the literary society movement is unique in that it brought women together with the express purpose of writing and reading their own work. There is a real difference between the individual literary production that occurred prior to the 1830s, in which black women were writing in isolation and often without any public audience, and the collective literary production that occurred in organizations during the 1830s. In these societies, black women were not only establishing themselves as writers who were often published in the anti-slavery and black press, but they were establishing themselves as intellectuals. The literary societies of the 1830s laid the foundation for a black female intellectual tradition in the United States.

Elite black women struggled with the ideological challenge of being black, female, and literary. This struggle brought them to the point of formal organizing and sustained their efforts throughout the lifetime of these associations. Their literary lives had a dual significance, an individual meaning that was unique to each member and a corporate identity that was shared by the group. The latter generally was reflected in the purpose and goals stated in an organization's constitution. The public declaration prescribed and proscribed socially acceptable modes of thinking.

For literary women, the organizing goals were in line with the political, social, and experiential ways in which they saw themselves, allowing us to see through corporate identification the personal meanings offered by literary associations.

In 1936, Dorothy Porter explored the history of black literary societies in the antebellum North for the first time. She presented literary groups as another form of organizing among free blacks during this period and contended that an understanding and recognition of these groups was vital to an understanding of the history of black education. The literary societies, male and female, established throughout the North provided resources that often encouraged and supported black education efforts. Prior to the inclusion of black children in public school programs, the black community, with the help of some of its philanthropic friends, established institutions to educate youth. But there was also illiteracy among the black adult population. Evening schools and weekend classes were created to address this need. In Philadelphia, several of the individuals affiliated with the literary societies also were active as educators in the community. Although no particular correlation can be drawn between literary society membership and a specific occupation such as teaching, the social standing of many members separated them from those struggling to attain basic literacy. After all, the literary groups were not literacy classes. They demanded a basic level of skill and interest. The fact that several club members were active supporters of literacy and black education attested to the links between their political interests and their literary pursuits.

In Philadelphia, those who formed organizations during the 1830s shared an overwhelming concern with both mental improvement and racial uplift. Members pushed themselves to read, write, and debate according to a high level of excellence. But their focus often was centered on Southern slavery, or the ways in which the lives of poor Northern blacks could be improved. The individuals who came together to form these groups shared an interest in the future of the race, a corporate meaning evident in the surviving records. The strong connection between literary groups and anti-slavery organizations was especially notable. Porter argued that the anti-slavery organizations weakened the literary societies by pulling away their members to attend abolitionist lectures and by calling upon their leaders to head up abolitionist programs.[7] But even as membership in, or leadership of, multiple groups and organizations may have taxed the black elite, it also strengthened the entire range of activities as activists shared resources and pooled efforts. A core group of leaders, while perhaps over-burdened and over-committed, enabled the various groups and organizations to work seamlessly together. After all, these were the same people who had been working, living, and socializing together for years.

Since Porter's 1936 article, black antebellum literary societies often have been noted as part of the institutional infrastructure that defines Northern elite communities. Literary societies are defined in relation to their anti-slavery roots and goals. The implication is that these organizations augmented and supported the central work of abolition. The limited work that has been done on black women in the antebellum North continually places anti-slavery activism at the center of these women's lives.[8]

Certainly during the 1830s, black women were preoccupied with abolitionism, but to center it as the single motivation of their activism is too simple. These women were not one-dimensional individuals. Although racial violence and discriminatory legislation reminded them that they shared the burden of race with slaves, their elite status created another distinct dimension. In the antebellum culture of Philadelphia, literary club members were educated women who valued education and intellectual advancement for itself. Although opportunities for formal schooling were restricted by sex and gender, these women continued to further their own education by establishing literary societies. Education among free blacks most often is considered in terms of opportunities for children and evening classes for adults; in both cases, individuals strived to gain basic literacy and mathematical skills. But many members of the community also wished to expand their education beyond rudimentary skills. They were interested in reading classical works as well as those of contemporary authors. Much of their reading was done for their own pleasure and to further their own knowledge. And yet, the history and literature they read affected the way they formulated their attack on slavery. Literary societies were a cultural arena for this type of adult education.

The initial impetus to organize a black female literary society is difficult to chart. According to an article on the Female Literary Association that was published in the *Liberator*, it all began at a meeting on September 17, 1831.[9] We have few details of this meeting, but an address was given in which the speaker recommended the establishment of a black female literary society. Three days later, on September 20, several individuals met and adopted the constitution that created the Female Literary Association of Philadelphia. The idea of such a society also had been recommended earlier that year by the abolitionist William Lloyd Garrison when he spoke before the free people of color in Philadelphia. Garrison suggested that reading, debating, and literary societies would help strengthen moral improvement. He noted in particular, "Let the women have theirs—no cause can get along without the powerful aid of women's influence."[10] Certainly by 1831, the topic of black women's literary societies was a popular one. Many people were eager for them to exercise their energies in this direction.

The preamble to the Female Literary Association was interesting in the way in which the new organization was presented. It revealed three concepts that characterized the literary association movement of the 1830s, and perhaps the entire antebellum era:

> Conscious that among the various pursuits that have engaged the attention of mankind in the different eras of the world, none have ever been considered by persons of judgement and penetration, as superior to the evaluation of the intellectual powers bestowed upon us by the God of nature, it therefore becomes a duty incumbent upon us as women, as daughters of a despised race, to use our utmost endeavors to enlighten the understanding, to cultivate the talents entrusted to our keeping, that by so doing we may in a good measure, break down the strong barrier of prejudices, and raise ourselves to an equality with those of our fellow beings, who differ from us in complexion but who are with ourselves children of one eternal parent, and by his immutable law, we are entitled to the same rights and privileges; therefore, we whose names are hereunto subscribed, do agree to form ourselves into a society for the promotion of this great object, to be called "The Female Literary Association of Philadelphia."[11]

The preamble had two elements that one would expect to find. The first was the goal to "break down the strong barrier of prejudices." This was in line with the anti-slavery sentiment of the black elite noted earlier. Deeply affected by the ideology of moral persuasion, they believed that they could lead lives that refuted the claims of racial inferiority upon which prejudice was based. Inasmuch as literacy was considered a weapon against slavery and discrimination, the advanced skills employed in the literary clubs would accomplish even more in this fight against inequality.[12] In addition, the members hoped to "raise ourselves to an equality with those of our fellow beings." This line evoked the concept of racial uplift that was gaining force at the beginning of the 1830s. By mid-decade, this community ideal had found a home in the American Moral Reform

Society. Slavery and racial discrimination were believed to have deni-grated the black race. As free people of color, the black elite became ardent supporters of racial uplift. The goals of uplift included purging the free community of any questionable and immoral habits as they also fought to free the slaves from their demoralizing state. The literary club made clear that blacks were fully capable of civilized pursuits. Neither of these goals was surprising in the context of the political world of the black elite. Both reflect a corporate significance for the club members and the race.

A third goal, however, has received far less attention. It was the women's avowed purpose "to enlighten the understanding, to cultivate the talents entrusted to our keeping." In other words, they were committed firmly to "the cultivation of the intellectual powers." This was a very individual goal, the purpose of which was to attract like-minded people. While they hoped to attain social and corporate goals, intellectual growth involved individual advancement and its immediate benefit was intangible, obvious only to the individual.

Noted for the success of numerous community endeavors and ardent community building, Philadelphia's antebellum black community set the standard for creating viable institutional structures in the midst of racial exclusion. Black women's role in this process was both front-line, as in the case of the Philadelphia Female Anti-slavery Society and the free produce movement, as well as supportive, as with the Female Vigilance Commit-tee. But in terms of intellectual curiosity and growth, no model was avail-able. This image of the literary club as breaking new ground makes the story especially fascinating. As part of their activist careers, these clubs mirrored anti-slavery, moral reform, and other organizational activities, but they also laid the foundation for a black female intellectual tradition in the United States.

Three black female literary societies were formed in Philadelphia dur-ing the 1830s. The Female Literary Association was established in 1831, the Minerva Literary Association in 1834, and the Edgeworth Literary Asso-ciation sometime prior to 1837. The Female Literary Association had the distinction of being the first black female literary society in the United States. The fact that its constitution was published, and thus preserved, in the *Liberator* enables us to understand this group better. The preamble explicitly stated what the founding members wanted to accomplish within the larger society. As representatives of a "despised race," they hoped to discourage prejudices and uplift the race while cultivating their own intellectual talents and interests.

The purchasing committee of the Female Literary Association included a group of elected officials who were responsible for buying "suitable books" for the association and submitting the bills to the treasurer. This committee was central to the direction of the entire association because they determined what books would be available to the members. The treasury was built by annual subscriptions and membership fees of $1.50. This was not a small price to pay in the 1830s. It cost $2.00 to receive an annual subscription to abolitionist newspapers such as the *Liberator* and *Pennsylvania Freeman.* With weekly meetings that required occasional literary contributions and an annual fee of $1.50, the society demanded a major commitment from its members.[13] Yet for women who had the means and the interest, the association also offered great opportunities. Moreover, many members had an active interest in anti-slavery as well as literature, and membership in the Literary Association bought them access to a variety of black and abolitionist newspapers as well as books on the subject purchased by the group.

The Committee of Examination defined what the Library Association actually *did* during its meetings. In the absence of meeting minutes, these glimpses of club life are essential to analyzing the organization. According to the association's constitution, this committee was responsible for inspecting and reading aloud at meetings any paper that was placed in the "box," where members were to submit their writing. Business meetings were held on the last Tuesday in every month, but "those devoted to reading and recitation" were "to be held once in every week."[14] A major activity of the Female Literary Association, then, was the submission and presentation of their own original work. In addition, members could choose to recite the work of another.

While the concept of women gathering to share and encourage one another in their literary efforts was not foreign to white society, it was a bold step for black women in the 1830s. There were few published women poets or novelists. For the most part, women's writing was considered a respectful pastime, but not a significant intellectual pursuit. This was particularly true for black women, for whom there was no arena where they were considered serious writers. And yet, several of the women who were members of the literary clubs were talented and prolific. As literate black women in the North, the club members had heard of and probably read

Phillis Wheatley's *Poems on Various Subjects, Religious and Moral*, printed in 1773. Wheatley was the first black American to publish a book. Born free in Africa, enslaved and transported to America, Wheatley was a talented poet. Writing during the revolutionary era, Wheatley's work was both political and sentimental. This combination was visible again in the works of Philadelphia's literary women. Did members of female literary societies read Wheatley? They would have been familiar with her work, which was advertised and reprinted in newspapers during the nineteenth century.[15] The parents of many of the literary women were young adults when she published her text, and the publication caused a stir across America and England. The corporate memory of the black community would have preserved Wheatley to the extent that literary women would have been aware of her accomplishment, even if they had not read her work. Wheatley was, no doubt, one example of educational possibility and recognized accomplishment.

Both Wheatley and the literary club women suffered from the absence of a black literary tradition on which to build. There was not a canon that Wheatley could contribute to, and her work often was criticized as being imitative of neoclassical and other white-authored works of her time. And, indeed, Wheatley did not define a black women's literary style, although she demonstrated that such a style could exist. The women who came after her had Wheatley, but little else. They too used the social issues that concerned them as the inspiration for much of their work.

One obvious difference between Wheatley and the literary club women is reflected in the frontispiece to Wheatley's book. Wheatley is portrayed alone at a writing table with a quill in one hand and her chin contemplatively in the other. She did not have a community of literati with whom she could share her writings and from whom she could receive criticism. She was a solitary writer who worked without the support of like-minded individuals. Certainly, Wheatley had a community of friends and acquaintances who influenced her work, but it was not a literary community with which she could share ideas and commiserate. The act of gathering to share their writings influenced literary society women in unique ways. As members, they were expected to write, to share, to listen, and to criticize, reflecting a progressive step away from the solitary production of earlier writers whose works were always in danger of extinction. Literary society women moved toward a tradition of writing that would be preserved and built upon.

The Female Literary Association of Philadelphia was not alone in its commitment to the promotion of reading and writing among free blacks. A variety of different types of clubs shared similar goals. Debating organizations, lyceums, lectures, and mental improvement groups often engaged in comparable activities. When the Female Literary Association was founded in Philadelphia in 1831, three men's reading groups already were established. The African Literary Society was founded around 1824; the Rush Education Society in 1827; and the Colored Reading Society for Mental Improvement around 1828. Meanwhile, similar organizations formed in black communities across the northeastern United States. In the January 7, 1832, edition of the *Liberator*, the editor noted a recent visit to a newly formed organization, the Afric-American Female Intelligence Society of Boston, which was very similar to its Philadelphia counterpart. The constitution's preamble was brief, but included a firm commitment to social uplift, which the authors proclaimed was based on "a natural feeling for the welfare of our friends."[16] This subtle reference to the uplift of the black community is common in the constitutions of most of the organizations referred to as literary or reading groups. Still, they took different forms and held various agendas. The activities ranged from reading literature and writing essays to efforts at spreading moral behavior and encouraging education in the community at large. Some groups were focused primarily on this larger community, while others sought the uplift of the race through the mental and intellectual improvement of their own members.

As a form of adult education, the groups differed in their pedagogy. For example, the Female Literary Association of Philadelphia read literature, but their meetings were occupied with the recitation of original and copied works as well as critiques of these writings. The men's New York Philomathean Society, founded in 1826, spent their meetings listening to prepared debates on pre-selected questions. The presiding officer appointed two members selected by their succession on the membership roll to debate each side of the question.[17] Other organizations, such as the Adelphic Union established in Boston in 1837, were committed to literary and scientific improvement. They attempted to acquire philosophical, chemical, and astronomical apparatus to aid in the presentation of public lectures.[18] The 1830s was a time of expansion in the fields of science, and black intellectual leaders were eager to guarantee that blacks were not left totally ignorant of these new fields. So what made 1830s Philadelphia ready ground for the rise and success of literary societies?

The convergence of anti-slavery, racial uplift, and black intellectualism defined Philadelphia during the 1830s. While all three ideals had been nascent in the free black community for some time, by 1830 they were articulated as community goals. For most free blacks in the Northeast, anti-slavery was a constant political goal. It was in this decade that organized abolitionism grew exponentially, as blacks took a more determined stand against white gradualism and colonization.

The Philadelphia women who organized the Female Literary Association, the Minerva Society, and the Edgeworth Literary Society hoped to engage in activities that would expand their own mental capabilities. Yet they also used these skills to engage actively in political discussions regarding slavery and the rights of blacks. Even as the clubs expanded their influence by engaging in public debates on some of the nation's most controversial topics, they never lost sight of the educational basis upon which they had been established. At their root, these groups were community forms of adult education, and members were the initial benefactors. But as lectures and debates were opened to the public, the entire community could benefit from the effort and expertise of such organizations. The interest and commitment to public lectures demonstrated the way in which the black elite wanted to make education and knowledge available to the larger community. Undoubtedly, the elite believed that they were best prepared to deliver talks and engage in debate, but in the 1830s, there was a real concern that everyone be made aware of the issues that affected them.

The world of black female activism is "hidden in plain view."[19] No extant collections of meeting minutes or membership rosters are available. Yet in the minutes of male organizations, the columns of black and abolitionist newspapers, and the observations of contemporaries, black female activism was recorded clearly. The same names emerge again and again in the historical sources. And yet, there are women whose names arose only once or twice. This reflected the range of involvement within the community. There were individuals and families who were deeply involved and others who were involved in singular activities, or not at all. Not all of these women made a career of intellectual activities, but their commitment and dedication was still important to the success of literary organizations.

As a self-defined space based on literacy, intellectualism, activism, and production, literary clubs were also political spaces. This is not a reference to their political opinions or affiliations, but rather a claim that these organizations, activities, and ownership directly challenged dominant ideas regarding blacks and particularly black women. One of the traditional factors in a successful institution is its ability to attract dynamic leadership. Black women's literary clubs did not so much attract leadership, as create their own. The experience and opportunity to be a part of such leadership formation was essential to the future success of black women's organizations. As founding members and executive officers, black women took on responsibilities that previously had been given to whites and men. The meaning and significance of these groups thus exceeded their activities and proceedings.

Moreover, during the 1830s, literary organizations were established throughout the free black community with such frequency that it can best be characterized as a movement. The popularity and growth of black organizations was a reflection of the community's concern with abolitionism, uplift, and intellectualism. Abolitionism was strengthened by the rhetoric of the American Revolution. Racial uplift was connected with the growing reform movement of the time. But black intellectualism, particularly black female intellectualism, was a relatively new idea that was impaired by the widespread stereotype of black mental inferiority. And yet, it was in the black literary club movement of the antebellum era that the roots of black intellectualism were established firmly.

While club women were proponents of an integrated vision for black Americans, within their literary groups they were able to create a unique space for themselves. Whether intentional or not, the fact that the Female Literary Association of Philadelphia was an all-black, all-female group gave the women the ability to have ownership of their space. Within the organization, they dictated the agenda and the program. Black literary societies were in fact spaces of ownership. They generally met in black school rooms, church basements, or private homes. They were self-sufficient and independent. Through their constitutions, they set specific standards for membership, controlling who could join. Once an individual joined the group, she was called upon to contribute to the financial maintenance and intellectual growth of the group. The founding members conceptualized their association as an active collaboration of like-minded individuals. They discouraged itinerant members who participated when it was convenient. Dedication and commitment meant that each member would feel invested in the group.

In May 1832, a guest delivered a speech before the Philadelphia Female Literary Association regarding female education. The speaker promoted a liberal and classical education among women in addition to the basic skills that currently were being taught.[20] Occasions such as this enabled women to engage not only with the literary ideas and figures that they encountered in their reading, but with the primary social and political issues of the day. By embracing and asserting their political selves, these women were creating and reinforcing a foundation for black women's activism. Prior to the literary explosion of the slave narrative, black literary women already were writing poems and prose that brought attention to the debasing experiences of enslaved women, mothers, and children. In black female literary associations, their activism and intellectualism held equal ground. They established an intellectual tradition that was rooted firmly in their struggle to fight racism, end slavery, and uplift the race.

Notes

1. *Freedom's Journal*, March 16, 1827.

2. Maria W. Stewart, "Religion And The Pure Principles Of Morality, The Sure Foundation On Which We Must Build," in *Maria W. Stewart: America's First Black Woman Political Writer*, ed. Marilyn Richardson (Bloomington: Indiana University Press, 1987), 37. Subsequent references are to this text; *The Liberator*, January 7, 1832.

3. William L. Andrews, Frances Smith Foster, and Trudier Harris, eds., *Oxford Companion to African American Literature* (New York: Oxford University Press, 1997), 175, 301, 639.

4. Sterling Stuckey, *Slave Culture: Nationalist Theory and the Foundations of Black America* (New York: Oxford University Press, 1987), 129, 137; Darlene Clark Hine and Kathleen Thompson, *A Shining Thread of Hope: The History of Black Women in America* (New York: Broadway Books, 1998), 105.

5. William Lloyd Garrison used this phrase in an address to free people of color in June of 1831. Stewart's pamphlet was published in October 1831.

6. John Shields, ed., *The Collected Works of Phillis Wheatley* (New York: Oxford University Press, 1988).

7. Dorothy B. Porter, "The Organizational Educational Activities of Negro Literary Societies, 1828–1846," *The Journal of Negro Education* 5 (October 1936): 575.

8. See Julie Winch, "You Have Talents—Only Cultivate Them: Philadelphia's Black Female Literary Societies and the Abolitionist Crusade," in *The Abolitionist Sisterhood: Women's Political Culture in Antebellum America*, ed. Jean Fagan Yellin and John C. Van Horne (Ithaca, N.Y.: Cornell University Press, 1994); Marie Lindhorst, "Politics in a Box: Sarah Mapps Douglass and the Female Literary Association, 1831–1833," *Pennsylvania History* 65 (Summer 1998).

9. *The Liberator*, December 3, 1831.

10. William Lloyd Garrison, *An Address Delivered Before the Free People of Color, in Philadelphia, New York and other cities, During the month of June, 1831* (Boston: Stephen Foster, 1831), 14.

11. *The Liberator*, December 3, 1831.

12. Shirley Wilson Logan, "Literacy as a Tool for Social Action among Nineteenth-Century African-American Women," in *Nineteenth-Century Women Learn to Write*, ed. Catherine Hobbs (Charlottesville: University Press of Virginia, 1995), 180.

13. *The Liberator*, December 3, 1831.

14. Ibid.

15. *Genius of Universal Emancipation*, March 24, 1827 and December 4, 1829.

16. *The Liberator*, January 7, 1832.

17. *The Liberator*, June 4, 1831.

18. *The Liberator*, January 2, 1837.

19. Jacqueline L. Tobin and Raymond G. Dobard, Ph.D., *Hidden in Plain View: A Secret Story of Quilts and the Underground Railroad* (New York: Anchor Books, 2000).

20. *The Liberator*, June 9, 1832.

Chapter 7

"A Sign unto This Nation"

Sojourner Truth, History, Orature, and Modernity

CARLA L. PETERSON

O f all the women studied in this book, Sojourner Truth is undoubtedly the best known, having achieved, along with Harriet Tubman,
almost legendary status. Yet the fact remains that much of Truth's life and
work is clouded in historical uncertainty, leaving us unable to answer
many questions about her with any real assurance. If knowledge of a historical figure comes to us mediated by the perceptions of contemporaries
and later historians, this is especially true of Truth. Given her illiteracy,
meant here the inability to read and write, Truth has not left us with any
writing of her own; moreover, facts and interpretations of events in her
life have often been multiple, contradictory, and sometimes unverifiable.
Such written documentation has ensured Truth's continued presence in
the historical record, yet it has also meant that she has in a sense become
an overdetermined historical figure. My organization of this chapter deliberately reflects this sense of overdetermination—of the degree to which
Truth comes to us as always already interpreted by others from their
own situated and partial perspectives. Thus, I start by examining the written record surrounding Truth and then later proceed to speculate about
those aspects of her life that lie beyond writing, including, of course, her
speeches.

What we know of Truth suggests that her adult life was marked by a
relative isolation from the black community. If Truth, like other black
women of this period, was locked out of the social institutions of the black

male leadership, it also appears that she was never an integral member of black society. After her emancipation from slavery, she affiliated with several white-dominated communitarian societies in what seems to have been an attempt to constitute a social group for herself denied by the experience of slavery. Subsequent to their failure, Truth appears to have moved largely in white abolitionist and feminist circles, giving two white women permission to write the story of her life. Given her inability to read and write, we may well wonder whether Truth's illiteracy was not in some sense the source of her dependence on white reformers. These dependent relationships were, however, extremely complex, centering on issues of control over self-representation. Indeed, although Truth appears to have been locked out of the economy of "writing," she nonetheless emphatically insisted throughout her life on her own historical agency expressed in different modes of "writing" as well as in other cultural forms rooted in African and African-American traditions. Misunderstood by the dominant culture, these latter forms were often dismissed as merely quaint. And yet Truth's engagement with her contemporary culture, with its technological developments in particular, was such that she may be marked as truly modern.

Truth's Search for Community

Much of our information about Sojourner Truth's life derives from the 1850 biography, *Narrative of Sojourner Truth*, written by Olive Gilbert, a rather inconspicuous member of white abolitionist circles and a friend of William Lloyd Garrison. In the 1870s, the book was revised slightly and considerably enlarged by Frances Titus—whom Truth had met in the 1860s while both women were working to resettle the freed slaves—to include Truth's activities during the 1850s, the Civil War, and Reconstruction.[1]

Truth was born Isabella Bomefree in Ulster County, New York, in 1797, to James and Betsey (or Mau-mau Bett) Bomefree, who were the slaves of a Dutch man, Colonel Hardenbergh. In the late eighteenth century, New York State could not yet lay claim to being "free" territory but in fact relied on slave labor in its urban and, even more prominently, rural industries. Thus, the Bomefrees engaged in forms of field work not altogether dissimilar to those described by Olmsted in his travel accounts of seaboard-state slavery. Moreover, as Margaret Washington has noted, Dutch slaveowners tended to be strong defenders of slavery, harsh in their treatment of their slaves and reluctant to pass manumission laws in the wake of American independence.[2] Isabella's parents were believed to have been of unmixed African ancestry, her mother in particular of pure Guinea Coast blood. If this supposition is accurate, James and Mau-mau Bett might well have been part of the re-Africanization of Northern slavery that occurred between 1740 and 1770 due to a temporary shortage of indentured white labor from Europe; in any event, it was most certainly they who were responsible for imparting to Isabella those elements of African culture that are evident in her speech patterns, belief system, and behavior.

While still a young child, Isabella was separated from her parents and sold at a slave auction. After yet a further sale, she was bought in 1817 by a John J. Dumont, with whom she resided until 1826. During this time, she was married (not legally, of course, and not altogether happily) to an older slave named Thomas by whom she had several children. According to Gilbert's *Narrative*, Dumont had promised Isabella that "if she would do well" he would manumit her one year before legal emancipation set for July 4, 1827, but when the time came he reneged on his promise, reluctant to "give up the profits of his faithful Bell" (39). With a determination that was to become characteristic of her, Isabella "concluded to take her freedom into her own hands, and seek her fortune in some other place" (41); in her escape, she left her children with her husband, whom she felt was in a better position to provide for them. Her departure led her to the nearby Van Wagenen family, where she remained long enough to recover her son, Peter, who had been sold illegally into slavery in the South. With Peter, she then struck out on her own in the hope—"of course . . . not in her power" according to Gilbert—"to make to herself a home, around whose sacred hearthstone she could collect her family, as they gradually emerged from their prison-house of bondage" (71).

Isabella's search for "home" led her first to New York City, where she lived an isolated and uncertain life emblematic of the difficulties facing unskilled African Americans who had been excluded from the economic expansion sweeping the North and for whom the meaning of freedom thus remained undefined. Gilbert's account of Isabella's life in New York at that time is remarkably similar to Harriet Jacobs's later autobiographical narration of her years there. Like Jacobs, Isabella served as a domestic in the home of a wealthy family, the Latourettes: "She worked for them, and they generously gave her a home while she labored for others, and in their kindness made her as one of their own" (86). Despite, or perhaps because of this kindness, Isabella found herself isolated from the African-American community, worshiping at a white Methodist church and unable to supervise the upbringing of her son, who eventually fell prey to the temptations of the city. Her troubles gradually resolved themselves once her son agreed to become a seaman, thus following an occupational pattern common to young black men of this period who found themselves at the bottom of the urban workforce.[3] And her isolation decreased when she agreed to accompany Mrs. Latourette on her visits to the Magdalene Asylum, an early association composed primarily of white women moral reformers devoted to the rehabilitation of New York prostitutes.[4] Finally, around this same time, Isabella left the white church in order to join the African-American Zion's Church; it was at this church that she unknowingly sat beside a sister from whom she had been separated by slavery, leading her to lament when later informed of this fact: "Oh Lord, . . . what is this slavery, that it can do such dreadful things? what evil can it not do?" (81).

Such a lament reflects Isabella's acute sense of loneliness and suggests her longing to experience some semblance of family life denied her by slavery. This longing, I would argue, finds outward expression in Isabella's repeated efforts to become part of a communal society whose values are based on notions of collectivity and mutual sharing.[5] If such a hunger for community constituted for Isabella an attempt to overcome the fragmentation of family life engendered by slavery, it also might have been due to her inability to compete successfully in the capitalist economy brought about by the Jacksonian market revolution in the urban Northeast. Just as importantly, finally, it also might have been indicative of a desire—however unconscious—to reconstitute some form of African social life, centered on the compound and on a commitment to the collectivity rather than to the individual household, that might have come to Isabella through her elders.[6] Indeed, in the 1830s and 1840s, Isabella came to participate in two very different communal experiments that flourished briefly in the Northeast, the kingdom Matthias in New York and the Northampton Association in Massachusetts; in the late 1850s, she became part of the spiritualist community of Harmonia located near Battle Creek, Michigan; finally, in the aftermath of the Civil War, one of Isabella's chief projects was to relocate the freed slaves in self-contained communities on land set aside for them in the West by the federal government.

The kingdom Matthias was an enthusiastic religious movement that emerged briefly in New York during the early 1830s. Claiming to be a Jew, a man by the name of Robert Matthews had renamed himself Matthias and fashioned himself rather eccentrically as an Old Testament prophet in dress, behavior, and speech. While nonbelievers dismissed him as a fanatic and "grotesque," Isabella, who like many other illiterate slaves had memorized large portions of the Bible, seems to have been able readily to fit him into the traditions of Old and New Testament prophecy. Thus, according to Gilbert, at her first sight of him, Isabella's "early impression of seeing Jesus in the flesh rushed to her mind" (90). Moreover, Matthias's oratorical style, which was grounded like that of many slave preachers in the oral traditions of the Old Testament, undoubtedly resonated with familiarity in Isabella's ears. Finally, the prophecies themselves, which pronounced "vengeance on the land, and that the law of God was the only rule of government," differed little in style or content from the jeremiads delivered by such radical antebellum African-American leaders as David Walker in the 1820s and 1830s (89). Yet events were gradually to reveal a dark underside to Matthias's kingdom not unlike the later sexual practices of John Humphrey Noyes's Oneida community. The kingdom broke up in 1835 under charges of adulterous practices that encouraged "match spirits" freely to cohabit with one another regardless of marital status and after the discovery of the fatal poisoning of one of its members, Mr. Pierson. Despite her implication in this scandal and the consequent negative publicity, Isabella appears never to have become embittered against Matthias; in fact, her self-naming shortly thereafter as "Sojourner Truth" may well have constituted an indirect tribute to Matthias, who referred to himself variously as a "traveller" and the "Spirit of Truth."

Truth's other early experiment with communal living was with the Northampton Association, where she resided from 1843 to 1846. An outgrowth of the transcendentalist movement, the Northampton Association drew to it many white abolitionists, including William Lloyd Garrison's brother-in-law George Benson, and adopted as its primary goal the achievement of social and economic equality. Opposed to the capitalist system that encouraged class divisions and hierarchies, fostered competition among individuals, and degraded labor in favor of "speculative pursuits," it established itself as an organization that made no distinction "on account of color, ... [or] between the strong and the weak, the skilful and unskilful, ... the rich and the poor," and that sought to restore dignity to labor.[7] Operating a silkmill and a sawmill, the association was initially controlled by two companies, an industrial community and a stock company, but shortly before Truth's arrival decided to do away with this double arrangement to make the decision-making process of its affairs more communal: "Last year labour and capital held joint sway. This year, as an experiment, labour has exclusive control."[8] Few specific facts are known about Truth's years there, but it appears that she was thoroughly at home in this Fourierist community and was devastated when the association broke up.

Indeed, like the kingdom Matthias, the Northampton Association eventually foundered and once again left Truth without a home. After the dissolution of the kingdom Matthias in 1835, Truth had temporarily abandoned the idea of acquiring a home. Adopting the name Sojourner Truth—emphasizing the importance of travel in the telling of truth, and maintaining, perhaps in a tacit acknowledgment of Matthias's continuing power over her, that "the Spirit calls me there, and I must go"— Truth became an itinerant preacher, exhorting in particular the Millerites, followers of a millenarian movement that predicted the end of the world in 1843 (100). In 1846, after the demise of the Northampton Association, Truth decided to return to her earlier itinerant ministry. She struck out on her own, crisscrossed the Northeast, and penetrated into Ohio and Indiana, following her call "to 'lecture,' . . . [and] 'testifying of the hope that was in her'" by speaking to large audiences composed primarily of religious devotees of the Second Great Awakening and participants in the temperance movement (101). Given the frenetic pace of her travels, it is not surprising that, according to Gilbert, her worried children's "imaginations painted her as a wandering maniac" (109).

Truth's Liminality

The facts of Truth's biography thus suggest a tension in her life between active participation in communitarian experiments and the solitary stance of the lone traveler. If, on the one hand, Truth longed to be enfolded within the warmth of family and community, on the other hand she was to discover that she could best achieve the leadership position to which she aspired in antebellum evangelical and anti-slavery movements by positioning herself as an isolated figure on the margins. Yet both these spaces of travel and communal experiment must be viewed as liminal ones. First

of all, the very fact of itinerancy constitutes a form of self-marginaliza-
tion in its dislocation of home and disruption of quotidian habits. Second, Truth's travels in the 1830s and 1840s took her into those marginal
spaces of the Second Great Awakening in which hierarchies between rich
and poor, black and white, male and female, urban and rural break down
in the face of a collective religious experience. Finally, the two established
communal experiments in which Truth participated may be seen as reflective of Turner's notion of liminal *communitas,* which exists "in contrast . . .
to social structure, as an alternative and more 'liberated' way of being socially human, a way both of being detached from social structure . . . and
also more attached to *other* disengaged persons."[9] Moreover, since both
these communities were predominantly white, Truth could only occupy a
marginal and ambiguous position within them; here too, she found herself, ultimately, alone.

Truth was to occupy this same ambiguous position in the two organized
movements with which she became affiliated in the 1850s—the Garrison-
ian antislavery movement at whose behest she lectured in the company
of such abolitionists as Garrison, Putnam, the Britisher George Thompson (and Frederick Douglass early on), and the women's rights movement
led by Elizabeth Cady Stanton and Susan B. Anthony. Indeed, it would
seem that the black urban elite that constituted the vanguard of the
community's abolitionist and racial uplift movements viewed Truth's refusal to conform to middle-class social conventions and her determination to flaunt her subaltern origins with a great deal of uneasiness. For
example, in a retrospective account of his first meeting with Truth in the
1840s, Douglass described her as "a genuine specimen of the uncultured
negro . . . [who] cared very little for elegance of speech or refinement of
manners . . . [and] seemed to feel it her duty to trip me up in my speeches
and to ridicule my efforts to speak and act like a person of cultivation
and refinement."[10] It is difficult to ascertain whether it was Truth's adamant
nonconformism or the elite's disdain, or a combination of both, that separated her from the community of black social activists.

In striking contrast, as Nell Painter has noted, whites appear to have
been quite comfortable with Truth, as her demeanor seemed to conform
nicely to their image of the black woman.[11] In their perception of her,
Truth was alternatively and overdeterminedly constructed as either invisible or visible, constituting either lack or surplus. In the kingdom
Matthias, for example, Truth's blackness enabled her to witness events

and conversations hidden to others: "To this object, even her color assisted [given] the manner in which the colored people, and especially slaves, are treated; they are scarcely regarded as being present" (91). But as a woman lecturer, Truth was fully exposed to the public gaze and perceived as unruly and excessive. It is this form of visibility, rather than Truth's invisibility, that is reproduced in the many contemporary published accounts of her, forging a reputation that would last well beyond her death in 1883. Thus, in Gilbert's *Narrative,* Truth's views are termed "curious and original" (101), her style "peculiar" (110), her "modes of expression" "singular and sometimes uncouth" (114), her "figures" "the most original and expressive" (114); finally her voice is rendered as "powerful and sonorous" (119). All these traits converge to suggest an unruliness and excess of body and speech that make of Truth an "entertainer" (119) who attracts the curious gaze of the public. In their narratives, Gilbert and Titus invite their contemporary readership to just such a form of gazing.

Writing Truth's Life: The Ethnobiographies of Olive Gilbert and Frances Titus

Unlike the other women studied in this book, Truth did not possess the requisite skills to represent herself in writing. While the exact status of her literacy is currently undergoing reevaluation by certain historians, it remains clear that Truth never engaged in any sustained act of literary self-representation.[12] Freely acknowledging her subaltern status, she permitted two white women writers to tell her life story so that she could sell it at a profit after her lectures and thereby support herself. Truth had in fact already had early experience with the difficulties of attempting black testimonial. At the two trials that marked the demise of the kingdom Matthias in which Pierson's death and the adulterous relationships of the match spirits were investigated, Truth was forbidden to take the stand to testify either in her own defense or on behalf of others; instead, the court relied exclusively on the testimony of the kingdom's white members. It was only at the end of the Civil War that Truth finally was able to give legal testimony and win a trial that would result in the integration of streetcars in Washington, D.C. (187). For the African-American subject, white testimony was of course often problematic and suspect; indeed, the pamphlet literature engendered by the two kingdom Matthias trials foregrounds the unreliabilty of white representations and interpretations of blackness, especially when these concern issues of black female power and sexuality. On the one hand, Truth's very blackness led the journalist William Stone to view her as a witch. Editor of the New York *Commercial Advertiser*, Stone spoke out on many of the controversial issues of the day, agitating against women's rights and suffrage, mediating between Masons and anti-Masonic forces, advocating both the emancipation and colonization of slaves, and exposing impostors such as Matthias. Incriminating Truth in the blackberry poisoning of Mr. Pierson, Stone referred to her as "the most wicked of the wicked." On the other hand, this same racial difference led Gilbert Vale, a less well-known journalist and editor of *Citizen of the World*, to claim that, because of the lack of an appropriate match spirit, Truth, in contrast to the white women in the kingdom, had not engaged in any sexual relations and was consequently chaste.[13]

To define their role as white amanuenses offering a testimonial of Truth's life, both Olive Gilbert and Frances Titus chose to portray themselves as women who have "achieved" Culture by writing on behalf of a child of Nature whose attributes are chiefly physical and thus "ascribed." In his preface to Gilbert's 1850 *Narrative*, Garrison had largely averted his gaze from Truth, relegating her to the frame of his text while focusing his discussion on the ways in which other nations currently gaze in disgust at slaveholding America. In contrast, in her preface to the 1878 edition, Titus relied on a series of natural images, first temporal and then geographic, to explain Truth's perdurance. If Truth is as old as the U.S. century (1776–1876), if she has experienced a physical rejuvenation since the end of the Civil War, it is because she is a natural object able to withstand the ravages of time: by means of analogy, her body becomes the palms of Africa, her blood its rivers fed by tropical fires, her life the sun itself. If African Americans, as children of Nature, are admitted to have the potential of achieving Culture, this potential remains future; they stand yet "on the Pisgah of freedom, looking into the promised land, where the culture which has so long been denied them can, by their own efforts, be obtained" (vii).

Titus's choice of language in the preface, much like the language of the narratives themselves, reinforces the dichotomy between ascribed Nature and achieved Culture. Titus as narrator relies heavily on the established discourse of the King James Bible while rendering Truth's speech and biblical quotations in an African-American idiom. As John Wideman has pointed out, such a dichotomy between white literary frame and black dialect is prevalent in much nineteenth-century writing—white and black—and works to hierarchize speech usage. The white literary frame is seen as a "matured mode of literate expression," while black dialect appears "infantile" and thus "inferior"; yet the white frame is necessary because it contains what is otherwise chaotic, renders respectable that which it places inside it.[14]

Undertaking a testimonial of Truth's life, Gilbert and Titus composed what I will call, following Philippe Lejeune, an "ethnobiography," defined as the "autobiography of those who do not write."[15] Interestingly, neither woman signed her narrative. It is possible, of course, to interpret this lack of signature as an index of narrative self-authorization such that the life story is seen to narrate itself. Yet both Gilbert's and Titus's self-perception was as essentially private women; for example, in an 1870 letter to Truth, Gilbert described herself as "not so public a personage as yourself . . . [M]ine is a very quiet mark compared to yours" (277, 276). Thus, literary anonymity here seems to point to questions of public authorship faced by nineteenth-century women writers. If a written signature implies the actual nonpresence of the signer, it also marks, as Derrida has noted, his or her "having-been-present in a past now" and suggests a "transcendental form of nowness (*maintenance*)" that is inscribed not only in the signature's singularity but in its iterability and reproducibility as well.[16] It is this lack of transcendental nowness that is denied to the woman writer who dares not sign her text but can only leave the trace of a continued nonpresence.

The complexity of female authorship is reinforced further here by the printer's notation "Published for the author," which inscribes a certain ambiguity in the term "author": is the author Sojourner Truth, the author of her own life, or Gilbert/Titus, the author of the narrative of the life of Sojourner Truth? If this notation seems to confuse the identity of the author, suggesting some form of authorial collaboration and the presence of a "floating writing" in the narrative, the text itself dispels such speculations as it firmly establishes the separate existence of, and gap between, author and ethnographic subject. For Gilbert's and Titus's ethnobiographies focus on a cultural subject who has been excluded from writing, and curiously inquire, "What is on the other side of writing?" Establishing itself as a written text composed by those who can write for those who can read, the ethnobiographies isolate the subject and her culture, turning her into a commodity, exploiting and reifying her by means of various constructed images, including that of Harriet Beecher Stowe's "Libyan Sibyl."[17]

If there is no signature that explicitly reveals the authorship of the ethnobiographies, the structure and style of Gilbert's and Titus's narratives themselves suggest authorial presence and control such that writing itself becomes a form of signature. Indeed, the differences between the two writers' use of narrative conventions, stances, and strategies indicate a particularized textual construction that is related not only to the individual personality of each author but to the historical moment of narrative composition as well. Though written in the third person, Gilbert's 1850 *Narrative* relies heavily—yet with interesting modifications—on the conventions of the slave narrative and the spiritual autobiography that typified African-American writing in the antebellum period. In its focus on a single heroic individual, Gilbert's text, like the slave narrative, underscores the uniqueness of its subject; but, unlike the slave narrative, it does not emphasize her representativeness. Moreover, as we shall see, uniqueness here is located in the peculiar forms of Truth's oral speech rather than the ex-slave's acquisition of literacy and consequent ability to write. Like the slave narrative, too, Gilbert's ethnobiography is a chronological account that attends foremost to the moral growth of its subject, tracing Truth's increasing awareness of the evils of slavery (underscored here, as in the slave narrative, in a separate chapter on slave horrors), her determination to resist slavery, and finally to escape it. These conventions of the slave narrative are doubled by those of the spiritual autobiography that record Truth's spiritual growth and conversion in a discourse that echoes Bunyan's *Pilgrim's Progress* and insists that the subject has a soul and is worthy of biographical notice. What is perhaps most significant is that, in its focus on Truth's individuality, Gilbert's narrative (and Titus's as well) refuses to foreground Truth's search for community but focuses instead on those events that isolate her and mark her as extraordinary.

In contrast, Titus's ethnobiographical narrative eschews chronological progression to ground itself in the conventions of documentary writing, reproducing in its latter part approximately fifty pages of newspaper columns culled from the abolitionist, feminist, and mainstream press and another fifty pages of private and public correspondence. Carleton Mabee has suggested that such a narrative method is indicative of Titus's relative lack of education and literary sophistication.[18] If indeed the case, this very lack sharply counteracts the ideological function of the naturalizing images that structure Titus's preface as well as Stowe's inserted essay, "The Libyan Sibyl." Indeed, in her narrative Titus relied on some of the more notable journalistic trends that were developing in mid-nineteenth-century America: the democratization of news whose focus is now broadened to include all social spheres, the increasing emphasis of news on elements of human interest, and finally the belief that news can provide objective, value-free, and impartial reportage.[19]

Gilbert's and to a lesser extent Titus's ethnobiographies both make explicit the mediating function of the narrator. Gilbert grounds her narrative authority to interpret and generalize in her frequent claim to having been an eyewitness to the practices of slavery: "And the writer of this knows, from personal observation, that . . ." (34). She freely offers editorial comments on various events in Truth's life, even transforming narrative description into commentary. Thus, her portrait of the old James Bomefree ("His hair was white like wool—he was almost blind—and his gait was more a creep than a walk") resonates with mythological overtones and endows him with a dignity that makes the account of his death particularly brutal: "[T]his faithful slave, this deserted wreck of humanity, was found on his miserable pallet, frozen and stiff in death" (22, 25). Finally, Gilbert manipulates narrative language by self-consciously setting limits to the expressible. At certain textual moments she insists that the intensity of Truth's emotions are beyond expression—"'Ah!' she says, with emphasis that cannot be written" (39). At others, she shifts from an ethnobiographical mode of narration grounded in facts to the more fictional discourse of sentimentality in order to raise what Margaret Washington has called the "indelicate subject" of black female sexuality.[20] As in Harriet Jacobs's later autobiography, sentimental conventions are invoked here to determine what in a black woman's life is, and is not, appropriately expressible: "From this source arose a long series of trials in the life of our heroine, which we must pass over in silence; some from motives of delicacy, and others, because the relation of them might inflict undeserved pain on some now living" (30).

Truth as Symbol: "Libyan Sibyl" and "Marie"

If Gilbert's and Titus's ethnobiographies confirm the authors' control over the writing process, they also reveal the degree to which Truth herself was aware of both the power of written language to authorize and interpret experience and her exclusion from this arena of power. In her narrative, Gilbert gives an account of Truth's conviction that God is a "great man" whose omniscience is manifested in his ability to write and in his written record of human activity: "She believed he not only saw, but noted down all her actions in a great book. . . ." By analogy, however, such omniscience is equally that of the white man, since God writes "even as her master kept a record of whatever he wished not to forget" (59). The power, but also danger, of "man's" written texts, Truth perspicaciously intuited, derives from the fact that subjective interpretations—"ideas and suppositions"—are always embedded in the written "records . . . of truth" (109), and that the reading of any written record itself invariably is accompanied by interpretation.

Truth's distrust of written texts, particularly insofar as they concerned her, is nowhere more evident than in her dismissal of Stowe's lengthy description of her in her article "The Libyan Sibyl," first published in the April 1863 issue of the *Atlantic Monthly* and then reprinted in Titus's narrative: "She would never listen to Mrs. Stowe's 'Libyan Sibyl.' 'Oh!' she would say, 'I don't want to hear about that old symbol; read me something that is going on *now*, something about this great war'" (174). Truth's attributed use of the term "symbol" is clearly derogatory and suggests her awareness of the dangers of analogy-making by means of figurative language. In his immensely popular *Lectures on Rhetoric and Belles-Lettres*, first published in 1783, the British rhetorician Hugh Blair began his chapter on the origin and nature of figurative language by insisting on the naturalness of figures of speech, on the impossibility that any user of language can speak or write without resorting to them. Yet the rest of Blair's chapter carefully proceeds to attend to the constructed nature of figures, analyzing both their structure and their effect on the listener/reader. Figures of speech are designed "to illustrate a subject, or to throw light upon it"; they are interpretive. If one of the advantages of the figure is its ability to present two objects together to our view without confusion instead of just one, even more significantly the figure may "often strike the imagination more than the principal idea itself"; at the extreme, it may even erase the idea in its own favor. Such an erasure is possible because figures, unlike "simple expression," are bodies: "As the figure, or shape of one body, distinguishes it from another, so these forms of Speech have, each of them, a cast or turn peculiar to itself." If Blair explicitly asserts that the creation of such figurative or bodied language is most characteristic of primitive peoples, of "savage tribes of men . . . much given to wonder and astonishment," his discussion implicitly suggests that it is just as or perhaps even more characteristic of civilized persons, of rhetoricians seeking to enrich, dignify, and illustrate their discourse. And Stowe's essay underscores just how easily bodied language may be put to use not only by savage tribes of men but by polite peoples writing *about* "savage tribes of men."[21]

Truth's attributed use of the term "symbol" to refer to Stowe's "Libyan Sibyl" is instructive, for it points to her awareness of the nature and function of figurative language, of the extent to which such language is inherently interpretive and thus can be used against that which it is meant to illustrate. As a figure, the symbol is one of the most bodied forms of language, in which a visible object is made to stand for or suggest something less visible and tangible. And, indeed, Stowe's use of figures in her essay to represent Truth emphasizes above all the material. Significantly, Stowe's text is framed at its beginning and end by bodies—by the verbal portraits of two pieces of sculpture to which Truth is analogized. In her introductory section, Stowe describes how Truth reminds her so forcefully of "Cumberworth's celebrated statuette of the Negro Woman at the Fountain" (151). But this brief allusion to Cumberworth's statue is then overshadowed by Stowe's later reference to William Wetmore Story's *Libyan Sibyl* that concludes the essay. Here Stowe informs the reader that it was an earlier conversation with Story about Truth that served as the genesis of Story's statue, which in turn provided her essay with its title.

Story's *Libyan Sibyl* is a massive female figure sculpted out of pure white marble. She is seated. The upper part of her body, which is nude, leans forward slightly; the lower part is covered by loose drapery. Her right leg is crossed over the left, and her right elbow rests on her knee while the palm of her right hand gently cups her chin. Her headdress is elaborate as is the pendant around her head; according to Jean Fagan Yellin, to Story's audience their designs of two interlocking triangles would have suggested the Seal of Solomon. In her analysis of the statue, Yellin argues that the Sibyl's pose is similar to that of Judea Capta, a figure representing the Jews in Babylonian captivity that also functioned as a type symbolizing "desolation" for both New England Puritans and nineteenth-century abolitionists. Yellin concludes that: "Story posed his sibyl in an attitude commonly assigned to defeated barbarians in Roman art [inviting] the viewer to consider parallels between the American enslavement

William Wetmore Story. *The Libyan Sibyl* (1861). *All right reserved, The Metropolitan Musem of Art*

of Africans and the Roman enslavement of defeated peoples—including the inhabitants of Britain and Jerusalem."[22]

In a letter to Charles Sumner reprinted in Henry James's *William Wetmore Story and His Friends,* Story himself offers an interpretation of his *Libyan Sibyl.* Significantly, even as he attends to the African woman's body, Story sanitizes her. She is conceptualized as "Libyan Africa of course, not Congo." Even more importantly, however, Story's description of his sibyl adheres closely to the dominant culture's view of the black woman by envisioning her doubly as masculine and feminine. For if her nude torso presents her as "large-bosomed," the sibyl is also a "very massive figure, big-shouldered, ... with nothing of the Venus in it." In his narrative commentary, finally, James offers us yet another interpretive paradigm through which to view the sibyl. Defining Story as "frankly and forcibly romantic," he argues that the artist sought in his work to offer "the observer a spectacle and, as nearly as possible, a scene" out of subjects "already consecrated to the imagination—by history, poetry, legend—and so offered them with all their signs and tokens, their features and enhancements."[23] To view the *Libyan Sibyl* as a representation of Truth, then, spectators needed to attend to such "signs and token" and thus engage in multi-layered typological interpretation.

Stowe ends her essay with a lengthy commentary on the *Libyan Sibyl* and its reception by the British press, and she gave her essay that title. Such an emphasis invites the reader to think of Truth in terms of Story's statue alone and to overlook Stowe's earlier comment that analogizes Truth to Cumberworth's statue. Indeed, at the beginning of her essay, Stowe recalled how in their first meeting Truth "gave the impression of a physical development which in her early youth must have been as fine a specimen of the torrid zone as Cumberworth's celebrated statuette of the Negro Woman at the Fountain. Indeed, she so strongly reminded me of that figure, that, when I recall the events of her life, as she narrated them to me, I imagine her as a living, breathing impersonation of that work of art" (151).

My research into the work of the relatively obscure French/British sculptor Charles Cumberworth (1811–1852) has led me to conclude that this statue of the Negro Woman at the Fountain might well be one of the artist's renderings of Marie, the female slave character in Bernardin de Saint-Pierre's *Paul et Virginie,* executed in the mid 1840s and exhibited at the Paris Salon of 1846. Unremarkable perhaps in its own right, Cumberworth's *Marie à la Fontaine* is remarkable in its contrast to Story's *Sibyl. Marie* is a full-standing bronze figure. She is fully clothed, although the bodice of her dress falls off her left shoulder to expose her left breast. Her left hand is placed akimbo while her right arm bends at the elbow in order to allow her right hand to hold aloft a large vase out of which protrudes what appears to be a profusion of vegetation. The left side of her dress is slightly raised and her feet are bare. Most significantly, in contrast to Story's *Libyan Sibyl,* Cumberworth's *Marie* is "Congo African"; her features are more

Charles Cumberworth. *Marie à la Fontaine* (1840s). Bronze sculpture. *Photo: Thierry Le Mage. Réunion des Musées Nationaux/Art Resource, NY*

markedly Negroid, her coloring is bronze, and a turban covers her head. As a representation of Truth, the statue is obviously mediated in its explicit reference to Saint-Pierre's fictional character. Unlike Story's *Libyan Sibyl*, however, it does not require multiple levels of interpretation in order for the viewer to read Truth through it. But given the *Libyan Sibyl's* peculiar representation of the African woman and greater fame, this statue undoubtedly better suited both Stowe's ideological purposes and her *Atlantic Monthly* readership than did Cumberworth's *Marie*.

Indeed, Yellin suggests that in her essay Stowe turned back to Story's statue to construct Truth not only as mysterious but also as passive and inhuman. I likewise would emphasize the degree to which Stowe's verbal description of Truth does indeed adapt itself to Story's marble portraiture but in somewhat different ways from those suggested by Yellin: a focus on the black woman's body that materializes her but also, in reinventing her through the imagination, dehistoricizes her. In the first part of her essay, Stowe reproduces in quotation marks (and in dialect, of course) Truth's narration of her own life. But if Truth insists on positioning herself as a subject in history, Stowe's later comments about her both materialize and dehistoricize her. Truth's bodied nature is emphasized throughout in Stowe's depiction of her, along with her grandson ("the fattest, jolliest woolly-headed little specimen of Africa that one can imagine," 152), as an "entertainer" to be gazed upon, a singer whose voice is intimately connected to her bodily energy (161). Stowe's description does not masculinize her as Frances Gage's would shortly do. But, much like Titus in her preface, Stowe repeatedly invokes nature images to analogize Truth's body to exotic African landscapes.[24] Thus, Truth's "African nature" is imaged as "those unexplored depths of being and feeling, mighty and dark as the gigantic depths of tropical forests, mysterious as the hidden rivers and mines of that burning continent whose life-history is yet to be" (170). What is especially signficant about these metaphoric and symbolic representations of Truth is the degree to which they privilege geography—first the geography of continent, then that of the body—over history, ultimately tending toward a dehistoricization of Truth herself. Stowe's use of landscape images resituates Truth in an African continent that has no history—"whose life-history is yet to be"—and is marked by a timeless materiality that comes to inhabit Truth's body: she is indifferently "calm and erect, as one of her own native palm-trees waving alone in the desert," or as quoted earlier, "mighty and dark as the gigantic depths of tropical forests," "mysterious as the hidden rivers and mines of that burning continent" (153, 170).

Dismissing such attempts to portray her in a bodied language as a de-historicized symbol, Truth insisted instead on relocating all representations of her in history and proposed herself as a sign possessing historical agency: "The Lord has made me a sign unto this nation, an' I go round a' testifyin', an' showin' on em' their sins agin my people" (152). In so doing, she refused to embody any abstract symbolic value but worked instead to inform herself about contemporary political events that she could then reinterpret to the people: "read me something that is going on *now*, something about this great war" (174); "I can't read a book, but I can read de people" (216).

As a sign, Truth sought a platform from which she could become a "doer of the word" and claim that right to give testimony on the state of the nation that had been denied her by the New York courts of law. Before turning to the issue of Truth's orature, her participation in oral rather than written literary traditions, however, we may want to question whether Truth, while herself not a writer, was not able in some way to take advantage of writing. I would like to suggest not only that Truth was able to make use of various technologies of writing but that it was her very lack of literacy that made possible her appropriation of different modes of "writing" and enabled her to enter "modernity"; no longer "primitive," she must be marked as "modern."

Truth as Sign: Autographs, Photographs, and Letters to the Editor

During the Civil War, Truth devised a highly interesting strategy through which she could in some sense engage in the process of narrative writing. Titus entitled her narrative of Truth "Book of Life," taking this title from a series of notebooks in which Truth had collected the autographs of friends in public life—William Lloyd and Helen Garrison, Amy Post, Wendell Phillips, Samuel and Abby May, Charles Sumner, Frederick Douglass—in the process attaching great significance to the written signature: "To all calling upon her, she asks the question, 'Don't you want to write your name in de Book of Life?' to which query, the counter one in relation to the same 'Book of Life,' is generally put, and Sojourner is usually gratified by the chirography of her visitor." (232–33). On the most immediate level, the signature functions here as a form of the documentary, testifying to the historical importance of the signers on the stage of national events. In addition, the signature points back self-referentially to the signer's own public authority and power, to what Derrida has called his or her transcendental nowness or *maintenance.* Even more significantly, however, Truth's "Book of Life," whose very title echoes biblical beliefs in God's omnipotence, underscores the degree to which the signer's signature confers power on the signatee—Truth—as well. First, the signatee's very existence is necessary in order for the signer to write and sign his or her writing. Second, the signatee inevitably comes to shape the form this writing takes, making the signer in a sense dependent on the signatee. Indeed, one could say that at the moment of writing the signer comes into existence only in relation to the signatee; thus, as they signed their autograph in her "Book of Life," Truth's friends and acquaintances received definition primarily in terms of their relationship to her. Third, the signatee can put the signer's signature to his or her own particular use. Most especially, we have seen how the signature, while singular, is of necessity also iterable, reproducible, and thus detachable; it may, in fact, come to function as a quotation. Thus, in her "Book of Life" Truth compiled the signatures as a series of quotations, providing her own frame for them and, in a sense, creating her own written text. And finally, by allowing Titus to publish the signatures in her narrative, she chose to give them a public existence.

In 1863, at about the same time that she became interested in collecting the signatures of friends in public life, Truth also agreed to have photographs made of herself, which she sold after her lectures much as she had sold copies of Gilbert's *Narrative* in the 1850s. The photograph thus came to function for Truth as a form of autobiography, of recorded testimony, of a signature both singular and reproducible, through which she once again hoped in some measure to enter the culture of writing. The photographs of Truth that remain in the historical record suggest an interesting ambiguity of cultural form that is again indicative of the problematics of self-representation faced by nineteenth-century black women in relationship to the dominant culture.

As Dan Schiller has noted, the new technology of daguerreotypy reinforced mid-nineteenth-century American ideologies of realism that asserted that artistic representation should and could be objective and true to nature. Photography thus became an important instrument of realism as the photograph was perceived to be strictly truthful, a nonsymbolic reflection of the objective world revealing Nature herself; in fact, its objectivity was believed to transform history itself into nature.[25] Despite such pronouncements about artistic naturalness, however, the photograph was, of course, a technological invention, a cultural artifact. The origins and development of the *carte de visite* photograph (a photograph mounted on a 2½-by-4-inch calling card) as well as the later cabinet photograph (mounted on a somewhat larger card measuring 4¼ by 6½ inches), both of which were favored by Truth, point to the cultural foundations of photography and suggest interesting social complexities. Created by the duke of Parma in 1857 as an innovative improvement on the more conventional calling card, the *carte de visite* was initially designed for an elite defined by its leisure-time social activities; but, transported to the United States, it was soon popularized and made democratic, becoming in the words of a contemporary photographer "the social currency, the sentimental 'greenbacks' of civilization."[26] At the height of its popularity, the *carte de visite* became an instrument of mass culture, a vehicle facilitating the accession of the private into the public sphere. For, just as private citizens could now transform themselves into writers and readily publish their views in newspapers in the form of letters to the editor, so now they could publicize themselves by means of the photograph.[27] In particular, the *carte de visite* and cabinet photograph became an inexpensive and easily available vehicle of publicity, a means of keeping oneself constantly in the public eye, for celebrities of all kinds—entertainers, politicians, military men, and professionals.[28]

Truth's use of the *carte de visite* and cabinet photograph suggests a willingness on her part to take advantage of this modern technological art form; and her appropriation of it once again points to its very ambiguity as a cultural artifact. One prevailing argument contends that the photograph can only be a commodity in a capitalist consumer society; it constitutes a consumable object whose relationship to the world is impersonal and open to exploitation by society. Yet if the social construction of the photograph implies commodification, it may also intimate resistance to commodification. In agreeing to have photographic images made of herself, Truth insisted on maintaining control over them by having them copyrighted in her own name and selling them on her own terms at profit. In a letter written to Oliver Johnson early in 1864 that she requested be published in the *National Anti-Slavery Standard*, Truth announced "that now I am about to have a new, and, I hope much better photograph taken of me, which a friend here is going to have copy-righted for my benefit; and when this is done I shall have letters written in answer to all those who have been sent, and enclose the required photographs." In a private letter sent shortly after to her friend Mary Gale, Truth expressed her concern about the quality of her photographic images: "I wanted to send you the best. I enclose you three all in different positions—they say here that they are much better than my old ones"; and she also explained her need to increase their cost to one dollar for three photographs, or thirty-five cents for one, due to the cost of paper, envelopes, and stamps.[29]

Moreover, if the photograph constitutes a commodified object to be bought and sold on the marketplace, at the same time it produces a subjective reality and may function as a more personal means of communication, as a form of writing. In other words, if the photograph is denotative, it is also connotative. An examination of some of Truth's photographic images suggests the extent to which they float between these two poles of denotation and connotation, creating a kind of ambiguity that impedes any reified categorization of Truth.

Truth's photographic consumers consisted in large part of those antebellum white abolitionists who continued to remain active in the fight for the civil rights of African Americans during and after the Civil War. In her photographs, Truth appears not as a child of Nature but as a historical being who inhabits the realm of Culture, thus returning us to a consideration of the cultural form and content of photography. For if on the one hand, the photograph seems to be a flat image, a mere mask, on the other it is a sign indicative of a historical reality; similarly, if it appears as an isolated fragment, a decontextualized quotation, it also takes its place within a cultural field as a culturally constructed image.[30] In the present instance, we have no way of knowing who was responsible for Truth's cultural presentation in her photographs, although we do know that she willingly agreed to their retouching. Examining her photographic images as a form of writing, however, we may nevertheless attempt to specify their cultural field and representation of the figure of the black woman.

The dozen or so photographs that we possess of Truth take pains to emphasize her femininity; indeed, several depict Truth knitting or present her against a background of feminizing elements taken from a domestic interior: a vase of flowers, a cloth-covered table, a mantelpiece, a carpet.[31] In most of the photographs, Truth is dressed in plain Quaker garb—a dark dress, covered by a white shawl, with a white bonnet on her head.

Sojourner Truth. Cabinet Card, 1864. *Courtesy the Sophia Smith Collection, Smith College*

Such a presentation accords fully with contemporary accounts of Truth's mode of dress, suggesting that she made no attempt here to appear different from her daily custom. Yet it does contrast in one detail with two well-known descriptions of her by white abolitionist women. In Stowe's essay, Truth is said to be wearing "a bright Madras handkerchief, arranged as a turban, after the manner of her race" (152), and Frances Gage's later account of Truth's appearance at a women's rights convention claims that "an uncouth sun-bonnet" covered her white turban.[32]

Sojourner Truth. *Courtesy of the State University of New York at New Paltz, Sojourner Truth Library*

In at least two photographs, however, Truth's appearance is more "folk" and more in accordance with Stowe's and Gage's conception of her: her vest, jacket, and skirt are of a plaid or striped material, a wooden walking stick is in one hand, a plaid bag hangs over the other arm. We have no way of knowing how much control Truth had over her choice of dress, whether it was dictated by her friends, the photographer, or Truth herself. Nor do we know what style of dress Truth might have preferred; is the supposedly better photograph alluded to in the letter to Oliver Johnson one in which Truth is dressed in folk clothes or one in which she is in Quaker garb and the trappings of conventional femininity are the most evident? This latter representational image was obviously designed to suggest both Truth's feminine nature and her evangelical mission; I would argue that it is meant to indicate acceptable class status as well. Yet if Truth does not appear in these photographs as one of the folk, neither does she, with her shawl, bonnet, and even glasses and knitting, reflect the genteel middle-class demeanor so evident in contemporaneous photographs of Watkins Harper, Shadd Cary, or Sarah Parker Remond. The effect of these photographs is to present Truth to the observer as a hybrid, to endow her with a social and cultural ambiguity that defies categorization and perhaps allowed her to challenge commodification.

There is yet a final ambiguity embedded in Truth's photographs that constitutes, I think, another form of resistance to commodification. It resides in the caption that accompanied them: "I sell the shadow to support the substance"—the shadow meaning the photographic image, the substance Truth's actual bodily self as well as the social causes to which she had committed herself. Yet it is also possible to reinterpret these two terms such that it is the absent person who becomes the shadow by virtue of her nonpresence, and the present photographic object that is now the substance. By substantiating herself in her photographs as an image for consumption by her white abolitionist audiences, Truth could remain a shadow elusive to everyone but herself.

Truth's request to Oliver Johnson that he publish her letter in the *Standard* indicates, finally, the extent to which she sought to appropriate, and manipulate, the newspaper as a modern technological instrument designed to gather and disseminate general information and, more particularly, to generate personal publicity. An 1864 letter dictated on her behalf to Rowland Johnson finds Truth asking for copies of the *Standard* so that the contrabands of Freedmen's Village might be informed of events of national importance. In the same letter, she requested that Johnson "publish my whereabouts, and anything in this letter you think would interest the friends of Freedom, Justice, and Truth, in the *Standard* and *Anglo-African*, and any other paper you may see fit" (180). Similarly, an 1871 letter to the *New York Tribune* suggests that information about Truth published in the newspaper has become the catalyst for the provision of yet more news: "Seeing an item in your paper about me, I thought I would give you the particulars of what I am trying to do, in hopes that you would print a letter about it and so help on the good cause" (239). Thus, from the 1850s on Truth appropriated the newspaper to fashion it into a nexus of information by, and about, her. Beyond that, as we shall see, she also endeavored to forge it into an instrument that would help her to reach out to those from whom she had become isolated in an act of imagining community.

Truth and Oral Culture

Our analysis of Gilbert's and Titus's ethnobiographies of "one who does not write" forces us to come to terms with the difficulty of recognizing and naming that which lies on the other side of writing. In an effort to open up our vision of the unwritten, I suggest that we speculate upon some of the ways in which Truth's life explodes beyond the narrative plots of the dominant culture, beyond writing itself, acknowledging at the same time the degree to which our knowledge of Truth's life always already is enmeshed in writing. What we discover is that elements of this life belonging to a culture beyond writing may be traced to African and African-American oral cultures. Yet while these are in fact present in the narratives written about Truth, they are not always explicitly named. For example, Truth's desire to overcome isolation and participate in communal social arrangements may be interpreted, as I suggested earlier, as an undefined yearning to return to an African social past that emphasizes commitment not to the individual or the nuclear family but to the collectivity that congregates in a compound where space is not bounded.

Along with Margaret Washington and Gloria Joseph, I would argue that Truth's epistemological worldview, ritualistic practices, and spiritual experiences contain residues of African oral culture.[33] Margaret Washington has shown that Truth's participation in Pinkster festivals, which merged Pentecostal rituals with African forms of entertainment, indicates the degree to which African traditions were immediately available to her. I would further suggest that Truth's conviction that God manifests himself in material objects such as the moon and the stars echoes James Gronniosaw's earlier account of the African belief that "there was no power but the sun, moon, and stars; that they made all our country."[34] These statements reflect an African perspective that holds that no distinction exists between spiritual and material worlds, but that animate and inanimate objects, spirit and matter, are bound together in one system ordered by God. Washington has also demonstrated that many of Truth's spiritual experiences, including her conversion in which she was visited by the Holy Wind, are not only Pentecostal but are grounded in Africanisms. It might thus even be possible to interpret Truth's affiliation with Spiritualism in the late 1850s as a natural extension of African religious beliefs that emphasize spirit communication and possession. Finally, Truth's belief in the primacy of the oral in the world at large, and more particularly in the religious world, which allowed her to converse freely with God in "her rural sanctuary" (60), corresponds to the African notion that the world is primarily one of sound in which speech can make the past present, vision a reality. The concept of words as "doing" is not only Christian but African as well.[35]

Gilbert's and Titus's recording in their narratives of selected speeches by Truth may be interpreted as an effort to neutralize the opposition between the one who writes and the one who does not.[36] Yet I would argue that it also opens the way for verbal Africanisms and African-Americanisms beyond the black dialect constructed by the dominant culture to infiltrate the narratives. Further, it intimates the presence of a double discourse addressed to a double audience, an immediate audience composed primarily of whites and, as I shall later suggest, a larger "absent" audience composed of her own people. An African-Americanism is already present in Truth's aspiration to transform herself into a "sign unto this nation." Indeed, to the African-American slave, the world was filled with signs that were not only to be read but functioned primarily as "calls to action."[37] Thus, Truth hoped that as a "sign" the nation would heed her "testifyin', an' showin' on 'em their sins agin my people" and be moved to action. As with all other public speakers—male or female, white or black—Truth needed carefully to assess the rhetorical context of her lecturing and to negotiate the complex relationship between self, situation, subject, and audience, a task particularly problematic, as we have seen, for black women. Indeed, the question facing Truth was whether it was possible for her to gain an audience, make herself heard, and maintain her authority while resisting commodification by the public gaze according to the terms and categories set up by the dominant culture.

As we have seen thus far, the dominant culture's perceptions and representations of Truth were foremost as an unruly material body. In accounts of her public speaking, most especially, emphasis was frequently placed on Truth's grotesque appearance and behavior: "She is a crazy, ignorant, repelling negress, and her guardians would do a Christian act to restrict her entirely to private life" (204). More often than not, Truth's grotesqueness is attributable to the dominant culture's masculinization of the black female body, already intimated in Story's commentary on his *Libyan Sibyl* and explicitly voiced by Olmsted in his description of slave women. In her narrative, for example, Gilbert records how to her owner, Dumont, Truth was above all a masculine laboring body: "*that* wench . . . is better to me than a *man*—for she will do a good family's washing in the night, and be ready in the morning to go into the field" (33). Most significantly, however, this social construction of Truth's body as masculine because laboring is often displaced by a biological one that results in a presumption of generic and/or sexual ambiguity. In Gilbert's narrative, we are told that a lawyer to whom Truth had appealed for help in recovering her son from slavery "looked at her a few moments, as if to ascertain if he were contemplating a new variety of the genus homo" (51). Even more dramatic was the reported incident at the 1858 anti-slavery meeting in Silver Lake, Indiana, where a Dr. Strain accused Truth of masquerading her essential biological masculinity as femininity: "A rumor was immediately circulated that Sojourner was an imposter; that she was, indeed, a man disguised in women's clothing." And as her oratory was perceived to issue directly from her body, Truth's voice was equally perceived as bodied and hence also masculine: "your voice is not the voice of a woman, it is the voice of a man, and we believe you are a man" (138). To remove such doubts about her body, Truth reportedly gave bodily testimony by revealing her breasts to the audience.

Julia Kristeva would contend that given such cultural constructions, Truth could only become an abject creature for whom writing "alone purifies from the abject."[38] Yet I would respond that Truth resisted, and even exploited, abjection by appropriating the act of public speaking and by subverting the dominant culture's constructions of black womanhood while seeming to accept them. In so doing, Truth exhibited no fear of exposing her body to the public gaze. For just as she rewrote the relationship between signer and signatee to allow the latter manipulative power over the written signature, so she strove in her public lecturing to reconfigure the relationship between audience and speaker in order to control the audience's gaze. If, as Stowe wrote in her "Libyan Sibyl" essay, the Beechers wished to gaze upon her as an "entertainer," Truth in turn insisted on reversing the power relationship embedded in this gaze: "Well, honey, de Lord bless ye! I jes' thought I'd like to come an' have a look at ye" (152). As an entertainer, Truth adopted the stance taken, in Victor Turner's formulation, by those who are weak and of low status (the court jester, for example) in order to embody the moral values of *communitas*, to insist on the need for an "open" rather than a "closed" morality, and thus acquire power.[39] Truth brought her open moral sense to bear on the historical problems of slavery, racism, women's rights, and the need to rethink current notions about black women, "the brave." For Truth, these issues were complicated further in the post-bellum period as African Americans sought to claim a place for themselves within the political economy of the nation and as gender relations between men and women within the black community became increasingly problematic.[40]

Truth's Speaking Style

Our knowledge of the form and content of Truth's speeches is constrained by our exclusive dependence on the written record, on our access to those speeches alone that were selectively chosen by the reporter, transcribed according to his or her linguistic preferences, and reprinted in the newspapers of the period, in Gilbert's and Titus's narratives, or in Stanton and Anthony's *History of Woman Suffrage*. Working with this written record left to us by history and acknowledging its corruption, I would suggest that it is still worth examining some of Truth's speeches to look for traces of the "native" culture, to place them within the context of both contemporary American oratorical traditions and African and African-American orature, to examine them as hybrid discourse.[41] Kenneth Cmiel has argued that by mid-century, antebellum American eloquence was dominated by a "middling culture" that mixed high and low styles, allowing classical rhetoric to be penetrated by such expressive modes as folk dialects, slang, plain speaking, jargon, bombast, and/or euphemism. While prominent public figures as diverse as Henry Ward Beecher and Abraham

Lincoln freely resorted to this "democratic idiom," pressure remained on the few women speakers of the period to continue employing a refined style. Truth refused to accede to this pressure, relying instead on dialect, folk expressions, and plain speaking to persuade her audiences. As a consequence, Cmiel interprets Truth's speaking style as part of this evolution of American oratory, comparing it to "the rustic dignity of Abraham Lincoln"; in the process, however, he neglects to consider the ways in which Truth's speech might well have been affiliated with other "native" oral traditions familiar to her from her childhood.[42]

Truth's links to African and African-American oral cultures may be located, as we have suggested, in her belief in the primacy of the spoken word, its importance as a mode of action rather than simply an articulation of thought, its magical power to create events, to make the past present, and vision reality.[43] Moreover, in such cultures, the oral word does not exist simply in a verbal context but in a larger human one that involves bodily presence. The voice is connected directly and intimately to bodily activity, giving rise to what Ong has called a "verbomotor lifestyle" and what I have characterized as Truth's "bodied voice." And, as Ong has remarked, verbomotor cultures readily lend themselves to highly rhythmic speech as they link bodily functions—breathing, gesture—to oral speech patterns.[44] Rhythmic discourse may in fact evolve into song. In an important chapter in his book, Carleton Mabee has emphasized the importance of song in Truth's speaking repertoire and has suggested her probable familiarity with "Juba," an "African-American dance, accompanied by singing, clapping, patting the hands on the thighs, and patting the feet on the ground." Finally, rhythmic discourse may lead to an alternation of song and speech characteristic of African oral culture and present in many of Truth's performances.[45] A post-bellum review in a Kansas newspaper, for example, commented that in her public speaking Truth demonstrated that "she has a poetic element in her nature, and has several times given forth her thought in spontaneous rhyme."[46]

Specific idiosyncrasies of speech also suggest Truth's close ties to African and African-American oral traditions. On the most general level, we may note orature's general stylistic inclination toward verbal accumulation and redundancy. Other devices reflect both the personal and communal tendencies of African oral narrative. On the one hand, the speaker may seek to affirm his or her own personal authority by "resort[ing] to a story that recapitulates his experience of coming to know: how he acquired his knowledge, when, from whom, whether any further evidence is available."[47] On the other hand, he or she also may employ verbal structures designed to cement community values. Call-and-response, for example, functions to involve the entire community in the performance and thus bring it together; proverbs work to reinforce the social values of the community, often allowing the speaker to position him- or herself as a teacher whose goal it is to bridge any gap that might have opened between different members or constituencies within the community.[48] Finally, African-American folk culture is characterized by the use of a deflationary form of humor designed to turn the social world, in particular black-white relations, on its head.[49]

In their reprinting, Truth's speeches were invariably contextualized by editorial commentaries that could only comprehend her language usage as "quaint," "peculiar," "singular," or "original." In so doing, they failed to recognize the presence in these speeches of an other/native cultural background. Those who ridiculed her bodily movements were unable to connect them to the verbomotor lifestyle of oral culture. Those who noted her penchant for "spontaneous rhyme" could neither understand how it related to her speech nor appreciate the cultural context that invited the conjunction of song and speech: "Her speaking is disjointed. . . . In fact, she talks in public just as she does all the time. There is not much connection, but she just drifts along."[50]

Such assessments of Truth's public speaking leave us with a series of unanswered questions. Was Truth indeed the naive child of Nature that her biographers and reviewers believed her to be? Or did she deliberately manipulate this naive persona as the most effective rhetorical stance available to her to speak to white audiences even though she was, according to Fred Tomkins, "able to speak in correct and beautiful English"?[51] Did she knowingly invent a double discourse that would allow her to reach beyond her white audiences to speak to those of her own race, particularly its women, thereby imagining community and working toward the creation of an African-American local place? Finally, did she suspect that the cultivation of such speech, in striking contrast to that of other black public lecturers of the period, could in fact function as yet another sign of modernity, that it could become what Werner Sollors has labeled a marker of ethnicity that relies on modern traditionalisms in order to insist on the cultural distinctiveness of the ethnic group?[52] In the remainder of this chapter, I offer a reading—speculative rather than definitive—of several of Truth's 1850s speeches in the hopes of enlarging our contemporary vision not only of Truth's oratory but more generally of the antebellum African-American culture that lay on the other side of writing.

Truth's Antislavery Speeches

Several of Truth's antebellum speeches address the issue of Southern slavery and Northern discrimination against free blacks, in the process seeking to redefine the place of African Americans in the political economy of the nation. In one lecture, delivered to a religious meeting around 1852 and reprinted in the *National Anti-Slavery Standard* and then again in Titus's narrative, Truth attacked the Constitution as a document that has failed to protect the rights of African Americans. In a pattern reflective of African oral traditions and belief systems, Truth began her speech with a personal account that, in affirming the primacy of the spoken word and the presence of God in the material world, also offered incontrovertible proof of the rightness of her own political position. Going out into "de fields and de woods," she examines a sheaf of wheat and asks God what is the matter with it. His response, "Sojourner, dere is a little weasel in it," allows Truth to analogize the ailing Constitution to the weevil-infested wheat: "Den I says, God, what ails *dis* Constitution? He says to me, "Sojourner, dere is a little weasel in it" (147). Truth's (conscious or unconscious) use of malapropism here most probably worked to undercut the seriousness of her message to her audience. Yet her metaphoric evocation of the weevil in the wheat, a common saying among African-American slaves warning of the presence of an informer within the community, functioned as a vigorous reminder of the resourcefulness of slave culture and undoubtedly resonated powerfully in the ear of an African American audience or readership.

In two other speeches, one reported in the December 10, 1853, issue of the *National Anti-Slavery Standard* and the other in the July 14, 1854, issue of the *Liberator*, Truth vehemently assailed the economic discrimination against free blacks in the North and the exploitation of slave labor in the South. To accomplish her ideological ends, Truth made use of the African-American verbal device that allowed her humorously to reverse the hierarchies of the social world while masking the aggressiveness of her satiric intent. She was thus able successfully to demonstrate how whites, convinced of their own racial superiority, in fact displace and abuse blacks

economically, betraying in the process their own moral and spiritual inferiority. Although the 1854 speech appears quite disjointed, it in fact
quite logically argues the case against white superiority in the moral, economic, and spiritual realms. It demonstrates how slaves have been able to
care for themselves "better than the white people had brought them up,"
how whites owe blacks so much for their labor that "if they paid it all
back, they wouldn't have any thing left for seed," how, given their many
tribulations on earth, God has reserved the rewards of heaven for blacks,
not whites.

In her 1853 speech in which she specifically addressed a black audience,
Truth focused her attention on economic issues, enumerating the many
menial occupations from which urban blacks were excluded—as waiters,
bootblacks, street cleaners, coachmen, and barbers. Rather than merely
complain about such economic discrimination, however, Truth proceeded
to point out the current deterioration of such services in urban centers
and consequently to argue the case for the inferiority of white labor. Broadening her argument, finally, she sought to reposition African-American
workers within the national political economy, contending, along much
the same lines as Shadd Cary and Watkins Harper, that blacks stand a
better chance of achieving economic independence in agrarian rather
than urban occupations: "I was lately lecturing out in Pennsylvania, the
farmers wanted good men and women to work their farms on shares for
them. Why can't you go out there?—and depend upon it, in the course
of time you will get to be independent."

Two other antebellum speeches of Truth's that have entered into the
written record focus on the issue of women's rights and were delivered at
the 1851 Woman's Rights Convention in Akron, Ohio, and the 1853 Broadway Tabernacle Convention, respectively, to primarily white female audiences. These speeches are important statements in Truth's broad-based
efforts to redefine the specific position of the black woman, the "brave"
who can claim privilege on the basis of neither whiteness nor maleness.
As she grappled with such redefinition, Trudi needed to situate the black
woman vis-à-vis the dominant culture's central construction of true
womanhood as well as the feminist-abolitionists' more marginal reconceptualizations of femininity. Truth's contempt for, and rejection of, the
cult of true womanhood is suggested in Titus's account of the 1858 antislavery meeting in Silver Lake, Indiana, in which her femininity was reportedly at issue. Whereas many of the white women present felt shame

at Truth's public exposure of her "private" sexual organs, Truth apparently felt none. In her speech, she reportedly redefined her breasts not as emblems of an essential femininity but as a sign of her public labor power, the socially enforced labor that had ensured the well-being of her masters' children and that thus differentiated her from white women: "her breasts had suckled many a white babe, to the exclusion of her own offspring" (139).

Truth needed, in addition, to redefine the black woman in relation to the feminist-abolitionists' construction of her. In her *Appeal to the Christian Women of the South* concerning the terrible condition of slaves, Angelina Grimké had spoken sympathetically of their plight and promised to "be faithful in pleading the cause of the oppressed" while urging "submission on the[ir] part" as the wisest policy. Both of Grimké's *Appeals* were, in fact, addressed specifically and exclusively to white women—South and North—suggesting that she was far more interested in rethinking the parameters of white women's culture than in forging a space for the "brave" to emerge into autonomous womanhood. Both Angelina and her sister Sarah, moreover, resorted to the analogy of "the slavery of sex" to define the obstacles that stood in the way of the full liberation of white women. Once again we are alerted here to the dangers that may inhere in the use of figurative language. The analogy of white women's lack of rights to slavery is valid to a certain extent: white women have no legal existence and cannot bring legal action, they cannot hold property but are themselves property, they have no control over their children, and so on. Nevertheless, there are ways in which this analogy is clearly invalid: the (white) *feme sole* possesses legal rights denied to the (white) *feme covert*, white women have the legal right of petition as well as education, those of middle-class status are maintained in a protected private sphere, their families are not customarily broken up, and so forth. Finally, it is important to note that in the construction of this analogy the slave is initially ungendered. As the analogy is expanded upon, this slave is most often gendered as male and the historical specificity of the female slave is thereby erased; if her special condition is addressed, she is invariably envisioned as victim.[53]

Truth's two antebellum women's rights speeches may be found in Stanton and Anthony's *History of Woman Suffrage*, but the 1851 speech (the famous "A'n't I a Woman" speech) has a longer and more complex publishing history. As Mabee has noted, at least four accounts of the speech were reported in newspapers shortly after the close of the convention, one in the June 6 issue of the *New York Daily Tribune,* another in the June 13 issue of the *Liberator,* still another in the June 14 issue of Jane Swisshelm's *Saturday Visiter,* and the longest in the June 21 issue of the *Anti-Slavery Bugle.* Frances D. Gage's "reminiscences" of the speech were not written until years later, when the essay appeared in the April 23, 1863, issue of the *Independent;* it was then reprinted in both Titus's narrative and Stanton and Anthony's *History.* Mabee has quite astutely questioned the accuracy of Gage's version of the speech as well as the veracity of some of the factual details provided in her editorial comments and has suggested that the 1851 *Anti-Slavery Bugle* version is probably a closer approximation of the speech that Truth actually gave.[54] We simply have no way of ascertaining what Truth actually said. What I propose to do is read Gage's reminiscences of Truth as a representation of a black woman by a white woman, and then compare them with the earlier 1851 *Bugle* speech.

As printed in the *History of Woman Suffrage,* Truth's 1851 and 1853 speeches are both contextualized by editorial narratives designed to place them in the proper historical and social context in which they were given. Both editorial narratives underscore the double burden of "color and sex" that Truth, and all black women, must bear (1:567). In particular, in her introductory comments to the 1851 speech, Gage relates the disgust felt by many of the women present that a "darkey" is to be allowed to speak: "Woman's rights and niggers! . . . Don't let her speak!" (1:115). In contrast, Gage emphasizes her own rejection of the irreconcilable contradiction between the concept of "woman" and that of "nigger," seeking instead to define Truth's specificity as a black woman. Yet Gage's use of bodied symbols here to portray Truth—"the Lybian Statue [sic]," "this almost Amazon form"—once again results in a dehistoricization of the black woman (1:115–16).

Truth's speech is an argument in favor of the equality of "woman." While it might give the appearance of disjointedness, as recorded by Gage it is in fact quite logically organized. Revising somewhat the African-American system of antiphony, it improvisationally but systematically "responds" to the "call" of male superiority made earlier by some ministers present at the convention. To their claim of man's superior intellect, Truth replies, from a position of open morality that relies on the wisdom of folk sayings, that men have the obligation to aid women in their acquisition of knowledge: "If my cup won't hold but a pint, and yourn holds a quart, wouldn't ye be mean not to let me have my little half-measure full?" To their argument that men are superior because of the manhood of Christ, Truth retorts that Christ originated not from a man but from God and a woman. And to the "theological view of the sin of our first mother," Truth responds that Eve "was strong enough to turn de world upside down all alone" (1:115, 116).

Yet the thrust of Truth's argument lies in the first part of her speech, in which she debunks the cult of true womanhood whereby "dat man ober dar say dat womin needs to be helped into carriages, and lifted ober ditches" in order to assert the worth and equality of black womanhood. In a series of statements, she affirms her masculine strength based on her ability to perform strenuous physical labor: "I have ploughed, and planted, and gathered into barns, and no man could head me." But in a second se-ries of rhetorical questions she pleads her identity as a woman—"and a'n't I a woman?"—an identity that remains incontrovertible given the fact of her motherhood: "I have borne thirteen chilern, and seen 'em mos' all sold off to slavery, and when I cried out with my mother's grief, none but Jesus heard me!" (1:116). Although at first glance it might appear that Truth here has adopted a paradigm similar to that of Frances Gage or Dr. Strain, in fact her construction of her own identity derives specifi-cally, as Jean Fagan Yellin has noted, from her historical experience as a slave whose productive and reproductive labor has been owned and ex-ploited by slaveholders. Indeed, the extent of Truth's difference from Gage may be measured in Gage's concluding editorial comment, "She had taken us up in her strong arms and carried us safely over the slough of difficulty turning the whole tide in our favor" (1:116–17). Yellin's observa-tion that Gage here "cast the black woman as a powerful rescuer and her-self and the other white women at the convention as powerless rescued female victims" must be further refined to emphasize that Gage has in fact placed black women in the same structural position as those men who help white women into carriages and lift them over ditches.[55]

As personal "reminiscences," Gage's account is constrained not only by her own social ideology but also by her memory and by the moment of narration itself. An exploration of this narrative moment indicates that Gage wrote her account shortly after the appearance of Stowe's "Libyan Sibyl" essay and while living on the South Carolina Sea Islands, where she had joined women like Charlotte Forten to work on behalf of the newly freed people. I would suggest that Gage's reminiscences were in fact highly influenced by these events such that the historical figure of Truth is overshadowed by other, contradictory, representational images. Thus, if Truth is ahistorically analogized to the Libyan Sibyl and the Amazon in the prefatory comments, the speech itself seems to assimilate her to the South Carolina slave characterized by a heavy black dialect and the use of the term "nigger," not present in the 1851 version nor, I believe, in any of Truth's other speeches. Thus, the opening lines read: "I tink dat 'twixt de niggers of de Souf and de womin at de Norf, all talkin' 'bout rights, de white men will be in a fix pretty soon" (1:116). The immediate effect of such dialect is to reinforce the image of Truth as a "darkey."

I would argue that Gage's reconstruction of Truth's speech rewrites Truth not only as a "darkey" but also as a masculine body seeking feminization implied in the repeated question "a'n't I a woman?" In contrast, the 1851 account offers an inversion of Gage's paradigm of a quest for feminization as it presents us first with Truth's synecdochic affirmation "I am a woman's rights," which is then followed by a series of statements that emphasize her capacity to do a man's work: "I have as much muscle as any man, and can do as much work as any man." Rather than begging for admission to a sphere of femininity acceptable to white women, Truth, here offers her audience a vision of black womanhood that records the ways in which the specific historical conditions of slave labor have insisted on masculinizing the "brave."

The second noteworthy difference between the two versions of this speech consists in the different placement and wording of the already quoted openings line of the "A'n't I a Woman" speech, which forms the concluding line of the 1851 version but in a different language: "But man is in a tight place, the poor slave is on him, woman is coming on him, and he is surely between a hawk and a buzzard." This sentence is significant in its evocation of slave and woman by means of a folk expression that is simultaneously standard English and African-American. In her juxtaposition of what Blair called "simple expression" and "figure of speech," Truth sought vividly to portray the white man's increasingly tense location vis-à-vis the two groups he has oppressed. The figurative expression "between hawk and buzzard" is a colloquialism of the dominant culture that suggests a positioning between two sufficiently similar but unpleasant entities that can only lead to indecision or paralysis. Yet "hawk" and "buzzard" are also figures from an African-American folktale in which the two vultures are seen as oppositional and come into conflict in a struggle for survival, the buzzard, a descendant of the powerful African "King Buzzard," always gaining the ascendancy.[56] To an African-American audience, this colloquialism can be read as the site where the two cultures overlap without converging and makes it possible to see the position of "slave" and "woman" not as symmetrical but as divergent and possibly hostile, thus undermining the kind of coalition that Gage's later 1863 narrative worked so hard to build.

Interesting parallels and divergences exist between Truth's 1851 speech and her 1853 New York convention speech. The latter one is a general plea for women's rights elaborated by means of some of the same figurative analogies employed by white feminist-abolitionists, in particular the figure of the pleading Esther.[57] But the language of Truth's speech also suggests the presence of other cultures—African and African-American—reaching out perhaps beyond her immediate audience of white women to the "brave." Thus, if Truth depreciatingly refers to herself throughout the speech as a "slave," a "colored woman," and an "aged woman" whose right to speak seems questionable, she in fact begins her speech with a powerful Africanism: "Is it not good for me to come and draw forth a spirit." In the Kumina, or "African dance," of the central African Bakongo tribe, the ritual ceremony is performed to the beat of drums and is led by a queen who, initiated into the mysteries of the religion, is both possessed by spirits and able to draw forth spirits.[58] Truth, then, implicitly positions herself here as a kind of African queen come to draw forth the spirit of her audience. Its spirit is, according to her, that of both a goose and a snake ready to hiss her. In this use of animal imagery, Truth shifts cultural ground to tap into a colloquialism of the dominant culture whereby the audience mocks the stage performer by hissing at him or her like a goose. Her additional evocation of the snake may be seen, however, as a kind of cultural convergence in which African, African-American, and American values alike interpret the snake as evil and demonic (1:567).

Aware that her audience might not recognize her power as the queen of the Kumina, Truth shifts the ground for establishing her authority as speaker by boldly laying claim to being a citizen of the State of New York. Despite the possibility that her audience might still hiss her "like snakes and geese," Truth's structuring of the rest of her speech suggests that she might in fact be striving to reach an audience of the "brave" that exists beyond her immediate one. For, interestingly enough, although Truth is addressing a "Woman's Rights" meeting, she bases her claim of citizenship on the fact of having been a slave: "I am a citizen of the State of New York; I was born in it, and I was a slave in the State of New York; and now I am a good citizen of this State." It is only after she has asserted the fact of her citizenship that Truth proceeds to speak out on the question of women's rights, allowing slave and woman to conjoin and finally produce the "colored woman." If the end of the 1851 speech had suggested the oppositionality of slave and woman in the figures of hawk and buzzard, here Truth attempts to collapse this opposition into a conflationary "we": "We have all been thrown down so low that nobody thought we'd ever get up again; but we have been long enough trodden now; we will come up again, and now I am here" (1:567). It is this same tension in her thinking between "slave" and "woman," conflict and coalition, that was to shape the politics of race and gender in Truth's post-bellum career as a public speaker and social activist.

Notes

1. My discussion of Sojourner Truth relies on the 1878 edition. All references to this edition are included parenthetically in the text. For a discussion of the minor changes made by Titus to Gilbert's portion of the *Narrative*, see Carleton Mabee, *Sojourner Truth: Slave, Prophet, Legend* (New York: New York University Press, 1993), 203.

2. Margaret Washington, "Introduction," *Narrative of Sojourner Truth* (New York: Vintage Books, 1993), xviii–xx.

3. Gary B. Nash, *Forging Freedom: The Formation of Philadelphia's Black Community, 1720–1840* (Cambridge: Harvard University Press, 1975), 146.

4. Nancy Woloch, *Women and the American Experience* (New York: Knopf, 1984), 172.

5. On this point see also Mabee, *Sojourner Truth*, 98. For a comprehensive history of Truth's relationship to communitarian experiments, see Wendy E. Chmielewski, "Sojourner Truth: Utopian Vision and Search for Community, 1797–1883," in *Women in Spiritual and Communitarian Societies in the United States*, ed. Wendy E. Chmielewski, Louis J. Kern, and Marlyn Klee-Hartzell (Syracuse, N.Y.: Syracuse University Press, 1993), 21–37.

6. For a discussion of the influence of African familial structures on the African-American family, see Niara Sudarkasa, "Interpreting the African Heritage in Afro-American Family Organization," in *Black Families*, ed. Harriette Pipes McAdoo (Beverly Hills, Calif.: Sage, 1988), esp. 40–44.

7. Alice Eaton McBee, *From Utopia to Florence* (Northampton, Mass.: Smith College, 1947), 20, 47, 44.

8. Charles A. Sheffeld, *The History of Florence, Massachusetts* (Florence: The Editor, 1895), 88.

9. Victor Turner, "Liminal to Liminoid, in Play, Flow, and Ritual: An Essay in Comparative Symbology," *Rice University Studies* 60 (1974): 82.

10. Quoted in Esther Terry, "Sojourner Truth: The Person Behind the Libyan Sibyl," *Massachusetts Review* 26 (Summer–Autumn, 1985): 442.

11. Nell Irvin Painter, "Sojourner Truth in Life and Memory: Writing the Biography of an American Exotic," *Gender & History* 2 (Spring 1990): 10.

12. See Mabee, *Sojourner Truth*, chapter 5.

13. William L. Stone, *Matthias and His Impostures* (New York: Harper and Brothers, 1835), 193; Gilbert Vale, *Fanaticism; Its Sources and Influence, Illustrated by the Simple Narrative of Isabella, in the Case of Matthias* (New York: G. Vale, 1835), 82.

14. John Wideman, "Frame and Dialect: The Evolution of the Black Voice in American Literature," *American Poetry Review* (September/October 1976): 35, 36.

15. Philippe Lejeune, *On Autobiography*, ed. Paul John Eakin, trans. Katherine Leary (Minneapolis: University of Minnesota Press, 1989), 196, 185.

16. Peggy Kamuf, *A Derrida Reader: Between the Blinds* (New York: Columbia University Press, 1991), 107.

17. Lejeune, *On Autobiography*, 189, 207–11.

18. Mabee, *Sojourner Truth*, 202–203.

19. Dan Schiller, *Objectivity and the News* (Philadelphia: University of Pennsylvania Press, 1981), 6–11.

20. Washington, "Introduction," xxix–xxxiii.

21. Hugh Blair, *Lectures on Rhetoric and Belles-Lettres*, 2 vols. (London: W. Strahan, T. Cadell, 1783), 1: 287, 281, 274, 283.

22. Jean Fagan Yellin, *Women and Sisters: The Antislavery Feminists in American Culture* (New Haven, Conn.: Yale University Press, 1989), 84.

23. Henry James, *William Wetmore Story and His Friends*, 2 vols. (Boston: Houghton Mifflin, 1903), 2:71, 77.

24. See also Painter, "Sojourner Truth in Life and Memory," 9–10, for comments about how Stowe depicts Truth as exotic and as an entertainer.

25. Schiller, *Objectivity and the News*, 88–95.

26. Robert Taft, *Photography and the American Scene* (New York: Dover, 1964), 143.

27. Walter Benjamin, "The Work of Art in an Age of Mechanical Reproduction," in *Illuminations*, ed. Hannah Arendt, trans. Harry Zohn (New York: Harcourt, Brace, and World, 1968), 232.

28. Taft, *Photography and the American Scene*, 149–50.

29. Letter to Oliver Johnson, *National Anti-Slavery Standard*, February 13, 1864; letter to Mary Gale, dated February 25, 1864, Sojourner Truth Papers, Manuscript Division, Library of Congress.

30. My comments on photography here owe much to discussions by Roland Barthes, *Image/Test/Music*, trans. Stephen Heath (New York: Hill and Wang, 1977); idem, *Camera Lucida: Reflections on Photography*, trans. Richard Howard (New York: Hill and Wang, 1981); John Berger and Jean Mohr, *Another Way of Telling* (New York: Pantheon Books, 1982); and Susan Sontag, *On Photography* (New York: Farrar, Straus and Giroux, 1977).

31. See Kathleen Collins, "Shadow and Substance: Sojourner Truth," *History of Photography* 7 (July–September 1983): 183–205, for the best and most comprehensive discussion of Truth's photographs to date.

32. Elizabeth Cady Stanton, Susan B. Anthony, and Matilda Joslyn Gage, *History of Woman Suffrage*, 6 vols. (Rochester, N.Y.: Fowler and Wells, 1881–1922), 1:115.

33. Washington, "Introduction," xxiv–xxix; and Gloria I. Joseph, "Sojourner Truth: Archetypal Black Feminist," in *Wild Women in the Whirlwind: Afra-American Culture and the Contemporary Literary Renaissance*, ed. Joanne Braxton and Andrée Nicola McLaughlin (New Brunswick, N.J.: Rutgers University Press, 1990), 38–40.

34. James Gronniosaw, *A Narrative of the Most Remarkable Particulars in the Life of James Albert Ukawsaw Gronniosaw* (Leeds: Davies and Booth, 1814), 7.

35. Lawrence W. Levine, *Black Culture and Black Consciousness* (New York: Oxford University Press, 1978), 58; Washington, "Introduction," xxvi–xxviii; Levine, *Black Culture and Black Consciousness*, 66, 158.

36. Lejeune, *On Autobiography*, 204.

37. Levine, *Black Culture and Black Consciousness*, 66.

38. Julia Kristeva, *Powers of Horror: An Essay on Abjection.* Trans. Leon S. Rudiez (New York: Columbia University Press, 1982) 23.

39. Victor Turner, *Ritual Process: Structure and Antistructure* (Ithaca, N.Y.: Cornell University Press, 1977) 109–10.

40. See also Jeffrey Stewart's comment that Truth laid a "claim to being the moral conscience of the nation." "Introduction," *Narrative of Sojourner Truth* (New York: Oxford University Press, 1991), xxxviii.

41. For other rhetorical analyses of Truth's speeches, see Janey Weinhold Montgomery, *A Comparative Analysis of the Rhetoric of Two Negro Women Orators: Sojourner Truth and Frances E. Watkins Harper* (Hays: Fort Hays Kansas State College, 1969); and Karlyn Korhs Campbell, "Style and Content in the Rhetoric of Early Afro-American Feminists," *Quarterly Journal of Speech* 72 (November 1986): 434–36.

42. Kenneth Cmiel, *Democratic Eloquence: The Fight over Popular Speech in Nineteenth-Century America* (New York: Morrow, 1990), 57–73.

43. Levine, *Black Culture and Black Consciousness*, 66, 158; and Walter Ong, *Orality and Literacy* (London: Methuen, 1982), 32.

44. Ong, *Orality and Literacy*, 67–68, 34.

45. Mabee, *Sojourner Truth*, 229–30; for a discussion on the alternation of song and speech, see Eileen Southern, *The Music of Black Americans*, 2nd ed. New York: Norton, 1983), 19.

46. Sojourner Truth Papers, Manuscript Division, Library of Congress.

47. Deirdre La Pin, "Narrative as Precedent in Yoruba Oral Tradition," in *Oral Traditional Literature*, ed. John Miles Foley (Columbus, Ohio: Slavica Publishers, 1981), 349.

48. On call-and-response, see Southern, *Music of Black Americans*, 19; on the function of proverbs in oral cultures, see Viv Edwards and Thomas J. Sienkewicz, *Oral Cultures Past and Present: Rappin' and Homer* (Cambridge, Mass.: Basil Blackwell, 1991), 168–72.

49. William D. Piersen, *Black Yankees: The Development of an Afro-American Subculture in Eighteenth-Century New England* (Amherst: University of Massachusetts Press, 1988) 107–13.

50. Sojourner Truth Papers, Manuscript Division, Library of Congress.

51. Fred Tomkins, *Jewels in Ebony* (London: 1866?), 6.

52. Werner Sollors, *Beyond Ethnicity: Consent and Descent in American Culture* (New York: Oxford University Press, 1986), 241–47.

53. Angelina Grimké, *Appeal to the Christian Women of the South* (New York: Anti-slavery Society, 1836), idem, *Appeal to the Women of the Nominally Free States* (New York: W. S. Dorr, Printer, 1837); Sarah Grimké, *Letters on the Equality of the Sexes and the Condition of Woman* (Boston: I. Knapp, 1838).

54. For the 1851 and 1853 speeches, respectively, see Stanton, Anthony, and Gage, *History of Woman Suffrage*, 1:115–17 and 1:567–68. Future page references to the speeches are included parenthetically within the text. For Mabee's analysis, see chapter 6 and n. 15. For a reprint of the *Anti-Slavery Bugle* version of the 1851 speech, see Mabee, *Sojourner Truth*, 81–82; Washington, 117–18; J. Stewarts, "Introduction," xxxiii.

55. Yellin, *Women and Sisters*, 81.

56. Levine, *Black Culture and Black Consciousness*, 92.

57. For a discussion on this use of the figure of Esther, see Yellin, *Women and Sisters*, 33, 40–41.

58. See Monica Schuler, *"Alas, Alas, Kongo": A Social History of Indentured African Immigration into Jamaica, 1841–1865* (Baltimore: Johns Hopkins University Press, 1980), 70–80.

Part III

Harper, Hopkins, and Shadd Cary
Writing Our Way to Freedom

Chapter 8

Narrative Patternings of Resistance in Frances E. W. Harper's *Iola Leroy* and Pauline Hopkins' *Contending Forces*

VANESSA HOLFORD DIANA

Against all . . . barbarities and abuses which degrade and dishearten them, the members of the National Association intend to agitate in the future as they have done in the past with such force of logic and intensity of soul that those who handicap and harass the race will either be converted to principles of justice or be ashamed openly to violate them.
—Mary Church Terrell[1]

Resistance is a political act. It is also a nonviolent strategy for changing a status quo that perpetuates race wars and violates civil rights. To resist means that one does not accept the belief system, the data as they are presented, or the rationalizations used to perpetuate the status quo around race relations.
—Maria P. P. Root[2]

At the close of the nineteenth century, black feminist activists turned to fiction writing as one tool of reform with which to fight gender and racial oppression. Anna Julia Cooper believed that literature was one important tool of social change in women's national reform efforts. She asked in 1892, "What is the key-note of the literature of these days? What

In memory of Eugenia C. DeLamotte

is the banner cry of all the activities of the last half decade? . . . It is compassion for the poor and unfortunate, and, . . . 'indignant outcry against the failure of the social machinery as it is, to ameliorate the miseries of men!'" This literary trend of critiquing corrupt "social machinery" and the expansion of social reform movements in general showed, according to Cooper, that "a 'mothering' influence . . . is leavening the nation."[3] Speaking of women's responsibility as reformers to lead the nation toward change, Frances E. W. Harper argued, "it is the women of a country who help to mold its character, and to influence if not determine its destiny; and in the political future of our nation woman will not have done what she could if she does not endeavor to have our republic stand foremost among the nations of the earth."[4] In these references to a national "mothering influence," Cooper and Harper voice a common belief in Victorian ideologies of gender: that American women must enact moral reform in the "saving" of America; both also suggest that storytelling can influence that reform. Harper's fictional character Frank Latimer argues that a novel can "inspire men and women with a deeper sense of justice and humanity," while Pauline Hopkins declares in the preface to *Contending Forces* that a successful novel can "[cement] the bond of brotherhood among all classes and all complexions."[5]

Cooper, Harper, and Hopkins all suggest that African-American writers must present their own stories in order to break the cycle of racist misrepresentation that contributed to the oppression of black Americans. Self-representation creates imaginative space for citizenship in Harper's 1892 novel *Iola Leroy* and Hopkins' 1900 novel *Contending Forces*. Both authors practice what Barbara Harlow has termed the "literature of resistance [which] sees itself . . . as immediately and directly involved in a struggle against ascendant or dominant forms of ideological and cultural production."[6] As resistance writers, both Harper and Hopkins depict female characters who are model reformers; in the fictional context, these women practice self-representation in such a way that they challenge their fellow characters (and, by extension, their readers) to take action. Harper's Iola Leroy determines to become an author in order to "do something of lasting service for the race" (197). Striving to become—to use Toni Morrison's terms—"the definers" rather than "the defined," both authors deconstruct specific racist and sexist misrepresentations of African Americans.[7] Speaking of Harper, Hopkins, and other African-American women writers at the time, Hazel Carby notes that literature was one arena in which "black women intellectuals reconstructed the sexual ideologies of the nineteenth century to produce an alternative discourse of black womanhood."[8]

As Claudia Tate has suggested in *Domestic Allegories of Political Desire*, female characters such as Harper's and Hopkins' enact what the authors define as an idealized political future, whether that future involves performing the seemingly conservative roles that the Cult of True Womanhood prescribed or behaving in ways revolutionary for women at the time. Both Harper and Hopkins present black women's contested relationship to the Cult of True Womanhood as a direct critique of the sexual violence committed during and after slavery. Although their heroines are in many ways independent, revolutionary women who perform acts of resistance, both authors' portrayals of female virtue, framed as appeals for enfranchisement and desegregation, often demand inclusion in Victorian definitions of "civilized" womanhood. Tate explains that "the highly noticeable exercise of conservative Victorian gender roles was a candid sign of the black middle-class' claim on respectable citizenship, just as the appropriation of bourgeois gender conventions in general were fundamental to the emancipatory discourse of nineteenth-century African Americans."[9]

Employing fiction as reform rhetoric required Harper and Hopkins to find innovative ways to work within the genre conventions available to them, especially those of women's sentimental domestic fiction, a genre that Claudia Tate and Jane Tompkins, among others, argue is already well-suited to political argumentation. Sentimental fiction is an especially effective medium in which to combine the persuasive techniques that Mary Church Terrell described in her address quoted at the opening of this essay as "force of logic and intensity of soul." Both Harper and Hopkins take innovative approaches to narrative conventions that especially lend themselves to metaphorical readings, such as the trope of the family tree, which encompasses representations of ancestry, family history, courtship, and parenting. Innovative presentations of the family tree critique the interdependent definitions of race, womanhood, and manhood used to deny black Americans recognized membership in the national family tree. Similarly, the tropes of idealized heroes and heroines also allow the authors to expose the faulty logic of the interrelated sexism and racism that fueled segregation and disfranchisement at the turn of the last century. Harper and Hopkins effectively shape their novels into resistance narratives through what I call twinning, a narrative structure that pairs or mirrors characters or events. Narrative twinning strategies create a composite portrait of characters and events that ultimately dramatizes collective rather than individual experience. These narrative twinning patterns encourage readers to understand individual characters and events to be representative of—in fact directly correlating to—larger patterns in and truths about American gender and race relations.

Harper and Hopkins challenge racist and sexist depictions of African Americans that characterized white supremacist rhetoric in the slavery era, when, as Gerda Lerner explains, justification for the rape of African-American women was based on the argument "that all black women were eager for sexual exploits, voluntarily 'loose' in their morals, and, therefore, deserved none of the consideration and respect granted to white women."[10] After slavery, African-American women continued to suffer under this stereotype; rape remained common, and the category of virtuous womanhood was reserved for white women only. Similarly, African-American men were excluded from mainstream definitions of manhood characterized by restraint and chivalry, as is evident in the prevalent stereotype of the black rapist, which was employed in much public discourse to justify lynching. To challenge these dangerous stereotypes, Harper and Hopkins critique white manhood by contrasting white male characters' moral corruption and hypocrisy with the idealized behavior of black male and female characters.

"Slavery's Shadows": Narrative Twinnings in Frances Harper's *Iola Leroy*

"Did not the whole nation consent to our abasement?"   —Iola Leroy in *Iola Leroy*

In *Iola Leroy*, Harper presents an extended critique of the nation's culpability in the historical oppression of African Americans while challenging the racist and sexist ideologies that contributed to that oppression. In using Iola's family tree as a metaphorical signifier of the national family tree, Harper undermines racist and sexist arguments that black women as a group possessed racially determined weak moral character and challenges white men's claims to moral superiority. Simultaneously, the domestic, private details of Iola's family tree expose fundamental flaws in mainstream (mis)understanding of America as a national family. One central representational strategy in *Iola Leroy* is the historicizing of power relationships between white men and black women, which Harper portrays through Iola's parents, Eugene Leroy, a slave owner, and Marie, his slave. Through their relationship, Harper introduces the power imbalance between them as a foundational paradigm for comparative consideration of *all* the male-female relationships in the novel.

For example, the narrator describes Iola's mother in terms of economic language; Marie was a slave "liable to be bought and sold, exchanged and bartered" before Leroy's decision to marry her (58). In this way, Harper enables readers to consider the daughter Iola's story in light of the power imbalance that comprises her lineage; she is born of a relationship perverted by the slave system, and both privilege and disempowerment are her "inheritance."

Harper dramatizes the relationship between individual and national moral culpability through Iola's father's failure to act responsibly toward his family. Leroy, as the novel's central Euro-American father, is a flawed patriarch, and his flaws become representative of national moral blindness. Despite his love for an African-American woman and despite the African heritage of his own children, Leroy never takes action to fight slavery, the system that eventually causes his family's destruction. Similarly, when he later dies and Marie is left powerless to defend herself or her children from Leroy's villainous cousin Alfred Lorraine, the nation's flawed legal system sanctions her suffering. As a failed symbolic protector, Leroy represents the failure of the national "law of the father" to protect all Americans, and Harper emphasizes that Leroy's and the nation's are both failed fatherings, in this case because both are complicit in the continuation of slavery. By creating Leroy as a representational figure in this way, Harper illustrates that—as Iola later will claim—the whole nation did consent to the abasement of African Americans. Like the shattered Leroy family, the nation, too, is characterized by disunion, suffering, and the denial of legitimate rights, as is evidenced by Harper's twinning of the Leroy's shattered family with multiple other shattered families in the novel. The "shadows" of slavery, as Harper calls slavery's far-reaching consequences, invade every home.

In tracing Iola's family history, Harper challenges definitions of white manhood that claim moral superiority through her repeated depictions of Euro-American men's violent disregard for African-American women. This is especially true in Harper's characterization of Lorraine, who—after Leroy's death—remands Marie and her children to slavery. Infusing the conventional villain of sentimental romance novels with political significance, Harper creates Lorraine as a spokesman for the popular refusal to recognize legitimate family ties between white men and enslaved black women. After learning that his cousin Leroy wants to marry a slave, Lorraine asks, "Why, man, she is your property, to have and to hold to all intents and purposes. Are you not satisfied with the power and possession the law gives you?" (51). Lorraine's question presents a perversion of marriage vows as he parodies "to have and to hold" in this context, which precedes Leroy's later vow, "until death us do part," suggesting that Leroy's words, too, are empty of the usual legal legitimacy of a marriage bond (58). Refusing to extend the category of family to a black woman, Lorraine denies not only Marie's place in his family, but also her right to a recognized, legal, socially sanctioned bond with a white man, because such a bond would require acceptance of Marie's right to citizenship, would legitimize her, and thereby render illegitimate the institution of slavery.

Harper's twinning of Marie's story with her daughter Iola's illustrates the persistence during Reconstruction of both overt and subtle racism and sexism toward black women. Like her mother, Iola is wooed by a white man, Dr. Gresham, who, despite his love for her, is nonetheless unable to recognize that his desire to have Iola live as a white woman and keep her African heritage a buried secret implicates him in larger systems of white supremacist thought and action. To Gresham's marriage proposal, Iola responds, "Doctor, I am not willing to live under a shadow of concealment which I thoroughly hate as if the blood in my veins were an undetected crime of my soul" (175). That Iola is free to refuse her white suitor where her mother Marie was powerless to do so illustrates a generational progression toward liberation, and the novel suggests that part of achieving liberation is acknowledging publicly the power disparities implicit in even the most benevolent relationships between white men and black women.

In revealing her past to Gresham, Iola directly challenges accusations of African-American women's moral degradation. She begins by describing herself in economic language twinning that which described her mother earlier: "I was sold from State to State as an article of merchandise" (89). She then goes on to speak from the knowledge her experiences have given her, using her personal testimony to represent the communal experiences of African-American women during slavery:

> I had outrages heaped on me which might well crimson the cheek of honest womanhood with shame, but I never fell into the clutches of an owner for whom I did not feel the utmost loathing and intensest horror. I have

> heard men talk glibly of the degradation of the negro, but there is a vast
> difference between abasement of condition and degradation of character.
> I was abased, but the men who trampled on me were the degraded ones.

Gresham responds, "But, Iola, you must not blame all for what a few have done." Her answer locates her personal experience in the national context of rape within slavery. She replies: "A few have done? Did not the whole nation consent to *our* abasement?" (89, my emphasis). Iola refuses to marry this white man who cannot see his role in her oppression.

Both Marie and Iola draw on their own personal histories to bear witness to a larger national trend of ongoing exploitation. Similarly, as Harper writes Marie's and Iola's stories, she addresses the next generation of black women readers and illustrates through example the passing on of moral understanding, modeling women's reform work. In projecting a secure self-image, Iola not only challenges white supremacist ideology, she also becomes a role model for black women readers to address internalized racism, for Iola's acts of self-representation give primacy to self-worth and pride. Iola finds empowerment in self-representation, in claiming and telling her story. Her willingness to speak openly even the shocking details of her story suggests another level of Harper's twinning—that of Iola Leroy and "Iola" (the pen name of Ida B. Wells), the outspoken African-American journalist who literally put her life at risk to protest against lynching.

If the novel is, as Pauline Hopkins claims, "a record of growth and development from generation to generation"(14), then Harper's decision to conclude her novel with the marriages of both Iola and her brother Harry represents that generational development within the historical continuum of the allegorical Leroy family tree. The ways Harper chooses to characterize those marriages, then, become her last words, a final set of oppositional representations that map out a program for healing of the national family. The central strategy Harper employs to enact this final resistance is the use of idealized characters. Courtship, marriage, and happy endings become ways of envisioning a liberated future while embracing commitment to social reform.[11]

In concluding a novel that charts the violation and shattering of multiple families with depictions of idealized marriages, Harper creates narrative locations that function as what bell hooks has called "homeplace," a location that enables African-American readers to imagine liberated selves.[12] Put another way, "domestic stories allowed black people of the post-

Reconstruction period 'to identify imaginatively with actions they would like to perform but [could] not in the ordinary course of events' given their exclusion from civil political participation."[13] Enabling imaginative identification is a central purpose of Harper's oppositional representation, which targets for African-American readers the interior discourses of self-doubt that have resulted from racist and sexist misrepresentations. Claudia Tate describes turn-of-the-century black artists' roles in contributing to the psychological health and political determination of their readers: "Central to the survival of African Americans, to the preservation of black culture and community, was finding strategies to withstand the persistent physical and psychological racial assaults. To mount a sustained struggle, black social activists and artists alike formulated strategies for fortifying the resolve of black Americans to continue the battle for freedom."[14]

Harper's presentation of idealized role models and marriages serves as one "strategy for fortifying the resolve" of her African-American readers by imagining activist selves who bring about both social change and personal healing. In individual characterizations, she utilizes twinning to offer evidence of African Americans' successful contributions to "the battle for freedom."[15] Characterizations of these marriages similarly offer evidence of individual characters' effective social impact. In the marriage of Iola Leroy to Frank Latimer, Harper represents idealized conceptions of black womanhood and manhood, terms she redefines as codes for practicing Christian democracy and idealized citizenship. Latimer "is more than a successful doctor; he is a true patriot and a good citizen. Honest, just, and discriminating, he endeavors by precept and example to instill into the minds of others sentiments of good citizenship. He is a leader in every reform movement for the benefit of the community; but his patriotism is not confined to race lines" (210). Harper's description of marriage suggests multileveled formations of a more perfect union: Formations of an ideal family are blurred with formations of an ideal nation. In her commitment to social activism, Iola finds in Latimer a perfect partner for her life's work: "Her noblest sentiments found a response in his heart. In their desire to help the race their hearts beat in unison. One grand and noble purpose was giving tone and color to their lives and strengthening the bonds of affection between them" (201). Removed temporarily from the context of public misrepresentations that would denigrate their manhood and womanhood, Frank Latimer and Iola Leroy are represented in a fictional homeplace where he is the "ideal of a high, heroic manhood . . . [who] belongs to the days of chivalry" (198), and she, "in the calm loveliness of her ripened womanhood, [is] radiant in beauty and gifted in intellect" (161). Their idealization performs the final "unsaying" of all representations that would dismiss their rights to citizenship; Harper imagines the nation as an extension of the idealized homes her characters create.

History Twinned in Pauline Hopkins' Contending Forces

"One hundred years ago . . . duplicated today" —Mrs. Smith, *Contending Forces*

Harper's *Iola Leroy* and Hopkins' *Contending Forces* share much in common. In both, family ties cross racial categories; in both, families are shattered as a result of racial and sexual oppression. In depicting the violent fragmentation of the Montfort family in the early nineteenth-century South, Hopkins dramatizes the brutal power relations of the slavery system. By echoing that brutality in the contemporary (Reconstruction era) tale, Hopkins shows those power relations' persistence in post-emancipation U.S. culture and illustrates the need to break historical patterns of sexual and racial oppression. The complex family histories that make up Hopkins' *Contending Forces* result from rape and forced family separations. Like Harper, Hopkins dismantles prevailing definitions of white manhood as superior to black manhood. Both novels critique white men's claims to such elements of chivalry as the protection of women and restraint of impulses.

The early nineteenth-century story that opens *Contending Forces* focuses on the white Montfort family, who are slave owners. Rumors arise that Grace Montfort may be of mixed race, a notion that her husband dismisses as unimportant, although he continues to participate in and profit from a system of white privilege that depends on concepts of "race" and "blood" for justification, enslaving people who may share his wife and children's racial lineage. The destruction of the Montfort family unit, like the destruction of the Leroy family unit, centers upon the role of a father who is directly responsible for slavery's continuance. Both novels dramatize white men's susceptibility to greed at the expense of their families. For example, Hopkins shows the corrupting influence of slavery on slave owner Montfort, who lets his greed rather than an internal moral code decide his actions. Like Harper's Eugene Leroy, Montfort fails to use his position of power to protest slavery:

> like all men in commercial life, . . . he lost sight of the individual right or wrong of the matter, or we might say with more truth, that he perverted right to be what was conducive to his own interests, and he felt that by owning slaves he did no man a wrong, since it was the common practice of those all about him. (22)

Montfort's greed and acceptance of "common practice" blind him to the wrongs he inflicts upon others, and he is therefore culpable in the suffering of his own family members.

While in sentimental fiction conventional depictions of positive patriarchal characters link fatherhood with protection, responsibility, and nationhood, Harper's and Hopkins' twinned narrative patterns illustrate white patriarchs ignoring moral imperatives of protection for the sake of profit, critiquing on a national scope the flawed morality of the nation's leaders. In both novels, the white father/protector is quickly killed off so that the mother, as a black woman, can be shown to be utterly unprotected under the slave system.

Another white man in Montfort's community, the villainous Anson Pollock, desires Grace Montfort and uses trumped-up charges to murder her husband so he can claim her for his own (which Grace's rumored African lineage makes legal). His murdering band, the "committee on public safety," an early portrayal of the Klan, justifies violence as a means of maintaining social "order." After the murder, Pollock's henchmen whip the naked Grace repeatedly, suggesting a sexual violation specific to slavery.

Using violence to emphasize the ongoing brutality of racial and sexual oppression and the careless shattering of families, Hopkins, like Harper, presents the violation of motherhood as evidence of the nation's moral corruption in allowing the slave system to persist. Based on the categories of race and difference used to justify slavery, Grace is legally reduced to the level of her black slave Lucy—described elsewhere as a "sister" to Grace. Now both women are slaves with no legal rights, articles of merchandise, who could by law be bought, sold, whipped, and raped at any time. That Lucy occupied this position throughout her life is not emphasized while the horror of Grace's tragic fall from virtuous wife and mother to violated woman takes place. But by seating the two women side by side, literally tied together, in Pollock's cart, Hopkins creates a visual deconstruction of race categories. In the allegorical tableau of the cart, readers see that these two "sisters" are indeed the same "race." Both Harper's and Hopkins' novels show white men denying women of color the protection afforded to white women under U.S. law and social practice. Like white feminists of the time, Hopkins targets the woman-as-property model upon which patriarchy is based, but she emphasizes the violent extremes to which that model is taken in the case of black women, thereby problematizing white feminists' claims to equal oppression with their "sisters" of color.

Harper and Hopkins include in Marie Leroy's and Grace Montfort's stories scenes that dramatize the horror behind broken family ties after presenting domestic scenes that establish both women's status as mothers befitting the angel-in-the-house imagery of the Cult of True Womanhood. Grace's relationship to her children is severed permanently at the moment when the seemingly white woman is violated and thus removed from the definition of True Womanhood that encompasses motherhood as well as sexual purity. Both Harper and Hopkins go to great lengths to emphasize the piety and purity of their violated black women characters. Anne duCille offers a useful analysis of such instances of seeming adherence to the Cult of True Womanhood by black women writers:

> the cultural interventions of many of these nineteenth-century novelists were propelled not by an accomodationist desire to assimilate the Victorian values of white society but by a profoundly political, feminist urge to rewrite those patriarchal strictures. For these, after all, were the values of the same social system that had enslaved an entire race, even as it declared the equality of all men—that had systematically raped, defiled, and degraded black women, even as it declared its deference for and defense of true womanhood.[16]

Hopkins reveals this hypocrisy by creating a plot shift that further blurs the distinction between Grace and Lucy. After Grace kills herself, "Pollock elect[s] to take Lucy in the place he had designed for Mrs. Montfort" (71). The slave sister becomes Pollock's unwilling mistress and a foster mother for Grace's children after their mother's death. While suicide or death by divine intervention made for convenient novelistic resolutions of violated womanhood in sentimental romances by white women, the reality of sexual exploitation during slavery was that many black women had to live with their violation, in part because they had children who depended on them. Unlike Grace, Lucy withstands her sexual violation to care for her foster sons, her motherly sacrifice challenging the exclusion of African-American women from the category of True Womanhood while emphasizing the interracial family ties that make up the nation.

Hopkins echoes Grace's violation with the twinned story of Sappho Clark, who, one hundred years later, is raped as a child by her white uncle, a story, reminiscent of *Iola Leroy,* that emphasizes the ongoing perversion of the family tree based on racist notions of human difference. When the young biracial girl, now pregnant, has been rescued from the brothel where her uncle left her after the rape, her outraged father confronts him. The uncle's response shows that, though slavery may no longer be legal, the time is not yet passed when African-American women are seen as objects of sexual service, able to be bought and sold. The uncle offers Sappho's father financial recompense for his daughter's sexual violation:

> Well ... whatever damage I have done I am willing to pay for. But your child is no better than her mother or her grandmother. What does a woman of mixed blood, or any Negress, for that matter, know of virtue? It is my belief that they were a direct creation by God to be the pleasant companions of men of my race. Now, I am willing to give you a thousand dollars and call it square. (260–61)

The uncle echoes here the common myth of the morally "loose" African-American woman, whom he sees in terms of ownership, while completely ignoring the incestuous perversion of his family connection to the girl.

According to Carby, Hopkins molds "Sappho's history into a paradigm of the historical rape of black women."[17] From the parallels between Grace's story and Sappho's, it becomes clear that African Americans cannot rely on the law to ensure justice. Harper and Hopkins present what Lauren Berlant calls "a different history," which "call[s] on people to change the social and institutional practices of citizenship to which they currently consent."[18]

Both of Hopkins' sexual predators, Anson Pollock and Sappho's uncle, are community leaders. Like the men who raped Grace, members of the unofficially sanctioned "committee on public safety," Sappho's uncle is legally empowered as a prominent member in the state senate; both crimes make mockeries of the law, divorcing legality from morality. When Sappho's father vows to pursue the proper legal means to seek justice by taking the uncle to court, the uncle responds by having him murdered. This moment of fratricide, in conjunction with incestuous child-rape, underscores the perversion of the American family tree in the name of racial separation. Repeatedly, these writers dramatize powerful white men, who come to embody a national patriarchy, denying the category of family and the protections that the category ideally affords to black Americans.

That rape and the threat of rape are recurring topics in both *Iola Leroy* and *Contending Forces* illustrates the directness with which Harper and Hopkins challenge representations of African-American women as willing participants in their sexual violation. Harper and Hopkins also deconstruct the racist stereotype of the black man as rapist. For example, Harper's narrator reminds readers that, during the Civil War, "fragile women and helpless children were left on the plantations while their natural protectors were at the front, and yet these bondmen refrained from violence" (8). By contrast, the slave owner who buys Iola Leroy "means to break her in" (31). In the words of Ida B. Wells,

> True chivalry respects all womanhood, and no one who reads the record, as it is written in the faces of the million mulattoes in the South, will for a minute conceive that the southern white man had a very chivalrous regard for the honor due the women of his race or respect for the womanhood which circumstances placed in his power . . . Virtue knows no color line, and the chivalry which depends upon complexion of skin and texture of hair can command no honest respect.[19]

Hopkins echoes Wells and Harper in her critique of sexual exploitation, when her character argues that rape "is *not* a characteristic of the black man, although *it is* of the white man of the South," a claim Hopkins supports through her violent twinned depictions of white men as rapists in both Grace's and Sappho's stories (298, emphasis in original).

Sappho's suffering because of racist and sexist misrepresentations of black women does not end with her childhood trauma; instead, shame infuses her self-perception and hampers her ability to claim her own family. Sappho must actively redefine virtuous womanhood in order to reclaim her identity as a mother. Hopkins illustrates the danger of internalized racism by showing Sappho accepting the belief that she is no longer virtuous after the rape, a belief that (temporarily) prevents her from mothering her child Alphonse and from marrying the story's hero, Will Smith: "feelings of degradation had made her ashamed of the joys of motherhood, of pride of possession in her child" (345). Accepting her own family history, including the violence from which Alphonse was born, is the struggle that Sappho must undergo before she can create a family of her own and forge a future. Hopkins juxtaposes motherhood and rape to emphasize the hypocrisy of men who would claim to protect and value the former while they eagerly perpetrate the latter.

Functioning as counterpoint to her characterization of white rapists, Hopkins' utilization of idealized black characters and happy endings to conclude *Contending Forces* functions politically in much the same way as Harper's conclusion. Her idealized characters disprove the stereotypes that would cast black Americans as creatures driven by sexual instinct. As duCille argues, in these marriages, "sexual desire is not *displaced* by social purpose but *encoded* in it—regulated, submerged, and insinuated into the much safer realm of political zeal and the valorized venue of holy wedlock."[20] Such encoding can be seen in Will Smith's desire for Sappho, which is characterized by restraint: "Although love had come to Smith like a flood sweeping all barriers before it, yet the very strength of his desire for her love but served to restrain desired action" (169). In employing this language of restraint, Hopkins alludes to popular discourse on masculinity while highlighting the contrast between Smith and unrestrained male sexual predators such as Pollock and Sappho's uncle.[21]

As in *Iola Leroy*, the marriages concluding *Contending Forces* position black couples' idealized romantic unions in the context of social activism, so that the characters of Sappho and her husband Will represent role models for "uplift" work while simultaneously forming a family unit in which to raise Sappho's son Alphonse: "Sappho was happy in contemplating the life of promise which was before her. Will was the noblest of men. Alphonse was to him as his own child. United by love, chastened by sorrow and self-sacrifice, he and she planned to work together to bring joy to hearts crushed by despair" (401). Will's idealized role as father to the previously unfathered Alphonse takes on allegorical proportions: "The ambition of [Will's] life was the establishment of a school . . . where the Negro youth of ability and genius could enter without money and without price . . . he would be *a father to the youth of his race*" (386, my emphasis). Parenting and responsible citizenship, in this connection, are shown to be the same act on different scales: the "uplifting" of the race. Just as some feminists at the turn of the century argued that the same (supposedly inherent) superior morality that fitted women to be successful moral leaders in the home simultaneously justified their increased political participation, so here idealized manhood is shown to be an essential element of citizenship on the levels of both family and nation. As black men who embody idealized manliness, "civilization," and restraint, Harper's and Hopkins' black heroes, along with their women counterparts, directly challenge the basic tenets of white supremacy.

By presenting egalitarian unions, Hopkins writes into the marriage stories of each couple an argument for both domestic and public responsibility. Commenting on the egalitarian nature of these idealized marriages, duCille says of the novel's conclusion, "as is so often the case in these African American revisions of the marriage plot, matrimony here means not submission and domesticity but partnership and race work."[22] Anne duCille explains that modern readers of these courtship tales may have trouble understanding both Harper's and Hopkins' decisions to conclude their novels with fairy-tale like marriages that ring of "happily ever after" sentimentalism:

> While modern minds are inclined to view marriage as an oppressive, self-limiting institution, for nineteenth-century African Americans, recently released from slavery and its dramatic disruption of marital and family life, marriage rites were a long-denied basic human right—signs of liberation and entitlement to both democracy and desire.[23]

Because Harper and Hopkins devote much of their novels to depicting the "dramatic disruption of marriage and family life," it makes sense that the resolution of each novel includes multiple marriages. These marriages not only signify entitlement to democracy as duCille notes, they also dramatize ways of *practicing* citizenship within a democracy. On both the domestic and national levels, the healing of the family tree signifies a first step in creating an ideal democracy in which all Americans are secure in their rights to life, liberty and the pursuit of happiness. Both Harper and Hopkins use the trope of the happily-ever-after ending to envision that ideal, suggesting that imagining the ideal is a prerequisite to achieving it.

Iola Leroy and Sappho Clark are not the only characters to wed at the end of their respective tales; in each, a female friend also weds in similar unions based on social activism. These twinned sets of marriages emphasize the communal characterization both Harper and Hopkins create throughout their novels. That four separate characters in each novel find in marriage the opportunity to create partnerships for "race work" emphasizes the representational function of each individual character. Similarly, twinned characters illustrate complimentary versions of that race work. Hopkins' Will Smith advocates higher education for young African Americans, while his twinned brother-in-law Dr. Lewis provides industrial training for his students.[24] Hopkins' twinned characters of Sappho and Dora, who "scattered brightness along with charitable acts wherever a case of want was brought to their attention," illustrate the success of women's cooperative efforts in "race work" (129). Similarly, Harper's twinned heroines Iola and Lucille Delany offer composite characterization as well. According to Frances Smith Foster, "separately, neither character could represent the African American experience. Together, the two women represented what Harper deemed the best potential of African American women."[25]

While the idealized marriages that conclude, *Iola Leroy* and *Contending Forces* may seem at first to celebrate patriarchy and insist upon heterosexual unions, the portrayals of relationships between heroines and heroes found in these texts are all significantly revolutionary as both feminist critiques of male dominance and radical revisionings of sexual politics. Like the earlier authors of women's slave narratives, Harper and Hopkins directly and honestly examine the role of sexual exploitation in black women's lives and in their struggles for autonomy. Both take great risk in presenting to their genteel readers disturbing truths associated with black women's sexual oppression at the time.[26] The risks that Harper and Hopkins take in discussing black female sexuality at all made possible the later celebration of black female sexuality in twentieth-century fiction such as Zora Neale Hurston's *Their Eyes Were Watching God.* Challenging Victorian conventions of decorum, both novels dramatize the roles of gender and race in power relationships between white men and black women by focusing on encounters characterized by sexual threat. Within these challenges to equations between white men's manliness, "civilization," and restraint lies an implicit questioning of the justification of white male power. As Bederman explains, "affirming the manly power of the white man's 'civilization' was one of the most powerful ways middle-class men found to assert their interwoven racial, class, and gender dominance."[27] But because these men's behavior falls far short of the prescribed code of self-restraint, readers are asked to question whether it is appropriate that corrupt white men inhabit positions of power.

Harper and Hopkins formulate their challenges to mainstream misrepresentations by combining "a force of logic and intensity of soul." As Terrell suggested, successful rhetorical strategies for change employ appeals to empathy and to reason, appeals that both authors construct by drawing largely from the conventions of sentimental romance fiction to represent African-American women's experiences from a resistant standpoint. Yet neither novel can be classified merely as an unconventional sentimental romance; both can be described more accurately as hybrid fiction that draws on conventional elements of such genres as sentimental romance, oratory, documentary, and slave narrative.[28] This weaving of elements from multiple genres is itself a revolutionary act of creative innovation and a political statement. Not only do Harper and Hopkins revise notions of biological and family inheritance in their critiques of sexism and racism, but they also revise understanding of literary inheritance—in both cases stressing the need to forge new possibilities out of old, externally imposed traditions and expectations.

As metaphor and as literal testimony, the family tree allows analysis of intersections between dominant constructions of gender and race. In exposing these intersections, Harper and Hopkins prefigure contemporary theorists who continue to explore the interrelatedness between these factors in identity. And yet these novels function as metaphorical representations does not diminish their impact as testimonies to individual suffering and survival. In *Yearning*, hooks describes a legacy of silenced African-American history that Harper and Hopkins, as resistance writers, challenge: "We have too often had no names, our history recorded without specificity, as though it's not important to know who—which one of us—the particulars."[29] In both *Iola Leroy* and *Contending Forces*, storytelling is precisely the act of naming names, specifying particulars, and bearing witness that hooks demands. Harper's and Hopkins' political critiques do not merely aim to influence change in the current legal system but also model for African-American readers ways of telling "the particulars" of one's own story to affirm one's right to justice.

Notes

1. Mary Church Terrell, "What the National Association Has Meant to Colored Women," in *Intimate Practices: Literacy and Cultural Work in U.S. Women's Clubs, 1880–1920*, ed. Anne Ruggles Gere (Urbana: University of Illinois Press, 1997), 137.

2. Maria P. P. Root, ed., *The Multiracial Experience: Racial Borders as the New Frontier* (Thousands Oaks, Calif.: SAGE Publications, 1996), 6.

3. Anna Julia Cooper, *A Voice From the South* (Oxford: Oxford University Press, 1988), 59.

4. Frances Harper, "Woman's Political Future," in *Intimate Practices*, 134.

5. Frances E. W. Harper, *Iola Leroy, or Shadows Uplifted*, in *The African-American Novel in the Age of Reaction: Three Classics* (New York: Mentor, 1992), 197; Pauline E. Hopkins, *Contending Forces: A Romance Illustrative of Negro Life North and South* (New York: Oxford University Press, 1988), 14. All further quotations from Harper's *Iola Leroy* and Hopkins' *Contending Forces* will be noted in the text with page number references in parenthesis following the quotations.

6. Barbara Harlow, "Narratives of Resistance," *New Formations* 1 (Spring 1987): 131–35.

7. Toni Morrison, *Beloved* (New York: Alfred A. Knopf, 1987), 190.

8. Hazel V. Carby, *Reconstructing Womanhood: The Emergence of the Afro-American Woman Novelist* (New York: Oxford University Press, 1987), 6.

9. Claudia Tate, *Domestic Allegories of Political Desire: The Black Heroine's Text at the Turn of the Century* (New York: Oxford University Press, 1992), 56.

10. Gerda Lerner, ed., *Black Women in White America, A Documentary History* (New York: Vintage Books 1992), 162.

11. See Ann duCille, *The Coupling Convention: Sex, Text, and Tradition in Black Women's Fiction* (New York: Oxford University Press: 1993); and Tate, *Domestic Allegories of Political Desire* for additional discussions of the functions of these happy endings.

12. See bell hooks's discussion of "homeplace" in *Yearning: Race, Gender, and Cultural Politics* (Boston: South End Press, 1990).

13. John Cawelti, quoted in Tate, *Domestic Allegories*, 7.

14. Tate, *Domestic Allegories*, 10–11.

15. For example, like the twinning of Iola with Ida B. Wells, Harper's decision to give the name Lucille Delaney to Iola's sister-in-law, the successful founder of a school for African Americans in the south, suggests a possible intentional twinning with Lucy Laney, an African-American educator who founded the Haines Normal Institute in Atlanta, which started with seventy-five pupils in 1886 and by 1940 had over a thousand pupils. See Lerner, *Black Women in White America*, 122–23.

16. DuCille, *The Coupling Convention*, 32.

17. Carby, *Reconstructing Womanhood*, 138.

18. Lauren Berlant, "The Queen of America Goes to Washington City: Notes on Diva Citizenship," in *The Queen of America Goes to Washington City: Essays on Sex and Citizenship* (Durham, N.C.: Duke University Press, 1997), 221, 223.

19. Lerner, *Black Women in America*, 203–204.

20. DuCille, *The Coupling Convention*, 45.

21. Gail Bederman discusses the importance of restraint to late nineteenth-century concepts of white manhood in her article "'Civilization,' the Decline of Middle-Class Manliness, and Ida B. Wells's Antilynching Campaign (1892–94)," *Radical History Review* 52 (1992 Winter): 5–30.

22. DuCille, *The Coupling Convention*, 42.

23. Ibid., 14.

24. Rather than portraying these DuBois and Washington representatives as in conflict, Hopkins suggests there is a place for both visions of the role that education will play in uplift work for black communities. Her focus, then, seems to be on cooperative efforts for race work.

25. Frances Smith Foster, *Written By Herself: Literary Production by African-American Women, 1746–1892* (Bloomington: Indiana University Press, 1993), 185.

26. As the critical uproar in response to Kate Chopin's *The Awakening* proves, turn-of-the-century American readers still did not expect polite *white* women writers to address in their fiction matters of female sexuality in any overt fashion, even when it related to a critique of marriage. For women writers of color to do so, then, was potentially quite shocking. See Sandra M. Gilbert's introduction to *The Awakening and Selected Stories* (New York: Penguin, 1986).

27. Bederman, "'Civilization'," 8–9.

28. According to Elizabeth Ammons, "Harper offers a novel that, in its formal self-fracturing, speaks to the inadequacy of any single inherited long narrative form—the slave narrative, the domestic novel, the nineteenth-century African American novel, the white antislavery novel, the tight high-culture Anglo-European art novel—to serve her purpose of writing a political novel about a black woman in the United States." See Ammons, *Conflicting Stories: American Women Writers at the Turn into the Twentieth Century* (New York: Oxford University Press, 1991), 27.

29. Hooks, *Yearning*, 116.

Chapter 9

"We Are All Bound Up Together"

Frances Harper and Feminist Theory

VALERIE PALMER-MEHTA

Frances Harper stands as one of the most prolific black feminist writers and orators of nineteenth-century American literary and political culture, yet her contributions to feminist philosophy and theory largely have been overlooked. Throughout her life, Harper passionately pursued justice for African Americans and for women, and her work reflects an unrelenting effort to disturb power disparities, to rearticulate social relationships, and to compel people to take purposeful action on progressive social issues. At a time when few women dared to speak in the public realm, let alone to promiscuous and integrated audiences, she was a much admired and sought after abolitionist and suffragist lecturer, traveling throughout the United States and Canada.[1] Literary critic Hazel Carby asserts, "Harper fought for and won the right to be regarded as a successful public lecturer, a career not generally considered suitable for a woman, especially a black woman."[2] Harper spoke on behalf of and was active in numerous organizations and movements dedicated to human rights and social justice, including the Underground Railroad, the National Association of Colored Women, the American Equal Rights Association, and a variety of state anti-slavery societies. Commenting on her oratorical legacy, Shirley Logan states, "Frances Ellen Watkins Harper emerges as perhaps the most prominent, active and productive black woman speaker of the nineteenth century."[3]

Although Harper was a well-respected political orator, she is best known for penning numerous volumes of poetry and prose, most notably *Poems on Miscellaneous Subjects, Iola Leroy,* and the recently rediscovered *Minnie's Sacrifice, Sowing and Reaping, Trial and Triumph.* According to Frances Smith Foster, "Harper generally spoke on the same themes about which she wrote—abolition, equal rights, temperance, education, community service, morality and personal integrity."[4] Harper's literary and oratorical accomplishments reflected her political concerns, as Paul Lauter points out: "Harper demonstrated in her life and work a fusion between her artistic and her political lives. She refused to separate the two . . . she stands as a model of integrated aesthetic and political commitment."[5] Harper's speeches and essays provide insight into her political and social perspective, and offer powerful analyses of the white patriarchal power structure in nineteenth-century America, serving as a clear, but perhaps unselfconscious, feminist philosophy.

Despite the significance of her ideas, Harper is still largely unknown to contemporary audiences. Scholarship that mentions or focuses on Harper's oratory has been located mainly within the discipline of literary study, and Harper's work is typically relegated to a few chapters in a larger body of work dedicated to resurrecting the rhetorical legacy of African-American women in the nineteenth century, an effort whose time is long overdue.[6] Few books have focused solely on Harper, but those that do have made significant strides in restoring Harper's life work, recovering her literary and oratorical accomplishments, and providing a history of her feminist activism.[7] Despite these efforts, there is still a lacuna in contemporary literature regarding the contributions Harper has made to feminist theory. Through an analysis of two of Harper's feminist speeches, as well as a variety of essays that intersect with the ideas presented in the speeches, my aim is to unearth the feminist philosophy and practice she laid out and to explore how her conceptualizations might inform feminist theory over a century later.

Harper presented the first speech, "We are all Bound Up Together" at the Eleventh National Woman's Rights Convention held at the Church of Puritans in New York on May 10, 1866, when she was forty-one. According to Foster, "this speech marked the beginning of Harper's prominence in national feminist organizations" and thus is fitting for an analysis of her feminist legacy.[8] Harper delivered her speech alongside a range of women's rights advocates such as Frederick Douglass, Lucretia Mott, Susan B. Anthony, and Elizabeth Cady Stanton. At the end of this meeting, which was the first women's rights convention held after the Civil War, the anti-slavery and women's rights societies merged under the name of "The American Equal Rights Association," whose purpose was to fight for universal suffrage.[9] Harper was unable to commit herself completely to women's suffrage or universal suffrage for reasons that will be explored in this essay.

Harper delivered her second speech, "Woman's Political Future," at the World's Congress of Representative Women of All Lands, held from May 15 to May 22, 1893. She was one of eight speakers addressing the "Civil and Political Status of Women." The event was held in conjunction with the Chicago World's Columbian Exposition.[10] As this speech was given when Harper was sixty-eight, her seasoned perspective and philosophy regarding women's rights, civil rights, and the experience of being an African-American woman in U.S. society can be gleaned from it. Melba Boyd refers to this speech as "Harper's political manifesto," and shortly after the speech was delivered, "a derivative women's club in Boston began publishing the journal *The Woman's Era*. Inscribed by the speech Harper delivered before the Congress in Chicago, it became the voice of black feminism."[11] The speech also represents one of the last extant speeches Harper delivered, although she continued to be active during the years between 1892 and 1900, publishing four volumes of poetry and one novel. From 1901 until her death from heart disease in 1911, public records suggest that Harper was largely quiescent.[12]

Second-wave feminist theorists often acknowledge the influence of those who have gone before them in the first wave, providing nods at particular activists such as Harper, but not investigating their contributions in any real depth. This chapter provides a starting point as well as a call for additional analyses of African-American feminist rhetoric, for as Olga Idriss Davis indicates, there is a "paucity of rhetorical scholarship on African American women's epistemology and ontology."[13] In investigating these two speeches and a variety of her published essays, I argue that Harper has made meaningful contributions to contemporary feminist theory and practice that have been overlooked. First, I begin by showing how Harper used compelling personal stories in order to demonstrate the political aspect of personal experiences, laying the groundwork for the contemporary feminist philosophy of making the "personal political." Second, I uncover the ways in which Harper uses essentialism strategically for political purposes, while maintaining an anti-essentialist stance and underscoring the experience of double oppression. Third, I show that Harper supported broad-based social change, a reformation of thought that would extend to practice, above (but not in lieu of) the reformation of institutions, policies, and laws, which have a tendency to allow old ways of thinking to remain in place even in the face of reform. In so doing, I hope to establish that Harper's contributions to feminist thought are as relevant and useful today as they were over a century ago.

The Personal Is Political

Lamenting the fact that Harper never left a diary or personal narrative, Foster states that "the absence of a personal narrative from her canon is consistent with the values that Harper expressed both in her private letters and her published literature."[14] Namely, "Harper advocated a life in which the personal and the public were merged in an effort to realize the moral, social and economic development of society."[15] Although scholars like Foster and Carla Peterson have pointed to Harper's collapsing of the personal and political spheres in her literary work, most of her extant speeches do not draw on her personal life even though their content could have warranted it. However, in the speech, "We Are All Bound Up Together," which she presented when speaking before the Eleventh National Women's Rights Convention, Harper chose to share poignant personal stories with her audience in order to demonstrate how women's personal lives were indeed political. Peterson states, "this address differs markedly from almost all of Harper's other speeches in the degree to which she sought . . . to ground her authority in personal experience and her subject matter in the revelation of intimate emotions."[16] It is telling, perhaps, that Harper would share such personal information in her speech before a women's rights convention, and not in other speeches at other venues.

Harper commences her speech "We Are All Bound Up Together" by advising the predominantly white audience that her life had been dedicated to dealing with issues of oppression as they related to race, rather than gender. Harper, as quoted in Foster, states, "I feel I am something of a novice on this platform. Born of a race whose inheritance has been outrage and wrong, most of my life had been spent in battling those wrongs. But I did not feel as keenly as others that I had these rights in common with other women, which are now demanded."[17] Harper prompts the audience to reflect on the "wrongs" experienced by African people in the United States, juxtaposing them with the "rights" that the predominantly white movement that women of the time were demanding. In this juxtaposition of wrongs and rights—the demanding of relief from wrongs as opposed to contemplating further rights—Harper underscores the comparatively privileged position in which white women found themselves as a result of their race and the "double oppression" or "multiple jeopardy" that Harper, and African American women, faced.[18] Born a free black woman in Maryland, Harper was acutely aware of the rights that she enjoyed which the slaves of the South did not possess. However, she recognized that even the rights she did have were uncertain. This is demonstrated aptly by an 1853 Maryland law that denied free blacks entry into the state, with the threat of enslavement. The law, which was a response to the Fugitive Slave Act of 1850, made it impossible for Harper, who had moved to Ohio and then to Pennsylvania, to visit her home state.[19]

Immediately following these remarks, Harper recounts a tragic situation that she had experienced, which prompted her to identify more readily with the women's movement and her white counterparts:

> About two years ago, I stood within the shadows of my home . . . My husband had died suddenly, leaving me a widow, with four children, one my own, and the others step-children. I tried to keep my children together. But my husband died in debt; and before he had been in his grave three months, the administrator had swept the very milk crocks and wash tubs from my hands. I was a farmer's wife and made butter for the Columbus market; but what could I do, when they had swept all that away? They left me one thing—and that was a looking glass! Had I died instead of my husband, how different would have been the result! By this time he would have had another wife, it is likely; and no administrator would have gone into his house, broken up his home and sold his bed, and taken away his means of support . . . I say, then, that justice is not fulfilled so long as woman is unequal before the law.[20]

In sharing this circumstance, Harper acknowledges the distinct experience of oppression as a woman, as this occurred as a result of her gender, not her race.[21] It is interesting to note that a woman as accomplished as Harper, who also had made a living from her publications and lecturing, chose to identify herself as "a farmer's wife" whose "means of support" was making "butter for the Columbus market," deferring her authority from the public realm to the domestic sphere. This is likely because she knew that the majority of women of her time were forced to operate almost exclusively within the private realm, and she wanted to highlight the implications of her situation for most women. Additionally, while the story of Harper's loss in a time of such grief is sufficiently compelling, it is punctuated further by the fact that she is left with only a "looking glass," or a mirror, underscoring how trifling women were considered at the time. In recounting this personal story, Harper utilizes her own experience as evidence to give political value to her feelings of oppression and to critique the ideological and material practices that supported the patriarchal power structure in the United States in the nineteenth century. By sharing this experience, she gives voice to women's collective alienation and thus makes the "personal political."

Later in the speech, Harper shares personal experiences that highlight the injustices she has faced specifically as an African-American woman. Drawing on a biblical reference, which was not unusual for Harper, she states, "I, as a colored woman, have had in this country an education which has made me feel as if I were in the situation of Ishmael, my hand against every man, and every man's hand against me."[22] Quoting from the Book of Genesis, Harper refers to the plight of Ishmael, who was the product of relations between Abraham and his maid, Hagar, an interaction sanctioned by Abraham's wife, Sarah, because it was assumed she was unable to bear children. Years later, Sarah does have a child, Isaac, and he becomes the favored son, while Ishmael and Hagar are forced to leave. The conflict that developed between the brothers, as well as their descendants, carries on today in the antagonism that exists between modern-day Arabs and Jews. By drawing on this example, Harper not only is comparing herself to a child who has been cast off and whose birthright has been conflict, but also is comparing the relationship between blacks and whites with the struggle between Arabs and Jews.

To demonstrate the prejudice she encounters on a daily basis, Harper explains that during the past spring when she was traveling from Washington to Baltimore, "they put me in the smoking car! Aye, in the capital of the nation, where the black man consecrated himself to the nation's defence, faithful when the white man was faithless, they put me in the smoking car!"[23] Harper explains that such treatment makes it difficult for her to determine where she should make her home. Harper states, "I would like to make it in Philadelphia, near my own friends and relations. But if I want to ride in the streets of Philadelphia, they send me to ride on the platform with the driver."[24] Harper continues, "One day I took my seat in a car, and the conductor came to me and told me to take another seat. I just screamed 'murder.' The man said if I was black I ought to behave myself."[25] Harper's experiences demonstrate how difficult and complex day-to-day life was for black women, so difficult in fact that traveling around town and the very decision of where to live in relative peace were interrupted and complicated by the power structure of her time, issues her white contemporaries did not have to negotiate. While Harper could have moved to Canada, as did her caregiver and uncle, the famous Reverend William Watkins, thereby foregoing "many of the distressing realities that controlled the lives of the less fortunate members of her race," she instead chose to remain in the states to fight for justice for African Americans and for women, suggesting her strength and tenacity, as well as her commitment to her political concerns.[26]

Black feminists long have recognized that everyday life is political, and this is evident in Harper's rhetoric as well as that of other black feminists in the first wave of the women's movement. According to Marsha Houston and Davis, Harper's words and actions, as well as those of nineteenth-century black feminists such as Maria Stewart and Sojourner Truth, helped germinate the feminist intellectual tradition of merging personal experiences with feminist philosophy, a practice that proliferates today. Indeed, African-American feminist and womanist thought "can be traced to the words of enslaved Black women in the South and the free women in the North who were their contemporaries. Because it began with ordinary women sharing the experiences of their everyday lives, Black women's intellectual tradition never has been merely the province of the academy."[27] Similarly, the authors of the Combahee River Collective Statement, Barbara Smith, Beverly Smith, and Demita Frazier, assert that the political aspect of personal life was a genesis of contemporary black feminism: "There is also undeniably a personal genesis for Black feminism, that is, the political realization that comes from the seemingly personal experiences of individual Black women's lives."[28] Smith, Smith, and Frazier specifically point to Harper and other nineteenth-century black feminist activists as influential in their conceptualization of oppression. "There have always been Black women activists—some known, like Sojourner Truth, Harriet Tubman, Frances E. W. Harper, Ida B. Wells Barnett, and Mary Church Terrell, and thousands upon thousands unknown—who have had a shared awareness of how their sexual identity combined with their racial identity to make their whole life situation and the focus of their political struggles unique."[29]

As these authors suggest, contemporary feminist thought and feminist rhetorical culture have been influenced by the black feminist tradition of merging the personal and public spheres, as demonstrated by nineteenth-century black feminist activists generally, and Harper specifically. While many of Harper's speeches do not include personal references even though the content intersected with her life, it is interesting that Harper elected to share such deeply personal experiences before this women's rights event, indicating the perceived utility of such a strategy, as well as the belief that her personal stories would be well received, suggesting some degree of trust in or identification with her audience. Perhaps this is because, as Lerner states, Harper "confidently expected white women to be more sympathetic and supportive . . . than were white men, a confidence which was not often justified."[30] Harper was consistently optimistic and even idealistic in her belief in the "eventual triumph of right," and she perceived that those who also were subordinated in the patriarchal power structure might better understand her circumstances and experience of oppression.[31]

Strategic Essentialism

While Harper's purposeful collapsing of the distinction between the personal and political spheres has been acknowledged, her use of strategic essentialism largely has been overlooked. In the speeches examined here, Harper has demonstrated the political utility of strategically essentializing certain elements of one's identity so as to gain a voice in the public sphere, while simultaneously advancing an anti-essentialist stance. Generally, this is what Gayatri Spivak has referred to as "strategic essentialism," a term that has resulted in much contentiousness among contemporary feminist theorists. Spivak argues that there is value in speaking to a collective essence or identity, while simultaneously recognizing that this is a strategy to achieve particular political ends. According to Donna Landry and Gerald MacLean, Spivak has praised the "*strategic* use of a positivist essentialism in a scrupulously visible political interest" and recognizes the hazards of deploying essentialism uncritically or unproblematically.[32] The success of Harper as an orator and instigator of social change demonstrates how the theoretical concept of strategic essentialism can work in practical circumstances.

In her 1893 speech to the World's Congress of Representative Women

of All Lands, "Women's Political Future," Harper moves between essentializing all women to troubling the very notion of essentialism itself. For
example, in her introduction to the speech, Harper brings all women together and appeals to a common essence when she praises women by saying "to-day we stand on the threshold of woman's era, and woman's work
is grandly constructive."[33] However, this notion of woman as an all-
encompassing, homogenous category is troubled later on in the speech
when Harper states, "Political life in our country has plowed muddy
channels, and needs the infusion of clearer and cleaner waters. *I am not sure
that women are naturally so much better than men that they will clear the stream by the
virtue of their womanhood; it is not through sex but through character* that the best influence of women upon the life of the nation must be exerted."[34] Rather
than perceiving all women as the harbingers of nurturance, reciprocity,
and intimacy, as suggested by the cult of true womanhood popular at the
time and by some radical feminist thought of the twentieth century, her
comments indicate that she did not think that women had a particular
essence by "virtue of their womanhood." As Carby points out, Harper
did not think that women were "naturally" better people than men or
that they necessarily would construct a better social world, unless they
developed their character, a social construct that could be cultivated by
any human being. Carby states, "Harper was convinced that it was possible for women to formulate alternative aims for a society . . . but did not
believe that women had a 'natural' claim to be the bearers of the highest
aspirations of humanity."[35] Because women were disadvantaged in the patriarchal power structure, Harper thought they might be more motivated
to cultivate the kind of character that would value and promote social
justice.

Similarly, by sharing the previously mentioned injustice resulting from
the death of her husband in "We Are All Bound Up Together," Harper
works to underscore the ways in which white and black women share experiences of oppression based on their gender. Then she advances an anti-
essentialist stance, as demonstrated by the comments that follow the
story of her loss. "I do not believe that giving the woman the ballot is immediately going to cure all the ills of life. I do not believe that white
women are dew drops just exhaled from the skies. I think that like men
they may be divided into three classes, the good, the bad, and the indifferent."[36] By moving between an essentializing story to anti-essentialist
remarks regarding white women, Harper's rhetoric functions to ally

women to a common cause, while also acknowledging differences among women, and separating out those who fight for change and those who do not. Logan refers to this maneuvering as a rhetorical strategy of convergence and divergence. "Harper emphasized convergence in her persuasive discourse in the context of the reality that many of her audiences were composed of men and women who did not share her cultural experience."[37] Logan states that Harper directed her audience's "attention to what they and those she represented did share in common, at the same time that she reminded them of what they did not."[38]

In the next section of the speech, Harper works to describe how black women's lives and experiences are very much different from those of white women. As she does this, she essentializes African-American women, while also prompting her audience to understand the experience of double oppression that black women face: "You white women speak here of rights. I speak of wrongs . . . Let me go to-morrow morning and take my seat in one of your street cars . . . the conductor will put up his hand and stop the car rather than let me ride."[39] The intersection of race and gender oppression—or double oppression—was not a concept that many first-wave white feminists overtly recognized or addressed. Indeed, once abolition had been accomplished and the issue of suffrage for black men and all women began to be addressed, many first-wave feminists strategically prioritized issues of gender over race and demonstrated, at best, a lack of concern regarding their intersection. In *Feminist Theory*, bell hooks argues that the "feminist emphasis on 'common oppression'" was essentially "an appropriation by conservative and liberal women of a radical political vocabulary that masked the extent to which they shaped the movement so that it addressed and promoted their class [and race] interests."[40] Harper recognized that the rhetoric and actions emanating from the first wave of the women's movement sometimes failed to address her experiences and interests as an African American woman in U.S. culture, including her negotiation of double oppression, and she attempted to make critical interventions by raising the consciousness of movement women and petitioning for them to join in the fight against racism.

Articulating the reality of racism and the experience of double oppression in the United States was particularly important since some high-ranking, visible members of nineteenth-century women's rights organizations were racist or, at the very least, presented themselves as appealing to racist ideology in their public discourse. For example, in a December 26,

1865, letter to the editor of the *National Anti-Slavery Standard* titled "This is the Negro's Hour," Elizabeth Cady Stanton appeals to racist ideology, as she responds to a speech given by Wendell Phillips in which he supported black male suffrage over woman's suffrage, by questioning why "Sambo" should receive this right before white women. Additionally, hooks reports that "Southern white suffragists rallied around a platform that argued that woman suffrage in the South would strengthen white supremacy. Even though woman suffrage would also grant Black women the right to vote, in the South white women outnumbered them by two to one."[41]

Perhaps such sentiments prompted Harper to ask, regarding black women's experience of racism in the United States in general and their treatment on street cars in particular, "Have women nothing to do with this?"[42] After Harper describes her encounter with racism on street cars, she recounts a similar encounter experienced by another black woman. "Not long since, a colored woman took her seat in an Eleventh Street car in Philadelphia, and the conductor stopped the car, and told the rest of the passengers to get out, and left the car with her in it alone, when they took it back to the station."[43] Here, Harper strategically essentializes African-American women's experiences to generate feminist consciousness regarding racism in U.S. society, white women's complicity in this oppression, as well as the multiple jeopardy that African-American women face. Harper does not attempt to describe the varying experiences among black women's lives to this audience or to advance an anti-essentialist stance regarding black women; one can surmise that attempting to overcome the ignorance surrounding African-American women's lives in general and the importance of gaining political alliances precluded getting into greater specifics at this particular period in time. Such rhetorical maneuvering, as well as her ability to bring to light the disparity between the lives of white women and black women, made Harper a beacon for black activists. Boyd reports, "representative of black feminist thought, she articulated and clarified the multi-faceted complexity of American repression as she guided the eager consciousness of young activists advancing into the twentieth century."[44] Indeed, Harper's words "profoundly affected the ideological perspective of emerging national black feminist organizations."[45]

Although the cultural milieu in which Harper lived is different than that which we experience today, there are also similarities that warrant discussion. The failure to address women's interlocking experiences of oppression and the varying needs of women across race, class, and sexuality was a gaping flaw in the first wave of the women's movement, just as it was in the second wave of the women's movement. As hooks argues, "to build a mass based feminist movement, we need to have a liberatory ideology that can be shared with everyone."[46] This can be accomplished "only if the experiences of people on the margin who suffer sexist oppression and other forms of group oppression are understood, addressed and incorporated."[47] While strides in this direction have been made in feminist circles, this exhortation is just as valuable today in both theory and practice as it was when Harper suggested it in the first wave of the women's movement and when hooks declared it in her critique of the second wave of the women's movement.

Transforming Social Thought

Perhaps Harper's most compelling contribution to contemporary feminist thought is her urging for broad-based social change over, but not in lieu of, reforms. Similar to Harper's use of strategic essentialism, this element of her feminist philosophy has been ignored. Harper's desire to transform social thought is a theme that runs throughout her speeches. However, it is "Woman's Political Future" and a variety of her essays that indicate why she perceives the transformation of public sentiment as so important.

The tone at the beginning of "Woman's Political Future" demonstrates that Harper is supportive of women's burgeoning political influence and that she sees this as a wonderful opportunity. She states, "If the fifteenth century discovered America to the Old World, the nineteenth is discovering woman to herself."[48] Harper's likening of the unfolding of women's political power to the discovery of the New World demonstrates how colossal she perceives this shift in power. At the same time, she reveals a desire to see women's influence produce different results than had been realized formerly in America:

> Little did Columbus imagine . . . the glorious possibilities of a land where the sun should be our engraver . . . so to woman comes the opportunity to strive for richer and grander discoveries than ever gladdened the eye of the Genoese mariner. Not the opportunity of discovering new worlds, but that of filling this Old World with fairer and higher aims than the greed of gold and the lust of power, is hers. Through weary, wasting years men have destroyed, dashed in pieces, and overthrown, but to-day we stand on the threshold of woman's era, and woman's work is grandly constructive."[49]

Given her moment in time and her experiences, as well as her rhetoric on abolition and the plight of African Americans in U.S. society, one can surmise that her remarks regarding "greed of gold" and "lust of power" are referencing the slave trade, which was a financial boon to slave dealers and to plantation owners.[50] The slave trade also provided those whites on the lowest rungs of the socio-economic ladder a degree of power, and the promise of never having to take the position at the bottom of the economic and social order as long as slavery was in place. Harper recognized this and she "advocated national education for all Americans. Her plea acknowledged the frustrated futility of the developing black population attempting human solidarity with the impoverished hostility of ignorant, poor whites; while political corruption benefited from racial and class conflicts."[51]

While Harper had worked alongside white abolitionists, she also recognized that white women had played an integral role in preserving slavery, as well as white supremacy and racism, and her speech suggests concern that similar perspectives might become manifest in women's budding political power. This concern is made plain in the following excerpt, as she discusses the possibility of extending voting rights to women:

> I do not think the mere extension of the ballot a panacea for all the ills of our national life. What we need today is not simply more voters, but better voters. To-day there are red-handed men in our republic, who walk unwhipped of justice, who richly deserve to exchange the ballot of the freeman for the wristlets of the felon; brutal and cowardly men, who torture, burn, and lynch their fellow men, men whose defenselessness should be their best defense and their weakness an ensign of protection."[52]

Harper recognized that white men had produced a political system that protected them from the consequences of lynching their fellow Americans, among other transgressions. Harper feared that extending the vote to white women might function simply to fortify the corrupt social order that already existed in the United States and under which African Americans languished. Indeed, white women were rewarded for supporting white supremacy and for assisting in the subjugation of African Americans with such things as monetary gain, social acceptance, and the prospect of power.

Such "rewards" often positioned white women in direct competition with black men, who sought similar "favors" from white men. Hooks asserts that "in white supremacist capitalist patriarchy, black males and white females are uniquely positioned to compete with one another for the favors white 'daddies' in power can extend to them."[53] This competition is demonstrated aptly in the aforementioned letter from Elizabeth Cady Stanton to the editor of the *National Anti-Slavery Standard*, "This is the Negro's Hour." Stanton writes,

> The representative women of the nation have done their uttermost for the last thirty years to secure freedom for the Negro, and so long as he was lowest in the scale of being we were willing to press his claims; but now, as the celestial gate to civil rights is slowly moving on its hinges, it becomes a serious question whether we had better stand aside and see 'Sambo' walk into the kingdom first.

In these remarks, Stanton demonstrates that she, and perhaps the other members of the women's rights movement for which she often spoke, were in direct competition with black men for power in U.S. society. Indeed, it was not only Stanton who had appealed to racist ideology on a number of occasions to support her claim for addressing women's suffrage first.[54] Carby reports that, "both Anthony and Stanton eventually compromised with and acceded to racist, exclusionary practices in order to court potential white female supporters in the Southern states."[55] Further, "the entry of white Southern women on terms which they dictated ensured that suffrage organizations became a white women's movement."[56] Bearing this in mind, it is not surprising that Harper was concerned about the ways in which white women would employ their bourgeoning political influence, and that she was asking women to strive for a better world than white men had produced. According to Paula Giddings, "as Harper saw it, the greatest obstacle to the progress of Black women was not Black men but White racism, including the racism of her White 'sisters.'"[57]

These issues begin to suggest why Harper was hesitant to throw herself squarely behind women's suffrage, and even universal suffrage. Harper states:

> I do not believe that the most ignorant and brutal man is better prepared to add value to the strength and durability of the government than the most cultured, upright and intelligent woman. I do not think that willful ignorance should swamp earnest intelligence at the ballot box, nor that educated wickedness, violence, and fraud should cancel the votes of honest men ... The hands of lynchers are too red with blood to determine the political character of the government for even four short years ... The ballot in the hands of woman means power added to influence. How well she will use that power I cannot foretell.[58]

While Harper evenly applies her skepticism to men and women, at the time all men had voting rights and all women did not. Consequently, her stance on voting rights evoked some displeasure among first-wave movement women. Additionally, previously Harper had lent her support to the Fifteenth Amendment, which enfranchised black men, but not women. Logan reports, "Harper's recognition that white feminists could not always be counted on to support blacks led her to support the Fifteenth Amendment, which, of course, barred racial but not gender discrimination in voting."[59] Indeed, "Harper was far from certain it was wise to sacrifice all to woman's suffrage when she did not trust the white women who stood to benefit most from it."[60]

Instead of throwing herself unquestioningly behind women's suffrage, Harper asserts, "*More than the changing of institutions we need the development of a national conscience, and the upbuilding of national character*," and women "influence, if not determine, its destiny."[61] This statement is significant, for here Harper valorizes broad-based social change, indicating that a transformation of thinking in society is more important than this particular institutional reform, and perhaps reforms in general. Carby states that "what Harper advocated was not an extension of 'womanly influence,' a feminization of society, but a total transformation of the social order achieved through a unity gained in the 'grand and holy purpose of uplifting the human race.'"[62]

Considering that emancipation freed African Americans from slavery, but not from the perils of racism, socio-economic discrimination, and lynching, and that black male enfranchisement was met by violence and trickery at poll offices, it is clear that Harper recognized the value of pushing for more than institutional reform, which did not ensure a change of public opinion or sentiment. For example, in her essay "The Woman's Christian Temperance Union and the Colored Woman," printed in the *African Methodist Episcopal Church Review* in 1888, Harper condemns the racial segregation of Woman's Christian Temperance groups in the South. She states, "The war obliterated the disparity between freedom and slavery. The civil law blotted out the difference between franchisement and manhood suffrage . . . With these old landmarks going and gone, one relic remains from the dead past, 'our social customs.'"[63] The social customs to which she is referring, of course, include the racism that promoted and justified segregation. Similarly, in the essay "The Colored People of America," which appeared in *Poems on Miscellaneous Subjects*, published in 1857,

Harper describes the experience of African Americans in the United States when she states that freed slaves "have only exchanged the iron yoke of oppression for the galling fetters of vitiated public opinion."[64] Harper recognized that when public sentiment did not change, reforms or changes in legal status could not fulfill the goal of generating social equity. Consequently, Harper suggests that an overhaul in thinking in society is a necessary aspect of producing lasting social change.

The importance of changing public opinion through the development of a national conscience is a perspective that is mirrored in several of Harpers' extant speeches and essays. She is concerned with influencing public opinion because, as she states in the introduction to "Our Greatest Want," published in the *Anglo-African Magazine* in 1859, "leading ideas impress themselves upon communities and countries. A thought is evolved and thrown out to the masses, they receive it and it becomes interwoven with their mental and moral life." Harper further states that, "In America, where public opinion exerts such a sway, a leading [idea] is success." And, according to Harper, the "greatest idea of the present age, [is] the glorious idea of human brotherhood."[65]

This notion of human brotherhood, which is made possible through the development of a national conscience/character, is grounded in Christianity, which Harper perceived as a foil for racist ideology. For example, in the speech "The Great Problem to be Solved," delivered on April 14, 1875, at the Centennial Anniversary of the Pennsylvania Society for Promoting the Abolition of Slavery, Harper states, "the white race has yet work to do in making practical the political axiom of equal rights, and the Christian idea of human brotherhood." Harper continues: "what we need to-day in the onward march of humanity is a *public sentiment* in favor of common justice and simple mercy."[66] In the introduction to the speech "Could We Trace the Record of Every Human Heart," delivered to the New York City Anti-Slavery Society on May 13, 1857, Harper explains the connection between Christianity and political objectives: "the law of liberty is the law of God, and is antecedent to all human legislation." Near the end of the speech, she underscores this notion by stating that "the message of Jesus Christ is on the side of Freedom."[67] Through the years and throughout her speeches and essays, Harper impressed upon her audience the importance of developing broad-based social change by cultivating public sentiment in favor of a human brotherhood (informed by Christian principles), which she believed would enable equality in all aspects of social and political life by serving as a foil to oppression and racism. According to Boyd, "Harper's spiritual beliefs underlined her feminist and abolitionist convictions. Radical Christianity constituted a spiritual system . . . that facilitated her political principles."[68] Harper's use of spirituality is characteristic of African-American's women's rhetoric. According to Dorothy Pennington, "the discourse of African American women is historically grounded in religion and spirituality."[69] Pennington further contends that "for African American women's discourse . . . the archetypal epistemic base is that of spirituality and religion."[70]

Just as Harper had seen the end of slavery, but not the end of brutality inflicted on African people, bell hooks lived in the aftermath of women's suffrage, affirmative action, and other civil rights and women's rights legislation and still witnessed and experienced sexist and racist oppression. Advises hooks, "reforms have helped many women make significant strides towards social equality with men in a number of areas within the present white supremacist, patriarchal system, but these reforms have not corresponded with decreased sexist exploitation and/or oppression. Prevailing sexist values and assumptions remain intact, and it has been easy for politically conservative anti-feminists to undermine feminist reforms."[71] Hooks laments the fact that "women involved with feminist reforms [during the second wave of the U.S. women's movement] were inclined to think less about transforming society and more about fighting for equality and equal rights with men."[72] Neither Harper nor hooks suggest that feminists should not strive for reform. Rather, they both suggest that a concomitant commitment to the transformation of U.S. social thought is vital if these reforms are to be sustainable and meaningful.

As both Logan and Carby indicate, Harper's preference for "the development of a national conscience" over and above suffrage evoked ire among other feminists, particularly Margaret Windeyer, who spoke at the convention immediately following Harper, and responded to Harper's speech as follows: "Women have no political present when they do not exercise the franchise . . . I can not conceive that the underhanded, secret influence which women try to have upon politicians is politics." Logan argues, "Windeyer understood influence to mean a form of suggestive discursive power deriving from a close relationship or from physical attractiveness. Harper meant much more."[73] Indeed, as indicated, Harper was referring to the cultivation of broad-based social change, a change in the national conscience of the American people, which Harper believed would be necessary to promote and sustain anti-racist, anti-sexist reforms. Rather than considering how Harper's perspective might be informed by Harper's experience of double oppression in the United States, and indeed in the first wave of the women's movement itself, Windeyer perceived her stance as a lack of loyalty to the feminist cause.

And perhaps Harper was not loyal to the feminist cause as white feminists were articulating it at that moment in time. There is little doubt that Harper had reservations regarding woman's suffrage because of the racism that was manifest in society and in the first wave of the women's movement, and this caused her, at times, to place issues of race before issues of gender. How could she be certain that white women would vote in a manner that would be consistent with her well-being, unless there was a massive overhaul in thinking in the United States? Racism caused her suspiciousness and uncertainty regarding women's suffrage, but this notion was often lost on or ignored by some of her white female contemporaries. Harper articulates her frustration with the ambivalence toward racism in the women's movement near the end of her speech. "How can any woman send petitions to Russia against the horrors of Siberian prisons if . . . she has not done all she could by influence, tongue and pen to keep men from making bonfires of the bodies of real or supposed criminals? O women of America . . . It is yours to create a healthy public sentiment; to demand justice, simple justice, as the right of every race; to brand with everlasting infamy the lawless and brutal cowardice that lynches, burns and tortures your own countrymen."[74] Harper was concerned that white women had not expressed sufficient concern regarding the lynchings taking place in America, and had even directed their attention to concerns overseas, while ignoring the atrocities taking place at home. Harper was one of many black feminists who "constructively criticized the reserve of those white feminists who refused to identify white male terrorism as a feminist issue."[75] It is hard to envisage how movement women could not be aware of Harper's concerns when she so clearly articulated them throughout her speeches. But it is clear that her concerns went unaddressed to such an extent that when forced to separate elements of her identity (which in itself suggests a problem with first-wave movement women's understanding of the interlocking elements of oppression), she felt the need to defer issues of gender to the more pressing issue of race as a matter of survival.

Harper's Feminist Philosophy

Harper's work spans some of the most critical junctures of nineteenth-century U.S. history, yielding great insight into the white supremacist patriarchal power structure of her time. Her observations and criticisms provide a purview into the experiences and plight of nineteenth-century African Americans and women, and their negotiation of a social world that was in great flux. This case study is a step toward rediscovering the feminist philosophy and practice Harper laid out and how her conceptualizations might inform feminist theory over a century later. How her vision may inform our future is also of consequence, and it is to this end that I now turn.

While most of Harper's extant speeches do not include personal experiences, her speech before the Eleventh National Women's Rights Convention contained deeply personal stories that she used to critique the legal, ideological, and material practices that supported the hegemonic power structure in the United States in the nineteenth century. By using experience as evidence, she dips into the everydayness of people's ordinary lives to suggest how sexism and racism debilitated the quality of life for and endangered many of its citizens, clearly demonstrating how the personal is political. Almost a hundred years later, the use of experience as evidence was a hallmark of the second wave of the women's movement; some activists and authors have pointed to persons such as Harper as one of the forebears of this tradition. The excerpts examined here support the claim that Harper was influential in developing this strategy; or, at the very least, that she presaged it.

Harper's use of strategic essentialism to develop political influence and alliances largely has been overlooked. While contemporary feminists have a tendency to regard any essentializing claims with suspicion and even irritation, often with good cause, Harper's rhetorical maneuvering demonstrates how one might use essentialism strategically to advance political agendas while simultaneously cultivating an understanding of double oppression and suggesting her audience's complicity in the state of black women's lives. Harper reveals that identities are constituted relationally within particular power structures and she is under no illusion that all women share a common ahistorical essence. She deftly moves between her identities, essentializing them in order to gain influence and to cultivate political alliances, while simultaneously calling attention to an anti-essentialist stance. In an intellectual juncture in which even "strategic" essential-ism can be met with ignominy, Harper provides a productive model to consider in the fight for social justice.

Harper's exhortations for transforming public sentiment in order to ensure lasting social change also have been ignored. Harper recognized that reform was compromised when the attendant environment would not support social justice or the instituted change. This advice is particu-larly compelling in our contemporary socio-political environment in which reforms increasingly are under attack because of a neo-conservative climate that is ambivalent at best toward issues of feminism and social justice. While Harper pushed for a transformation of social thought grounded in a Christian ideal of a human brotherhood, today feminists likely would find that particular conceptualization problematic for a variety of reasons. However, Harper's broader focus on changing public sentiment to support social justice for all people, in addition to fighting for reforms, is a fundamental concept that feminists are called to address. How this might be accomplished is, I think, a most pressing issue for feminists today.

Finally, Harper's discourse suggests a concern that still plagues femi-nism on multiple levels today. That is, Harper ultimately felt some dis-trust of white women because she sensed that they did not fully grasp her experience of double oppression, and did not fight as passionately and consistently against racism as she did. It would not be unreasonable to suggest that, over a hundred years later, African-American women might still feel this distrust. Indeed, Smith, Smith, and Frazier state, "We real-ize that the only people who care enough about us to work consistently for our liberation are us."[76] This statement obviously is troubling because it suggests the depths to which feminists and the feminist movements have failed to meet black women's needs, and have allowed black women to feel alone in the struggle for justice. Ultimately, many feminists do be-lieve that there is some value in a collectivity, or else books such as this one would not exist. The goal is to make the collective useful and atten-tive to the needs of all involved, particularly those who have felt margin-alized, ignored, and dehumanized by the collective. Harper said, "I felt the fight in me; but I don't want to have to fight all the time."[77] We must fight for each other's liberation with as much care, passion, and knowl-edge as we fight for our own.

Although Harper had her doubts regarding white women's propensity to stand behind their black sisters, she also had hope that they ultimately would; she remained cautiously optimistic. Consequently, she never stopped engaging all audiences, fighting for social change and passionately attempting to raise consciousness regarding her experience of double oppression in a white supremacist patriarchal society. Harper's tenacity is a lesson for all of us, as we engage each other, and attempt to generate scholarship that addresses the myriad needs of women across race/ethnicity, class, nationality, and sexuality. However, we must admit that Harper was an exceptional person; most people do not have the strength to fight such a one-sided battle as Harper. That is why it behooves women in positions of privilege to work harder to bridge the gap, to fight ignorance and trained incapacities, and to work collaboratively on a transformation of social thought conducive to the needs of all women and, indeed, all humans.

Notes

The Author would like to thank Sherianne Shuler and Edward E. Lee III for their helpful comments on this paper.

1. "Promiscuous" refers to audiences composed of both men and women. For a discussion of the difficulties faced by nineteenth-century women speakers, see Karlyn Kohrs Campbell, *Man Cannot Speak for Her,* volume I: *A Critical Study of Early Feminist Rhetoric* (Westford, Conn.: Praeger, 1989), 9–12. For information on the specific exigencies faced by African American women, see 145–56.

2. Hazel V. Carby, *Reconstructing Womanhood: The Emergence of the Afro-American Woman Novelist* (New York: Oxford University Press, 1987), 66.

3. Shirley Wilson Logan, *We Are Coming: The Persuasive Discourse of Nineteenth-Century Black Women* (Carbondale: Southern Illinois University Press, 1999), 44.

4. Frances Smith Foster, ed., *A Brighter Day Coming: A Frances Ellen Watkins Harper Reader* (New York: The Feminist Press, 1990), 37.

5. Paul Lauter, ed., *The Heath Anthology of American Literature* (Boston: Houghton Mifflin, 1998), 2053.

6. See, for example, Carby, *Reconstructing Womanhood;* Logan, *We Are Coming;* Shirley Logan, *With Pen and Voice: A Critical Anthology of Nineteenth-Century African-American Women* (Carbondale: Southern Illinois University Press, 1995); Carla Peterson, *"Doers of the Word": African-American Women Speakers and Writers in the North (1830–1880)* (New York: Oxford University Press, 1995).

7. See, for example, Foster, *A Brighter Day Coming;* Melba Boyd, *Discarded Legacy: Politics and Poetics in the Life of Frances E. W. Harper 1825–1911* (Detroit: Wayne State University Press, 1994), 187–227.

8. Foster, *A Brighter Day Coming,* 216.

9. Logan, *We Are Coming,* 57.

10. Ibid., 66.

11. Boyd, *Discarded Legacy,* 222, 225.

12. Harper delivered the speech "Enlightened Motherhood" about six months later, on November 15, 1892. The text of the speech can be found in Foster's *A Brighter Day Coming,* 12.

13. Olga Idriss Davis, "A Black Woman as Rhetorical Critic: Validating Self and Violating the Space of Otherness," *Women's Studies in Communication* 21 (1998): 78.

14. Foster, *A Brighter Day Coming,* 23.

15. Ibid., 25.

16. Peterson, *"Doers of the Word,"* 228.

17. Foster, *A Brighter Day Coming,* 217. For an extended version of this speech, see Boyd, *Discarded Legacy,* 114–16.

18. For discussion of these terms, see Marsha Houston and Olga Idriss Davis, eds., *Centering Ourselves: African-American Feminist and Womanist Studies of Discourse* (Cresskill, N.J.: Hampton Press, 2002); D. King, "Multiple Jeopardy, Multiple Consciousness: The Context of a Black Feminist Ideology," *Signs* 14 (1989): 42–72.

19. Foster, *A Brighter Day Coming,* 10.

20. Ibid., 217.

21. Logan, *We Are Coming,* 57–58.

22. Foster, *A Brighter Day Coming,* 218. The use of biblical allusions was characteristic of women's oratory in the nineteenth century. In *Appropriate[ing] Dress,* Carol Mattingly states that women who "blatantly broke conventional strictures against woman's private place [the home] immediately found their moral character questioned." Women speakers dealt with such charges by displaying knowledge of the Bible in their speeches and asserting, "that they were doing God's work." Lillian O'Connor, quoted in Carol Mattingly *Appropriate[ing] Dress: Women's Rhetorical Style in Nineteenth-Century America* (Carbondale: Southern Illinois University Press, 2002), 17.

23. Foster, *A Brighter Day Coming,* 218.

24. Ibid.

25. Ibid., 219.

26. Ibid., 3.

27. Houston and Davis, *Centering Ourselves,* 4.

28. Miriam Schneir, ed., *Feminism in Our Time: The Essential Writings, World War II to Present* (New York: Vintage Press, 1994), 178.

29. Ibid., 177.

30. Gerda Lerner, ed., *The Female Experience: An American Documentary* (New York: Oxford University Press, 1992), 355.

31. Foster, *A Brighter Day Coming,* 96.

32. Donna Landry and Gerald MacLean, eds., *The Spivak Reader* (New York: Routledge, 1996), 205.

33. Logan, *With Pen and Voice,* 45.

34. Ibid.; my emphasis.

35. Carby, *Reconstructing Womanhood*, 70.

36. Foster, *A Brighter Day Coming*, 218.

37. Logan, *We Are Coming*, 45.

38. Ibid., 46.

39. Foster, *A Brighter Day Coming*, 218.

40. Bell hooks, *Feminist Theory: From Margin to Center* (Cambridge, Mass.: South End Press, 2000), 6.

41. Bell hooks, *Ain't I a Woman: Black Women and Feminism* (Boston: South End Press, 1981), 170.

42. Foster, *A Brighter Day Coming*, 218.

43. Ibid., 218–19.

44. Boyd, *Discarded Legacy*, 221.

45. Ibid., 221–22.

46. Hooks, *Feminist Theory*, 163.

47. Ibid.

48. Logan, *With Pen and Voice*, 43.

49. Ibid.

50. See, for example, "Could We Trace the Record of Every Human Heart," originally published in the *National Anti-Slavery Standard* on May 23, 1857, and reprinted in Foster, *A Brighter Day Coming*.

51. Boyd, *Discarded Legacy*, 208.

52. Logan, *With Pen and Voice*, 44.

53. Bell hooks, *Reel to Real: Race, Sex and Class at the Movies* (New York: Routledge, 1996), 84.

54. For accounts of racism in the first wave of the U.S. women's movement, see Paula Giddings, *When and Where I Enter* (Toronto: Bantam Books, 1984), 65–68; and bell hooks, *Ain't I a Woman*, 170–73.

55. Carby, *Reconstructing Womanhood*, 68.

56. Ibid.

57. Giddings, *When and Where I Enter*, 66.

58. Logan, *With Pen and Voice*, 45.

59. Logan, *We Are Coming*, 59.

60. Ibid., 59–60.

61. Logan, *With Pen and Voice*, 44; my emphasis.

62. Carby, *Reconstrucing Womanhood*, 70.

63. Foster, *A Brighter Day Coming*, 284.

64. Ibid., 99.

65. Ibid., 102–104.

66. Ibid., 219–220; my emphasis.

67. Ibid., 100–102.

68. Boyd, *Discarded Legacy*, 70.

69. Dorothy Pennington, "The Discourse of African American Women: A Case for Extended Paradigms," in *Understanding African American Rhetoric: Classical*

Origins to Contemporary Innovations, ed. Ronald L. Jackson and E. B. Richardson (New York: Routledge, 2003), 293.

70. Ibid., 298.
71. Hooks, *Feminist Theory,* 159.
72. Ibid., 160.
73. Logan, *We Are Coming,* 68.
74. Logan, *With Pen and Voice,* 46.
75. Boyd, *Discarded Legacy,* 225.
76. Schneir, *Feminism in Our Time,* 179.
77. Foster, *A Brighter Day Coming,* 218.

Chapter 10

Mary Ann Shadd Cary

A Visionary of the Black Press

CAROL B. CONAWAY

Nineteenth-century black newspapers were sites of awareness, protest, and resistance, and created a valuable forum for political discourse within the black community, discourse that often developed and matured into distinct black social and political theories. Black newspapers addressed concerns across social class; they educated, united, and mobilized people to action in ways ranging from individual acts of resistance such as self-liberation to collective acts such as forming communities that valorized black culture, independence, and elevation.

In this chapter, I investigate the development of newspaper editor Mary Ann Shadd Cary's thought and activism. I explore the various concepts of nationalism that developed in the nineteenth century, the gender ideologies embedded in these theories, and her theory of "elevation" characterized by the concepts of emigration, education, and equality. Shadd Cary's position stood between what I call the "nativist-integrationists" such as Frederick Douglass who advocated that blacks remain in their native country, the United States, and assimilate with whites, and the "nationalist-separatists" such as Martin Delany who advocated emigration from the United States and the development of a black separatist and self-governing culture and political system.[1] Shadd Cary was an emigrationist-integrationist who advocated emigration to Canada and the formation of a racially integrated society in Canada West (the province of Ontario).

I argue that in many ways, Shadd Cary's stance in opposition to the separatist-emigrationists was sensible because her position recognized the drawbacks of striving for equality in a nation that had a structurally racist legal system and an entrenched legacy of racism. Yet by advocating emigration to Canada with its distinct legal system and history, she was able to envision the benefits of a continuity of North American black culture, and the practicality and basic fairness of racial integration.

The North American black press has a formidable tradition as a powerful protest medium and as a public forum for debates on black liberation, identity, racial uplift, assimilation, separatism, emigration, and nationalism. When Shadd Cary—teacher, orator, and social reformer—published the first issue of her newspaper, the *Provincial Freeman*, in Windsor, Ontario, in 1853, she became the first black woman in North America to found and edit a newspaper. As an editor, she entered the almost exclusively male profession of antebellum journalism and exhibited boldness that was uncharacteristic of most women at that time.[2] Shadd Cary's lived experience on the margins contextualized her newspaper texts as sites of awareness and resistance, that is, as instruments of protest used by a woman from the standpoint of "otherness." Angela Davis, bell hooks, Audre Lorde, Patricia Hill Collins, and many other black feminists have regarded "otherness" as a powerful position.[3] For example, Collins sees black women as ideal outsiders-within because they are both dually marginalized (as women and as blacks) yet able to move among a variety of communities. Thus, outsider-within positions "can produce distinctive oppositional knowledges that embrace multiplicity yet remain cognizant of power."[4]

As a site of protest and resistance, the black press reconfigures the power relations in political discourse. A Northern black woman, Shadd Cary initially occupies the position of "other," one whose location on the margins might be expected to signify a debilitating difference from those in the center who possess greater access to power and privilege. But Shadd Cary and the black press movement generally shift the center of knowledge production from whites to blacks in a relative but empowering way. By addressing each other instead of whites, they put themselves at the center of discourse. In this essay, I argue that this shift is reflected also in the focus on the ideology of self-reliance and that the black press and the annual conventions were living examples of self-reliance. Instead of allowing the dominant forms of communication to control the discourse, the existence of the black press and the dialogues they generated proved to be a way of moving the loci of discourse in the cultural experience, of blacks away from the racist white press and toward the development of theories and ideologies that reflected black culture, experience, and aspirations. Thus, for those blacks who were engaged in the discourse through a grass-roots medium that reached the masses, blacks were no longer entirely "the other." In the context of the broader abolitionist and anti-abolitionist North American discussion about what blacks should do for themselves, or what should be done about them, the black press enabled them to become their own center of focus regarding their personal social and political futures. While the focus remained there, the power of centrality accrued to blacks as well. In the words of bell hooks, they were able to move "from margin to center."

The Leadership of the Black Press in Antebellum Protest and Emigrationist Movements

Antebellum black protest movements were early sites of awareness, protest, and resistance and forums for political discourse within the black community, especially with regard to but not limited to slavery and racial uplift. Since the first black newspaper, *Freedom's Journal,* was published in New York City by John Russwurm and Samuel Cornish on March 16, 1827, the black press had been the vanguard of the abolition movement and a central site of African-American protest against the racism of white hegemonic society, including the rhetoric of the white press. The opening editorial on the front page of *Freedom's Journal* stated, "We mean to plead our own cause. No longer will others speak for us." It was a site where citizenship, abolition, and emigration debates were publicized widely.[5] While the white abolitionist press was opposed to slavery, it typically did not argue that blacks were equal to whites. The white abolitionist press had a paternalistic and condescending attitude toward blacks. Consequently, the values, initiatives, and political concerns of the black community went unreported.

Serving as its own resistive medium, the black press was an alternative forum for representing various currents in the black community and for offering contested visions of a better life for blacks. It was used to define black identity and to create a strong sense of unity by establishing a communication network among literate blacks and sympathetic whites. It also presented events from the black perspective, highlighted black achievement ignored by the mainstream press, and worked toward achieving black equality. Black newspapers provided forums for debate on full citizenship versus separatism and repatriation to Africa or to any of the Western hemisphere countries advocated by Shadd Cary or Martin Delany.[6]

Citing the seminal work of Benedict Anderson, historian and Shadd Cary biographer Jane Rhodes contends that antebellum black newspapers, including Cary's, created imagined communities across broad geographical spaces. These imagined communities were instrumental in facilitating collective identities that became the basis for emergent nationalisms.[7] Debates on citizenship, abolition, integration and separatism, and emigration would have been the province of the black elite only had it not been for newspapers and other publications. Historian Patrick Rael maintains that through all self-conscious acts of public political speech, black elites employed the tropes of racial uplift, elevation, and respectability as the tools to be used in an assault on white supremacist arguments of black inferiority.[8]

During this time of political ferment, the socially activist black press offered its own expanded vision of community, paving the way for the abolitionist and black liberation movements. As many as forty antebellum black newspapers in the United States and two in Canada West played a critical role in black politicization by becoming sites of debate and opinion. In her history of the early black press, Frankie Hutton describes the black press as forward-looking and socially responsible because it offered self-reflexive forethought from middle-class blacks on issues such as uplift, vindication, and aid to assimilation as a means toward black community-building and humanitarian activities.[9]

Leading the charge toward a newfound black press, Frederick Douglass's newspaper, the *North Star*, emerged in 1847 as the most influential black weekly in the United States. During its tenure from 1847 to 1851, it supported abolitionism, civil rights for blacks, women's rights, and numerous other reforms such as temperance. Through the *North Star*, Douglass became the leading spokesman for the abolition of slavery by means of politics and even violence, despite the fact that many of his readers and supporters were white abolitionists.[10] He often is considered the father of black journalism because he understood the importance of the press as a vehicle for black politicization and expression of black aspirations. For example, before publishing her own newspaper in 1853, Shadd Cary's correspondence on racial elevation was published in an issue of the

North Star in 1849, and excerpts from her pamphlet on black life in Canada, *Notes on Canada West*, appeared in the *North Star* in 1852. The black press stood at the forefront of the antebellum black protest movement against slavery, just as it stood at the forefront of the American black civil rights movement in the 1960s. Recognizing the immense power and reach of the black press, Shadd Cary decided that the only way that she could promulgate her distinctly radical views on the best strategy for black liberation and racial elevation was to publish the *Provincial Freeman*, the newspaper that she would own and edit.

The Provincial Freeman *as a Resistive Medium from 1853 to 1861*

Mary Ann Shadd Cary's newspaper editorials and correspondence are examples of nondominant narratives about racial, ethnic, gender, and class oppressions in the context of a mid-nineteenth-century society dominated by white men and women. Her discourse illuminates a new black collective comprising freeborn and newly liberated people struggling for survival in and recognition from a mostly white society. The collective was dominated by a black male establishment that assigned black women only secondary, passive roles. Shadd Cary's newspaper texts enable us to examine and interpret the discourse of an individual who was a middle-class, repatriated, light-skinned, mixed-race African-Canadian/African-American "uppity" woman—a woman with multiple oppressions that were interrelated and inseparable.[11] Most published research on gender and communication omits, erases, or distorts the experiences of nondominant women.[12]

I argue that Shadd Cary's racial and ethnic background, gender, class, and religion must be placed at the center of the analysis of her communicative texts so that we can understand her place within a specific cultural group. She was a middle-class black woman burdened by race and ethnicity, gender and sexism, and religion, yet privileged by her light skin color, education, and economic status. But her newspaper discourse privileged the voices of black African-Canadian/African-American men and women across classes, gender, skin hues, and circumstances. A review of several excerpts on racial elevation from her newspaper enables us to rethink feminist communication theories that compare black women's lived experience at the margins to the lived experience of dominant white women or to other nondominant women. Those theories do not consider fully the impact of black women's specific matrices of oppression that are embedded within their discourse.

Fundamental to the development of Shadd Cary's post-liberation racial elevation ideology were the interlocking oppressions of her race and ethnicity, gender, class, and religion. I argue that her life as a member of several nondominant groups in society bears study regarding how she overcame some constraints through the resistive medium of her newspaper. Shadd Cary used her newspaper to conceptualize a new social collective and order through multiple sites of identity and experience.

Shadd Cary created the *Provincial Freeman* as the vocal organ of her resistance to slavery and oppression. Sexism within the liberation movements compelled her to unite with two black men who also favored emigration to Canada. The Reverend Samuel Ringgold Ward and Alexander McArthur were listed as Editor and Corresponding Editor, respectively, on the masthead, concealing Shadd Cary's identity as editor and publisher. Initially, she identified herself as the "Publishing Agent, M. A. Shadd." Alternatively, she often signed her editorials by using her initials. Most of the time, she left her editorials unsigned, signaling her awareness that most black men and possibly some black women thought it was unseemly for a woman to be outspoken in the public sphere.

The *Provincial Freeman* was published first in March 1853 in Windsor, Canada West, later in Toronto, and finally in Chatham until 1861, when it ceased publication. That she was able to launch her newspaper was a triumph, because even white women were bound by the conventional roles that confined them to silence in the press or to writing and publishing poetry in the press to support their husbands' public roles.[13] The newspaper was published somewhat irregularly during its tenure because of its negative financial situation. Many subscribers were too impoverished to pay for their subscriptions. Shadd Cary, members of her family, and others associated with the newspaper often were engaged in fund-raising trips within Canada and the United States. Although many black newspapers were started but ceased publication within a short time, the *Provincial Freeman* is significant because it survived for several years, thanks to the commitment and resourcefulness of its dedicated staff.[14]

The newspaper's "Prospectus," published in the March 24, 1854, issue of her four-page broadsheet indicated that it would be devoted "to Anti-Slavery, Temperance, and General Literature," political opinion, articles and editorials "on all questions or projects affecting the people [largely blacks, but also whites] in a political way," and to support "the principles of the British Constitution or British Rule in the Provinces." Because the newspaper's circulation was extensive, it also was useful in assisting new arrivals to locate family members from whom they had been separated during their journeys into Canada.[15] Shadd Cary's newspaper provided a glimpse of what life in Canada was like to allay black fears about racism and the quality of life north of the border. As she visited black settlements in Canada and reported on them, she was in effect a "Colored Tourist" and public relations specialist when reporting on her travels and observations.[16]

Her "Prospectus" omitted any direct reference to gender. However, the indirect reference to feminism lay in her stated goal that the newspaper's readers would engage in moral reform activities—such as temperance—that were primarily the province of women, both black and white. When eventually the public outcry of her male foes forced her to step down as the newspaper's editor (she did so in title only), she openly confronted the men who had opposed her because of her sex: "To [my] enemies, we would say, be less captious to him than to us; be more considerate, if you will; it is fit that you should deport your ugliest to a woman" ("Adieu," *Provincial Freeman*, June 30, 1855). Then, addressing herself to black women solely, she shifted the discourse away from men and stated that black women had "broken the Editorial ice" for their class in America. She encouraged them: "So go to Editing, as many of you as are willing, and able, and as soon as you may, if you think you are ready." While she was a lifelong champion of women's equality, this was one of the rare instances in her Canadian newspaper when she openly directed her comments toward women. Nevertheless, she eagerly selected and published letters from other women that espoused her positions on women's rights.

As Shadd Cary conceived the *Provincial Freeman*, it was to play a large role in promulgating her thoughts on all urgent matters affecting the entire black community, especially the issues of emigration, separatism, integration, nativism, and equality, all of which she addressed within her three-fold definition of racial elevation.

Elevation: The Keys to the Kingdom

Shadd Cary's ideology of racial elevation (the term she used for racial uplift) comprised three main concepts: emigration to Canada, education, and equality with whites leading to a racially integrated society. Fundamental to all three concepts was the self-realization of ex-slaves and free black women and men that they would never be able to attain equal rights under the cover of law in the country that had enslaved them, the United States. Her solutions to the "Negro problem" were the same as those of other black abolitionists: reducing black dependency on whites, promoting education and agricultural investment, and promoting interracial and political organizing.[17] Frederick Douglass invited her to submit a letter to the *North Star* in January 1849 on the status of Northern blacks. That letter criticized black leadership failure by those who had been active in black life-improvement meetings and the black church. When she published her twelve-page pamphlet, *Hints to the Colored People of the North*, later that year, there was evidence that her developing ideology of self-help and self-reliance was rooted in her middle-class identity, upbringing, and political socialization.[18] Education, morality, and economic self-sufficiency—the values and behavior that she thought would cause whites to hold blacks in higher regard—were of paramount importance to her philosophy of black self-reliance and racial progress.

She expected that the black press in both the United States and Canada would provide the impetus and encouragement for the acceptance of her concept of racial elevation among its readership. Shadd Cary viewed the formidable tradition of black newspapers as a forum for political discourse within the black community to be at the forefront of racial elevation. Noting the comparatively large number of newspapers under the management of black men in her editorial dated June 23, 1855 (*Provincial Freeman*, "Newspapers by Colored People in the United States"), she stated that "this simultaneous introduction of 'instruments' [newspapers] to promote the elevation of colored citizens, must mean something [and we] concede to them the very greatest desire for the welfare of their people." However, she also was very wary of the American black press's intentions and expressed her frustration with regard to its nativist symbolism:

> They [black newspapers] are, without exception, we believe, advocates of the old, long tried, and long condemned policy of remaining in the United States, at all hazards, almost to a man, to make the white American give to them equal political and social privileges.

She thought that any black newspaper that supported nativist-integration rather than emigration to Canada was failing to acknowledge the history of white oppression in the United States. She viewed the black press with contempt for shirking its responsibility to lead, think independently, and inspire other blacks to do the same instead of being deluded by false hopes. She roundly criticized the black press in her editorial, "Newspapers by Colored People in the United States" (*Provincial Freeman*, June 23, 1855) when she wrote,

> If there is anything [black journalists for black newspapers] should ap-
> propriate to themselves from proximity with the Yankees, it is the philos-
> ophy of their progress, made up as they are in part of oppressed people,
> who have emigrated from other despotisms, and the absolute utility of
> emigration, as declared encouraged and promoted, by their wisest men.
> Instead of heeding calls for emigration, colored men reject emigration
> through speeches, and through the press, the most powerful means.

Shadd Cary claimed that because of the black press's failure to inspire black people to leave the United States, its readership consequently moved in circles without effecting change. But, in the same editorial, she predicted "Young colored America will move away of itself, by force of inherent and cultivated energy, at no distant day, and their journals will be obliged to follow suit." She believed that black emigration to Canada would force the black press to follow philosophically in their wake. Shadd Cary was convinced that it was the moral responsibility of the black press to lead the way to Canadian emigration just as it had led the way to abolitionism.

Emigration to Canada: Black Salvation

Shadd Cary was the only woman among the leading publicly outspoken emigrationists. Rhodes notes that Shadd Cary was quite comfortable with evoking masculinity as the ultimate symbol of black power and authority, while at the same time openly challenging black male supremacy and gen-dered authority and relying "on Victorian femininity to shield her from the attacks of her enemies."[19] Clearly, her enemies were not moved at all by her "Victorian femininity" when they launched their bare-fisted written attacks on this black woman. She was as outspoken as any man on what she con-sidered black deficiencies and the impotence of those who attended con-ventions on emigration and improving conditions for blacks and had al-most negligible results to show for it. Her criticisms partly account for her shifting the discourse of black survival away from nativist-integrationist theories to the radical theories of black emigrationist-nationalism.

Philosopher Tommie Shelby maintains that the definition of black nationalism has been contested often by black intellectuals. Loosely defined, it is an ideology including "the creation and control of separate institutions within the black community, black economic and political self-determination, and a belief that African Americans constitute an 'internal black nation' within the United States."[20] He contends that Black nationalism may include racial solidarity and group self-reliance, various forms of voluntary racial separation, and pride in the historic achievements of persons of African descent. It also may include a concerted effort to overcome racial self-hate and instill black self-love, militant collective resistance to white supremacy, the development and preservation of a distinctive black cultural identity, and the recognition of Africa as the true homeland of those who are racially black.[21]

Shelby argues that strains of black nationalism have become a constitutive component of the self-understanding of a substantial segment of the African-American population and that it is one of the oldest and most enduring traditions in American political thought.[22] But he also argues that there are two types of black nationalisms—strong and weak—rather than one overarching category. This distinction clarifies our understanding of the early nineteenth-century nationalistic theories of Shadd Cary and black leader Martin Delany.

Shelby argues that "strong black nationalism" treats the establishment of an independent black republic or a separate self-determining community as an intrinsic goal of black liberation struggles.[23] Strong nationalists advocate the development of a national identity, group self-reliance, and separatism to bring about racial justice and achieve "the political destiny of African Americans."[24] This might be attained in the formation of a self-governing black nation-state or a separate self-determining community within a multinational state.[25] Martin Delany was a strong nationalist who advocated black emigration from the United States to countries in Central and South America or the West Indies. He rejected emigration to Canada because he was convinced that the United States would annex Canada and impose its institutionalized racial oppression on black Canadians. Delany advocated emigrating to form a new nationality in a country where blacks were to be the predominant race and ruling political element.[26] Thus, blacks would govern blacks. He also proposed that only black elites immigrate to African countries to help Africans modernize their governments and accept the ways of Western civilization. As black nationalism evolved in the antebellum nineteenth century, though, it was less connected to a particular nation-state than to the unifying ties of skin color and culture. This latter concept is aligned more closely with Shadd Cary's "weak nationalist" theory rather than with Delany's theories.

Like strong nationalism, weak nationalism also "urges black solidarity and concerted action as a political strategy to lift or resist oppression."[27] This might be attained in the formation of a self-governing black nation-state. But weak nationalism also could mean creating a racially integrated society or even a "post-racial" polity, a political order where "race" has no social or political meaning.[28] This latter designation describes Shadd Cary's "weak nationalism" concerning emigration and integration, as well as the integrationist thought espoused decades later by W. E. B. DuBois and Martin Luther King, Jr.

Thus, both Delany and Shadd Cary were nationalists who prescribed different forms of nationalism as the penultimate strategy for black survival. But Shadd Cary found that Delany's typically separatist-nationalism was contrary to her integrationist-nationalism. Nevertheless, Shadd Cary and Delany agreed that Douglass's nativist-integration theory on the certainty of a racially integrated society in the United States was deluded at best. Shadd Cary's and Delany's theories were premised upon their belief that the institutionalized legal, cultural, and political racism of white Americans militated against racial equality and an elimination of racial oppression in the United States.

Between the years of 1853 and 1861, the *Provincial Freeman* embodied Shadd Cary's voice on emigration to communities in Canada where fugitive and free blacks settled prior to the American Civil War with the objective of living in a racially integrated society. Her correspondence, pamphlets, columns, and editorials on life in Canada West were written to attract the attention of the black elite and masses who sought an alternative to the institutionalized oppression they experienced in the United States.

Shadd Cary favored emigration to Canada, a country where there was a history of institutionalized freedom and full citizenship rights for repatriated black men and women. Like her father, Abraham Shadd, and the other elite participants in the black convention movement, she thought that Canada's history of black liberation and equal rights for all citizens offered blacks more hope than did remaining in the United States or emigrating to any other destination.[29] Once blacks crossed the border into Canada, they were guaranteed equal rights under the cover of law—institutionalized rights that emerged from the unique history of blacks in Canada, the country where slavery had been abolished since 1833.[30]

Canadian legal and social institutions granted the one percent black population full equality and enfranchisement. Canadian society was far less culturally racist than the white-dominated society of the United States. Black men were able to vote, own property, and hold office in Canada. Thus, conditions for black Canadians were far superior to those for enslaved and free blacks in the United States because Canadian legal, social, and political institutions valorized black culture, independence, and elevation. Shadd Cary made a sensible decision to advocate black emigration to a North American English-speaking country that guaranteed and protected the human and legal rights of blacks and that offered the opportunity for black economic development, self-fulfillment, and self-reliance.

Reflecting the influence of her father's philosophy, Shadd Cary held an integrationist view of emigration, believing that blacks had to become fully integrated in white society, and that racial integration was impossible in the United States. She contended that emigration to Canada rather than Africa, the Caribbean, or South America, as Delany and others had advocated, was the only reasonable option leading to a free, racially integrated society. Her approach to the struggle for freedom and equality was also contrary to Douglass's contention that the best hope for blacks lay in their remaining in the country that they had helped to build. While both Douglass and Shadd Cary advocated racial integration, they strongly disagreed on where that could be accomplished.

While the nationalist-emigrationist plan proposed principally by Delany and other separatist-nationalist leaders was progressive, historian Carla Peterson contends that Delany's agenda for women was conservative and that the radical black male view of black women emulated the gender ideology of the dominant white American culture—the cult of true womanhood. While Shadd Cary attended and made speeches at numerous male-dominated emigrationist conventions, most black women avoided participating in national and state conventions on emigration. Instead, they preferred "to reconfigure, as [Maria W.] Stewart had, the dominant culture's model of domestic economy to suit their particular purposes."[31] Peterson argues that beneath all of the emigrationist schemes lay the masculinist ideology of a Negro nationality that excluded any account of gender. Thus, the 1850s nationalist-emigrationist movement was "an intensely masculine one that excluded black women from its proj-

ect."[32] There is no account of what roles women were to play in emigration. Peterson argues that Delany and other radical emigrationists wanted
to exclude middle-class women from the public sphere (unless they were
missionaries) and keep them within the private sphere of the home, where
they were to educate children and instill strong morals in them. Women's
roles as wife and mother were to be passive outwardly, even though the responsibility for racial uplift fell on their shoulders.[33] Since this concept
of women's roles was a politically and socially conservative philosophy,
Peterson states that Delany's concept of new social relations for black
men and women in Africa "is couched in the rhetoric of class elitism and
gender exclusion that is depressingly reminiscent of traditional capitalist,
class-conscious, patriarchal social relations."[34]

However, Shelby interprets Delany's nationalist philosophy as it per-
tains to black women differently than Peterson does.[35] He contends that
Delany, a liberal egalitarian, valued and sought to encourage the cultivation of the moral virtue of "manhood" in both men *and* women. While
he concedes that Delany might have chosen an unfortunate term, Shelby
maintains that "manhood, as Delany understood it, is a quality of character that is not peculiar to men, as many women also value and embody
it." While Shelby also agrees that Delany did not have many traditional
patriarchal attitudes, he argues that Delany's thought, while sexist, had progressive elements regarding gender because he thought that women should
engage in business enterprises, be political entities in their own right, participate in the emigration conventions, and even become revolutionaries.[36]

Not all black men agreed with Delany regarding the place of women
in the emigrationist scheme. The rhetoric of Delany and others on the
place of women was countered by nativist-integrationist black male leaders such as William J. Watkins (Frances Ellen Watkins Harper's cousin)
and Frederick Douglass, as well as black women such as Maria W. Stewart, Harper, and Sarah Remond. According to Peterson, "they chose instead to develop their own cultural programs for their race and to forge
home within the local place of North America," the place blacks had
earned by right.[37]

While Shadd Cary was not a nativist-integrationist, as an advocate of
emigrationist-nationalism, she agreed with the nativists that women should
participate in the public sphere in addition to their role in the home, but
in Canada rather than the United States. Shadd Cary is an "outsider"
among most other black women by arguing that gender equality was pos-

sible only after emigration to Canada. Her newspaper texts reveal that Shadd Cary's "other" status pervades her editorials and other discourse. Confrontational and unconventional, she was marginalized by most black leaders. She was an "other" to most of her gender, to black American nativists, mostly black men, to blacks who advocated separatism, and to black nationalists who supported emigration to destinations other than Canada.

In an editorial titled "A Word about, and to Emigrationists" (*Provincial Freeman*, April 15, 1854), a response to Delany and other black separatists, Shadd Cary suggested that blacks were no better equipped than whites to govern a segregated nation. She refused to adhere to notions of black superiority or nobility, arguing instead that "colored men are as merciless as other men, when possessed of the same amount of pride, conceit, and wickedness, and as much, if not more ignorance. They make just as bad masters as the worst of the whites, in their best moods, and infinitely worse in their worst." She wondered what kinds of people would be attracted to an exclusive nation, and suggested that emigrationists should consider the opportunity to be "part of the Colored British nation. This nation knows no one color above another, but being composed of all colors, it is evidently a *colored* nation." Thinking pragmatically, she also wrote against emigration to Latin America, Central America, and the Caribbean because of the hot climate and because she was certain that blacks would be as exploited in the sugar cane fields as they had been in the American South as slaves. She also was firmly against the colonization schemes proposed by some white abolitionists, notably Harriet Beecher Stowe, the author of *Uncle Tom's Cabin*. To Shadd, the American Colonization Society's scheme was a barely hidden attempt to ship freed and fugitive slaves back to Africa rather than permitting them to remain in the United States.

Although many runaway slaves crossed the border into Canada, not all of these were determined to seek Canadian citizenship. Shadd Cary clearly stated that complete repatriation to Canada was a prerequisite to beginning the process of elevation. For example she wrote that

> emigrationists hold that political elevation, the bone of contention, and which cannot be secured without unnecessary sacrifice of time, energy and means in the land of their birth, can be obtained by removal to foreign and more liberal governments. (*Provincial Freeman*, July 5, 1856, "Emigration Convention")

She often lauded Canadian blacks, finding them superior to American blacks. In her article, "A Recent Tour" (*Provincial Freeman*, March 24, 1854), she reported on her six weeks' tour of some of the black settlements in Canada:

> Our tour satisfied us abundantly that the colored people of Canada are progressing more rapidly than our people in the United States, that the liberty enjoyed here makes different men of those once crushed and dispirited in the land of chains . . . that along with the other poor classes who come here, and improve themselves in wealth and status, the black people will also arise.

In her editorial "Our Free Colored Emigrants" (*Provincial Freeman*, May 20, 1854), she restated her admiration for repatriated blacks: "The people of whom we write, are a little more energetic than any to be found among those who will not occupy a more desirable field. Their determination to leave, settles that point. They are fully equal to those among whom they are now living."

Based on her observations, she thought that equality could not be denied, once black people, with their new identity as free persons, became self-reliant, especially economically. Furthermore, she believed that the move toward equality already was beginning to happen. She noted in the same editorial that black emigrationists were becoming businessmen who soon would find favor with Canadian whites because "they bring morally, intellectually, and peculiarly, the same as are brought by the better class of white emigrants." But she addressed both her black and white readership when she wrote that the black émigrés would not ask for more than equality. Centering the discourse on blacks, she wrote the following in her editorial "Slavery and Labor" (*Provincial Freeman*, August 29, 1855):

> We have never considered it any particular honor to associate with white people, simply because they are such. We are brothers. We hold that we can and ought to make our position physically, intellectually, and morally, as well as, politically, and socially, such, that our white brethren would, as naturally and readily seek our association, as we would theirs. It seems disgraceful to us, to ask more than equal rights of any people, and thank God, such we have here.

She must have been responding to or anticipating white Canadian backlash to what might have been perceived as a flood of black emigrants who were leaving the United States to escape slavery and racism. It is estimated that some forty thousand slaves made it to Canada via the Underground Railroad.[38]

Once the émigrés crossed the border into Canada West, it was Shadd Cary's expectation that they would become totally self-reliant, independent Canadian citizens. Self-reliance meant that both the black fugitives and free persons would not seek or accept charity from blacks or from whites, and they would not seek pity as if they were beggars. She advocated their owning businesses that conformed to the free market. As she wrote in her *Provincial Freeman* editorial of July 15, 1854 ("The Old Man and His Views") in a retort to her rival, Henry Bibb and his supporters:

> The [white] people will pay—and well—if the commodities suit—and in no way will the negro question be better received than to represent him as poor, miserable, pitiable, and likely to be until the 'problems are solved,' and as needing somebody to do for him after their fashion—which is undoubtedly the best for themselves.

Thus, emigration represented a unique opportunity for blacks to prosper, exercise their rights as citizens, and attain equality and racial integration. Although emigration to Canada was the first step to black liberation, it was not the last. Emigrants had to become educated if they were to become productive and earn a rightful place alongside their white Canadian counterparts.

Education: Acquiring the Knowledge that Led to Liberation

Shadd Cary defined education as the pursuit of knowledge that would enable black men and women to achieve their rightful place in society—equality with whites. She conceptualized education in two ways: religious and secular. She believed that black people should be educated first with regard to their relationship with God and Christ so that they would know what their duties and obligations were to their fellow women and men. In her editorial "The Way to do Colored Canadians Good" (*Provincial Freeman*, November 10, 1855) she wrote, "It is very clear to us, that God's plan to benefit a certain people, or our race, as a whole, is the very best one that can possibly be adopted, to secure that end." She maintained that the missionaries who had come to Canada West to teach secular matters first and religious matters second were completely mistaken with regard to developing a strong black citizenry.

Shadd Cary believed that black people needed to be educated on the "duties growing out of the relations, we sustain to God, our families, to the church and state" (*Provincial Freeman,* November 10, 1855, "The Way to do Colored Canadians Good"). With that knowledge, they would understand their duty arising from it. She argued that black people would be patriots, or lovers of "our country," once they knew "it, and [their] relations to it." The goal was "to have our country love us," which would occur only after black people did their duty to the country. At the very least, black citizens had to help refine Canadian society, develop its resources and defend its interests—in other words, attain and practice full-fledged citizenship.[39]

With regard to secular education, she espoused the more typical elements that other black writers deemed necessary for racial uplift. For example, in a brief review, "William Wells Brown at Philadelphia," published in the *Provincial Freeman* on January 20, 1854, of a speech given by a self-educated ex-slave who had just concluded a series of lectures in Philadelphia, she admonished black people to study literature as a means of elevation. William Wells Brown "[was] able, after so many years spent in slavery, to lecture to his brethren on [the arts, religion, and politics]. [This] ought to give [black people] renewed courage, and cause every colored person in the land to labour early and late for his own elevation." She thought that free black people paid too little attention to literature, "and thereby fail[ed] in obtaining that knowledge of the world and its affairs that is desirable." To Shadd Cary, school libraries were essential to bringing about social and political equality. In her *Provincial Freeman* editorial dated October 20, 1855, "The Future of the Colored Canadians," she lauded the school libraries: "[School libraries are] great auxiliaries, in the bringing about the final result [i.e., elevation]. They should be freely used by the aged and young...Reading clubs, and literary associations are fellow helpers in the good cause, and no city town, or settlement, should be without them."

She thought that the opportunity for black education pertained to all classes. This idea was rooted in her early teaching experiences and her acknowledgement of the opportunities that were denied her because of sexism and racism as well as those afforded her because of her education, training, and ties to the black elite.

Intellectual improvement and elevation were virtually synonymous in Shadd Cary's mind because education was to play a crucial role in racial elevation. In keeping with her integrationist ideology, she believed that racial elevation would occur only if schools were integrated and both black and white teachers engaged in teaching newly liberated black people how to be citizens and men and women of good character. She thought that whites would play a critical role in educating blacks and sharing citizenship with them. In her *Provincial Freeman* editorial dated November 3, 1855 ("The War Ended"), she wrote with uncharacteristic humility:

> We [black people] know there is much room for our improvement and we are desirous to improve; hence, our minds and hearts are open to receive intellectual and moral instruction, and our arms are extended to embrace those who may be sent or who shall come among us as the servants of Christ, for such purpose, whether they be white, or black, and come whence they may. We do not say so much, about what others may do for us, because, we would lose sight of own obligation, to do for ourselves.

While she undoubtedly would have deemed herself "a Christian woman," she also criticized Christianity because it was the same religion that justified the southern slavocracy. The slavocracy taught blacks Christianity, and the message that white Christians transmitted to slaves supported white patriarchy and white supremacy. Shadd Cary stressed that salvation and elevation were valuable for black people as much as for other peoples on earth. However, she informed both the missionaries she distrusted, as well as her black readers, that there was a limit as to how much and what type of education they should receive.[40]

In correspondence for the *Provincial Freeman* (February 16, 1856) signed "M. A. Shadd" from a convention she had attended on the condition of black people, she expressed her utter disdain for black missionaries who tried to stifle black advancement. She maintained that what black people heard from the pulpits was that life was short, that "man wants but little here below, nor wants that little long," and that if they sought worldly goods they would lose their souls." In her opinion, this was a self-defeatist strategy meant to keep blacks at the bottom of the racial hierarchy:

> So, as a remedy, or to out-wit the crafty white man, instead of getting hold of the knowledge that make him so potent, and defeating him on his own ground, it is thought best not to get too much property for him to take ... [Instead] the Emigrationist is seen walking down the terra firma of facts, passing by connections, pinning their faith to no man's garments, but taking common sense and the signs of the times for their guide, are either preparing to leave [the United States], have left, or are

determined to seize upon the nearest free soil that can be found to slave territory.

This point was particularly pertinent with regard to religion. Shadd Cary and Delany strongly agreed on the nature of white Christianity as it pertained to blacks: White missionaries were not to be trusted. But she thought that black missionaries were no more trustworthy than most of their white counterparts. In her opinion, the philosophies of black and white missionaries would be major impediments to the realization of black self-reliance.

She also argued that the settlers did not need what she termed "complexional help" from whites or blacks. According to Shadd Cary, "complexional help" meant that blacks were not to receive special treatment from either whites or blacks simply because they were black *or* because of their skin hue. They were to receive the same education that whites received— nothing more, nothing less.

> We would help ourselves, while, we look to others, to do their duty. Nor do we desire, strictly speaking, a complexional help. Our interest, as a class, don't [sic] need it, nor does that of our country, nor of humanity, as a whole, demand it. (*Provincial Freeman*, June 24, 1854, "A Missionary among the Fugitive Slaves")

In Shadd Cary's opinion, the education most needed by blacks in Canada was a good British education taught by teachers who were British at heart, using British school books and religious instruction in the churches of the province without denominational distinction. The teachers were to be qualified black or white preachers rather than by the "ignoramuses" she despised (*Provincial Freeman*, April 25, 1857, "The Things Most Needed"). Complementing those essentials was a sound political education. She thought that black people should be indoctrinated in the principles and policy of Canadian Conservative politics and should be active citizens fully engaged in preserving the common weal.

Thus, Shadd Cary espoused that if black émigrés were to be educated properly, they would have to leave all things American back in the proslavery, Negro-hating, segregated, Yankee republic. To become citizens equal to whites in Canada, black people had to avail themselves of religious and secular education that made them fully independent, self-reliant, refined men and women who forsook charity and anything else that bore resemblance to the shackles of the enslaved mind. Only then would they attain the most desired goal—social and political equality.

Equality: The Road to Racial Integration

The third concept of Shadd Cary's ideology of racial elevation and self-reliance is equality. Once black men and women immigrated to Canada, a country that guaranteed liberation, citizenship, education, and opportunity, she thought they would be self-reliant and equal to whites in every respect. Equality would lead to black assimilation in a racially integrated society—an impossible achievement in the racist institutions and discriminatory culture of the United States. Once Canadian blacks achieved equality and were self-reliant and independent, she believed that they would control their destiny and actualize the seemingly endless possibilities for individual and collective development. In an egalitarian Canadian society, she believed that the position of black people would "ultimately be the same as that of [the position of] their white fellow citizens" ("The Future of the Colored Canadians," *Provincial Freeman*, October 20, 1855). Her view of such a society was that "a perfect equality among the people of different nations in [Canada] is the will of God, hence positively certain." How would whites recognize that their black compatriots were equals? She imagined that the increasing influence of black piety, intelligence, and wealth would make it abundantly and irrevocably clear that whites and other emigrants, despite their "complexional distinctions" were social and political equals.

The egalitarian Canadian society also would be an integrated one. Shadd Cary opposed racial separatism or "complexional distinctions." In fact, she was an ardent supporter of intermarriage between the races:

> Amalgamation is proper, and its results most happy. It is a part of the divine arrangement, and hence the different nations should practice it. It is the blending of the beauties of nature. It is the imparting of force and dignity to man and beast. It adds to those, who practice it, those varieties which may be regarded as the spice of life." ("Amalgamation," *Provincial Freeman*, November 17, 1855)

As a mixed-race woman, she thought that amalgamation would perfect the world: "The hope of the world is in the amalgamation of nations, for the Gospel of Christ is in the doctrine of ONE BLOOD!" Her mixed-race status, as well as her Protestant beliefs, shaped her views on racial unity and miscegenation. It is likely that she was aware that her skin hue and the Protestant ethic were at least partially responsible for her elevated position in the black hierarchy.

If equality could not be attained in the lifetimes of the then-adult settlers, she predicted it surely would be attained by the settlers' children.
"Our children will as certainly seek and find their level, which will be the
white boys and girls of their generation, as water finds its level and wind
its equilibrium" (*Provincial Freeman*, October 20, 1855, "The Future of the
Colored Canadians"). Although such a result was "morally certain," adult
black men and women might serve as role models and sources of inspiration toward that end. Their charity toward others, their union and
progress would promote the common weal of "our country, the happiness of our race, and the glory of Christ." She envisioned the virtuous life
in much the same way that her father had envisioned it: a life and livelihood based upon industry, knowledge, and morality—concepts embedded in Shadd Cary's ideology of self-reliance. Thus, black men in Canada "should possess good farms, and cultivate them properly, or the
mechanic art, and use it, or the professions, as ministers of religion, as
doctors, or lawyers, &c." (*Provincial Freeman*, October 20, 1855, "The Future
of Colored Canadians"). Education would cast the minds of black
youths as it did those of white youths. She thought that when this happened, black youths would admire the intellectual features of white youths,
and white youths would admire the intellectual features of black youths.
This prediction took no account of white racist beliefs about blacks, even
those of the Canadian whites whom she idealized. It was her vision of the
Canadian utopia that she hoped to help bring about through her writings
and speeches.

Thus, Shadd Cary thought that a racially integrated society in Canada
West would be realized, but not until black people were thoroughly educated on and steeped in the white cultured mind. "Intellectual feasts, and
fattenings of the lecture room . . . elevate, and dignify the character of the
aged and young, of the black, and the white." But then she rather naively
predicted that perfect equality would be the result in Canadian society.
Finally, in the same editorial, she expressed her profound belief that "these
things exist, among us, in common, for the white and colored people. If
they be equally used, by both classes, the result must be the SAME, since
mind is mind." In addition to using libraries and literary societies—an
idea probably influenced by black American elites in Philadelphia and
New York—she recommended that blacks seek innocent amusements
and attend the numerous moral concerts. She expressed her faith that
God had brought black people to Canada to enjoy the blessings of emi-

gration and education leading to a society where "PERFECT EQUALITY MUST BE THE ULTIMATE RESULT!" Shadd Cary told black Canadians that their brethren, God, their children, and their country expected much from them. This optimism was typical of her aspirations for the émigrés as they struggled to become exemplary citizens intellectually and morally. Not for an instant did she ever conceptualize black Canadians as victims. As far as she was concerned, the black future lay in black hands. Thus, she absolved white Canadians of almost any responsibility for working toward a more just and equal society.

Once free black persons attained equality, Shadd Cary thought that they would have equal responsibilities in society, as well as "a higher tone of thought, than to serve a class of tyrants for reduced wages, and to speculate upon, and imitate the fashions and follies of a people who despise and decide you" (*Provincial Freeman*, "The Future of Colored Canadians," October 20, 1855). She thought that equality also meant that men and women had become independent and self-respecting people. Independence meant not relying on whites or well-meaning, misguided black people—such as missionaries. But she was aware that subtle racism emanating from white liberal Canadians was just as threatening to blacks as overt racism. An example of her indignation and disgust over subtle racism can be seen in the way she responded to a white journalist, Thomas Henning, who wrote about his visit to the black Elgin settlement for the *Toronto Globe*:

> I might say much more of a similar encouraging character regarding this settlement, but enough has been told to prove that under proper management the black man is as capable of success, even in agricultural pursuits as the white one, and that the social and moral habits of the Ethiopian, when properly directed, are not inferior in any respect to those of the European. ("A Visit to the Elgin Settlement," *Provincial Freeman*, October 6, 1855)

From the tone of her response, Shadd Cary's outrage at such chauvinism, racism, and paternalism was quite palpable: "Indeed, is it true that the colored people cannot succeed, only as they have some white man to control them? It is anything but true. The boot is on 't other' leg. They have not succeeded, because WHITE MEN would not allow them to; and especially is that true of our people in Canada." In just a few sentences, she courageously shifted the discourse centering whites to centering blacks. She boldly countered Thomas Henning's racist conclusions and from her site as "other" produced a counter-argument vindicating blacks and putting the blame where it belonged—on white racism. This was a moment of the black press at its finest—fighting back against white supremacy, disparagement, and contempt while embodying the voice of the black collectivity. Shadd Cary's newspaper embodied her voice, bristling with indignation at even the suggestion that blacks could be successful *only* under white supervision and management, a situation reflecting white Southern Americans' justification for slavery. In the same editorial, she directed her brethren "to wipe off such an everlasting stigma. Let it no longer be said, that you must be put 'under proper management' to succeed."

In her editorial "Plastering &c." (*Provincial Freeman*, July 19, 1856), she maintained that those blacks who resided in Canada and became independent citizens equal to whites were now in a position to help their kinsmen in the States rather than expecting help from them: "As a class of men not in service to any man, [black Canadian emigrants] have just emerged from oppression; and as the bone and sinew of a powerful and increasing class, they will ... help to shape the destiny of this continent." This statement reconfigured power relations between blacks and whites. Instead of white charity, she envisioned black philanthropy. Also, she strongly believed that black people would "disown the dogged custom of staying in the background, until permission is given to leave, [and] they [would] gravitate into this freer sphere" (*Provincial Freeman*, May 20, 1854, "Our Free Colored Emigrants"). This statement reflected Shadd Cary's personal philosophy inherited from her father: Seek freedom at all times and at all costs. It also was meant to empower American blacks still in the throes of slavery to liberate themselves and settle in the "freer sphere" of Canada.

In the same editorial, she denounced the bigotry that "invites credence for the absurd notion [that] color must be a bond of union among colored, when the theory and practice of the white races contradicts such an idea." This belief was in direct opposition to the theories that black separatist-emigrationists espoused, and in effect posited that there was no such thing as racial identity. This was part of her emigrationist-integrationist theory—that integration would lead eventually to racial amalgamation and a color-blind society in Canada. It was contrary to Delany's separatist-emigrationist assertion that integration was impossible in a white-dominated society.

There is evidence in her editorials that Shadd Cary placed Native Americans beneath blacks in the hierarchy of nondominant groups. For example, in her *Provincial Freeman* editorial of May 20, 1854, "Our Free Colored Emigrants," she compared black émigrés to Native Americans and contended that black men had a "progressive character, and in glazing contrast with the red man, they go onward, planning improving, accumulating and enlarging." Rather than portraying the "black men" and the "red men" as having a common enemy, she instead considered that red men must be less than black men because, in her opinion, they did not make any progress in fighting white racism and exploitation. This criticism revealed her racial and ethnic chauvinism and her apparent ignorance of the differences and commonalities in black and red oppressions. She thought that only black emigrants had made the right choice—leaving the United States rather than continuing to endure white oppression as the "red man" had done. Black emigrants in Canada had chosen British ground—"the only ground on which they can make despots feel the forces of their words and actions . . . Now, what is to prevent them from living in the future?" Her idealization of black life and progress in Canada affirmed her optimism regarding black acceptance by a predominantly white society. Perhaps her enthusiasm was meant to attract American blacks to the Canadian Eden, but it is also likely that she zealously sought any positive signs that blacks had a promising future in their newly adopted country.

Despite her very strong opinions regarding the promise of an egalitarian society in Canada, Shadd Cary wrote little in her editorials to promote women's equality per se. However, there were subtle messages from her regarding "woman's place" in the antebellum United States. For example, in her editorial "Praiseworthy Example" (*Provincial Freeman*, April 19, 1856), she expressed her support for a black women's guild that would give the women a substantive role in a church dominated by black men:

> The colored daughters of the Church in New Haven it will be seen, have set a praiseworthy example to their fairer sisters. In one organization which they have not inappropriately entitled the "Sisterhood of the Good Angels" its prospectus tells us that its design is "that woman may be the helpmate of man in the noblest of enterprises, the advancement of the Redeemer's Kingdom on earth;" and no doubt there are many ways in which pious and devoted woman [sic] may legitimately exert themselves for such an object.

She supported the Sisterhood's effort to assume more responsibility in the church rather than remaining passive participants, and justified their expanded role by providing a history of notable female predecessors who had been important "attendant women called assistants, ministers or servant, whose services, however, were in no wise ministerial." She thought that "colored women appear to be peculiarly adapted" for taking such an assertive step—an incredible understatement. But the closest she came in this editorial to endorsing such a step for other black women was to indicate that both black men *and* women were "striving together for the faith of the Gospel" and closing with her hope that importance of women's role in the black church would be recognized and acknowledged: "We wish it, let them be assured with all our heart, God speed."

Her discretion on gender matters should not discount the magnitude of her highly visible role as the female owner and editor of a newspaper that reached both a black and white readership. Without editorializing in the antebellum period on women's equality, she was the perfect model of black women's autonomy in the public sphere. As her biographer Jane Rhodes states, "hers is less a tale of bravery or cunning, and more a narrative of tenacity, political acumen, and striving for social change under difficult circumstances . . . a woman who simultaneously fought for—and with her people."[41]

Although she was a contemporary of Frances Ellen Watkins Harper, Charlotte Forten, and Sarah Parker Remond—all of whom were freeborn, educated, and thoroughly European in their outlook and bearing—she received comparatively little recognition for her very few explicit writings in her newspaper on black women's autonomy.[42] The efforts for which she is well known regarding women's equality occurred after the end of the Civil War when she returned to the United States to work for women's rights and racial uplift. In the post-bellum period, she actively worked for and spoke out about women's equality and suffrage until she died in Washington, D.C., in 1893.

Conclusion

Between 1853 and 1861, Mary Ann Shadd Cary was an extraordinary voice for and leader of the emigration movement as well as an outspoken abolitionist, an advocate of temperance and self-reliance, and a discrete but committed exponent of women's equality. She was the foremost leader of the emigration movement of fifteen thousand blacks to Canada between 1850 and 1860.[43] Her thoughts on racial elevation preceding that of other nineteenth-century black women such as Mary Terrell, Anna Julia Cooper, and others began the concerted effort for racial uplift. Her positions on morality, temperance, virtue, self-reliance, frugality, entrepreneurship, and racial integration were rooted in three fundamental pillars of her philosophy of black elevation: emigration, education, and equality. But because of her radicalism regarding emigration to Canada, her sphere of influence was less than that of Douglass and others who insisted that the destiny of black people was to remain in the United States rather than repatriation. A stubborn, feisty visionary, she imagined a Canadian utopia for fugitive and free blacks living among whites who would grow to think of their black brethren as equals in all respects.

Her immediate remedy to black marginality was equality with whites, rightfully earned by achieving exemplary citizenship, self-reliance, morality, spiritual, and secular education—none of which was possible, in her opinion, without emigration to Canada. Some of her newspaper texts show a peculiarly unsophisticated worldview—as if white racism could be dissolved easily once blacks appeared to be on equal footing with their white cohorts in Canada. At times, her editorials and columns also exhibit her middle-class prejudices and privilege. But from her position as "other," she powerfully shaped the discourse of an oppressed collectivity that emancipated itself and seized the reins of its own destiny.

Invariably, Mary Ann Shadd Cary's alternative antebellum political discourse allows us to explore nondominant narratives about equality and emancipation within the context of a gendered and cultural experience. Although traditional content analyses within communication studies emphasize the power of the mainstream press—a press that historically has privileged the voice of white, upper-class men—Shadd Cary's black press underscores the importance of new directions for research on the communication of nondominant women. In this case, the gendered, racial, and national narratives provided within Shadd Cary's writings need not create a unified and harmonious vision within feminist, nationalist, or ethnic camps. Instead, by centering ethnic culture within the broader matrices of race, ethnicity, class, gender, nation, and generation, Shadd Cary moves beyond simple tropes and essentialism about suffrage or emancipation. New articulations abound from this visionary approach toward black women's communication. As feminist communication scholar Marsha Houston explains, the advantage of placing women's ethnic cultures at the center of our analysis of women's communication is that we can uncover the diversity of experience *within* cultural groups.[44] Shadd Cary's newspaper writings serve this aim by helping us understand how a new social collective was conceptualized through multiple sites of identity and experience within the black press.

Notes

I am very grateful to Ann Bookman, Marla Brettschneider, and Julie Frechette for their astute criticism, suggestions, and generosity regarding this essay. I am especially indebted to Kristin Waters for her expertise, editing, criticism, teaching, unwavering support, and generosity at every stage in the development of this essay.

1. These distinctions emerged through a series of conversations that I had with Kristin Waters about capturing the differences and similarities between and among the various positions.

2. In 1848, Jane Swisshelm was the first white woman in the United States to found and edit a newspaper, *The Saturday Visitor* of Pittsburgh.

3. See, for example, Angela Y. Davis, *Blues Legacies and Black Feminisms: Gertrude "Ma" Rainey, Bessie Smith, and Billie Holiday* (New York: Pantheon Press, 1998); bell hooks, *Feminism Is For Everybody* (Cambridge, Mass.: South End Press, 2000); hooks, *Ain't I a Woman; Black Women and Feminism* (Cambridge, Mass.: South End Press, 1983); hooks, *Feminist Theory: From Margin to Center* (Cambridge, Mass.: South End Press, 2000); Audre Lorde, *Sister/Outsider: Essays and Speeches* (Trumansburg, N.Y.: Crossing Press, 1984); Patricia Hill Collins, *Black Feminist Thought: Knowledge, Consciousness, and the Politics of Empowerment* (New York: Routledge, 1991).

4. Patricia Hill Collins, *Fighting Words: Black Women and the Search for Justice* (Minneapolis: University of Minnesota, 1998), 8.

5. Jane Rhodes, *Mary Ann Shadd Cary: The Black Press and Protest in the Nineteenth Century* (Bloomington: Indiana University Press, 1998), 220.

6. Ronald L. F. Davis and B. J. Krekorian, "The Black Press in Antebellum America," in *Slavery in America*, published online by New York Life, http://www.slaveryinamerica.org/history/hs_es_press.htm.

7. Rhodes, *Mary Ann Shadd Cary*, 220, citing Benedict Anderson, *Imagined Communities: Reflections on the Origin and Spread of Nationalism* (New York: Verso, 1987), 38–39, 62–63.

8. Patrick Rael, *Black Identity and Black Protest in the Antebellum North* (Chapel Hill: University of North Carolina Press, 2002).

9. Frankie Hutton, *The Early Black Press in America, 1827 to 1860* (Westport, Conn.: Greenwood Press, 1993). See also Carter Bryan, "Negro Journalism in America before Emancipation," *Journalism Monographs* 12 (September 1969).

10. Davis and Krekorian, "The Black Press."

11. See Paula Gunn Allen, *The Sacred Hoop: Recovering the Feminine in American Indian Traditions* (Boston: Beacon Press, 1986); and bell hooks, *Feminist Theory*.

12. Marsha Houston, "The Politics of Difference: Race, Class, and Women's Communication," in *Women Making Meaning: New Feminist Directions in Communication*, ed., L. Rakow, (New York: Routledge, 2006).

13. Rosemary Sadlier, *Mary Ann Shadd: Publisher, Editor, Teacher, Lawyer and Suffragette* (Toronto: Umbrella Press, 1995), 74.

14. Ibid.

15. Ibid.

16. This appellation for Shadd Cary is attributed to Carla L. Peterson in *"Doers of the Word": African-American Women Speakers and Writers in the North (1830–1880)* (New Brunswick, N.J.: Rutgers University Press, 1998).

17. In January 1849, Shadd Cary had written and published a long letter in Douglass's *North Star*. She strongly criticized black leaders and herself for the lack of progress in improving the horrible conditions for Northern blacks, despite numerous meetings on the issues, and she admonished black leaders to say little and do much. In the same letter, she also strongly criticized the black church by implying that it encouraged black submission to rather than independence from whites.

18. Rhodes, *Mary Ann Shadd Cary*, 22.

19. Ibid., 63.

20. See, for example, Michael C. Dawson, *Black Visions: The Roots of Contemporary African-American Political Ideologies* (Chicago: University of Chicago Press, 2001), chapter 3; and Dean E. Robinson, *Black Nationalism in American Politics and Thought* (Cambridge: Cambridge University Press, 2001), chapter 7. These texts are cited in Tommie Shelby, *We Who Are Dark: The Philosophical Foundations of Black Solidarity* (Cambridge, Mass.: The Belknap Press of Harvard University Press, 2005), 24.

21. Shelby, *We Who Are Dark*, 24.

22. Shelby maintains that these strains are ingrained deeply within the black political consciousness and argues that it is more important to see contemporary black nationalism as an extension of, rather than a radical rupture with, traditional beliefs of the group—that these strains run so deep that an "uncompromising and comprehensive attack on them will surely be met with hostility or suspicion, if it is taken seriously at all." Shelby, *We Who Are Dark*, 25. See also, James Clyde Sellman, "Black Nationalism in the United States," in *Africana: The Encyclopedia of the African and African American Experience*, ed. Kwame Anthony Appiah and Henry Louis Gates, Jr. (New York: Basic Civitas Books, 1999), 256–57.

23. Shelby, *We Who Are Dark*, 38.

24. Ibid., 28.

25. Martin Delany, Marcus Garvey, Elijah Muhammad, Malcolm X, the Black Power movement, Afrocentric proponents, hip hop, and Farrakhan, for example, are what Shelby characterizes as strong nationalists.

26. Peterson, *"Doers of the Word,"* 112.

27. Shelby, *We Who Are Dark,* 28.

28. Ibid.

29. Beginning in 1830 and throughout the mid-nineteenth century, meetings (conventions) were held primarily in Philadelphia, Cleveland, Delaware, and Canada West (Ontario) on issues pertaining to black survival and elevation, including emigration. In the First, Second, and Third Annual Conventions held in Philadelphia in 1831, 1832, and 1833, respectively, emigration was debated, but by the Third Annual Convention in 1833, the delegates were more interested in discussing black abolitionism than they were in discussing emigration issues.

30. According to Wilson, enslaved blacks had been present in Canada since 1628, but by the early 1700s, there was little need for slave labor in the colony. By the mid-eighteenth century, a relatively mild system of slavery existed in Canada compared with the United States. Harsh punishment, family separation, and abject deprivation were unacceptable in Canadian society. The main influx of slaves from the United States to Upper Canada was from the 1780s to 1793. Among the slaves who arrived in Canada through the 1780s were African-American Loyalists who had fought actively for the British during the American Revolution. In 1790, an act of the Imperial Parliament (that is, the British Parliament acting on colonial matters) assured prospective white emigrants to Canada that their slaves would remain their property, but that they were to be freed after nine years of service. That act stipulated that slaves' children were to remain with their mothers. Upon attaining the age of twenty-five, enslaved children were to be freed.

Wilson maintains that the Slave Act of 1793 gradually ended slavery in Upper Canada before Britain did the same in 1807. African Canadians had been overwhelmingly loyal to the British during the War of 1812 and they served with distinction. Their allegiance impressed Canadians and hastened the end of slavery. In 1833, the newly elected Imperial Parliament passed the Imperial Act to abolish slavery throughout the empire, effective August 1, 1834—twenty-nine years before Lincoln's Emancipation Proclamation freeing some of the slaves in the United States took effect. W. R. Wilson, "An Act to Prevent the Further Introduction of Slaves," *Historical Narratives of Early Canada,* 2005, accessed online on 2-27-06 at http://www.Uppercanadahistory.ca/lluc/lluc3.html. See Roy P. Basler ed., *The Collected Works of Abraham Lincoln* (Ann Arbor, Mich: Lincoln Society, University of Michigan Press, 1953. Accessed online at http://www.hti.umich.edu/thelincoln/. The Emancipation Proclamation, written and issued in 1852, did not take effect until January 1, 1863. It did not free all of the enslaved. Slaves in the Confederate states who were not back in the Union by then would be freed. But slaves in the Border States were not affected.

31. Carla L. Peterson, *"Doers of the Word,"* 112.

32. Ibid., 115.

33. Ibid., 112.

34. Ibid., 116.

35. Tommie Shelby, *We Who Are Dark,* 34.

36. Robert S. Levine, *Martin Delany, Frederick Douglass, and the Politics of Representative Identity* (Chapel Hill: University of North Carolina Press, 1997), 14.

37. Carla L. Peterson, *"Doers of the Word,"* 116.

38. Ryerson University School of Journalism, "Diversity Watch Group," http://www.diversitywatch.ryerson.ca/backgrounds/blkhtm.

39. Fourth, she believed that colored people needed instruction on heaven that could be used on earth—"how to use the latter to obtain the former (*Provincial Freeman*, November 10, 1855, "The Way to do Colored Canadians Good").

40. Delany also strongly urged blacks to think for themselves. Shelby notes that "Delany was particularly dismayed when blacks allowed whites, even those sympathetic to black interests, to think for them; and so he consistently urged blacks to resist white paternalism." This point was particularly pertinent with regard to religion. In Delany's opinion, blacks had "unthinkingly accepted their oppressor's interpretation of Christianity, an interpretation that encouraged passivity in the face of subordination and exploitation." Shelby, *We Who Are Dark*, 35, citing Martin R. Delany, *The Condition, Elevation, Emigration, and Destiny of the Colored People of the United States, Politically Considered* (Baltimore: Black Classic Press, 1993), 10, 25–30, 170–71, and 190–91.

41. Rhodes, *Mary Ann Shadd Cary*, xiv.

42. Ibid.

43. Paula Giddings, *When and Where I Enter: The Impact of Black Women on Race and Sex in America* (New York: Bantam Books, 1984), 69.

44. Marsha Houston, "The Politics of Difference: Race, Class, and Women's Communication," in *Women Making Meaning: New Feminist Directions in Communication*, ed. L. Rakow (New York: Routledge, 2006), 45–59.

Part IV

Anna Julia Cooper
A Voice

Chapter 11

Anna Julia Cooper

A Voice from the South

MARY HELEN WASHINGTON

Given Anna Julia Cooper's unparalleled articulation of black feminist thought in her major work, *A Voice From the South by a Black Woman of the South*, published in 1892; given her role as a leading black spokeswoman of her time (she was one of three black women invited to address the World's Congress of Representative Women in 1893 and one of the few women to speak at the 1900 Pan-African Congress Conference in London); given her leadership in women's organizations (she helped start the Colored Women's YWCA in 1905 because of the Jim Crow policies of the white YWCA and in 1912 founded the first chapter of the Y's Camp Fire Girls); and given the fact that her work in educating black students spanned nearly half a century, why is Anna Cooper a neglected figure, far less well known than such distinguished contemporaries as Frances Harper, Ida B. Wells, and Mary Church Terrell? One of her biographers, Dr. Paul Cooke, suggests that Cooper's role as a scholar limited her public profile: "Cooper was continually the scholar. She was in the library when Mary Church Terrell was picketing the drugstores and cafeterias in downtown Washington, D.C. She chose the lesser limelight, while Terrell chose the Civil Rights route and carried the media."[1] In her personal and professional life Cooper made similar choices for the "lesser limelight." In middle age, in the prime of her intellectual and professional life, she adopted five small children. She was a principal and teacher at the renowned Dunbar High School in Washington, D.C., for years, and in her retirement, she continued her life's dedication to the "education of neglected people" by starting a night school for working people who could not attend college during the day. In 1982, when Louise Hutchinson, staff historian at the Smithsonian Institution, completed her biography of Cooper, she called for an official Smithsonian car and hand-delivered the first copy of the biography to Mrs. Regia Haywood Bronson, the eldest of the five children: Anna Cooper had adopted in 1915. Then in her late seventies, Mrs. Bronson took the book from Hutchinson, and holding it to her breast, she rocked back and forth with tears streaming down her face, but not saying a word. When Hutchinson asked her why she was crying, Bronson said, "Nobody ever told me Sis Annie was important."[2]

In her first and only full-length book, *A Voice From the South by a Black Woman of the South,* Cooper wrote prophetically about the dismissal of the intellectual: The thinker who enriches his country by a "thought inestimable and precious is given neither bread nor a stone. He is too often left to die in obscurity and neglect."[3] But the exclusion of Cooper from black intellectual history is more than simply disdain for the intellectual. The intellectual discourse of black women of the 1890s, and particularly Cooper's embryonic black feminist analysis, was ignored because it was by and about women and therefore thought not to be as significantly about the race as writings by and about men. (As a black Catholic priest said to me when I asked about the position of women in the church, "We're here to talk about black Catholics, not about feminism.") Cooper thought differently, maintaining, in fact, that men could not even represent the race. At the heart of Cooper's analysis is her belief that the status of black women is the only true measure of collective racial progress. Because the black woman is the least likely to be among the eminent and the most likely to be responsible for the nurturing of families, it is she, according to Cooper, who represents the entire race:

> Only the BLACK WOMAN can say "when and where I enter, in the quiet, undisputed dignity of my womanhood, without violence and without suing or special patronage, then and there the whole *Negro race enters with me.*"[4]

A Voice From the South begins with this dramatic challenge to the prevailing ideas about black women, and Cooper never softens that uncompromising tone. She criticizes black men for securing higher education for themselves through the avenue of the ministry and for erecting roadblocks to deny women access to those same opportunities:

while our men seem thoroughly abreast of the times on almost every other subject, when they strike the woman question they drop back into sixteenth century logic...I fear the majority of colored men do not yet think it worth while that women aspire to higher education.[5]

If black men are a "muffled chord," then black women, writes Cooper, are the "mute and voiceless note" of the race, with "no language—but a cry."

Cooper is equally critical of the white women's movement for its elitism and provinciality, and she challenges white women to link their cause with that of all the "undefended." Always she measures the ideals and integrity of any group by its treatment of those who suffer the greatest oppression.

The feminist essays that comprise the first half of *A Voice From the South* are extremely compelling for contemporary readers. And yet I must confess to a certain uneasiness about Cooper's tone in these essays, a feeling that while she speaks *for* ordinary black women, she rarely, if ever, speaks *to* them. I find myself wondering how Cooper imagined the relationship between herself, an articulate, powerful speaker and writer—an intellectual—and the woman she describes as a "mute and voiceless note," "the sadly expectant Black Woman." Clearly, she sees herself as the *voice* for these women, but nothing in her essays suggests that they existed in her imagination as audience or as peer.

We must remember that the emphasis on social uplift by educated nineteenth-century women was the direct result of their own perilous social position. As Mary Church Terrell explains, the motto of the National Association of Colored Women—"Lifting As We Climb"—grew out of the recognition by elite black women that they were tethered to the destinies of the masses of disadvantaged black women: "Colored women of education and culture know that...the call of duty,...policy and preservation demand that they go down among the lowly, the illiterate and even the vicious, to whom they are bound by the ties of race and sex...to reclaim them."[6] We "have determined to come into the closest possible touch with the masses of our women," Terrell continues, because the womanhood of the race will always be judged by these groups. While Terrell's open condescension seems offensive, the discreet distance Cooper maintains between herself and those "mute and voiceless" black women is probably the result of the same vulnerability Terrell felt. To counteract the prevailing assumptions about black women as immoral and ignorant, Cooper had to construct a narrator who was aware of the plight of uneducated women but was clearly set apart from them in refinement, intelligence, and training.[7] And there were other vulnerabilities. As a woman, Cooper had to fight against both black and white men who posed tremendous obstacles to her own education. As a single woman for nearly all of her adult life (she was widowed after only two years of marriage), she was considered, like all women, to be a sexual being whose personal and professional activities had to be circumscribed. And as a passionate and committed feminist, she had to struggle against the masculinist bias in black intellectual circles and against the racism among white feminists. These circumstances help us to understand the limitations of Cooper's writings. Her voice is not radical, and she writes with little sense of community with a black and female past. But in the light of her special vulnerabilities— and that is how we must examine Cooper's life and work—it is all the more remarkable that she develops in *A Voice from the South,* with her critique of dominant groups, an analysis that asserts black womanhood as the vital agency for social and political change in America.

Born Annie Julia Haywood in 1858 in Raleigh, North Carolina, Cooper was the child of a slave woman, Hannah Stanley Haywood, and her white master, George Washington Haywood. In a brief autobiographical statement of her early years, Cooper wrote, "My mother was a slave and the finest woman I have ever known . . . Presumably my father was her master, if so I owe him not a sou & she was always too modest & shamefaced ever to mention him."[8] Cooper knew very well that Haywood was her father, because in 1934, when she requested information about her family tree from Haywood's nephew, he wrote back that "Wash" Haywood, who was a prominent and successful lawyer in Raleigh until the Civil War, had "one child by his slave Hannah without benefit of Clergy."[9] When the Episcopal Church opened St. Augustine's Normal School and Collegiate Institute for the newly freed slaves in 1868, Annie Haywood, then about nine and a half years old, was among the first to enter, her admission perhaps reflecting the social and cultural standing of the Haywood family.

As a teenager, Cooper began protesting against sexism when she realized that men, as candidates for the ministry at St. Augustine's, were given preferential treatment, while women were steered away from studying theology and the classics. She complained to the principal that "the only mission open before a girl . . . was to marry one of those candidates." Writing of that experience in *A Voice,* she remembered the difficulties a black girl faced in her struggle for education and how easy the way was made for males:

A boy, however meager his equipment and shallow his pretentions, had only to declare a floating intention to study theology and he could get all the support, encouragement and stimulus he needed, be absolved from work and invested beforehand with all the dignity of his far away office. While a self-supporting girl had to struggle on by teaching in the summer and working after school hours to keep up with her board bills, and actually to fight her way against positive discouragements to the higher education.[10]

In 1877, at the age of nineteen, Cooper did in fact marry one of those candidates for the ministry, George Cooper. His death two years later left her a widow, which ironically allowed her to pursue a career as a teacher, whereas no married woman—black or white—could continue to teach. She began writing letters to Oberlin in 1881 to request free tuition and to apply for employment so that she could earn her room and board. As at St. Augustine's, Cooper rejected the distinctly inferior "Ladies Course" at Oberlin and, like many of the women, chose the "Gentleman's Course," which she says sarcastically caused no collapse at the college, though the school administrators thought it was a dangerous experiment: "[It] was adopted with fear and trembling by the good fathers, who looked as if they had been caught secretly mixing explosive compounds and were guiltily expecting every moment to see the foundations under them shaken."[11]

Cooper attained a B.A. and later an M.A. at Oberlin, and in 1887, as one of the few blacks with a graduate degree, she was recruited by the Superintendent for Colored Schools to teach at Washington's only black high school—first known as the Washington Colored High School, then as M Street High School, and finally as the famous Dunbar High School.[12] For several decades the school educated the children of the aspiring black middle class and gained a reputation for having both high academic standards and a deep-seated snobbery based on class and color. During her initial tenure at M Street, where she was first a math and science teacher (she later taught Latin) and then the school principal, Cooper was in the midst of a male and racist stronghold that would eventually bring about her humiliating expulsion from the school. According to a former student at the school, Annette Eaton, Cooper might have expected male hostility:

You must also remember that as far as the Negro population of Washington was concerned, we were still a small southern community where a woman's place was in the home. The idea of a woman principal of a high school must account in some part for any reaction Dr. Cooper felt against her.[13]

Cooper became the principal of M Street in January 1902, when she was forty-four years old. At the time, Booker T. Washington's program of vocational and industrial training was emerging as *the* model for black education and consequently was playing into the prejudices of whites who believe in black intellectual inferiority. By contrast, Cooper staunchly maintained M Street's orientation toward preparing black youth for college. In defiance of her white supervisor—Percy Hughes, who told her that colored children should be taught trades—Cooper sent several of her students to prestigious universities, including Harvard, Brown, Oberlin, Yale, Amherst, Dartmouth, and Radcliffe. During her tenure as principal, M Street was accredited for the first time by Harvard. For her intransigence, Cooper became the central figure in the "M Street School Controversy" and was eventually forced to resign. A letter by Annette Eaton testifies to the role of white racism in Cooper's dismissal.

> If you could smell or feel or in any way sense the aura of D.C. in those days, you would know that it only took her daring in having her students accepted and given scholarship at Ivy League schools to know that the white power structure would be out to get her for any reason or for no reason. It was pure heresy to think that a colored child could do what a white child could. I well remember a year when I was in the fourth grade and Bill Hastie in the eighth, when the Board of Education decided to check the reading competency of D.C. students. All schools were told to select their best fourth grade and eighth grade readers, and send them to a special Board meeting. Bill and I were sent, were told to read until we were stopped, and naively did so. I was told later that I didn't miss a word until I got to the twelfth grade level. Heaven only knows how far Bill went. But the Board never held that test again. My great-grandfather was on the Board at the time, so the story became a family legend. I cite it only to show you what resentment existed in the city whenever the Negro children succeeded in any way, or surpassed the whites. So I must fix Dr. Cooper's removal on the ill-feeling created among the power structure in education because of the way her students stood up. And then, you must remember that she was out in front, highly visible, and therefore caught the brunt of the hatred that really belonged to her faculty.[14]

Cooper was brought before the D.C. Board of Education in 1905 and, according to the minutes of the Board meeting, she was charged with the following: (1) refusing to use a textbook authorized by the Board; (2) being too sympathetic to weak and unqualified students; (3) not being able to maintain discipline (two students had been caught drinking); and (4) not maintaining a "proper spirit of unity and loyalty."

The Cooper case was reported extensively in two prominent Washington newspapers, the black *Washington Bee* and the white *Washington Post.* There was considerable support for her side. A delegation that included former Congressman George H. White of North Carolina sat in on the Board's deliberations and waited until after 10 P.M. to speak on Cooper's behalf. The Board claimed to have "damaging testimony" that "cast some aspersion upon Mrs. Cooper's record in North Carolina," but such evidence never materialized. The dispute dragged on for almost a year until 1906 when the Board voted to dismiss her.[15]

Racism aside, the sexism behind this decision was apparent to all who understood the male-dominated D.C. school system of spoils that did not include black women in its inner circles. As Annette Eaton points out, among the factors in Cooper's dismissal, three were the result of sexual politics:

> First, AJK [*sic*] was a woman, a "condition" very much frowned upon in Washington school circles, especially at the secondary or administrative level. It was O.K. for women to be elementary school teachers and principals, but they were not supposed to aspire to any higher rank. Second, she had been married, and married women were not wanted, or even for a time allowed, to teach. She got away with it because she was a widow, but I remember even as early as my elementary school days, my mother could not get a teaching position until she divorced my father. The third factor is that she rented out a room in her house to a man (teacher, I think) named John Love, and the whole city of Washington was rife with the gossip that she was having an affair with him. I suspect I that it was this, and not the quality of her teaching, that caused my mother to refuse to let me study Latin under her.[16]

The rumor of Cooper's alleged affair with John Love was another example of the Victorian double standard: Since women's behavior, no matter how innocent, could be sexualized, it had to be contained and repressed. Single women especially were victimized. When Fannie Jackson taught at the Philadelphia Institute for Colored Youth in the 1880s, she had to hire the janitor to escort her home in order to avoid the appearance of impropriety. In 1883 Lucy Ellen Moten was refused the position of principal of Washington's Minor Normal School because the all-male Board of Trustees felt that the tall, elegant mulatta "cut too fine a face and figure" for the job. Moten appealed to one of the trustees, the eminent Frederick Douglass, who told her he would intercede for her if she agreed to give up dancing, playing cards, going to the theater, entertaining gentlemen callers—and her fine clothes. She agreed to all conditions and got the job.[17]

John Love and his sister Emma, orphaned as teenagers, had been taken in by Cooper as her foster children. They were still living with Cooper several years later, along with four women teachers, who, according to the 1902 census data, were "boarders" in her home, of which she was listed as owner and "head of household." Indeed, John Love, who by this time was a teacher of English and history at M Street, did eventually fall in love with Cooper. There was a thirteen-year difference in their ages; by 1906, Love would have been thirty-five years old and Anna Cooper an attractive forty-eight-year-old woman.

Students at M Street were very much aware of their closeness; as Annette Eaton indicated, some parents went so far as to refuse to let their children study Latin under Cooper because of the suspected affair. A former student said that John Love supported Cooper by maintaining discipline at M Street, and another student, ninety-five years old at the time of her recollection, crossed her index and second fingers to indicate the closeness between Love and Cooper. Both of them were dismissed from M Street at the same time, and each took teaching jobs in the Midwest, Cooper in Jefferson City, Missouri, at the all-black Lincoln University. Apparently, during their exile, John Love wrote to Cooper with a proposal of marriage, which she refused. The love letters from Love to Cooper appear to be lost. Her grandniece, Regia Bronson, who was the eldest of the children Cooper adopted and who died shortly after I began my research, apparently threw the letters out in a wave of housekeeping, but not before she told one of Cooper's biographers, Dr. Paul Cooke, about their existence. Perhaps the age difference deterred Cooper from returning Love's affection, or perhaps she simply felt the romance was improper since she had formerly been his guardian. For many years, they worked and taught together as professional and intellectual comrades, but in her writings the only reference that I could find to John Love is in her account of the weekly soirees with the Grimké family: "Mr. Love, especially, had a fine baritone voice, and a favorite from him was 'O Rest in the Lord, Wait Patiently for Him' from Mendelssohn's Elijah."

In 1910 a new superintendent of M Street summoned Cooper back to resume her position as a Latin teacher. She was fifty-two years old, and the next fifty years of her life (she died at the age of 105 in 1964) were as active as the first. Perhaps to assuage the humiliation of her exile, Cooper began to study for her doctorate at Columbia. Before she could complete Columbia's one-year residency requirement, she adopted, in 1915, five orphaned children, who ranged in age from six months to twelve years and were the grandchildren of her half-brother. She brought all five children from Raleigh to Washington, where she had bought a new home "to house their Southern exuberance." As difficult as it was to become the mother of five at age fifty-seven, Cooper tackled it with characteristic resolution and defiance:

> With butter at 75 cents per lb. still soaring, sugar severely rationed at any price and fuel oil obtainable only on affadavit in person at regional centers, the Judge at Children's Court . . . said to me: "My, but you are a brave woman!" Not as brave as you may imagine, was my mental rejoiner—only stubborn, or foolhardy.[18]

In spite of a newly acquired mortgage, a family of five small children, and a full schedule of teaching, Cooper continued—"for 'Home Work,'" as she called it—to work on her doctorate, this time with the Sorbonne. Once she enrolled the children in boarding schools, she began to study summers in Paris, and in 1924, having requested a sick leave from her teaching job, she went to Paris to fulfill the residency requirements. Apparently the leave had not been granted, and after fifty days in Paris she received this cable from a friend: "Rumored dropped if not returned within 60 days."[19] Not willing to risk the loss of her retirement benefits or income, Cooper returned to her classroom "5 minutes before 9 on the morning of the 60th day of my absence," greeted by the applause of her students. Despite these obstacles from her supervisors at M Street (now Dunbar High), Cooper defended her dissertation in the spring of 1925 and was awarded a doctorate from the University of Paris. At the age of sixty-seven, she was the fourth American black woman to receive a Ph.D. (The other three were also associated with M Street School. Georgiana Rose Simpson and Eva B. Dykes taught there, and Sadie Tanner Alexander was a former student.)

Cooper continued to write well into the 1940s, but she never again singled out black women as her major subject, nor did she ever again take the explicitly feminist stance that she did in *A Voice.* The critical questions to ask about Anna Cooper's career are these: What happened to her early feminist voice in the years after *A Voice* was published? What stymied the development of a fully mature feminism? What happened to the critical position she took against male privilege in *A Voice?* What of her steadfast resolve that "there be the same flourish of trumpets and clapping of hands" for the achievement of women as for men?[20]

We can speculate that a life of professional uncertainty and of financial insecurity made it difficult for her to continue her writing. Cooper came of age during a conservative wave in the black community, a period in which Afro-American intellectual and political ideas were dominated by men. In the very year that Cooper published *A Voice From the South*, Frederick Douglass, when asked by historian M. A. Majors to name some black women for inclusion in Majors' biographical work on black women, responded: "I have thus far seen no book of importance written by a negro woman and I know of no one among us who can appropriately be called famous."[21] Five years later in 1897, when leading black intellectuals such as Francis Grimké, W. E. B. Du Bois, and Alexander Crummell formed the prestigious American Negro Academy "for the promotion of Literature, Science, and Art," they limited their membership to "men of African descent."[22] Deeply committed to the intellectual and moral goals of the ANA, Cooper reviewed the opening meeting for the February 1898 issue of *Southern Workman,* in which she noted the exclusion of women with the simple comment, "Its membership is confined to men." She did not comment further, even though she knew that outstanding black women intellectuals were being denied membership. Nor did she comment on the obvious exclusion of women from the masculine imagery of the ANA, which was determined to rescue and elevate "black manhood."

In spite of the reverential way she referred to her male colleagues—Douglass, Du Bois, Grimké, and Crummell in particular—her distinguished counterparts rarely returned the compliment in print. Cooper's relationship with Du Bois underscored how women got left out of black political life. She obviously knew and respected the eminent Dr. Du Bois. She was one of the few black women to address the 1900 Pan-African Congress, which Du Bois helped to organize. She wrote to him at least three times, once in 1936 to ask if he would publish her biographical sketch of her friend Charlotte Grimké. Du Bois said it was too long, although he praised the idea. When she suggested he run it in three serials (probably in the *Crisis*), he neither answered nor returned her notes for the sketch. She wrote to him in 1929, urging him to write a response to *The Tragic Era,* a racist book on Reconstruction by Claude Bowers:

> It seems to me the Tragic Era should be answered—adequately, fully, ably, finally, and again it seems to me *Thou* are the man! Take it up seriously thro

the Crisis and let us buy up 10,000 copies to be distributed broadcast thro the land.

Will you do it?
Answer
Faithfully,
Anna J. Cooper

Du Bois' famous book, *Black Reconstruction,* was the result of his response to Cooper's urgings.[23]

In another poignant letter, written on October 27, 1929, she wrote Du Bois about her regrets at not being able to attend the Pan-African Congress that year: "But why oh why don't you have your Congresses in summer time when working people might go with out having their heads thrown to the crows."[24]

I cannot imagine Du Bois being similarly faithful to Anna Cooper, offering to publicize her work, or being willing to hawk 10,000 copies of one of her speeches on women's equality, nor can I imagine that any of the male intelligentsia would have been distraught at not being able to attend the annual meetings of the colored women's clubs. In a compassionate and generally progressive essay called "On the Damnation of Women," Du Bois sympathetically analyzes the oppression of black women, but he makes no effort to draw on the writings of black women intellectuals for their insights into the problems facing black women. In fact, in a remarkable oversight in this essay, Du Bois quotes Cooper's brilliant observation that "only the black woman can say 'when and where I enter'" and attributes the statement *not* to her but *anonymously* to "one of our women."[25]

Though the embryonic black feminist viewpoint suggested in *A Voice* was never fully developed in any of her subsequent writings, Cooper maintained a natural feminist sensibility that made her—at least occasionally—an outspoken critic of patriarchal politics. Once asked by a white friend why the men of her race seemed to outstrip the women in mental attainment, Cooper said that men's intellectual superiority was merely an illusion created by their posturing: "'the women are more quiet. They don't feel called to mount a barrel and harangue by the hour every time they imagine they have produced an idea."[26] She instinctively rebelled against the power males exerted over female life, even when that male was a trusted friend. In 1936, the Reverend Francis Grimké, one of the most respected men in Washington and a good friend of Cooper's, sent her a copy of a sermon called "Suicide or Self-Murder," which he had preached after the death of feminist writer Charlotte Perkins Gilman. The sermon was a judgmental and condemnatory pronouncement of Grimké's deep regret that Gilman had failed to bear her afflictions with Christian courage and patience. Cooper's reply to Grimké's moralism, dated April 9, 1936, shows her unwillingness to have a female life subjugated by a male text. She strongly objected to Grimké's depreciation of Gilman's achievements by focusing only on her death:

> I wish in the leaflet on Frances [sic] Perkins Gilman you had given your readers more of the life history of your subject . . . I am sure the facts in that life, leaving out its tragic end, would have been full of inspiring interest and stimulating encouragement. But you are always *the preacher* you know and *must* draw your moral for the benefit or the confusion of the rest of us poor sinners. I forgive you.[27]

If Cooper was unwilling to have women's lives subordinated to male texts, she was equally unwilling to have black lives dominated by white texts. It is important to understand that Cooper's criticism was mainly directed at a system of white male power. As a literary critic, she was uncompromising in her denunciation of white control over the black image, and she took on such nineteenth-century establishment figures as William Dean Howells, Joel Chandler Harris, and George Washington Cable. She blasts Howells and Harris in *A Voice* for attempting to portray black people and black culture in their work, even though they were arrogantly ignorant about that life: "[They] have performed a few psychological experiments on their cooks and coachmen, and with astounding egotism, and powers of generalization positively bewildering, forthwith aspire to enlighten the world with dissertations on racial traits of the Negro."[28]

Cooper made this same complaint against white critics of the 1940s whose power and position made them the arbiters of what was "authentic" black life. Black critics were afraid to criticize Richard Wright's *Native Son* once it was selected for the Book-of-the-Month Club because, in Cooper's words, it was so "richly upholstered by cash and comment." She was also angered that praise from the white poet Vachel Lindsay had made criticizing Langston Hughes nearly impossible:

> It is the curse of minorities in this power-worshipping world that either from fear or from an uncertain policy of expedience they distrust their own standards and hesitate to give voice to their deeper convictions, submitting supinely to estimates and characterizations of themselves as handed down by a not unprejudiced dominant majority.[29]

Everywhere in *A Voice From the South,* Cooper is concerned about the un-restrained power of a dominant majority to crush the lives of the weak and powerless. As Hazel Carby points out in her essay on black women intellectuals at the turn of the century, Cooper's position was never nar-rowly confined to the women's issue because she saw this dominance of the strong over the weak as the critical issue, and she saw that tendency to abuse power in the labor and women's movements, both of which were deeply entrenched in "caste prejudice" and hostile to the needs and in-terests of black women.[30] The sympathy of the labor movement for "working girls" never included black working women who were confined to the most menial and strenuous physical labor:

> One often hears in the North an earnest plea from some lecturer for "our working girls" (of course this means white working girls) . . . how many have ever given a thought to the pinched and down-trodden colored women bending over wash-tubs and ironing boards—with children to feed and house rent to pay, wood to buy, soap and starch to furnish—lugging home weekly great baskets of clothes for families who pay them for a month's laundrying barely enough to purchase a substantial pair of shoes![31]

While Cooper believed strongly in the power of the women's move-ment to challenge patriarchal power, she was not naive about the capacity of white women to condone and perpetrate race prejudice. Knowing how deeply the South had influenced the women's movement, she devotes an entire chapter in *A Voice* to attacking the white supremacist ideas that had crept into the movement. Women emancipators must first be released from the "paralyzing grip of caste prejudice," Cooper asserts, and she takes on movement leaders Susan B. Anthony and Anna B. Shaw for their failure to take a strong stand against racism.[32] What precipitated this cen-sure was the refusal of a women's culture club, of which Shaw and An-thony were members, to admit a "cream-colored" applicant to what Cooper called "its immaculate assembly." Cooper felt that as leaders Shaw and Anthony had the power, which they failed to use, to telegraph down the lines of their networks clear disapproval of such attitudes and behavior. She was further troubled by a speech entitled "Woman Versus the In-dian," in which Shaw complained that white women were humiliated at being treated less courteously than "Indians in blankets and moccasins." Cooper responded:

> Is not woman's cause broader, and deeper, and grander, than a blue stock-ing debate or an aristocratic pink tea? Why should woman become plain-

tiff in a suit versus the Indian, or the Negro or any other race or class who have been crushed under the iron heel of Anglo-Saxon power and selfishness?[33]

For Cooper, the greatest potential of the women's movement lay not with white women but with the women who were "confronted by both a woman question and a race problem." And it is precisely at this juncture of racial and sexual politics that we would expect Cooper to make her strongest statements in *A Voice*. Her language, when she speaks of the special mission of black women, is beautiful and stirring, almost evangelical: "But to be a woman of the Negro race in America, and to be able to grasp the deep significance of the possibilities of the crisis, is to have a heritage, it seems to me, unique in the ages."[34] The rhetoric is compelling, but the ideas in this section of *A Voice*, where Cooper tries to connect race and gender issues and to place black women at a pivotal point in that discussion, are disappointing. She is never able to discard totally the ethics of true womanhood, and except for the one passage about black laundry women, she does not imagine ordinary black working women as the basis of her feminist politics. While she admits that black women are an "unacknowledged factor" in both race and gender issues, she insists that their quiet and unobserved presence as they stand "aloof from the heated scramble [of politics]" will eventually make itself felt. Here Cooper is falling back on the true womanhood premise that women need not possess any actual political power in order to effect political change; in true womanly fashion, black women could pressure their husbands to vote the right way by whispering "just the needed suggestion or the almost forgotten truth."[35] The dictates of true womanhood confined women's authority to the domestic realm where they could supposedly derive power from their ability to influence their husbands.[36] Such drawing-room scenarios were hardly relevant to the lives of most black women. Even the examples Cooper gives of black women leaders (Sojourner Truth, Amanda Smith, Charlotte Forten Grimké, Frances Harper) are undermined by the genteel language of true womanhood: They are "pleasing," or "sweet," or "gentle," or "charming," or with a "matchless and irresistible personality."[37]

How did Cooper, a woman who in some ways is so clear-eyed about the need to resist the subordination of women in all its forms, get trapped in the ideological underbrush of true womanhood? As some historians of women's history would claim, many of the tenets of true womanhood did lay the groundwork for a more radical form of feminism, and Cooper obviously expected black women to be at the forefront, if not the helm, of social change. As a middle-class black woman, Cooper, like all of her contemporaries—Fannie Jackson Coppin, Frances Harper, Mary Church Terrell, Ida B. Wells, Josephine St. Pierre Ruffin—had a great stake in the prestige, the respectability, and the gentility guaranteed by the politics of true womanhood. To identify with the issues and interests of poor and uneducated black women entailed a great risk. Cooper and her intellectual contemporaries would have to deal with their own class privilege and would undoubtedly alienate the very white women they felt they needed as allies. Burdened by the race's morality, black women could not be as free as white women or black men to think outside of these boundaries of "uplift"; every choice they made had tremendous repercussions for an entire race of women already under the stigma of inferiority and immorality.

When Cooper is willing to speak out of her own personal experience, to probe her own pain, anger, and victimization, as she does in one of the early essays in *A Voice*, "The Higher Education of Woman," her own real outrage surfaces. At the time she was writing *A Voice*, Cooper had been a self-supporting widow for nearly fourteen years, and she undoubtedly knew how difficult life was for a professional woman. As an intellectually curious and exceptionally bright young girl, she had already experienced the discouragements planted in the way of the "exceptional" female: "I constantly felt (as I suppose many an ambitious girl has felt) a thumping from within unanswered by any beckoning from without."[38] With her own struggle for an education as a background, she understood what little encouragement there was for female development, and she was insulted by the advice to women of her class to "merely look pretty and appear well in society." Her own private poll of colleges that admitted black women revealed a striking inequality between black men and black women: By 1890 Fisk had graduated only twelve black women; Oberlin, five; Wilberforce, four; Atlanta, one; Howard, none. Imagine how difficult it must have been for black women intellectuals of Cooper's day to fight against the racism that roadblocked almost every avenue to education for women and to contend as well with the sexism in "their own little world" that denigrated their attempts at intellectual growth. Passionately committed to women's independence, Cooper espoused higher education as the essential key to ending women's physical, emotional, and economic dependence on men:

> I grant you that intellectual development, with the self-reliance and capacity for earning a livelihood which it gives, renders woman less depen-

dent on the marriage relationship for physical support (which, by the way, does not always accompany it). Neither is she compelled to look to sexual love as the one sensation capable of giving tone and relish, movement and vim to the life she leads. Her horizon is extended. Her sympathies are broadened and deepened and multiplied.[39]

Education, Cooper continues, will change woman's relationship to marriage, enabling her to see herself as a power broker and not merely as a grateful beneficiary. The question shall not be "'How shall I so cramp, stunt, simplify and nullify myself as to make me eligible to the honor of being swallowed up into some little man?'" The question instead "now rests with the man as to how he can so develop his God-given powers as to reach the ideal of [this] generation of women?"[40] The humor and irony she brings to the question of how intellectual women will fare in the matrimonial market makes Cooper seem remarkably progressive for a nineteenth-century woman. When asked if higher education would make women less desirable to men, she first says, tongue-in-cheek, that she realizes that only men think this a most weighty and serious argument. Then she dismisses the question with the sarcastic rejoinder that "strong-minded women could be, when they thought it worth their while, quite endurable."[41]

If there is a serious flaw in this feminist position, it is that it often bears so little relation to the lives of black women of the 1890s, most of whom were sharecroppers, struggling farmers, or domestic servants, few of whom could aspire to anything beyond an elementary education. But it was typical of black publications and black writers of this period to treat black women's lives as though they were merely reflections of leisured white women's. In *We Are Your Sisters: Black Women in the Nineteenth Century*, Dorothy Sterling reports that there were articles in the black press on the latest fashions and advice on how to be a submissive wife.[42] Although her sympathies were with the poor and uneducated, Cooper's images in *A Voice* are almost entirely of privileged women: the struggling, ambitious intellectual, those fatally beautiful Southern mulatto women, a "cream-colored" aspirant to a white culture club, and an artist whose application to the Corcoran museum school was rejected because of her race.

Cooper and her contemporaries saw themselves in the 1890s, "the Women's Era," as avatars of the progress of black women. As "representative" women, they had dual and conflicting roles: They had to "represent" as advocates that class of American women who were victimized by every social and political policy created by the American power structure, and they had to "represent" the progress that black women were making toward greater refinement, good taste, intelligence, and religious development.[43] And even these efforts were met with contempt and obstructions. Fannie Barrier Williams, in a speech to the 1893 World's Congress of Representative Women, addressed black women's intellectual progress since the Emancipation and declared that every movement of black American women toward intellectual and cultural growth was met with hostility: "If we seek the sanctities of religion, the enlightenment of the university, the honors of politics, and the natural recreations of our common country, the social alarm is instantly given and our aspirations are insulted."[44] Sensing perhaps that she was addressing a sympathetic audience, Cooper also spoke before this same congress and broached a sensitive and potentially damaging subject—the sexual violation of black women. In a speech that could not have taken more than five minutes to deliver, Cooper revealed what is often concealed in *A Voice:* her passionate concern for the poorest black women and her unshakable belief that they were waging a heroic struggle for the necessities of life—for knowledge, for bread, for dignity, and for the simple right of possession of their own bodies.

Without women like Fannie Barrier Williams, Ida B. Wells, Fannie Jackson Coppin, Victoria Earle Matthews, Frances Harper, Mary Church Terrell, and Anna Julia Cooper, we would know very little about the conditions of nineteenth-century black women's lives, and yet the black intellectual tradition, until very recently, has virtually ignored them and devalued their scholarship as clearly subordinate to that produced by black men.[45] These women were activists as well as intellectuals: They worked as teachers, lecturers, social workers, journalists, and in women's clubs. They were more committed to the idea of uplift than to their own personal advancement, partly because they could not isolate themselves from the problems of poor black women. If at times their language betrays their elitism, they were nevertheless forced to give expression to the needs and problems of the least privileged in this society.[46] Cooper wrote in a college questionnaire in 1932 that her chief cultural interest was "the education of the underprivileged," and indeed the fullest expression of her feminism and her intellectual life is to be found in her work as an educator. Still, I do not want to minimize the accomplishment of *A Voice From the South.* It is the most precise, forceful, well-argued statement of black feminist thought to come out of the nineteenth century. Ironically, Cooper and other black women intellectuals were very much like poor black women who were engaged in the most difficult and poorly rewarded physical labor: They did the work that no one else was willing to do.

Notes

1. Interview with Dr. Paul Phillips Cooke, Washington, D.C., May 1985.

2. Louise Daniel Hutchinson, staff historian, Anacostia Neighborhood Museum of the Smithsonian Institution. Mrs. Hutchinson told me this story in a telephone interview, May 1985.

3. Anna Julia Cooper, *A Voice From the South by a Black Woman of the South* (New York: Negro Universities Press, 1969), 136. (Originally published in Xenia, Ohio: Aldine Printing House, 1892.)

4. Ibid., 31.

5. Ibid., 75.

6. Mary Church Terrell, in *Twentieth-Century Negro Literature; or, a Cyclopedia of Thought on the Vital Topics Relating to the American Negro, by One Hundred of America's Greatest Negroes*, ed. D. W. Culp (Naperville, Ill.: J. L. Nichols & Co. 1902), 174–75. Cited in Bert Loewenberg and Ruth Bogin, eds., *Black Women in Nineteenth-Century American Life: Their Words, Their Thoughts, Their Feelings* (University Park: The Pennsylvania University Press, 1976), 23.

7. An excellent discussion of the pressure felt by nineteenth-century black women to defend themselves against the charge of immorality is found in Paula Giddings, *When and Where I Enter: The Impact of Black Women on Race and Sex in America* (New York: William Morrow and Company, Inc., 1984).

8. An undated autobiographical account of her birth by Anna J. Cooper, Courtesy Moorland-Spingarn Research Center, Howard University. Reprinted in Louise D. Hutchinson, *Anna J. Cooper: A Voice From the South* (Washington, D.C.: Smithsonian Press, 1982), 4.

9. Anna Julia Cooper papers, courtesy Moorland-Spingarn Research Center, Howard University.

10. Cooper, *A Voice From the South*, 77.

11. Ibid., 49.

12. Among the distinguished graduates of Dunbar High School were Benjamin O. Davis, the first black U.S. general; Judge William Hastie, a U.S. appeals court judge and the first black governor of the Virgin Islands; Dr. Charles Drew, who devised the method of storing blood plasma in banks; Senator Edward Brook of Massachusetts, the first black U.S. senator since Reconstruction; Robert Weaver, secretary of the U.S. Department of Housing and Urban Development under President Kennedy; and Eleanor Holmes Norton, chair of the federal Equal Employment Opportunity Commission under President Carter.

13. Letter from Annette Eaton to Leona C. Gabel, 1977. Smith College Archives.

14. Letter from Annette Eaton to Leona Gabel, October 11, 1977. Smith College Archives.

15. Hutchinson, *Anna J. Cooper*, 67–84.

16. Letter from Annette Eaton to Leona Gabel, September 4, 1977. Smith College Archives.

17. Telephone interview with Louise D. Hutchinson, May 1985.

18. Anna J. Cooper, *The Third Step*, 5. Anna Julia Cooper Papers, courtesy Moorland-Spingarn Research Center, Howard University.

19. Ibid., 6.

20. Cooper, *A Voice From the South*, 78, 79.

21. Letter from Frederick Douglass to M. A. Majors, August 26, 1892. Reprinted in Dorothy Sterling, ed., *We Are Your Sisters: Black Women in the Nineteenth Century* (New York: W. W. Norton, 1984), 436.

22. Alfred A. Moss, Jr., *The American Negro Academy: Voice of the Talented Tenth* (Baton Rouge: Louisiana State University Press, 1981), 38.

23. Letter to W. E. B. Du Bois, 1929. Anna Julia Cooper Papers.

24. Letter to W. E. B. Du Bois, October 27, 1929. Anna Julia Cooper Papers.

25. W. E. B. Du Bois, "On the Damnation of Women," in *Darkwater: Voices from within the Veil* (New York: Schocken Books, 1969), 173.

26. Cooper, *A Voice From the South*, 74.

27. Letter to Francis Grimké, April 9, 1936. Anna Julia Cooper Papers.

28. Cooper, *A Voice From the South*, 186.

29. News article on Wright and Hughes. Anna Julia Cooper Papers.

30. Hazel Carby, "'On the Threshold of Woman's Era': Lynching, Empire, and Sexuality in Black Feminist Theory," *Critical Inquiry* 12 (Autumn 1985): 262–77.

31. Cooper, A Voice from the South, 254–55.

32. Ibid., 116.

33. Ibid., 123.

34. Ibid., 144.

35. Ibid., 137–38.

36. For a discussion of the ideology of true womanhood, see Barbara Welter, "The Cult of True Womanhood: 1800–1860," in *Dimity Convictions: The American Woman in the Nineteenth Century* (Athens: Ohio University Press, 1976), 21–41.

37. Cooper, *A Voice from the South*, 141.

38. Ibid., 76.

39. Ibid., 68–69.

40. Ibid., 70–71.

41. Ibid., 72.

42. Sterling, *We Are Your Sisters*, 434.

43. This list of attributes is suggested by a speech given by Fannie Barrier Williams to the World's Congress of Representative Women in 1893 entitled

"The Intellectual Progress of the Colored Women of the United States Since the Emancipation Proclamation," reprinted in Loewenberg and Begin, *Black Women in Nineteenth-Century American Life*, 272.

44. Ibid., 277.

45. The first contemporary documentation of the intellectual tradition of nineteenth-century black women was Loewenberg and Bogin's *Black Women in Nineteenth-Century American Life* in 1976.

46. Ibid., 21.

Chapter 12

A Singing Something
Womanist Reflections on Anna Julia Cooper

KAREN BAKER-FLETCHER

God and Reform

For Anna Julia Cooper, the most sacred and noble lesson of the Gospels was love for one another regardless of color. This, in her view, was the most important message of Christ's teaching. Only in receiving all of God's people equally, she suggested in her choice of scripture, can one receive Christ. She implied that those who claim to be Christians and limit their understanding of equality to people of their own race are not true Christians at all.

In her essay "Has America a Race Problem? If So, How Can It Best Be Solved?" Cooper wrote of race as being like a family.[1] Like other women in the Black women's club movement, she was concerned about White attempts to exterminate Black men and women. Following the lead of Ida B. Wells-Barnett, she and her contemporaries sought an end to the practice of lynching. Extermination of the race, particularly in the South, was a real threat. There is no need, she argued, to exterminate others:

> Men will here [in America] learn that a race, as a family, may be true to itself without seeking to exterminate all others. That for the note of the feeblest there is room, nay a positive need, in the harmonies of God. That the principles of true democracy are founded in universal reciprocity, and that "A man's a man" was written when God first stamped His own image and superscription on His child and breathed into his nostrils the breath of life.[2]

In the harmonies of God, race is not at all problematic, because all of humankind bears God's image and is God's child. These are familiar principles to contemporary readers. But Cooper wrote during a time when Black writers were challenging the White supremacist views of those who identified with the Ku Klux Klan, the "night riders," for the first time. She wrote during a period when many White Americans openly questioned the humanity of Black Americans. To claim that Black people were created in the image of God undoubtedly sounded as radical to the ears of many White Americans then as the Black liberationist claim that God is Black sounds to many White people today.

Criticizing White supremacist claims, Cooper contended that the supremacy of one race could not ultimately prevail in America, a continent "held in equilibrium by such conflicted forces and by so many and such strong fibred races."[3] She questioned the viability of racial supremacy on American soil, arguing that with its multiracial makeup America would inevitably be required to recognize God's image as being stamped on all races. In 1925, in her doctoral defense, "Equality of Races and the Democratic Movement," Cooper argued against theories that democracy, progress, and equality manifested themselves only in Western civilization. For Cooper, these principles were not the property of a superior race. Rather they were innate principles given to all humankind:

> Is it not reasonable to grant that if our theory regarding the elite of nations is not sufficiently comprehensive to include a nation with such a creditable recommendation, that we should either enlarge our definition to harmonize with the facts or else treat the subject of Equality not as an abstraction but as it manifests itself uniquely in Europe and in America? A better hypothesis it seems to me, would be the postulate that progress in the democratic sense is an inborn human endowment—a shadow mark of the Creator's image, or if you will an urge-cell, the universal and unmistakable hall-mark traceable to the Father of all.[4]

"Progress in the democratic sense," she hypothesized, was an "inborn human endowment" and "a shadow mark of the Creator's image." Democratic progress could be traced right back to God. It was an ordained, God-given reality in human history. Further, humankind was endowed with such principles. In this way, humanity is created in God's likeness. Democratic progress most essentially had to do with freedom and equality. In a nutshell, then, human beings were created fully equal and free by their Creator, God.[5]

Moving beyond classical metaphors of "image," Dr. Cooper further referred to humankind's likeness to God as a "*Singing* Something." This "Singing Something" distinguishes humankind from apes. Democratic principles in humankind are also like a divine spark capable of awakening at any moment and "never wholly smothered or stamped out." Democratic principles, like an "urge-cell," a "divine spark," a *Singing* Something, surge forth from era to era calling for reform.[6] Thus, Cooper argued, the racial group or nation that supposes to play God by dominating the earth takes on a terrible responsibility.[7] She warned of the revolutions that met dominating governments in Russia, China, Turkey, Egypt, and the Gandhi movement in India as examples of the power of democratic principles of freedom and equality in the human spirit.

Where is God's presence evident for Cooper? God is in the very *movement* of reform. God is in this *Singing* Something in human being that rises up against injustice and moves onward toward a full realization of freedom. God is the power of freedom and equality that moves them forward. What is striking about her metaphor is that one can conceptualize God as a liberating voice within human being. Such words are suggestive for contemporary liberation theology. They suggest that something of the liberating voice of God rises up and speaks through those who resist domination. It eventually flares, comes to voice, and rises up.

This has empowering implications for liberationist and womanist theologies. To conceive of God's message of freedom and equality as innate in the human spirit is empowering for the silenced and voiceless, for those whose knowledge has been trampled down to the underside of history, for those whose voices have been muted in the history of the Western Church with its distortions of the Gospel. If this divine message of freedom and equality that sparks and sings within humanity can never truly be suppressed by a dominating race or nation, then the proper role of the Church is to empower the politically powerless to find their voices. The movement toward freedom and equality is part of an unquenchable universal process. For Christians Jesus exemplified these principles in his work and teachings.

Cooper and Nineteenth-Century Feminism

When Anna Cooper published *A Voice from the South* in 1892, women did not have the right to vote, and for a woman to speak in the public sphere to mixed-sex audiences was considered unladylike. Women's proper place was seen as the domestic sphere, and women had few property rights. African American women did not have the right to vote and were denied equal opportunities in the economic and educational spheres.

Because women in the Black women's club movement were both Black and female, they were sympathetic to human rights issues for both women and for the Black community. Similarly, White feminists had compared the lot of White women in America to slavery. Mid-century, many had been abolitionists. Early White feminism emerged in part out of sexist reactions to White women abolitionists. But by the end of the nineteenth century, White feminists such as Carrie Chapman Catt and Elizabeth Cady Stanton had taken on a White supremacist ideology in order to argue for White women's qualifications to vote over and against those of Blacks, European immigrants, and Native Americans. Stanton argued that White women were more qualified to vote than illiterate Black men. Black women found themselves excluded from the White women's movement, particularly in the South. Afraid that Southern women would be offended by Black women's presence at conventions, Northern White women discouraged and often barred Black women from attending meetings.[8]

"There is no grander and surer prophecy of the new era and of woman's place in it, than the work already begun … by the Women's Christian Temperance Union (WCTU) In America," Cooper asserted.[9] She saw the WCTU as prefiguring women's increasing power as a moral factor. As for Black women, she argued that in such a transitional, unsettled period, their status seemed "one of the least ascertainable and definitive of all the forces which make for our civilization."[10] Colored women, "confronted by both a woman question and a race problem," were "an unknown or unacknowledged factor in both." All the same, she argued, colored women should not be ignored. White feminists ought to include Black women's rights in the women's movement.

Black women's opinion was valuable, Cooper explained, as demonstrated by the writer and lecturer Frances Ellen Watkins Harper, by preachers Sojourner Truth and Amanda Berry Smith, and by the poet/reformer Charlotte Forten Grimké. Their analysis and possible solutions for the problems of racism and sexism were invaluable. Cooper asserted that Negro women were "able to grasp the deep significance of the possibilities of the crisis," a unique heritage in human history.[11] Her most famous statement on Black womanhood is still quoted today: "Only the Black woman can say, 'When and where I enter, in the quiet, undisputed dignity of my womanhood, without violence and without suing or special patronage, then and there the whole *Negro race enters with me.*'"[12]

In the thought of Anna Cooper, the Black woman was the vital and essential element in the regeneration of the race. Similarly, for Cooper, women worldwide across races and culture were the fundamental agents in the development of a race or culture. Why? Because women as mothers were the trainers, teachers, and educators from the moment they educated young children at their feet. Thus, they were the earliest influence for all those who would become women and men. In her chapter on "The Higher Education of Women," Cooper suggested that even silent, educated Christian women had influence and power, as did vocal women who taught: "The earnest well trained Christian young woman, as a teacher, as a home-maker, as wife, mother, or silent influence even, is as potent a missionary agency among our people as is the theologian; and I claim that at the present stage of our development in the South she is even more important and necessary."[13] Christian faith and intellectual development in Cooper's view made for a woman who would be foundational in the regeneration of a race or a society. Cooper's understanding of the nobility of womanhood, particularly of women as mothers, was characteristic of the era in which she wrote. In popular literature and in early women's movement circles there was a strong ideal of true womanhood, particularly of motherhood. The more conservative view was that women's sphere was domestic, man's sphere public.[14] Women influenced men and children morally in the domestic sphere, passing on in subtle, gentle ways their civilizing influence. Early feminists did not reject the ideal of the true woman as being endowed with greater moral wisdom and strength. Rather, they employed the ideal of true womanhood, reforming it like clay, to further their arguments for the women's movement. Precisely because women were endowed with greater moral feeling they should be involved in the public sphere. Women's powers of moral persuasion, early feminists argued, were greatly needed in government and in education.

There was tension between early White and Black feminists, because White feminists found it to their political advantage to adopt racist and supremacist rhetoric to further their cause. Barbara Andolsen points out that race and class prejudice underlay White feminist appropriation of the myth of True Womanhood. White suffragists chose to manipulate the belief that Anglo-Saxons were uniquely qualified to create good governments to advance the case for women's voting rights.[15] White supremacist and classist ideologies were implicit in much of the White feminists' appropriation of the myth of True Womanhood:

> White feminists openly manipulated white supremacist ideology in order to persuade Anglo-Saxon men to share political power with Anglo-Saxon women. They appealed to a more subtle form of race and class prejudice when they invoked the American myth of True Womanhood . . . The True Woman was almost certainly the wife of a well-to-do male (usually white and native-born) whose economic success made it possible for her to reign as queen of the home. Poor women, Black women, and immigrant women often led lives that precluded the development of a "refined," "feminine" character.[16]

Cooper's *A Voice from the South* was all the more significant as a feminist text because it sought to address the feminist concerns of Black women in a social environment in which White feminists on the whole found the inclusion of Black women problematic to the furtherance of their cause. Cooper employed the myth of True Womanhood to meet the needs and experience of her ideal of the Black woman. Her voice was that of a Black feminist. She took a model of womanhood originally meant to be descriptive of conservative, White, middle-class womanhood and reshaped it to her perception of Black women's needs and experiences. Cooper chided Black men, White men, and White women for presuming to speak for Black women. She published A *Voice from the South* to present the concerns of Black womanhood in the voice of a Black woman from the South. Anna Cooper's voice was unique because she presented an early feminist perspective on race and gender and because she demanded an inclusive conceptualization of women's issues as universal issues in the movement for human freedom.

On the one hand, Cooper, like liberation theologians today, argued from the standpoint of particularity. She spoke with great strength and consciousness from the standpoint of Black womanhood, aware of her particular dignity in the midst of race and gender oppression. She was aware of Christianity as her particular religious framework and focus. On the other hand, she was conscious of the interrelationship of the problems of Black Christian women and women of diverse cultures and religions.[17] She found it essential to return to a universal standpoint. There are certain universal truths, eternal verities, she argued, that are essential to human life in all religions—like freedom and benevolence.

Freedom: A Universal Birthright

In her essay "Woman versus the Indian," Cooper set forth some of her most acerbic criticisms of racism in the White feminist movement. But Cooper was not simply critical. She wanted to get on with a fuller vision of the task at hand—the task of human freedom. Therefore, she presented constructive ideas on Christ and freedom from a Black, feminist perspective.

The context for Cooper's critique and constructive analysis of the problem of racism in the women's movement is her response to a speech presented by Methodist preacher Anna Howard Shaw. Cooper inveighed a harsh critique against Shaw's speech "Indians versus Woman," charging that the topic was indicative of a more general "caste" mentality in America.[18] She first expressed admiration for Shaw and applauded her for her attitude toward Black women. She recognized, for example, Shaw's and Susan B. Anthony's efforts on one occasion to include Cooper in a meeting of Wimodaughsis (a women's club for women, mothers, daughters, and sisters) despite racial opposition:

> In the National Woman's Council convened at Washington in February 1891, among a number of thoughtful and suggestive papers read by eminent women, was one by the Rev. Anna Shaw, bearing the above title [Woman versus the Indian]. That Miss Shaw is broad and just in principal [sic] is proved beyond contradiction. Her noble generosity and womanly firmness are unimpeachable. The unwavering stand taken by herself and Miss [Susan B.] Anthony in the subsequent color ripple in Wimodaughsis ought to be sufficient to allay forever any doubts as to the pure gold of these two women.[19]

But Cooper's expression of admiration for Shaw serves as a basis for expressing profound disappointment in the racist overtones of Shaw's speech.[20] Shaw argued that women's ability to vote had been overlooked, while a share in government had been granted to Native American men—who in her view were less civilized and less capable of government. Although elsewhere Shaw applauded the innate moral character of Native Americans, Cooper was offended by the racism of Shaw's views on Native American men's ability to vote.[21] Cooper paraphrased the racist arguments that White women used to plea for suffrage:

> The great burly black man, ignorant and gross and depraved, is allowed to vote; while the franchise is withheld from the intelligent and refined, the pure-minded and lofty souled white woman. Even the untamed and un-

tamable Indian of the prairie, who can answer nothing but "ugh" to great economic and civic questions is thought by some worthy to wield the ballot which is still denied the Puritan maid and the first lady of Virginia.[22]

In Cooper's judgment, such argumentation amounted to a suit of "Eye vs. Foot," each of which is a vital, necessary part of one body, one organism. She argued that women should not be plaintiff in a suit versus the Indian, Negro, or any other race or class "crushed under the iron heel of Anglo-Saxon power and selfishness."[23] Her interpretation of the Gospel as revealing a universal principle of human freedom is central to her argument for social justice across racial and gender lines. This birthright, she argued, belongs to women and men of every race. And to the extent that it belongs to each gender and to every race of human being, this birthright of freedom transcends race and gender even as it belongs to and is the concern of each one.

Cooper called attention to the need for White women to apply the Golden Rule by recognizing that freedom is not the exclusive right of an individual group or person. While she was aware of the needs of particular groups, she saw herself as engaged in a universal cause for freedom: "The philosophic mind sees that its own 'rights' are the rights of humanity. That in the universe of God . . . the recognition it seeks is . . . through the universal application ultimately of the Golden Rule."[24]

Women, men, and persons across color lines, Cooper argued, are created sacred, in the image of God.[25] With a keen sense of the rights and dignity of the individual, she challenged White women to recognize individual human rights across racial lines. "Let her [woman] try to teach her country that every interest in this world is entitled at least to a respectful hearing, that every sentiency is worthy of its own gratification," she prophetically proclaimed. Believing that people of all races are created in the image of God, Cooper further argued for the sacredness of the rights of individuals, proclaiming that:

> when the image of God in human form, whether in marble or in clay, whether in alabaster or in ebony, is consecrated and inviolable, when men have been taught to look beneath the rags and grime, the pomp and pageantry of mere circumstance and have regard unto the celestial kernel uncontaminated at the core . . . then is mastered the science of politeness, the art of courteous contact, which is naught but the application of the principal [sic] of benevolence, the back bone and marrow of all religion; then woman's lesson is taught and woman's cause is won.[26]

All, she argued, are worthy of a hearing. All are created in the image of God and are sacred. Thus women must extend benevolence—the backbone and marrow of all religion—to persons of every race and class. Cooper saw the women's movement as a continuation of a never-ending reform. She suggested that reform in each age is embodied in a different movement. White women, she argued, must recognize their continuity with a larger movement than the one they were most immediately aware of. This movement that courses throughout the ages, in Cooper's thinking, was the movement of freedom—the very birthright of humanity:

> The cause of freedom is not the cause of a race or a sect, a party or a class,—it is the cause of human kind, the very birthright of humanity. Now unless we are greatly mistaken the Reform of our day, known as the Woman's Movement, is essentially such an embodiment, if its pioneers could only realize it, of the universal good. And specially important is it that there be no confusion of ideas among its leaders as to its scope and universality.[27]

Cooper saw the women's movement as a particular embodiment of a universal good. In the process it was necessary to remember one's interconnectedness with the good of others across race, class, and gender.[28] Cooper made reference to the parable of the Good Samaritan in her argument for universal human rights. She demanded that White suffragists ask, "Who is my neighbor?" Cooper agreed with Shaw's and Anthony's concerns for women's suffrage, as long as they affirmed a Christian theology that emphasized universal principles and a "love of neighbor," regardless of class, race, or sex. White women, she argued, must be inclusive in their understanding of who the right of freedom belonged to. They needed to recognize "the red woman" and "the black woman" as their neighbors. Cooper contended that "it is important and fundamental that there be no chromatic or other aberration when the teacher is settling the point, 'Who is my neighbor?'"[29]

Cooper argued that a woman who claimed or desired to be a teacher of morals must clear her eyes of "all mists" in order to see clearly "Who is my neighbor?"[30] She portrayed White women as having their vision blurred by mists. She saw their failure to see the humanity of Black women and other women of color as a problem of vision, which needed correction. White women, she suggested, had misperceived the Gospel. Only with corrected vision could they fully see their neighbors and the Gospel's message of freedom.

Further, Cooper asserted that women must understand that the world needs to hear their voice on social issues, specifically in the realm of morals. The world must hear not only the voice of White women on moral and social reform, however, but the voices of women of color in America and around the globe: "It is not the intelligent woman vs. the ignorant woman; nor the white woman vs. the black, the brown, and the red,—it is not even the cause of woman vs. man. Nay, 'tis woman's strongest vindication for speaking that the world needs to hear her voice."[31]

As for Black women, only Black women themselves, Cooper argued, are able to speak on behalf of Black women. She criticized White women, White men, and Black men who would attempt to speak for Black women. I would like to introduce here some of the possible reasons for the use of the word "voice" in the singular. Feminist and womanist theologians today are conscious of religious and cultural pluralism. To speak of the "voice of the Black woman" sounds odd to our ears, because we are aware of the multiplicity of women's voices across and within different cultures.

Cooper lived in a world in which there was an organized group of Black women, many of whom were well-educated, who traveled on the lecture circuit to speak out on issues of racism and sexism. Whether or not participants in the Black women's club movement agreed on every method for attaining racial uplift, they agreed on common issues and goals. These women spoke, wrote, and acted on social issues in "solidarity." And, to the extent that they spoke, wrote, and acted on issues of racism and sexism in solidarity, it is understandable that Cooper saw herself as being part of one voice, one movement, one cause. She was part of a minority group of educated, outspoken women who found it necessary to speak in relative unity on social issues in order to be heard.

Cooper's intention was to speak in solidarity with other Black women as a representative voice. What is problematic is that her audience is a middle-class audience. While she claims to speak on behalf of Black women, including the masses, she rarely appears to speak with or to them. While she was aware that there were many voices among Black women, she tended to speak for them. Why? She probably considered it an act of altruism and benevolence. Undoubtedly she felt that since she was in a position to gain an audience it was her responsibility to speak for those who did not have the opportunities for publishing and speaking that were available to her and her peers. Today, womanists must seek ways of standing in solidarity with an entire people across class lines by insisting on an audience for a diversity of voices.

Gender Roles

Cooper's conception of woman as the essential element in the progress and regeneration of a race rests on two presuppositions: first, women are the earliest educators of women and men—the world's future leaders; and second, women as the dominated sex across race and culture have a stronger moral sensitivity, are more greatly endowed in feeling, and because of their own domination ought to have greater sympathy for the weak and the dominated. She further believed that women should extend their sympathy to all the world's dominated by working against socioeconomic and political inequality.

I have discussed Cooper's concept of Christ as a depositor of ideals, in the form of the Gospel, which requires millennia for its growth and ripening in human civilization and culture. As for women, Cooper saw the historical Jesus as laying down a code of morality equal for men and women. She interpreted the life and death of Christ as giving men a guide for the estimation of women as equals and friends as well as helpers:

> By laying down for woman the same code of morality, the same standard of purity, as for man; by refusing to countenance the shameless and equally guilty monsters who were gloating over her fall,—graciously stooping in all the majesty of his own spotlessness to wipe away the filth and grime of her guilty past and bid her go in peace and sin no more . . . throughout his life and in his death he has given to men a rule and guide for the estimation of woman as an equal, as a helper, as a friend, and as a sacred charge to be sheltered and cared for with a brother's love and sympathy, lessons which nineteen centuries' gigantic strides in knowledge, arts, and sciences, in social and ethical principles have not been able to probe to their depth or to exhaust in practice.[32]

This syncretism of a concept of equality between men and women on the one hand and traditional models of women as helper and men as protectors on the other hand were characteristic of nineteenth-century feminist argumentation.[33] In Cooper's case, her emphasis on women's need for protection, care, and shelter was meant to counter the overriding abuse of Black women in the South.[34]

Black women were not accorded the same rights over their bodies as middle-class White women. To the contrary, they were stereotyped as having no sexual morals and therefore as unworthy of respect.[35] So Cooper presented Christ's formula and example for relations between the sexes as one in which women were treated and respected as equals, friends, and helpers and as worthy of respect and protection.

For Cooper, equality between men and women did not abolish gender distinctions in terms of attributes or roles. She described "man" as physically superior and more cooly rational. But, she clarified, man had abused his physical strength and rationalism to coldly dominate the "weaker" sex and weaker cultures. Woman, on the other hand, stood for the preservation of the deep, moral forces of social righteousness. Therefore, Cooper asserted, "In the era now about to dawn, her sentiments must strike the keynote and give the dominant tone. And this because of the nature of her contribution to the world.[36] Cooper portrayed this "dominant tone" as different from male political domination:

> Her kingdom is not over physical forces. Not by might, nor by power can she prevail. Her position must ever be inferior where strength of muscle creates leadership. If she follows the instincts of her nature, however, she must always stand for the conservation of those deeper moral forces which make for the happiness of homes and the righteousness of the country. In a reign of moral ideas she is easily queen.[37]

The language of "dominant tone" to describe the potential compassion in women's leadership is problematic in moving away from systems of domination. What is most helpful is Cooper's concept of a society that realizes social, political, economic, and ontological equality among human beings with compassion. Essentially, Cooper accepted the ideal of woman as the conservator of deep moral forces that made for the happiness of homes and the righteousness of American government and culture. She described women as inferior in areas where leadership depended on "strength of muscle." But here Cooper's wit was at play once again. Cooper decried leadership created by strength of muscle. For Cooper, "woman's cause is the cause of the weak." Cooper criticized Anna Howard Shaw for the disparagement of the weak implied in her speech "Indians versus Women" by arguing that "woman should not, even by inference, or for the sake of argument, seem to disparage what is weak. For woman's cause is the cause of the weak."[38]

By "the weak," Cooper meant those who did not strive to attain greatness and power through physical domination. She meant all those who are dominated by patriarchal, imperialistic, and racist rule, including women. The weak included White women, Native American women and men, people of African descent around the globe, and Asians. She had in mind persons who were lacking physical strength and military power. Today, liberation theologians would refer to these various groups as "the oppressed." Cooper's critique of domination was a critique of European and American imperialism. She opposed the subjugation of women and people of color around the globe.

Cooper based her argument against women's disparagement of the weak on the premise that the rights of all the weak are interrelated. She chided Shaw, explaining that "when all the weak shall have received their due consideration, then woman will have her 'rights,' and the Indian will have his rights, and the Negro will have his rights, and all the strong will have learned at last to deal justly, to love mercy, and to walk humbly."[39]

Moreover, Cooper reminded her White feminist audience of the principle of neighborliness in a truly Christian society. When all have learned the universal principles of justice, mercy, and humility, she argued, then, "our fair land will have been taught the secret of universal courtesy which is after all nothing but the art, the science, and the religion of regarding one's neighbor as one's self, and to do for him as we would, were conditions swapped, that he do for us."[40] Critical of militarism and conquest of one nation by another, she decried "brute force" against Black Americans, Africans, Native Americans, and the Chinese. Even in her dissertation, she described the Haitian military revolt as a necessary but unfortunate response to France's militaristic, imperialistic failure to follow its own democratic principles.

Inner, moral strength was preferable to physical strength, Cooper thought—it belongs to the order of justice. The weak, she asserted, are more merciful than the strong. They have a greater understanding of mercy. The strong, that is those who historically have been oppressive, must learn to be merciful from the weak. Cooper suggested that woman's lesson of mercy could work in symmetry with man's task of truth and that man's ideal of rightness together with woman's ideal of peace would result in a more just world.[41]

Anna Cooper saw the nineteenth-century women's movement as the beginning of a new era in which civilization would realize positive social developments. She gave a long but eloquent description of the variety of social injustices women's contributions would correct in the twentieth century. "Religion, science, art, economics, have all needed the feminine flavor; and literature, the expression of what is permanent and best in all of these, may be gauged at any time to measure the strength of the feminine ingredient," she argued.[42] Envisioning a world that included women's leadership, she sharply contrasted such a world against a male-dominated society and challenged theological, social, economic, and political absurdities such as infant damnation, an impersonal God, economic inequality in marriage, and supply and demand economics. She put it this way:

> You will not find theology consigning infants to lakes of unquenchable fire long after women have had a chance to grasp, master, and wield its dogmas. You will not find science annihilating personality from the government of the Universe and making of God an ungovernable, unintelligible, blind, often destructive physical force; you will not find jurisprudence formulating as an axiom the absurdity that man and wife are one, and that one the man—that the married woman may not hold or bequeath her own property save as subject to her husband's direction; you will not find political economists declaring that the only possible adjustment between laborers and capitalists is that of selfishness and rapacity— that each must get all he can and keep all that he gets, while the world cries laissez faire and the lawyers explain, "it is the beautiful working of the law of supply and demand"; in fine, you will not find the law of love shut out from the affairs of men after the feminine half of the world's truth is completed.[43]

Women's half of the world's truth would balance the scales of justice. Cooper asserted that it is "transmitting the potential forces of her [woman's] soul into dynamic factors that has given symmetry and completeness to the world's agencies."[44] She challenged women to generate a new kind of civilization. Women must demand that principles of peace and mercy work together with ideals of truth and righteousness to generate a society that is merciful in its attitudes toward children, believes in a God of peace rather than of physical force, gives equal property rights to women, and declares economic justice for working people. The feminine principles of love, peace, and mercy would complete the world's truth. There would be sympathy for the weak. There would be an amelioration of social situations, compassion for human suffering:

> Nay, put your ear now close to the pulse of the time. What is the keynote of the literature of these days? What is the banner cry of all the activities of the last half decade? What is the dominant seventh which is to add

richness and tone to the final cadences of this century and lead by a grand modulation into the triumphant harmonies of the next? Is it not compassion for the poor and unfortunate, and as Bellamy has expressed it, "indignant outcry against the failure of the social machinery as it is, to ameliorate the miseries of men"?[45]

In Cooper's writings, compassion for the poor and unfortunate is a standard of justice, the dominant seventh that adds richness and tone. Women, because of their own domination, have no excuse for a lack of sympathy. The very value of women is their ability to sympathize with the rest of the world's weak, that is, the rest of the world's oppressed peoples. Women, from their own experience, Cooper suggested, understand the problem of domination. Their experiential understanding of the failure of domination and of the call for compassion as a standard of justice is a vital element in the regeneration of a society.

Although Cooper claimed that neither women nor men were superior to the other, she portrayed women as the best potential leaders of a new era. She conceded that there are compassionate, feeling, sympathetic men but clarified that such men learn these virtues at some mother's feet. The masculine virtue of intellect and the feminine virtue of sympathy emerge as most vividly embodied in women in her early essays. Educated women, in her view, were the future leaders of the new era. She employed gender-typing as a literary device to argue for women's leadership.

Women would herald in a more compassionate social order. Cooper suggested that women are a vital element of the reign of God, because she went on to state that Christianity is part and parcel of the social amelioration she envisioned. True Christianity is on the side of the poor and the weak. It too is "brought to the bar of humanity and tried by the standard of its ability to alleviate the world's suffering and lighten and brighten its woe."[46] In other words, Christianity is not exempt from God's judgment. It is a religion among religions. It is not sacred in and of itself. It is a human cultural institution that seeks to attain knowledge of who God is.

Christians are imperfect in their understanding of who God is and the meaning of God's revelation in history. They participate in God's activity of alleviating the world's suffering imperfectly and with great difficulty. Cooper asks, "What else can be the meaning of Matthew Arnold's saddening protest, 'We cannot do without Christianity, . . . and we cannot endure it as it is'?"

Notes

1. Anna Julia Cooper, "Has American a Race Problem? If So, How Can It Best Be Solved?" In *A Voice from the South*, ed. Mary Helen Washington, Schomburg Library of Nineteenth-Century Black Women Writers (1892; New York: Oxford University Press, 1988), 168.

2. Ibid. Cooper used traditional, that is, masculine, language to describe humankind and God. She was in keeping with her social-historian context.

3. Ibid., 165.

4. Anna Julia Cooper, "Equality of Races and the Democratic Movement," privately printed pamphlet, Washington, D.C., 1945, 4–5.

5. See ibid., 4–9. Cooper refuted the notion of her examiner, Dr. Bougle of the Sorbonne, that there were certain "elite" nations and races who were "privileged as the most advanced to carry the torch of civilization for the enlightenment of the 'Backward races.'"

6. Ibid.

7. Ibid., 5.

8. See Barbara Andolsen, *"Daughters of Jefferson, Daughters of Bootblacks": Racism and American Feminism* (Macon, Ga.: Mercer University Press, 1986), 31–35. She quotes Stanton: "American women of wealth, virtue and refinement, if you do not wish the lower orders of Chinese, Africans, Germans and Irish, with their low ideas of womanhood to make laws for you ... demand that woman, too, shall be represented in the government."

9. Ibid., 134. The Women's Christian Temperance Union, founded in 1874, developed into a major movement within the nineteenth-century women's movement. Under Frances Willard's leadership, it became one of the greatest women's organizations in the United States. The WCTU endorsed suffrage as early as 1887. See Paula Giddings, *When and Where I Enter: The Impact of Black Women on Race and Sex in America* (New York: William Morrow, 1984), 91.

10. Andolsen, *"Daughters of Jefferson, Daughters of Bootblacks,"* 134.

11. Ibid., 144.

12. Cooper, "Womanhood a Vital Element in the Regeneration and Progress of a Race," in *A Voice from the South*, 31.

13. Cooper, "The Higher Education of Women," in *A Voice from the South*, 79.

14. See Barbara Welter, *Dimity Convictions: The American Woman in the Nineteenth Century* (Athens: Ohio University Press, 1976), 21–41. Early to mid-nineteenth-century women's magazines and religious literature (1820–1860) presented ideals of True Womanhood: women's purity, piety, submissiveness, and domesticity. Feminists used the ideal of women's piety and purity to argue for women's natural abilities as leaders in society as well as in the home.

15. See Barbara Andolsen, *"Daughters of Jefferson, Daughters of Bootblacks,"* 21. Andolsen has written an incisive study of racism and sexism in the nineteenth-century women's movement.

16. Ibid., 45.

17. In "Womanhood a Vital Element in the Regeneration and Progress of a Race," 9–11, Cooper was critical of Islam's subjugation of women. Later, in "The Gain from a Belief" (in *A Voice from the South*, 301–302), she positively cited Mohammed as an example of the power of religious belief. Cooper compared Christ and Buddha as breaking caste systems in "Has America a Race Problem? If So How Can It Be Solved?" in *A Voice from the South*, 154–55. Cooper held that religion, in all its diversity, was the source of all ideas on the fulfillment of human potential.

18. For information on Anna Shaw's attitude toward Native Americans, see Barbara Andolsen, "Racism and Nativism," in *"Daughters of Jefferson, Daughters of Bootblacks,"* 31–33. Andolsen notes that in their descriptions of Native Americans whom they had observed in South Dakota in 1890, White women suffragists Anna Shaw and Carrie Chapman Catt perpetuated the notion that Indians were less capable of self-government than White women, dwelling on details that made Native Americans seem less civilized. Although she claimed no moral superiority, Shaw found it repulsive that Native American men—far less civil than White women according to the Euro-American standard—were granted a share in government, while White women were disfranchised.

19. Cooper, "Woman versus the Indian," in *A Voice From the South*, 80.

20. See Andolsen, *"Daughters of Jefferson, Daughters of Bootblacks,"* 33–34; from Anna Howard Shaw, "Indians versus Women," *Woman's Tribune*, May 9, 1891.

21. Ibid.

22. Cooper, "Woman versus the Indian," 123. See also Andolsen on Cooper, *"Daughters of Jefferson, Daughters of Bootblacks,"* 41–42.

23. Cooper, "Woman versus the Indian," 123.

24. Ibid., 118.

25. Ibid., 120–22.

26. Ibid., 124–25.

27. Ibid., 120–21.

28. Cooper's rhetoric is similar to that of the Social Gospel, which emphasized the Fatherhood of God and the brotherhood of man to call attention to the significance of human interconnectedness and social feeling.

29. Cooper, "Woman versus the Indian," 121.

30. Ibid.

31. Ibid.

32. Cooper, "Womanhood a Vital Element in the Regeneration and Progress of a Race," 17–18.

33. See Andolsen, *"Daughters of Jefferson, Daughters of Bootblacks,"* 44ff.

34. Ibid. See also p. 62.

35. Ibid.

36. Cooper, "The Status of Woman in America," in *A Voice from the South*, 133.

37. Ibid.

38. Cooper, "Woman versus the Indian," 117.

39. Ibid.

40. Ibid.
41. Cooper, "The Higher Education of Women," in *A Voice from the South,* 57.
42. Ibid., 57–58.
43. Ibid.
44. Ibid.
45. Ibid., 58–59.
46. Ibid.

Chapter 13

Arguing from Difference

Cooper, Emerson, Guizot, and a
More Harmonious America

JANICE W. FERNHEIMER

At the end of the nineteenth century amidst the failure of Radical Reconstruction of the 1870s and the rise of Jim Crow laws beginning in the 1890s, Americans were vying to establish their cultural and intellectual status both at home and abroad. The North and South had been competing for political dominance in American culture since pre–Civil War times. After the Civil War, the "fall" of the South, and the abolition of slavery, however, the question of what constituted legitimate, authentic American culture became important not only on a national level, but on an international one as well. Who would be responsible for representing America abroad? As Americans moved West to fulfill their Manifest Destiny, making their imprint on the physical land, they also were embroiled in a deep cultural battle on the intellectual front. This conflict is reflected in the development of the higher education system and the curriculum it instituted. Since the beginning of the nineteenth-century, Americans such as essayist Ralph Waldo Emerson were trying to create and establish an American cultural identity and body of knowledge separate and distinct from America's English, ancestral heritage. In addition, African Americans and others were trying to carve space for themselves within that newly forming American landscape and tradition.

Creating such a space was and in some ways continues to be an especially difficult challenge for African-American intellectuals, because their very existence defies the assumptions most deeply held by dominant white racist discourse and ideology. Even as late as the 1880s, just a few decades after slavery was abolished and the period of Reconstruction officially had ended, many whites still had a hard time recognizing that blacks were indeed fully human, much less capable of advanced intellectual thought. Many believed that blacks were not simply intellectually inferior and therefore uneducable, but worse still, that they were not even capable of civilized conduct in the absence of the social framework that slavery had provided. It is against this backdrop that Anna Julia Cooper's text *A Voice from the South* (1892) enters the scene.[1] This chapter will provide a close reading of Cooper's "Has America a Race Problem? If So, How Can It Best Be Solved?" in an attempt to demonstrate how her conceptual and rhetorical sophistication enable her to work within familiar vocabularies such as those set forth by Emerson and others, in order to advance strong arguments for the necessity of African-American presence in and cultural contribution to America. She successfully deploys the conceptual frameworks of Social Darwinism, nativism, determinism, Nature, and religion as well as the rhetorical forms of anaphora and anthypophora, to argue not only that difference but also the existence and use of free speech are vital, integral elements that contribute to America's dominance and superiority over the European traditions from which America evolved.[2]

Contributing Her Voice to an Intellectual Tradition

Anna Julia Cooper is only one of many black intellectuals of the period who was attempting to reconcile the disconnection between America's ideals as expressed in the Declaration of Independence and Constitution, and the social reality, which did not yet reflect these lofty goals. This topos of the ideal as expressed in official documents, in contrast with the reality of the social structures in place, had been a popular and effective rhetorical tact employed by African-American men and women alike since the abolitionist debates of the 1830s, 1840s, and earlier. And Cooper was not alone in using it in this period. In the numerous battles that African Americans were waging—for basic civil rights, for educational opportunities, for the chance to speak at the World Columbian Exposition at Chicago in 1893—this topos was readily available and skillfully employed. In 1892 alone, many of Cooper's contemporaries also were publishing works to combat the racism and false assumptions undergirding American misconceptions of blacks. In the fight against lynching, Ida B. Wells published *Southern Horrors: Lynch Law in All Its Phases,* and in the battle against racism, Frances Ellens Watkins Harper published *Iola Leroy* that same year. Eleven years later, W. E. B. DuBois would publish *The Souls of Black Folk* (1903), which addressed issues similar to those in Cooper's text. Though she shares many rhetorical strategies with her peers, what sets Cooper apart are her sophisticated intellectual and theoretical developments— her emphasis on the necessity of African-American presence and voice along with her insistence that difference, to the extent that it is a "problem" at all, is a welcome and beneficial one.

In order to better understand how sophisticated her argument is, it is helpful to put Cooper in context. In the essay "DuBois, Emerson, and the 'Fate' of Black Folk," Brian Bremen argues specifically for the benefit of reading Emerson and DuBois in light of one another, and I would like to argue that reading Cooper in light of all three emphasizes how her work not only participates in but also pushes forward the cultural conversation of her time.[3] Linking Emerson and DuBois through the recurrent phrase "double-consciousness" employed by both, Bremen argues that "not just DuBois' idea of double-consciousness" but "nearly all of *The Souls of Black Folk* needs to be read in direct dialogue with Emerson's essay [Fate]" (81). Ultimately, Bremen contends that "DuBois' strategy in *The Souls of Black Folk*—to 'merge his double self into a better and truer self'— empowers Blacks merely by reshaping cultural assumptions about their souls, as it keeps intact the structure of power in Emerson's essay ['Fate']" which therefore makes DuBois' strategy "less oppositional than it is complicit in the production of Emerson's hierarchical 'kingdom of culture'" (87).

In contrast to DuBois, I contend that Cooper *does* make oppositional claims. Cooper's revision of Emerson's "book of Nature" helps redefine American culture and locate a place for African Americans within it. Writing more than ten years before Du Bois, Cooper does not simply make space within the existing cultural structure, thus reifying its power and requiring African Americans to subscribe to it. Instead, like Wells in her campaign against lynching, Cooper works at the level of first premises to redefine American culture entirely. Cooper thus not only makes space for African Americans on their own terms, but also legitimates their centrality and necessity to the nation's well-being. By arguing from the vantage point of difference, Cooper establishes a place for "Negroes" on physical, rhetorical, and political planes in American culture.

The Textual Context

Anna Julia Cooper's text *A Voice From the South* contains a carefully arranged series of essays.[4] As a whole, the text advocates a place for African-American women in particular and African Americans as a race within a larger American context. While each chapter reads "as though it were written for a special occasion or in response to a particular problem of the day," the origins of only two of the essays can be verified.[5]

Amongst the unidentified pieces, "Has America a Race Problem? If So, How Can It Best Be Solved?" seems to be one of the most innovative and provocative. It may in fact be that which is most responsible for earning *A Voice* its positive reviews in the press at the time of its original publication. The *Detroit Plaindealer* wrote that "there has been no book on the race question that has been more gently and forcibly written by either white or black authors."[6] Here the seemingly paradoxical "gently and forcibly" reflects the way Cooper's strong voice employs paradox itself to make her point that difference is essential. The *Kingsley Times* (Iowa) pronounced it "one of the most readable books on the race question of the South."[7] Like the *Plaindealer,* the *Times* also praises the text for its coverage of the "race question." Yet despite the fact that her contemporaries recognized the "race problem" as central to the text as a whole, and in spite of the essay's particular rhetorical savviness, it has received the least critical attention of all the pieces. Most major critical works devoted to Cooper make little or no mention of it, yet "Has America a Race Problem? If So, How Can It Best Be Solved?" sets forth one of the most interesting and intellectually complicated arguments of the collection. In it, Cooper emphasizes the importance of both physical presence and the vocal voice; she argues that both the "race problem" and the role the Negro plays in sustaining it are necessary for the health, wealth, and continued development of the American nation as a whole.

The essay's position within the text is also significant in that it comes directly after "The Status of Woman in America" and thus begins the second part of *A Voice.* Immediately preceding the essay "The Negro as Presented in American Literature," the "Race Problem" essay thus sets the stage for the argument this later essay sets forth: that there need to be black voices in American literature. Here, scholar Karen Baker-Fletcher's reading of the title and subtitles employed in *A Voice from the South* proves instructive. Baker-Fletcher reads the text's division in terms of the musical metaphors implied by the words themselves.[8] The first half of *A Voice*, subtitled "Soprano Obligato," contains essays on womanhood, whereas the second half "deals with the question of the problem of race in American culture, literature, and economics" (136). The "Soprano Obligato" thus "describes the voice of the Black woman as a counter-melody that stands out in the listener's ear and is used to add drama" while also connoting the "separateness" and "isolation of the voices of such women" (136). The musical implications resonate on a political level as well in the essay "Has America a Race Problem," where it is no longer just the voices of women, but the voice of the African-American race as a whole that provides the counter-melody, the drama, the difference necessary for America's progression. The essay's position within the second half of the text whose subtitle, "Tutti ad libitum," "describes the Black community as a whole, its men and women, as an improvisational movement" seems apt (136). By emphasizing the multiplicity of voices, the necessity of making them heard, and the benefit of difference, Cooper's use of music and voice enable her to better make the argument for the ultimate goal of harmony achieved by preserving and highlighting difference.

Throughout *A Voice* as a whole, but in particular in "Has America a Race Problem? If So, How Can It Best Be Solved?" Cooper uses European history and Western culture to enter what Kenneth Burke terms the ongoing "conversation of history."[9] In this essay, she inserts herself into an intellectual tradition that continually debates the nature of social circumstance, as well as the potential benefits and disadvantages of certain races and civilizations in history. Working against a tradition that sees African Americans as intellectually inferior, she quotes from famous and respected intellectuals: Cornelius Tacitus, Hippolyte Adolphe Taine, Ernest Renan, Edward Bellamy, Frances Guizot, and William Shakespeare among them, to demonstrate both her familiarity with the canon and her own academic achievement as an African-American woman. This "name-dropping" enables her to create an authoritative ethos as a speaker familiar with and fluent in the conversation of Western, classical culture.[10]

Once she has earned the respect and trust of her audience, she can then push what is "familiar" in a new direction. She uses several dominant discourses including Social Darwinism, determinism, nativism and

Nature—employed by other recognized intellectual figures such as Spencer
and Emerson—both to ground her in a familiar intellectual tradition and
to enable her to carefully shift the underlying assumptions upon which
these traditions are based. The general movement of the argument can be
broken down into three primary rhetorical shifts: 1) from a focus on European History and the ways that difference enables progress; 2) to the
progressive evolution of society developing on American soil with an emphasis on the uniquely American capacity to enable voice and speech even
to the least powerful groups; 3) to the universal realm of progressive
movement where God ultimately plays the most significant role. By focusing on the ways that her essay can be read in dialogue with Emerson's
1856 essay "Fate" and Guizot's "Lecture II. History of Civilization," we
can see more clearly how her text works within familiar cultural paradigms to set forth some radical ideas.[11] Her use of rhetorical devices such
as anaphora and anthypophora work in conjunction with the musical
metaphors of harmony, tones, and notes to redefine America's "race problem" as a divinely inspired, necessary consequence of European political
and historical development.

Cooper begins the piece at the global—what she terms "world"—
level so she can incorporate and address the widest possible audience, as
"everyone" lives in the same world. By setting up a series of dichotomies
that she later blurs, however, she both enables a wide audience to identify
with her claims, and then subtly shifts the premises upon which those
claims are based. This strategy allows her to bring what might be a resistant audience along with her. She writes: "There are two kinds of peace
in this world. The one produced by suppression, which is the passivity of
death; the other brought about by a proper adjustment of living, active
forces" (Cooper, 149). She begins at the global level and in Socratic fashion sets up the *modus differenci* into which this world can be divided—two
kinds of peace. The first set of oppositions consists of the two ways to
achieve peace in the world: either by "suppression" and "death" or by
"proper adjustment" of "living" and "active" forces. However, Cooper
soon further specifies her partition from divisions of the world, to those
between nations and individuals. She continues: "A Nation or an individual may be at peace because all opponents have been killed or crushed;
or, nation as well as individual may have found the secret of true harmony
in the determination to live and let live" (149). Within just two brief sentences she moves from the two kinds of world peace to that which is pos-

sible on the national and individual level. This subtle shifts allows the idea of "live and let live" to apply not only to the level of national but also to individual harmony, thus suggesting that there are multiple forces at work in both whole nations and individuals. Structurally, these national and individual terms parallel one another; consequently not only should nations let others within their midst "live" but individuals should too.

It is important to note that from the inception of her argument, Cooper introduces a concept that will be key throughout: harmony. Most people think of harmony as the pleasant combination of forces, the unity of notes or chords to produce a pleasing sound. Indeed the first four definitions in the online *Oxford English Dictionary* support such an understanding: Harmony is defined as "[t]he combination of musical notes, either simultaneous or successive, so as to produce a pleasing effect; melody; music, tuneful sound." Cooper, however, is using "harmony" in its original sense as "[t]he combination of (simultaneous) notes so as to form chords; that part of musical art or science which deals with the formation and relations of chords; . . . and, in strict modern use, from counterpoint . . . the combination of melodies."[12] *The Harvard Brief Dictionary of Music* defines counterpoint as "music consisting of two or more melodic lines sounding simultaneously. The term comes from the Latin *contrapuntas,* properly *punctus contra punctum,* meaning 'note against note' or, by extension, 'melody against melody.'"[13] And it is both the simultaneity and the sounding against one another that Cooper emphasizes in her argument here as these musical terms are applied to racial elements of the American polity. It is at the individual level that people must sound their own voices, their own melodies, and in order to make harmony possible they must do so simultaneously. From this individual level, she moves back to a "natural," more universal one, but does so while emphasizing not only that harmony is divinely inspired and natural but also that it involves necessarily opposed forces:

> Now I need not say that peace produced by suppression is neither natural or desirable. Despotism is not one of the ideas that man has copied from nature. All through God's universe we see eternal harmony and symmetry as the unvarying result of the equilibrium of opposing forces. Fair play in an equal fight is the law written in Nature's book. And the solitary bully with his foot on the breast of his last antagonist has not warrant in any fact of God. (150)

In this passage, Cooper exploits the concepts of "nature," "harmony," and "God's design" to argue for the natural, implicitly democratic, state of nations where all people are equal. Linking "God's universe" with "harmony" and "symmetry" highlights this sense of equality, as does Cooper's repetition of "fair" and "equal." By establishing that despotism is both "unnatural" and "undesirable," she earns a place for her ideas within the framework of an already existing discourse—"state of nature" theory—but she does so by shifting the focus of the oppositional forces. "Nature's Book" or the "Book of Nature" would be familiar to any intellectual audience of her time, because it is a concept discussed by Emerson himself—the man who Matthew Arnold termed author of the "most important work done in prose" in his 1884 lecture of the same name.[14]

Revising Emerson's "Book of Nature"

In his 1856 essay "Fate," Emerson introduces the "Book of Nature" and the idea of necessarily oppositional forces: "Man is not order of nature . . . but a stupendous antagonism, a dragging together of the poles of the universe."[15] However, Emerson talks about these oppositional forces functioning on the individual level. Even the very words he chooses— "antagonism" in contrast to Cooper's "oppositional," which suggests balance and equality, and "dragging together" instead of Cooper's "harmony"— emphasize the competitive lens through which Emerson sees the world. In her piece, Cooper plays on the terms Emerson set forth, but shifts them slightly to meet her argument's needs. While Emerson speaks specifically about the individual, Cooper extends these ideas more broadly to encompass the nation as a whole, thus making both individual and nation part of God's universal and natural plan. By shifting the focus from the individual to the national and global level, Cooper can successfully carve out a place for blacks within that nation and "world," something that Emerson's understanding of progress seems not to allow.

By emphasizing God's universe and the "harmony" and "symmetry" observed throughout it, Cooper appeals to both "Natural" and "Divine" law to set the premises for her case. In the next paragraph, she uses examples from the natural, scientific world to corroborate her claim: "[t]he beautiful curves described by planets and suns in their courses are the resultant of conflicting forces" (150). She invokes the principles of not only "centripetal" and "centrifugal" forces, but also the "counterbalances" of "alkali" and "acid." Indeed, she points out that the very "air we breathe" and "water, the bland fluid we cannot dispense with" are the result of "proper equilibrium" and "constant conflict" respectively (150). Once she establishes that the very basics of life—air and water—and the most natural of all laws are based upon these ideas of equilibrium achieved through tension and conflict, she then shifts the rhetorical plane from the scientific to the historical (151). Here she finally sets forth the thesis she had been delaying up until this point of the essay. It is only after she demonstrates that her interpretations work on the global or international, national, and individual levels, as well as the Divine one, that she specifically states the argument that the essay as a whole will amplify: "Progressive peace in a nation is the result of conflict; and conflict, such as is healthy, stimulating, and progressive, is produced through the co-existence of radically opposing or racially different elements" (151). Her definition of progressive peace is an extension of her understanding of harmony, and operates similarly—in order for it to exist there must be conflicting elements sounding themselves simultaneously.

Working from this understanding that both difference and simultaneity are necessary to produce harmony, she extends the concept of Emerson's individual to the level of nation, and then strategically interprets the multiplicity of races in marked contrast to the progressive model that Emerson sets forth in "Fate." Emerson writes: "You have just dined, and however scrupulously the slaughter-house is concealed in the graceful distance of miles, there is complicity, expensive races—race living at the expense of race."[16] Here Emerson understands the difference of races as part of a necessary hierarchy where some races are privileged and "expensive," and others are expendable, sacrificed to preserve those in the privileged position. For Emerson, "[t]he book of Nature is the book of Fate . . . when a race has lived its term, it comes no more again."[17] His understanding reflects a linear and teleological concept that can justify such "race extinction" as the necessary sacrifice required to enable the "progress of the expensive race."

But Cooper understands racial difference and world progress very differently, and thus makes no allowance for genocide. For her, difference is something "healthy, stimulating, and progressive." In fact, she repeats the term "progressive," using it first to describe the kind of healthful peace in a nation that comes from the balance of opposing elements, and then again to describe the kind of "conflict" that would create such a nation. Cooper invokes the first person "I" to admit to her audience that she can visualize no other reason why such difference would exist: "I confess I can see no deeper reason than this for the specializing of the racial types in the world" (151). While Emerson sees the relationship between the races as necessarily competitive and hierarchical, where one is sacrificed to preserve another; Cooper sees the relationship as symbiotic, where such competition exists only to mutually benefit all groups involved. Cooper emphasizes the mutuality and reciprocity of healthy conflict and the stimulation and progression such salubrious co-existence offers—a both/and concept. In contrast, Emerson thinks in terms of either/or. When race lives at the expense of race—as it does for him—healthy co-existence is simply not an option.

Both Emerson and Cooper understand that different races may have different functions; however, because Emerson's basic assumption includes a belief that some races are inherently more valuable than others, he draws conclusions that border the genocidal. He writes: "[t]he population of the world is a conditional population; not the best, but the best that could live now; and the scale of tribes, and the steadiness with which victory adheres to one tribe and defeat to another, is as uniform as the superstition of strata."[18] He quotes Knox's *Fragment of Races,* to emphasize the idea that "[e]very race has its own *habitat,*" consequently, if you "[d]etach a colony from the race" "it deteriorates to the crab."[19] He uses this understanding to explain both why "Americans" are so successful on American soil and why others perish there. He writes, "The German and Irish millions, like the Negro, have a great deal of guano in their destiny. They are ferried over the Atlantic and carted over America, to ditch and to drudge, to make corn cheap and then to lie down prematurely to make a spot of green grass on the prairie."[20] Thus, the "fate" of Emerson's races, determined to "lie down prematurely," stands in stark contrast to the roles that Cooper imagines for them.

While Cooper also discusses the importance of race and place, her understanding is, once again, a much more positive one:

> Whatever our theory with reference to the origin of the species and the unity of mankind, we cannot help admitting the fact that no sooner does a family of the human race take up its abode in some little nook between mountains, or on some plain walled in by their own hands, no sooner do they begin in earnest to live their own life, think their own thoughts, and trace out their own arts, than they begin also to crystallize some idea different from and generally opposed to that of other tribes of families. (152)

In contrast to Emerson, who sees some races as "branded" to become guano on the hill, and then left to die out, Cooper recognizes that "each race, has its badge, its exponent, its message branded in its forehead by the great Master's hand which is its own peculiar keynote, and its contribution to the harmony of nations" (152). Again, her emphasis on the need for harmony shifts the focus away from linear time and landlocked space into the realm of greater possibility—the creative and productive arts. Her metaphor is not one of "shit" but music—"keynotes" and "harmony" as opposed to "drudgework" and droppings. The niche each race finds enables its members to "live their own life, think their own thoughts, and trace out their own arts" each of which is in necessary, but productive opposition to other races' imaginings. Like Emerson, she also recognizes that certain patterns result in stagnation and death, but for Cooper this only comes about precisely when difference is eliminated: "Left entirely alone,—out of contact, that is with other races and their opposing ideas and conflicting tendencies, this cult is abnormally developed and there is unity without variety, a predominance of one tone at the expense of moderation and harmony, and finally a sameness, a monotonous dullness which means stagnation,—death" (152). Here, Cooper uses more musical terms to speak about the need for diversity, carefully emphasizing that one tone should not predominate lest one risk the failure of musical texture. Here univocality results in "sameness," "monotonous dullness," and consequently "stagnation,—death."

Moreover, Cooper does not take the term "American" for granted as Emerson does. Emerson's understanding of America seems to exclude different races, assuming that the white descendents of the British merely had been geographically misplaced. Yet Cooper uses history to illustrate that in fact, different races are just as—if not even more—American than these "newcomers" who Emerson privileges. First, she exposes the belief system that one must ascribe to in order to accept the logical conclusions of Emerson's argument, then she skillfully lays out the premises of her own syllogism, and uses anthypophora to argue enthematically that America always has been multivoiced, and therefore, necessarily must be democratic and republican. She quotes Shakespeare's *Macbeth*, without identifying it, to introduce her opposition's argument concerning America:

> Here surely was a seething caldron of conflicting elements. Religious intolerance and political hatred, race prejudice and caste pride—"Double, double toil and trouble; Fire burn and cauldron bubble." Conflict, Conflict, Conflict. America for Americans! This is the white man's country. The Chinese must go, shrieks the exclusionists. Exclude the Italians! Colonize

the blacks in Mexico or deport them to Africa. Lynch, suppress, drive out, kill out! America for Americans! (162–63)

However, she only introduces these nativist ideas in order to successfully refute them by asking the question: "Who are Americans?" (163). She then uses history to expand the definition accepted by the nativists who she impersonates. Skillfully employing anthypophora, Cooper answers her own question by asserting that the red men who "used to be owners of this soil" also "[h]ave the best right to call themselves 'Americans' by law of primogeniture. They are at least the oldest inhabitants of whom we can at present identify any traces" (163). This first definition, concerning the Native Americans, is one based on indigenousness, in which case the "red men" certainly trump the newly located Europeans.

For those unwilling to accept the "red men," she offers yet another interpretation. She argues that "the settlers" themselves were not clear on the definition of Americannness: "The first settlers seem to have been almost as much mixed as we are on this point; and it does not seem at all easy to decide just what individuals we mean when we yell 'America for Americans'" (164). Her historical examples thus enable her to argue that difference is nothing new to the American nation: "[t]he fact is this nation was foreordained to conflict from its incipiency. Its elements were predestined from their birth to an irrepressible clash followed by the stable equilibrium of opposition" (164). Her use of the words "foreordained" and "predestined" enable her to connect this progression, this "natural" state of the nation's birth with the Divine will. Of course, here, when Cooper uses Fate, she does so to underscore the importance of rather than eliminate the possibility for difference and diversity. She reiterates the importance of and historical precedence for the existence of myriad voices and people to emphasize the democratic "nature" of America:

> Exclusive possession belongs to none. There never was a point in its history when it did. There was never a time since America became a nation when there were not more than one race, more than one party, more than one belief contending for supremacy. Hence no one is or can be supreme. All interest must be consulted, all claims conciliated ... America is not from choice more than of necessity republic in form and democratic in administration. (164)

Her skillful use of anaphora where she repeats the phrase "there was never" both emphasizes and links the two main points she is attempting to demonstrate to her audience that America has never been homogenous and that there always has been more than one, race, party, belief "contending for supremacy." She follows this repetition with that of the first word "all." The "there never was" sentences call attention to times in the past and foreclose the possibility for imagining a nostalgic, univocal America that once was. The "all" statements that follow them draw attention to the inclusiveness Cooper wants to emphasize: "all voices, all claims," thus driving home her initial point that "exclusive possession belongs to none."

Guizot as Corroborating Ethos

It is not only Cooper who understands difference this way. In fact, she marshalls in the well-known and respected François Guizot to back up the claims she makes.[21] Referenced in the works of Arnold, Emerson, and many other thinkers, lecturers, and philosophers of the time as well, Guizot was quite influential. Cooper quotes extensively from his "Lecture II. History of Civilization" to corroborate the fact that multiplicity of both race and voice are beneficial to the nation. She includes numerous historical examples from ancient to contemporary Europe to make her case. She begins with Guizot's examples of Egypt and Greece: "[n]ow I beg you to note that in none of these systems was a RACE PROBLEM possible. The dominant race had settled that matter forever" (154).

Here she picks up where Emerson's argument must inevitably lead. If one race lives at the expense of other races, ultimately, the other races die out to support "the" race. She emphasizes, however, that anytime this exclusivity has existed, historically, that particular nation has not fared well: "It was the tyranny and exclusiveness of these nations, therefore, which brought about their immobility and resulted finally in the barrenness of their one idea. From this came the poverty and decay underlying their civilization, from this the transitory, ephemeral character of its brilliancy" (155). Her use of words like "immobility," "barrenness," "poverty," and "decay" underscore the negative repercussions of exclusivity. Indeed Greece, which traditionally gets held up as the most "advanced and civilized" of ancient cultures, the producer not only of many cultural artifacts but even the model of classical education in which Cooper was trained, is here cited as an example of the disadvantage of homogeneity: "Not even Greece with all its classic treasures is made an exception from these limitations produced by exclusiveness" (156).

Additionally, Cooper uses Guizot's words to demonstrate the negative effects such homogeneity has on a race's culture as well: "This character of unity in their civilization is equally impressed upon their literature and intellectual productions . . . They all seem the result of one same fact, the expression of one idea . . . The same character of unity and monotony shines out in these works of mind and fancy, as we discover in their life and institutions" (156). Not only are national, political life, and institutions not served well, but the culture such nations produce is also inferior. This is a particularly important argument for Cooper to make, especially since the next essay in *A Voice*, "The Negro as Presented in American Literature," argues for the entrance and legitimate place of black voices within the American literary and cultural scene. Since cultural and institutional supremacy rest on the multiplicity rather than the monotony of voice, here Cooper explicitly links America's progression with the responsibility to speak: "Here you will not see as in Germany women hitched to a cart with donkeys; not perhaps because men are more chivalrous here than there, but because woman can speak. Here labor will not be starved and ground to powder because the laboring man can make himself heard. Here races that are weakest, if they so elect, make themselves felt" (167). Again her use of anaphora and repetition of "here" keeps the focus on American soil, while her use of words like "speak," "make heard," and "make felt" put emphasis on the active agency available to even those in what she sees as disadvantaged positions: women, labor, and "weak" races. Of course her insistence that even "weaker" races make themselves heard and felt rests on the assumption that there are weaker races and that they are indeed allowed to exist.

Consequently, she returns to working within an Emersonian vocabulary, reiterating her argument against the idea of "race living at the expense of race" and instead re-reading God's will through her symbiotic lens:

> And the last monster that shall be throttled forever methinks is race prejudice. Men will here learn that a race, as a family, may be true to itself without seeking to exterminate all others. That for the note of the feeblest there is room, nay a positive need in the harmonies of God. (168)

Calling "race prejudice" a "monster" couches it, linguistically at the very least, outside the "natural" about which she has spoken throughout the essay. To deepen this metaphor, she uses a simile to compare "race" to a "family." This domestic metaphor works well to emphasize the interdependent nature of relationships. Moreover, it instantiates on the level of race, the argument she makes about God's relationship to individuals. Here she explicitly argues against genocide, insisting rather that "a race, as a family, may be true to itself without seeking to exterminate all others." She repeats her argument that there is "room" for physical presence, but more than that there is actually a "positive need." Again, by invoking musical terminology, she is able to link not only the weakest races but also the need for them with divine will and inspiration. Her enthymeme can be diagrammed in the following logical progression: "if God's voice can be interpreted as the true voice, and His harmony has room and need for weak races, then truly there is room for all races." Her reasoning and use of musical metaphor thus force her audience to reach the same logical conclusion.

Just as in the beginning of her essay she delays the announcement of her thesis, waiting until after she has emphasized God's role, here too at its near conclusion, she first emphasizes the divine order and then announces her main point loud and clear. She finally ends her piece with another instance of repeated anthypophora:

> Has America a Race Problem? Yes. What are you going to do about it? Let it alone and mind my own business. It is God's problem and He will solve it in time . . . What can you or I do? Are there not duties and special lines of thought growing out of the present conditions of this problem? Certainly there are. (171)

These four questions, asked and answered, strengthen the connection between God's design and America' race problem. Though she begins the passage invoking God's will, which might suggest that one can simply stand back and wait for the divine plan to unravel, Cooper develops the rest of the paragraph to urge her audience members subtly but strongly to live up to the challenge of making their voices heard. Not wanting to leave her audience without a way actively to help bring God's will about, she emphasizes that there are "duties" and "special lines of thought" that can help to put God's plan into effect. She concludes with a tour de force of rhetorical eloquence:

> *Imprimis;* let every element of the conflict see that it represent a positive force so as to preserve a proper equipoise in the conflict. No shirking, no skulking, no masquerading in another's uniform. Stand by your guns. And

be ready for the charge. The day is coming, and now is, when Americans must ask each citizen not 'who was your grandfather and what the color of his cuticle,' but '*What can you do?*' Be ready each individual element,— each race, each class, each family, each man to reply '*I engage to undertake an honest man's share.*' (171)

The entire passage is written in command form addressed to individuals: "let, stand, be ready," are just a few of the specific actions Cooper urges her audience to take. She repeats the word "no" three times to exhort her audience not to shy away from their obligations. Instead they must "stand" and "be ready." By using the phrase "the day is coming" in the eternal present and following it with "now is," in the actual present, Cooper, like God himself in Genesis, imaginatively, if not actually, calls a state of affairs into being simply through the power of her voice and words. She commands her audience to shift the focus of their questions from those obsessed with the race of others, to those which focus on their own, individual potential for action: "What can you do?" Again she uses anaphora to underscore the importance of "being ready." She repeats the word "each" four times to call attention to the many registers of identity through which people can act—as a race, class, family, individual.

In this section, she urges her audience to stand up for themselves, to speak, to represent themselves both in body and voice. She assures her audience that God will take care of the big picture, as long as each of them does his individual part, "God and time will work the problem. You and I are only to stand for the quantities *at their best*, which he means us to represent" (171). Here again, she emphasizes that it is God's will for each person to represent his or her best qualities, for by doing so, he will help bring God's plan into fruition. And it is from this position of the divine that Cooper concludes: "We would not deprecate the fact, then, that America has a Race Problem. It is guarranty [sic] of the perpetuity and progress of her institutions, and insures the breadth of her culture and the symmetry of her development. More than all, let us not disparage the factor which the Negro is appointed to contribute to that problem" (173). Here she uses the third person "we" to link herself with her audience. She continues with the command not to "disparage" the Negro's divinely appointed role. The last sentence of the essay reads: "And the historian of American civilization will yet congratulate this country that she has had a Race Problem and that descendants of the black race furnished one of its largest factors" (174). Writing in the conditional, Cooper asserts that a future historian will "congratulate" America not only for her "Race Problem" but also for the fact that the "descendants of the black race furnished one of its largest factors." Using paradox, Cooper bewilders her audience with her words, thus concludes with the seemingly impossible idea that a problem is worth congratulating. By projecting into the future, Cooper literally creates imaginative space for the reality she hopes to bring about through her words.

Employing such rhetorical strategies as repetition, anaphora, and anthypophora, Cooper successfully redefines and redeploys the word "problem" as "solution;" and thereby demonstrates how the presence of a "race problem" is actually beneficial to and necessary for the health of the nation. Quoting other important intellectuals throughout her essay, Cooper equates her own intellectual and rhetorical power with theirs. By revising Emerson's "Book of Nature," Cooper works within a vocabulary familiar to the audience that she wants to persuade, but ultimately turns it against itself just as she manipulates the word "problem" into a kind of solution. Her musical metaphors provide a strong antidote to the nativist and Social Darwinist explanations she counters. This chapter has only begun to examine the rhetorical force of one of the essays in *A Voice from the South*, yet even this brief glimpse suggests that American and African-American studies have a lot to learn from the woman who Baker-Fletcher terms "A Singing Something." Cooper's use of musical metaphor and the other essays in *A Voice* warrant closer examination. Though she has been relatively overlooked compared to other African-American intellectuals of her time, it is time for scholars to pay greater attention to Anna Julia Cooper's life and works.

Notes

1. Anna Julia Cooper, *A Voice from the South* (1892; New York: Oxford University Press, 1988). All references to this text refer to this edition.

2. According to Gideon Burton, anaphora is the "repetition of the same word or group of words at the beginning of successive clauses, sentences, or lines" and anthypophora, also referred to as hypophora, is "a figure of reasoning in which one asks and then immediately answers one's own questions. Reasoning aloud. Anthypophora sometimes takes the form of asking the audience or one's adversary what can be said on a matter, and thus can involve both anacoenosis and apostrophe." For more information on rhetorical terms, see also Gideon Burton, *The Online Rhetoric*, http://rhetoric.byu.edu/.

3. Brian A. Bremen, "DuBois, Emerson, and the 'Fate' of Black Folk," *American Literary Realism* 24 (Spring 1992): 80–89. All further references are to this text.

4. Several of these essays were first or later delivered orally to a variety of audiences and still contain marks of their orality even in their published, written form. See also Shirley Wilson Logan, "'Women of a Common Country, with Common Interests' Fannie Barrier Williams, Anna Julia Cooper, Identification and Arrangement," in *We are Coming: The Persuasive Discourse of Nineteenth-Century Black Women* (Carbondale: Southern Illinois University Press, 1999).

5. Anna Julia Cooper's third chapter, "Womanhood: A Vital Element in the Regeneration and Progress of the Race," was first delivered as a speech to the Episcopal Clergy in 1886. The fourth chapter, "The Higher Education of Women," was given as a presentation to a convention of the American Conference of Educators in 1890 and then later published in the Southland in 1891. See also Charles Lemert and Esme Bhan, *The Voice of Anna Julia Cooper: Including A Voice From the South and Other Important Essays, Papers, and Letters* (New York: Rowman & Littlefield Publishers, 1998), 46. They note that Cooper did not provide information for the other pieces in *A Voice* and "none is discernable in the archives" (46).

6. Louise Daniel Hutchinson, *Anna J. Cooper: A Voice from the South.* (Washington, D.C.: Smithsonian Institute Press, 1982), 104.

7. Ibid.

8. Karen Baker-Fletcher, *A Singing Something: Womanist Reflections on Anna Julia Cooper* (New York: Crossroad Press, 1994). All references in this paragraph are to this text.

9. Kenneth Burke, *Philosophy of Literary Form* (Berkeley: University of California Press, 1973), 110.

10. For more information on her educational training, see Hutchinson, *Anna J. Cooper;* Baker-Fletcher, *A Singing Something;* and Todd Vogel "The Master's Tools Revisited: Foundation Work in Anna Julia Cooper," in *Criticism and the Color Line: Desegregating American Literary Studies,* ed. Henry B. Wonham (New Brunswick, N.J.: Rutgers University Press, 1996).

11. Ralph Waldo Emerson, "Fate," in *The Portable Emerson,* ed. Carl Bode and Malcolm Cowley (New York: Viking Penguin, 1981), 346–75.

12. *Oxford English Dictionary Online,* "Harmony," http://dictionary.oed.com/cgi/entry/00102740?single=1&query_type=word&queryword=harmony&edition=2e&first=1&max_to_show=10. Accessed May 7, 2003.

13. Willi Apel and Ralph T. Daniel, eds. *The Harvard Brief Dictionary of Music* (New York: MJF Books, 1960), 72.

14. Matthew Arnold, *Discourses in America* (London: Macmillan and Co., 1885), 196.

15. Emerson, "Fate," 358.

16. Ibid., 349.

17. Ibid., 354.

18. Ibid.

19. Ibid.

20. Ibid. I am greatly indebted to Brian Bremen for his insightful instruction of Emerson's essays. Much of what I have written here has grown out of conversations with him.

21. François Guizot, *The History of Civilization in Europe* [1828], translated by William Hazbitt, edited by Larry Seidentop (New York: Penguin, 1997).

Part V

Leadership, Activism, and the Genius of Ida B. Wells

Chapter 14

"I Rose and Found My Voice"

Claiming "Voice" in the Rhetoric of Ida B. Wells

OLGA IDRISS DAVIS

Ida B. Wells stands as one of the premier personas on the canvas of American social and political discourse. Her work embodies a rhetorical tradition established by Black women who told their stories of survival in pre-emancipatory Black female slave narratives.[1] Ida B. Wells extends Black women's rhetorical tradition by creating a body of political discourse that not only serves to resist hegemonic discourses of power, but crafts a theoretical framework for critically explicating the American/Western ideology of Black sexuality that exoticizes, commodifies, politicizes, and polices Black heterosexual male and female bodies.[2] Wells centers public address in the same discursive manner found in the pre-emancipatory narratives of slave women: through an ethnic culture of survival. Placing Wells' oratory in the culture out of which it emanates provides an insightful examination of Black female dimensions of her discourse. Valuing Black women's tradition of survival explores critical voice as central to the survival of the Black community and celebrates a rootedness in narrative experience as rhetorical foundation.

"Voice" is an illuminating concept for exploring the strategy of resistance and reclamation in the public discourse of Ida B. Wells. The notion of "voice" offers the space to emphasize the ongoing interplay between Black women's oppression and Black women's activism within the matrix of domination as a response to human agency. In examining the discourse of African-American women speakers, rhetoric is viewed as a symbolic act going beyond the mere style of a speaker, and rather creates a site of struggle for inclusion and survival. Furthermore, because of its public acknowledgement of the ethical and emotional dimensions of public discourse, "voice" becomes a celebration of the value and beauty of otherness, which in turn reveals the public and private spheres of experience.[3] Similarly, a womanist conceptual framework offers insight into African-American women's rhetorical spaces. By embracing a commitment "to the survival and wholeness of entire people, male *and* female,"[4] a womanist perspective seeks to illuminate the liberatory strategies of Black women in our attempts to transcend essentialist ideologies that neglect our experiences, lives, and critiques from the discourse of human communication.[5]

This chapter reveals how the notion of "voice" informs our understanding of the rhetoric of Ida B. Wells. Engaging Wells's political discourse from this notion points to her rhetorical strategies of negotiating the space of otherness through the public act of storytelling. She challenged the master narrative of lynching by employing a liberatory discourse to the spaces of hatred and indifference in which Black female political consciousness and political solidarity are maintained. By celebrating a racial and gendered consciousness of self and claiming "voice" as a rhetoric of survival and resistance, the rhetoric of Ida B. Wells stands as a model of progressive means for change in the context of community.

In this chapter, I first discuss voice as a rhetorical strategy of otherness. I will parallel Wells's use of voice to the rhetorical "voice" located in Black female slave narratives and extend the notion of rhetoric as a site of struggle in Black women's ways of knowing and theorizing the world. Second, to help clarify the situatedness of Wells's public address in the continuum of African-American women's rhetorical tradition, I explore the relationship between her rhetorical voice and a culture of resistance. Finally, I argue that the critical voice of Wells's rhetoric reflects her unique position of being *both* African American *and* a woman, both of which serve to inform her moral responsibility and counter the discursive powers of domination.

Rhetorical Voice as Otherness

Much of what has been written historically and in literary analysis of Ida B. Wells begins with a background of her public life, and situating the private sphere of experience of the first twenty-five years of her life provides a perspective on the public sphere that later informed her public address. In the rhetorical tradition of Black female slave narrators, Ida B. Wells wrote about her life as a journey of declaring self.[6] It was in her writings and speeches that Wells found her place in the continuum of Black women's intellectual and rhetorical traditions. She advanced both traditions while simultaneously redefining them based on her skills as well as what was needed for the times.

What is meant by Black women's intellectual and rhetorical traditions? By an intellectual tradition, I am referring to that point in history in which Black women were acknowledged as human beings of rational thought and cognitive abilities. The tradition of intellectual prowess began in 1772, when Phillis Wheatley faced a committee of astute, erudite, white, male examiners skeptical of the authenticity of her work. After a lengthy oral defense, she proved her authorship of a book of poetry and in 1773 became the first published African American and African-American woman author in the Western world. Similarly, a century later, it would be Black women in nineteenth-century pre-emancipatory America who would create a rhetorical tradition through the telling of their stories of lived experience in the genre of slave narratives. Through narrative discourse, Black women created a liberating persona while discursively crafting an intellectual identity through persuasive strategies in emancipatory efforts against pro-slavery arguments. The significance of both of these traditions is that Black women defied the belief that they were creatures unable to think, create ideas, rationalize, and most specifically to use language as a *written* form of persuasive discourse.

My interest here lies in the rhetorical aspect that Black women— unlike the Greek male elite of Aristotle's time who defined rhetoric as "a good man speaking well"—had to prove themselves *first* as *humans,* then as speaking *and writing* humans capable of crafting, through discourse, an empowering persona that supported abolitionist efforts while redefining their image in all of the world. In both instances, these traditions embraced a legacy of struggle and resistance that Black women knew and understood. To enter into the continuum of the legacy meant that Ida B. Wells was destined to locate herself in the rhetorical and intellectual traditions.

The public voice of African-American women is a discourse of surviving oppression. From the time of slave narratives to the time of Ida B.

Wells to the present day, Black women craft discourse as a way of responding to hegemonic oppression and as a vehicle for resistance and change.[7] The relationship between discourse and resistance informs the cultural struggle for self-definition and personal respect in relation to the complexities of American life and culture. That complexity is most crystallized in the experience of otherness.

"Otherness" is the embodied space of difference. It is a constructed, performed space of identity between the "who" society crafts you to be and the "who" you determine to become. Otherness is an ongoing dialectic between discourse and ideology. As dialectic informs rhetoric, otherness informs ideology through discourse and as such, responds and transforms ideology within the context of narrative framework of lived experience. "The story" of ourselves and our relationship to others in our world "powerfully influences the problems and possibilities of our language."[8] "Otherness" as a rhetorical strategy employs "voice" as a dialectical opposition to the ideologies of the time and becomes the shaping of narrative experience into a public discourse that redefines the prevailing ideologies of the period. "Otherness," in a rhetorical space, provides a presence of otherness that creates discourse into "the word made flesh." Of presence as a rhetorical choice to support evidence, Perelman and Olbrecht-Tyteca state:

> By the very fact of selecting certain elements and presenting them to the audience, their importance and pertinency to the discussion are implied. Indeed such a choice endows these elements with a *presence* that is an essential factor in argumentation and one that is far too much neglected in rationalistic conceptions of reasoning.[9]

The presence of Ida B. Wells in the realm of public address grew to prominence as she crafted her campaign that later became the anti-lynching movement, a life-long commitment to telling the lived experience of the "other": "I am only a mouthpiece through which to tell the story of lynching and I have told it so often that I know it by heart. I do not have to embellish it; it makes its own way."[10]

The voice of "otherness" embodies a multiple consciousness that informs the ways in which the "other" negotiates the interplay among social, cultural and political locations. Ida B. Wells navigated the terrain of racism and sexism to employ a unique rhetoric that maintained advancement and activism. Like the foremothers, she claimed resistance to subjugation and oppression in her daily lived experience. For example, segregation on trains in Tennessee was a contested issue during the period of Reconstruction, and the debate over African Americans securing access to public accommodations and fair court trials escalated during the late 1880s. In May 1884, Wells was to embark on what some critics say "was the beginning of Wells Barnett's lifelong public campaign against the inequities and injustices faced by Blacks throughout the South."[11] She purchased a first-class ticket on the Chesapeake, Ohio, and Southwestern Railroad for a trip from Memphis to Woodstock, Tennessee. She had obtained a teaching position in the town of Woodstock, just ten miles north of Memphis, and rather than traveling by mule she now went to work by train. Unbeknownst to her, shortly after she would take a seat in the ladies' car, an experience would occur to change her life forever:

> When the train started and the conductor came along to collect tickets, he took my ticket, then handed it back to me and told me that he couldn't take my ticket there. I thought that if he didn't want the ticket I wouldn't bother about it so went on reading. In a little while when he finished taking tickets, he came back and told me I would have to go in the other car. I refused, saying that the forward car was a smoker, and as I was in the ladies' car I proposed to stay. He tried to drag me out of the seat, but the moment he caught hold of my arm I fastened my teeth in the back of his hand. (18)

She was being relegated to the "Colored" train car, where blacks were permitted to sit. However, explaining that she had paid for first-class accommodations and would not give up her seat, Wells

> braced my feet against the seat in front and was holding to the back, and as he had already been badly bitten he didn't try it again by himself. He went forward and got the baggageman and another man to help him and of course they succeeded in dragging me out. They were encouraged to do this by the attitude of the white ladies and gentlemen in the car; some of them even stood on the seats so that they could get a good view and continued applauding the conductor for his brave stand ... When I saw that they were determined to drag me into the smoker, which was already filled with colored people and those who were smoking, I said I would get off the train rather than go in—which I did. Strangely, I held on to my ticket all this time, and although the sleeves of my linen duster had been torn out and I had been pretty roughly handled, I had not been hurt physically. (19)

Later, she testified in court that the conductor, "said to me that he would treat me like a lady but that I must go into the other car, and I replied, that if he wished to treat me like a lady, he would leave me alone."[12] As a result of the dehumanizing attack on the train, Wells filed a lawsuit against the railroad company and won, but later the suit was repealed and the assault on her character cast her as a troublemaker.

Wells also faced the necessity of negotiating stereotypes of gender in the face of racist Victorian images of Black womanhood. The tradition of the ancestral voice reflects in Wells's narrative,

> [My] good name was all that I had in the world. I was bound to protect it from attack by those who felt they could do so with the impunity because I had no brother or father to protect it for me. [I was] one southern girl born and bred, who had tried to keep herself spotless and morally clean as my slave mother had taught me. (22)

Learning to negotiate the cult of true womanhood of the nineteenth century was a daunting challenge. The challenge was to recognize a discursive framework of ideal womanhood—docile, gentle, innocent, pure, modest, and pious—while simultaneously crafting a racial and gendered identity within the sexual mores of the times. The notion of a proper sphere for women—the home and her husband—found Wells as an unconventional woman who carved an existence for herself through hard work, independence, and intellectual prowess, not only as a woman but also as an African-American woman. Of this inner dialectic of race and gender Rosemary Bray observes:

> The parallel pursuits of equality for African Americans and for women have trapped black women between often conflicting agendas for more than a century. We are asked in a thousand ways, large and small, to take sides against ourselves, postponing a confrontation in one arena to address an equally urgent task in another . . . despite the bind, more often than not we choose loyalty to the race rather than the uncertain allegiance of gender.[13]

For Ida B. Wells, rhetoric was a dynamic process of negotiation. She learned to use symbols as a means to affect change while negotiating resistance to dominant forces of hegemony and subjugation. She rose and found her voice by discovering the rhetorical act of shared experience while internalizing a sense of social responsibility and community uplift.[14]

The notion of *rising* suggests activism—that one is in social decline or debasement. To *find* her voice implies that somehow it was lost, obscured, abandoned, needing to be claimed, retrieved, taken back, healed. To find voice means to search and locate ancestral ideas to challenge words that are an affront to human dignity and self-identity and finally, it suggests that Ida B. Wells's voice was taken back *by* her and *for* her and the community of which she was a part. The taking back of voice was not a request of return from perpetrators and co-optors. Rather, she took back her voice in defiance of a system that endorsed a master narrative that created the heinous crime of silencing voices of the oppressed. To rise, find, and claim one's voice under extreme conditions of subjugation and degradation, characterizes African-American women's rhetorical tradition. That tradition is inherently social and political, inextricably linked to power and hegemony, and the tradition occurs through a collective process of political struggle. Ida B. Wells reveals the person in whom the continuum of struggle, survival, and resistance manifests such a rhetorical tradition.

Critical Voice as Cultural Resistance

Ida B. Wells rose to become one of the most brilliant orators and political organizers of the twentieth century, known for her efforts in creating the anti-lynching movement in the 1890s and taking an activist role in women's suffrage. The rhetoric of Ida B. Wells is a continued story of the lived experience and social reality of being of African descent in nineteenth-century America. Before Wells embarked on a career as a noted and controversial journalist, she was a storyteller. She told her story of mob violence and lynching throughout the United States and Britain. Wells learned the art of the story from her ancestral heritage of Black women. This symbolic expression of narrative or, the telling of one's story, is what Hortense Spillers calls "a symbol-making task to confront the suppression of the enslaved woman's existence and of her realities."[15] In other words, the narrative provided Black women and men a chance to declare a chronological space among the human race and to claim a central tenet of identity—to redefine the discontinuities of exclusion by creating a space of existence. In the tradition of her female ancestral heritage, Ida B. Wells named, claimed, and redefined the story of discrimination and lynching in American society. Of the power of storytelling, Williams observes:

> To be a Storyteller . . . is to assume the awesome burden of remembrance for a people, and to perform this paramount role with laughter and tears,

joy and sadness, melancholy and passion, as the occasion demands. The Storyteller never wholly belongs to himself or herself. The Storyteller is the one who sacrifices everything in the tellings and retellings of the stories belonging to the tribe.[16]

Ida B. Wells assumed her ancestral role in the continuum of Black women's cultural tradition by becoming a "keeper of the culture" with storytelling that confronted the conscience of white people and challenged the dominant discourses that mythologized the Black race as savagery. She speaks of the silence of the North in respect to lynching thus: "Before leaving the South I had often wondered at the silence of the North. I had concluded it was because they did not know the facts, and had accepted the southern white man's reason for lynching and burning human beings in this nineteenth century of civilization" (77).

Lynching became an effective means for maintaining white superiority at the expense of black inferiority until such activists as Wells and others organized black and white resistance to lynching. The story of lynching became as much a defining experience in America as that of slavery. For Wells to take on the role of storyteller as a means of advancing justice for her people meant shaping a public address unlike any other of our theoretical exemplars. Wells shaped lived experience of African Americans in terms of moral, ethical, and community narratives. Those narratives raised the consciousness of audiences in America and throughout the world. Public address as *story* is a way to craft, shape, redefine, and challenge a master narrative of inferiority and discrimination to a subjective voice of resistance poised for symbolic means of change. Wells wrote of the demise of three black men to lynching and began her inquiry into lynching with these sentiments: "The more I studied the situation, the more I was convinced that the Southerner had never gotten over his resentment that the Negro is no longer his plaything, his servant, and his source of income" (70).

Wells believed that lynching was an act of political and economic repression that served to hold both Blacks and women in their respective places in the social hierarchy.[17] Hall notes that whites continually felt themselves under siege, and lynching served to reinforce the hierarchical power relationships based on race and gender.[18] Furthermore, lynching persisted as much to reaffirm solidarity and demonstrate power to whites themselves as to punish and intimidate Blacks.

Wells's anti-lynching campaign began as a response to the brutal lynching of Thomas Moss, Calvin McDowell, and Henry Stewart, three business partners of the People's Grocery Company and friends of Ida B. Wells. During Reconstruction, Blacks began making economic gains in the South. Moss and his business partners opened a grocery store to patrons of the Black community and sold at prices competitive to the white store owner across the road. Their crime was not rape, but rather that they were successful, Black, and defended their property against ransackers of the white community.

In Wells's 1893 speech, *"Southern Horrors: Lynch Law in All Its Phases,"* she attempts to heighten consciousness, change perceptions, stimulate imagination, and garner action within her audience through anti-lynching discourse. This speech tells of the horrors of lynching and mob violence while denouncing the lynching mentality of upstanding white community citizens. Wells narrates the Black community's symbolic resistance as it responds to the lynching of three of its upstanding Black businessmen:

> The Afro-Americans of Memphis denounced the lynching of three of their best citizens, and urged and waited for the authorities to act in the matter and bring the lynchers to justice. No attempt was made to do so, and the black men left the city by thousands, bringing about great stagnation in every branch of business. Those who remained so injured the business of the street car company by staying off the cars, that the superintendent, manager and treasurer called personally on the editor of the *Free Speech,* asking them to urge our people to give them their patronage again. Other business men became alarmed over the situation and the *Free Speech* was run away that the colored people might be more easily controlled. A meeting of white citizens in June, three months after the lynching, passed resolutions for the first time, condemning it. But they did not punish the lynchers. Every one of them was known by name, because they had been selected to do the dirty work, by some of the very citizens who passed these resolutions. Memphis is fast losing her black population, who proclaim as they go that there is no protection for the life and property of any Afro-American citizen in Memphis who is not a slave.[19]

This excerpt demonstrates Wells's rhetoric as narrative of the voiceless. She creates a space that is indicative of Black women's culture of resistance. Finding her voice in the "Southern Horrors" speech reveals that Black women's discourse is a *story* of "rhetorical strategies of women who transformed the ordinariness of daily life into a rhetoric of survival not only for themselves but for generations to come."[20] Wells reveals how the everyday life of the Black community of Memphis is transformed when ordinary daily life happenings such as riding street cars becomes an act of resistance and challenges the system of domination. Boycotting becomes a symbolic act of defiance and shows the economic influence of the Black community. Symbolically, it demonstrated that African Americans were an economic force to be reckoned with, bringing the mainstream business community to its knees. Their symbolic act at once declared their presence as citizens while actively demonstrating their collective community of economic power. Boycotting not only disempowers white supremacy but empowers the Black community with a vision of economic power in community economics. That is to say, the notion of creating Black business communities owned by and for African Americans was forthcoming in the expansion of Black Americans to the West. As a response to Jim Crow segregation, Wells saw this vision of economic empowerment and encouraged the opportunities it would bring. She notes in her diary:

> I wrote this interview for the next issue of the *Free Speech* and in the article told the people to keep up the good work. Not only that, I went to the two largest churches in the city the next Sunday, before the paper came out, and told them all about it. I urged them to keep on staying off the cars. Every time word came of people leaving Memphis, we who were left behind rejoiced. Oklahoma was about to be opened up, and scores sold or gave away property, shook Memphis dust off their feet, and went out West as Tom Moss had said for us to do.[21]

By boycotting and creating a mass exodus out of the city, Black communities throughout the South defied the indifference and disrespect displayed to them by white citizens and city officials. Furthermore, community members defined themselves as "exodusters," on their way to the West, wherein greater opportunities for freedom and economic empowerment allegedly awaited them. Wells told the story of a people destined to redefine their existence as free people and spoke to the moral and ethical dimensions of American democracy:

> A large group who were not able to pay railroad fare left with their belongings in wagons, as in early years others had hit the trail. The men said they would walk, with their dogs and guns, and the women and children rode in wagons that were not even covered. About three hundred persons were in this particular party. When time came for them to be ferried across the Mississippi River a large number of friends were on the bluff to see them go. Many silent but observant white men were there and saw that bond of quiet, determined people leaving home and friends to seek

some place in our great democracy where their lives, liberty, and property would be protected. (55–56)

Resistance then, becomes a "discourse of experience" that illuminates a culture of struggle and survival. Wells's public address becomes the storyteller's voice that reveals a dialectical tension between white Southern resentment of Black freedom and the quest for Black American economic empowerment and social uplift. On an occasion to speak with Frederick Douglass, Douglass questioned Wells about her calm demeanor before speaking to an audience. She answered him with the confidence of a storyteller and the wisdom of an ancestral griot:

> The citizens of Providence, Rhode Island, next united to have a monster meeting there. Not only was I one of the chief speakers, but they sent to Washington for Mr. Douglass—who came and gave great honor to the occasion. As we sat in the anteroom waiting for the meeting to begin, Mr. Douglass said: "Ida, don't you feel nervous?" and I said, "No, Mr. Douglass." He said, "For the fifty years that I have been appearing before the public I have never gotten over a nervous feeling before I have to speak." And I said, "That is because you are an orator, Mr. Douglass, and naturally you are concerned as to the presentation of your address. With me it is different. I am only a mouthpiece through which to tell the story of lynching and I have told it so often that I know it by heart. I do not have to embellish; it makes its own way." That's exactly how I felt about the matter and that to my mind at least explained my utter lack of nervousness from that day way back in Aberdeen, Scotland, when I was unexpectedly thrust on the platform without my manuscript. (231)

Ida B. Wells embodied the storyteller's voice in the tradition and zeal of her foremothers. Her voice embodied both the struggle and the progress in the pursuit of human rights. I now examine how the rhetorical "voice" of Wells evidences a womanist perspective by navigating the dialectic of oppression and activism.

Claiming the Story: Creating Community through a Humanistic Vision

One of the tenets of womanism is to create a humanistic vision of the world through community building and activism. The rhetorical choices made by Ida B. Wells in her anti-lynching movement as well as in the development of African-American women's suffrage campaigns point to the underlying need to create community in the midst of claiming the story by telling it from the perspective of the lived experiences of the voiceless other. One such example of Wells's community building efforts was her first engagement of public address. She notes in her autobiography of having "no knowledge of stage business," and this would be her "first appearance before a New York audience" (80). Known throughout Black communities of the East coast for her journalistic fortitude and protests against lynching, Wells recalls: "Having lost my paper, had a price put on my life, and been made an exile from home for hinting at the truth, I felt that I owed it to myself and to my race to tell the whole truth now that I was where I could do so freely" (69). Several prominent Black women of New York and Brooklyn wished to show their communities' appreciation by inviting Ms. Wells to speak at Lyric Hall on October 5, 1892. Her newspaper columns were forceful indictments on the American judicial system and "race" women were determined to keep the monetary resources available for Wells to continue her activist work. It was the first time that Ida B. Wells would speak before an audience of hundreds. She was terrified. Of her speech in Lyric Hall, Wells writes:

> The testimonial was ... to be the greatest demonstration ever attempted by race women for one of their number ... Yet the best womanhood of those two cities responded wonderfully to their appeal. It resulted in the most brilliantly interesting affair of its kind ever attempted in these United States ... When the committee told me I had to speak I was frightened. I had been a writer, both as correspondent and editor, for several years. I had some little reputation as an essayist from schoolgirl days and had recited many times in public recitations which I had committed to memory ... But this was the first time I had ever been called on to deliver an honest-to-goodness address. (78–79)

She evokes the ancestral memory of a griot and reports the stories of her community so that her audience may never forget the horrors of a time past in America. As a novice, her trepidation to speak in public is compounded by the task of negotiating the public and private spheres of experience:

> Although every detail of that horrible lynching affair was imprinted on my memory, I had to commit it all to paper, and so got up to read my story on that memorable occasion. As I described the cause of the trouble at home and my mind went back to the scenes of the struggle, to the thought of the friends who were scattered throughout the country, a feeling of loneliness and homesickness for the days and the friends that were

> gone came over me and I felt the tears coming . . . I kept saying to myself
> that whatever happened I must not break down, and so I kept on reading.
> I had left my handkerchief on the seat behind me and therefore could not
> wipe away the tears which were coursing down my cheeks. The women
> were all back of me on the platform and could not see my plight. Noth-
> ing in my voice, it seemed, gave them an inkling of the true state of affairs.
> Only those in the audience could see the tears dropping. At last I put my
> hand behind me and beckoned even as I kept reading. Mrs. Matthews, the
> chairman, came forward and I asked her for my handkerchief. She brought
> it and I wiped my nose and streaming face, but I kept on reading the story
> which they had come to hear. (78–80)

Wells's experience underscores the notion of the public and private spheres
of experience analyzed through a womanist perspective. The public sphere
of experience reveals Wells's attempt to presents her public persona within
the framework of the traditional masculine style rhetoric—style, credibility, rational appeals, control of one's emotions, while at the same time
crafting a new persona within a new public space that affirms her telling
the stories of horrific experiences of her community. As discussed earlier,
a storyteller situates herself and experience in the belongingness of the
tribe. Storytelling means to assume the range of memory and emotions
sacrificing everything in the retelling of the story.[22] While the public
space is comprised of an audience, it is an audience that co-creates a *safe
space* to resist the hegemonic differences of proper (masculine) decorum
of speechmaking, and allows for community acceptance and appeal. Wells
continues:

> I was mortified that I had not been able to prevent such an exhibition of
> weakness. It came on me unawares. It was the only time in all those trying
> months that I had so yielded to personal feelings. That it should come at
> a time when I wanted to be at my best in order to show my appreciation
> of the splendid things those women had done! They were giving me tan-
> gible evidence that although my environment had changed I was still sur-
> rounded by kind hearts. (80)

Although driven out of her community in Memphis, Tennessee, Wells
found community in a safe space of Black women activists dedicated to
promoting the ancestral cause of freedom. Of this safe space, Patricia
Hill Collins writes, "Extended families, churches, and African-American
community organizations are important locations where safe discourse
potentially can occur . . . This space is not only safe—it forms a prime
location for resisting objectification as the Other."[23] Sondra O'Neale ex-

plains the space of self-definition through the legacy of Black women's cultural tradition thus: "In this space black women . . . go about the business of fashioning themselves after the prevalent, historical black female role models in their own community."[24] Wells demonstrates that the private sphere, of experience conjoins with the public sphere giving clarity to the notion that the "personal is political." The private sphere, however, reveals the legacy that she embodies—the legacy of telling the story of her people's culture of struggle and survival. Moreover, the safe space of Lyric Hall assisted in co-creating meaning among audience and speaker, while presenting new meanings of self-definition and resistance in support of Black women's activism. Wells concludes her novice experience by illustrating the "fruits" of community coalition resulting from her speech:

> So many things came out of that wonderful testimonial. First, it was the real beginning of the club movement among the colored women in this country. The women of New York and Brooklyn decided to continue that organization, which they called the Women's Loyal Union. These were the first strictly women's clubs organized in those two cities. Mrs. Ruffin of Boston, who came over to that testimonial, invited me to be her guest in Boston later on. She called a meeting of the women at her home to meet me, and they organized themselves into the Woman's Era Club of that city. Mrs. Ruffin had been a member of the foremost clubs among white women in Boston for years, but this was her first effort to form one among colored women . . . Several years later, on a return visit to New England, I helped the women of New Haven, Connecticut, to organize their first club . . . Second, that testimonial was the beginning of public speaking for me. I have already said that I had not before made speeches, but invitations came from Philadelphia, Wilmington, Delaware, Chester, Pennsylvania, and Washington, D.C. (80–82)

Wells goes on to say that a final result of her first speaking engagement at Lyric Hall was the meeting of Miss Catherine Impey of Somerset, England, who later invites her abroad. That voyage to England serves as the beginning of a worldwide campaign against lynching. Collins points out that:

> These institutional sites where Black women construct independent self-definitions reflect the dialectical nature of oppression and activism . . . African-American women have traditionally used Black families and community institutions as places where they could develop a Black women's culture of resistance.[25]

In her work at home and abroad, Wells uses the rhetorical act of storytelling to build bridges in the universal community and to promulgate a culture of resistance. Though she locates Black women's community, Wells recognizes the nationalistic aspect of "race" women, yet sees the need for social change by placing the rhetoric of lynching in the broader world community. Bernice Johnson Reagon observes, "at a certain stage nationalism is crucial to a people if you are going to ever impact as a group in your own interest. Nationalism at another point becomes reactionary because it is totally inadequate for surviving in the world with many peoples."[26] Wells attempts to refute the historically held notion that the Black race is the most denigrated of all species, and uplifts the image of her race by citing the personal experiences of men, women, and children as victims of mob violence:

> The alleged menace of universal suffrage having been avoided by the absolute suppression of the Negro vote, the spirit of mob murder should have been satisfied and the butchery of Negroes should have ceased. But men, women, and children were the victims of murder by individuals and murder by mobs, just as they had been when killed at the demands of the "unwritten law" to prevent "Negro domination." Colored women have been murdered because they refuse to tell the mobs where relatives could be found for "lynching bees." Boys of fourteen years have been lynched by white representatives of American civilization. In fact, for all kinds of offenses—and, for no offenses—from murders to misdemeanors, men and women are put to death without judge or jury; so that, although the political excuse was no longer necessary, the wholesale murder of human beings went on just the same. A new name was given to killings and a new excuse was invented for doing so.[27]

In this speech, Wells embraces the notion of forging universal bridges for the construction of community as a complex and challenging endeavor. The complexities of Black women's actions in constructing community are the basis of Wells's rhetoric. While she attempts to construct the audience of Black members, she simultaneously speaks to the "human community" by challenging their notions of morality and ethics, and appeals to familial ties within the human family.

Wells's rhetoric also demonstrates how culture and community are linked with studies of rhetorical discourse that take into account the larger mosaic of gendered and cultured lives within a dialectic of power and resistance. Ida B. Wells demonstrated a tradition of Black women's rhetoric that constructs new forms of community and creates realities that resist structures of domination. It is within this legacy that she leaves an indelible mark for scholars—a message that encourages deeper exploration of how African-American women create, negotiate, challenge, and change the cultural realities as we rise to find our collective voice.

Conclusion

This chapter offers a new perspective on the public address of Ida B. Wells. Its aim is to reveal how the notion of "voice" informs our understanding of Wells's rhetoric from a negotiated space of otherness through the public act of storytelling. First, Black women's rhetorical tradition provided a context within which Ida B. Wells maintained the legacy of Black women's resistance and activism. Second, the rhetorical voice of otherness yields the notion that "voice" of Black women resisted traditionally held assumptions of race, culture, and experience. Finally, examples of her rhetoric reveal the ways in which Wells created community in a womanist tradition of care and coalition building.

Examining Wells rhetoric as a continuum of African-American women's rhetorical tradition provides new ways to appreciate her rhetoric as a lens through which the rhetorical "voice" shapes our understanding of ethnic culture, community building, and lived experience. The public and private spheres of experience in Wells's early life revealed a multiple consciousness of the ideological perspectives of the times and informed her sense of survival and resistance in the struggle to achieve human dignity and American justice. Not only did the ideologies of nineteenth-century America shape her, but she in turn provided a dialectical opposition to the systems of power insistent on maintaining the subjugated social positions of African Americans and women. In rising to find her voice, she claimed an existence of self, community, and narrative discourse that redefined, reconstructed, and transformed the myth of the master narrative of lynching.

Wells's use of the African-American female rhetorical tradition provided a paradigm for the rootedness of her public address. This rootedness was in the spirit-voice of her ancestors. Wells never forgot nor underestimated the culture of community as evidenced in her tireless efforts to reach out to the Black race as well as forging bridges abroad. In remembering her place in the continuum, she told the story of what it means to be Black, to be a Black woman, to be a Black woman American in a land "that defines human by being white and male for starters" and within a land that acknowledges rhetorical prowess and effectiveness by standards crafted by and for whites and males.[28]

Her voice was a political statement of the private and public spheres of the experience of survival. Wells centers experience at the core of knowledge and meaning and redefines the social construction of the immoral institution of lynching. In addition, Ida B. Wells continues the African-American women's rhetorical tradition through her autobiographical narrative and efforts of collective activism among Black women. The rhetoric of autobiography provides generations beyond her time to review the experience of oppression and strategies for transforming social reality into a public discourse of resistance.[29] As in Black female slave narratives, the autobiography was a personal-rhetorical artifact that unites with the collective voice in a major effort to expose white oppression.[30] The autobiography of Wells points to that transcending aspect of Black female slave narratives: to continue the ancestral continuum of transforming lives by keeping the stories of collective experience alive. Of the relationship between narrative and community Clifford G. Christians notes: "Communities are woven together by narratives that invigorate their common understanding of good and evil, happiness and reward, the meaning of life and death. Recovering and refashioning . . . word forms help to amplify our deepest humanness."[31] Ida *Bell* Wells is the "carillon" that calls, even now, for *our* response to lived experience that challenges moral responsibility, ethical awareness, and human consciousness throughout time—beyond her days.

Notes

1. Olga Idriss Davis, *It Be's Hard Sometimes: The Rhetorical Invention of Black Female Persona in Pre-Emancipatory Slave Narratives* (Ph.D. dissertation, University of Nebraska, 1994).

2. Hazel V. Carby, *Reconstructing Womanhood: The Emergence of the Afro-American Woman Novelist* (London: Oxford University Press, 1987), 111.

3. Eric King Watts, "'Voice' and 'Voicelessness' in Rhetorical Studies," *Quarterly Journal of Speech* 87, no. 2 (May 2001): 179–96.

4. Alice Walker, *In Search of Our Mothers' Gardens: Womanist Prose,* (New York: Harcourt Brace Jovanivich, 1983).

5. Olga I. Davis, "A Black Woman as Rhetorical Critic: Validating Self and Violating the Space of Otherness," *Women's Studies in Communication* 21, no. 1 (Spring 1998): 77–89.

6. Davis, *It Be's Hard Sometimes,* 13.

7. Olga I. Davis, "Theorizing African American Women's Discourse: The Public and Private Spheres of Experience," in *Centering Ourselves: African American*

Feminist and Womanist Studies of Discourse, ed. Marsha Houston and Olga I. Davis, (Cresskill, N.J.: Hampton Press, 2002), 36.

8. Mark Lawrence McPhail, *Zen in the Art of Rhetoric: An Inquiry into Coherence* (Albany: SUNY Press, 1996).

9. Chaim Perlman and L. Olbrechts-Tyteca, *The New Rhetoric: A Treatise on Argumentation* (Notre Dame: University of Notre Dame Press, 1969), 40.

10. Ida B. Wells Barnett, *Crusade for Justice: The Autobiography of Ida B. Wells*, ed. Alfreda M. Duster (Chicago: University of Chicago Press, 1987), 44–45. Future references cited parenthetically in text are to this edition.

11. Linda T. Wynn, "Ida B. Wells Barnett," in *Notable Black American Women*, ed. Jessie Carney Smith (Detroit: Gale Research, 1992), 183.

12. Wells Barnett, *Crusade for Justice*, 19–21; "Ida Wells v. Chesapeake, Ohio, and Southwestern Railroad Company," March 31, 1885, Manuscript Court Record, 21.

13. Rosemary Bray. "Taking Sides Against Ourselves," *New York Times Magazine*, November 17, 1991, 56.

14. Jacqueline Jones Royster, *Southern Horrors and Other Writings: The Anti-Lynching Campaign of Ida B. Wells, 1892–1900* (Boston: Bedford Books, 1997).

15. Hortense Spillers, "Foreword," in *Six Women's Slave Narratives*, H. L. Gates (New York: Oxford University Press, 1988), xi.

16. R. Williams, "Foreword," in *The Rodrigo Chronicles: Conversations about America and Race*, ed. R. Delgado (New York: New York University Press, 1995), xi–xv, xi.

17. Emilie Maureen Townes, "The Social and Moral Perspectives of Ida B. Wells-Barnett as Resources for a Contemporary Afro-Feminist Christian Social Ethic" (Ph.D. dissertation, Northwestern University, 1989).

18. Jacquelyn Dowd Hall, *Revolt against Chivalry: Jessie Daniel Ames and the Women's Campaign against Lynching* (New York: Columbia University Press, 1979).

19. Ida B. Wells, "Southern Horrors: Lynch Law in All Its Phases," in *Man Cannot Speak for Her: Key Texts of the Early Feminists*, vol. 2, ed. Karlyn K. Campbell (New York: Greenwood Press, 1989), 414–15.

20. Davis, "A Black Woman as Rhetorical Critic," 77–89.

21. Miriam DeCosta-Willis, *Memphis Diary of Ida B. Wells*, (Boston: Beacon Press, 1995).

22. Williams, "Foreword," xi–xii.

23. Patricia Hill Collins, *Black Feminist Thought: Knowledge, Consciousness, and the Politics of Empowerment* (New York: Routledge, 1991), 95.

24. Sondra O'Neale, "Inhibiting Midwives, Usurping Creators: The Struggling Emergence of Black Women in American Fiction," in *Feminist Studies/Critical Studies*, ed. Teresa de Lauretis (Bloomington: Indiana University Press, 1986), 139–56.

25. Collins, *Black Feminist Thought*, 95.

26. Bernice J. Reagon, "Coalition Politics: Turning the Century," in *Home Girls—A Black Feminist Anthology*, ed. Barbara Smith (New York: Kitchen Table Press, 1983), 358.

27. Wells, "Southern Horrors," 3.

28. Elsa Barkley Brown, "Imaging Lynching: African American Women, Communities of Struggle, and Collective Memory," in *African American Women Speak Out on Anita Hill-Clarence Thomas*, ed. Geneva Smitherman, (Detroit: Wayne State University Press, 1995), 116.

29. Olga Idriss Davis, "Life Ain't Been No Crystal Stair: The Rhetoric of Autobiography in Black Female Slave Narratives," in *Black Lives: Essays in African American Biography*, ed. James L. Conyers, Jr. (New York: M.E. Sharpe, 1999), 151–59.

30. Sidonie Smith, *Where I'm Bound: Patterns of Slavery and Freedom in Black American Autobiography* (Westport, Conn.: Greenwood Press, 1974), 2–3.

31. Clifford G. Christions, "Ethics and Politics in Qualitative Research," in *Handbook of Qualitative Research*, eds. Norman K. Denzin and Yvonne S. Lincoln (Thousand Oaks, Calif.: Sage, 2000), 147.

Chapter 15

The Emergence of a Black Feminist Leadership Model

African-American Women and Political Activism in the Nineteenth Century

MELINA ABDULLAH

For Black women, leadership is designed to restructure the existing power system. As such, a model of leadership emerged among Black women activists that is rooted in Black feminism. The development of a Black feminist leadership model can be traced at least as far back as the nineteenth century. During this period, Black women birthed their own movements, developing unique definitions and forms of leadership as illustrated through the Black women's club movement and the anti-lynching movement.

This chapter investigates the model of leadership developed by Black women in the nineteenth century and identifies the major features of this praxis using examples from the anti-lynching and Black women's club movements. Several recent studies assert that Black women engage in leadership styles that are specific to the intersectional socio-political spaces that they occupy.[1] However, to date, little work has been done to historicize the development of Black women's leadership. The early work of Black women through the overlapping anti-lynching and club movements builds a leadership model that is rooted in traditional African gender roles and has been shaped by the history of American slavery. This model, at its core, is a Black feminist one in that it seeks to encompass the simultaneous realities of race, gender, and class, and eradicate all forms of oppression that accompany multi-axis identities. The distinctive form of leadership developed here takes on a radical approach—favoring fundamental transformation over limited reform.

Although Black feminist organizing is rooted in precolonial African tradition, the nineteenth century marks the earliest point at which there is substantial documentary evidence of Black women working in an organized manner toward their own empowerment. Works by Ivan Van Sertima and Nah Dove are especially valuable in affirming that the legacy of Black women's leadership precedes their arrival in the United States and in making connections between the traditions of precolonial continental and diasporic Africans.[2] Slave narratives suggest that there also was some level of group organizing led by Black women in the United States in earlier periods.[3] However, slavery severely restricted the communication and movements of slaves, making organized group action difficult. Similarly, organizing among free Blacks was limited by the lack of a critical mass and the black codes that were established to serve as a constant source of intimidation and crush any visible organizing efforts. Thus, while some examples of Black feminist leadership can be identified prior to the nineteenth century, they are more likely to have existed through everyday acts of resistance, escapes, and individually initiated rebellions.[4]

For Black women, who recognize their intersectional identities, oppressed as women, as Black people, and as members of the poor and working class, leadership functions to bring about a transformation in how power and resources are allocated as opposed simply to working to maintain the status quo or lobby for reform. Thus, Black feminist leadership as a radical concept has required an alternate leadership model. The leadership that emerges from this Black feminist conceptualization carries with it four core tenets: 1) it seeks to bridge theory with practice, with each constantly informing the other, 2) it is proactive and not simply reactive, 3) it adopts a group-centered approach in which all members share the responsibility of leadership and collectively "own" the movement, and 4) it utilizes both traditional and nontraditional forms of activism.

Black and Woman: The Problem with the Ranking of Oppressions and the Hierarchical Approach to Comparative Discrimination

During the nineteenth century, change movements generally focused on either race-based or gender-based empowerment. One of the core challenges of Black women's involvements in such efforts has been the implicit requirement of "choosing" either a racial identity or a gender identity—as if the categories are somehow mutually exclusive. This has meant that Black women, in a sense, must rank their oppressions. While Black women generally have chosen Blackness over womanhood when forced, there remains the frustration of never being able to fully address the whole of Black womanhood. Black women experience the world as both Black and woman simultaneously. Thus, the attempt to force a choice between racial or gender identity denies a part of one's very existence.

The interlocking systems of oppression have always been a part of Black women's everyday lives. In slavery, the Black woman endured both racial and sexual dehumanization. With the process of dehumanization the distinguishing element of American slavery, Black women and Black men both were rendered "socially dead" beings.[5] However, in addition to this shared racial oppression, Black women also experienced sexual dehumanization. The common practice of rape offered both psychological and material benefit for White slaveholders—as rapist conquerors and owners of any resulting children.

In addition to the appropriation of the Black woman's body for White male pleasure and economic gain, there was a hypocritical process of de-feminization of the Black woman that enabled Whites to justify her oppression and exploitation. If she were seen as a woman, as feminine, there would be an implied humanity (albeit a lower order than man). Thus, there is a disturbing paradox. While it is her womanhood that contributes to her value as "property" based on her ability to reproduce, the acknowledgement of womanhood would require that Black women become "human."

As socially dead, sexually exploited, defeminized beings, Black women served as the "lowest common denominator" in the American social and political hierarchy.[6] However, rather than serving as a foundation and bridge between Black empowerment and women's movements, Black women were subject to both racist and sexist oppression even within gender-based and race-based organizations. White women denied Black women full entrance into the suffrage movement, viewing Blackness as detracting from one's identity as a woman. Thus, the only "true" woman was a White woman. During the same period, many "race men" asked Black women to set aside gender and focus solely on racial empowerment. "Even though African American women were victims of both racism and sexism, they were being put into a position of having to choose which oppression was more debilitating."[7] As a result, Black women were forced to choose between African-American patriarchy and White female racism.

Exclusion of women from the decision-making process was practiced widely within Black empowerment movements. Still, Black women always have asserted their right to full participation. With few exceptions, Black men in leadership positions included Black women in organizations and movements.[8] However, when faced with the question of whether to address the particularity of Black women's conditions, Black men, almost without exception, chose to deny the intersectional identities of Black women, instead seeing them as a sort of specialized arm of the Black male vanguard.

More blatant acts of exclusion occurred in the suffrage movement where White women dominated. While some organizations allowed Black women in the room, they were not seen as having the capacity to speak for all women, nor was their particular status as Black women seen as an area that the suffragists needed to address. While the early coalition between first-wave feminists and early movements for Black empowerment offered promise—especially for Black women who found themselves on the cusp of two movements—growing tensions between Black men and White women were exacerbated with the passage of the Fifteenth Amendment when Black men were granted the right to vote ahead of women.[9]

The breakdown of the coalition left Black women in a suspended state. They remained participants in race-based movements and fought for inclusion in gender-based movements, but found themselves along the periphery of both. This marginal status within the male-dominated Black empowerment movement and White-dominated women's organizations may have encouraged the development of a Black feminist leadership model in the nineteenth century.

There are two clear illustrations of Black feminist leadership in the nineteenth century: the anti-lynching movement and the Black women's club movement. Through these examples, we begin to understand more clearly ways in which Black feminist leadership is manifested.

The Anti-Lynching Movement

Following the withdrawal of federal troops from the South and the end of Reconstruction in 1877, White southerners increasingly viewed Blacks as a threat to White society. No longer the legal property of White owners, Blacks increasingly were subject to mob violence, for no material loss was suffered by Whites as a result of their death or injury. Lynching surged during this period. From 1882 to 1903, 2,060 Blacks were lynched.[10] In fact, between 1892 and 1920, more people were lynched than were executed legally.[11] Lynching served two purposes—one psychological and the other material. First, lynching grew out of mob violence where the intense anger harbored by individuals was compounded through large group or mob settings.[12] Lynching served to satiate the hatred toward and fear of Blacks held by many Whites of all classes, but especially the White working class who sought to affirm their position of societal superiority. The second and perhaps more important purpose that lynching served for Whites was to preserve the material benefits that accompanied Whiteness. Where it is commonly held that Black men were lynched for alleged acts of sexual aggression against White women, only 25 percent of those Black men who were lynched were even accused of rape.[13] Many more were targeted because of their economic successes.[14] Thus, lynching not only was a tool designed to instill fear and maintain the social racial hierarchy; it also was used to preserve the White monopoly on wealth.

Although lynching was practiced under slavery and during the Reconstruction period, several political factors contributed to the surge in lynching in the late nineteenth century. In 1877, the United States government withdrew its troops from the South, marking the end of Reconstruction. This was followed by the 1883 Supreme Court ruling that struck down the Civil Rights Act of 1875, making the protection of Black rights against the acts of private citizens beyond the scope of federal governmental duty.[15] This refusal to protect Blacks against other private citizens contributed to a public tone that condoned mob violence.

The movement to stop mob violence and lynching during the post-Reconstruction period and into the twentieth century was considered one of the most radical efforts of the time. Despite the actual accusations and motivations of lynch mobs, the public perception was that "justifications" for lynching were grounded in the notion that victims were, themselves, the perpetrators of crimes and deserving of the torturous acts inflicted upon them. Challenges to lynching meant revisiting the alleged crimes and questioning the behaviors of all parties involved. Most notably, lynch mobs often justified their actions by alleging that the Black men who were lynched had raped or sexually assaulted White women. By questioning this allegation, the anti-lynching movement was thought to be also questioning the virtue of White women.

Nonetheless, Black women and men were driven to challenge lynching for the sake of their very lives and survival of their community. Anti-lynching activism took place in many forms, from the armed protection of Black inmates by Black townspeople, to the outmigration from Southern towns to Northern and Western areas where lynching was less common.[16] Anti-lynching was a movement that rallied the efforts of the nameless, faceless Black masses who would work tirelessly for their collective right to life.

This sort of individual anonymity—which stands at the center of Black feminist leadership—makes the identification of solitary leaders difficult. By design, the group-centered component, advocated most explicitly by Ella Baker in the 1960s, diminishes the visibility of individual leaders, making each member a partner in the larger movement.[17] This group-centered approach, while not clearly outlined or identified as such by organizers in the nineteenth century, remained central to their organizing efforts. As the Black feminist model emerged, the centering of the "leader" becomes less important and thus the work of many leaders remains undocumented. However, such an approach leads to more-enduring, collectively owned movements, and serves a practical purpose as a protective mechanism, shielding individual organizers from repercussions of their actions. "They left no records, wrote no books, organized no conferences, but they helped to establish a tradition of political activism among black women."[18] In order to research the way that individual leaders functioned in such a movement, we begin with those who did leave records as their contributions to the collective effort: public lecturers and journalists. At the center of the movement stood Ida B. Wells-Barnett.

A Pen Mightier than a Sword: The Activism of Ida B. Wells

In her work "Black Women Journalists in the South, 1880–1905," Gloria Wade-Gayles discusses how journalism was used by Black women as a method of social and political empowerment for Black people generally and Black women specifically. Journalism was a particularly valuable tool for Black women because of three key factors: 1) exposure and access to writing opportunities, 2) the relatively high political and social impact of written words, and 3) the relatively minimal risk that accompanied this form of activism. Black women often gained exposure to and experience in journalistic writing by working for church publications. Some used these experiences to transition into journalism careers for more widely circulated periodicals, mainly Southern Black newspapers and journals.[19]

Ida B. Wells followed this model, beginning her work as a journalist by writing for a church paper in 1887.[20] Through the weekly contribution of articles, Wells gained exposure that resulted in the offering of a position as editor of the Memphis *Free Speech and Headlight,* a position she accepted with the contingency that she would become partner—purchasing one-third ownership in the paper.[21] Wells began her career embracing the notion of "objective" journalism. Her early writings sought to expose the injustices and inequality of the segregated Black educational system along with other challenges faced by southern Blacks. She increasingly became committed to the anti-lynching movement following the 1892 "Lynching at the Curve" where three Black grocery store owners were murdered because of the economic threat that they posed to a competing White grocer; one of the victims was a close friend of Wells's. This personal connection with lynching brought about a shift in her journalistic style. Whereas in previous pieces on lynching Wells thought that the horror of lynching could be addressed by informing an ignorant White public of Black innocence and highlighting the morality of a "higher class" African Americans, with the lynching of her friends in 1892, her approach evolved. She no longer sought to shroud herself in the cloak of "objectivity," but used her writing to tell the particular truths of Southern Blacks. She saw her writing as a form of activism in itself and, as such, developed a style that was more aggressive and confrontational than other Black women leaders of the era.[22] She quickly became the voice of African Americans in the South and found herself at the center of the anti-lynching movement. "[M]ost turn of the [twentieth] century anti-lynching activities revolved around the efforts of Ida Wells."[23]

Her central role in the anti-lynching movement does not negate her commitment to group-centered leadership, however. Rather than viewing herself as a leader among followers, Wells viewed her work as her way of contributing to a larger movement. As her reputation as a leader grew and her work began to encompass other forms of activism, including public speaking, she held that she was simply doing her part for the masses that she represented. In a conversation with Frederick Douglass, she spoke of this philosophy, downplaying her importance as an individual. When

Douglass expressed concern about how well his pending public address would be received, Wells responded by defining herself as a tool of the movement rather than an orator. "That is because you are an orator Mr. Douglass, and naturally you are concerned as to the presentation of your address. With me it is different. I am only a mouthpiece through which to tell the story of lynching."[24] The goal of her writing and public addresses was to disseminate information in a way that would compel action, that would give the receivers of her words the resolve to stand up against lynching at all costs. In fact, her advocacy of specific actions, including the armament of Black Southerners, the economic boycott of White businesses, and the outmigration of African Americans from oppressive Southern states is indicative of two additional tenets of Black feminist leadership: taking a proactive as opposed to a simply reactive posture and the use of both traditional and nontraditional methods.

While writing and public speaking were her main forms of activism, Wells also engaged in other actions and placed herself firmly in the midst of the movement. As she pushed her readers and audiences to carry out particular acts of resistance, she also did so herself. For example, she often used her writing to encourage Blacks to take up arms. "The lesson this [lynching] teaches and which every Afro-American should ponder well, is that a Winchester rifle should have a place of honor in every black home, and it should be used for the protection which the law refuses to give."[25] This was not simply rhetoric for Wells, but a prescription that she also followed.

> I had bought a pistol the first thing after Tom Moss was lynched, because I expected some cowardly retaliation from the lynchers. I felt that one had better die fighting against injustice than to die like a dog or a rat in a trap. I had already determined to sell my life as dearly as possible if attacked. I felt if I could take one lyncher with me, this would even up the score a little bit."[26]

This simultaneous commitment to serving as a catalyst for mass action and her willingness to engage in the action herself begins to distinguish Wells as an early example of a Black feminist leader. While Ida B. Wells was one of several well-known public speakers and journalists of the time, the way in which she viewed her role distinguished her from others—especially Black men, White women, and White men.[27] Where fellow journalists, such as T. Thomas Fortune, viewed their writing as their activism and as evidence of their leadership, Wells viewed this work as only a part of her commitment. She spoke and wrote not of what "they" must do, but what "we" must do. It is this perspective that compelled her to follow her own instruction in arming herself, leaving the South, filing lawsuits, and lobbying public officials.[28]

As with most political awakenings, Wells was prompted by a personal experience with a particular traumatic event. Although her work became more politicized following the 1892 lynching of Moss, McDowell, and Stewart, her activism was not limited to a reactionary posture. Her work in the anti-lynching movement was proactive in that it sought to transform the social and political realities of Blacks by humanizing them in the eyes of Whites, challenging the law to protect them, and standing among the masses to claim the right to life. Wells also bridged theory with practice, with each continuously informing the other. This is evidenced in the shift in approach between her early career as a journalist and her later work. Early on, she ascribed to a more accommodationist theory, believing that if she demonstrated the virtue of a certain class of Blacks to Whites that she would appeal to their sense of righteousness and succeed in stopping "unwarranted" lynchings. However, following the "Lynching at the Curve," she recognized the unwillingness of Southern Whites to see Blacks as human and thus shifted both her theory and her approach to a more radical one, advocating economic sanctions and self-defense.

This example is also illustrative of the third element of her leadership model—the use of both traditional and nontraditional methods. A more traditional approach was taken by Wells as she worked within the existing system, using her voice as a writer and public speaker to compel shifts in policy and public action. However, she was not limited by the parameters of acceptability, and regularly engaged in actions that were more protest-driven, beyond those outlets defined by dominant society; such is the case with economic boycotts and Black armament.

This combined traditional/nontraditional approach (often referred to as inside participation and outside agitation) carried with it the greatest possibility for substantive change. There is a symbiotic relationship between the two methods. Participation within a system that was designed to exclude and oppress carries with it, at best, the opportunity for limited reform. However, traditional participation sets the stage for transformative change in two ways. First, it chips away at the system of oppression, in a sense weakening the hold of the oppressor's boot on the neck of the oppressed, increasing the possibility of revolutionary change. Second, the push for favorable policy provides a mechanism through which demands made by the "outside" might be realized. Similarly, nontraditional approaches serve as a very real threat to the existing system, making the reformist demands presented by "insiders" appear much more reasonable. The outside approach also stands as an outlet that enables organizers to "vision" the world that they would like to see rather than being restricted by the constraints of the current system. Thus the combined practice of both traditional and nontraditional methods was essential to moving a transformative agenda forward.

The final component of the emerging Black feminist praxis is group-centered leadership. While journalism and public speaking are much more individual than collective behavior, Wells recognized the power of mass action. Enduring substantive change never results solely from the actions of an individual; transformative change derives from group action. Thus, Wells saw her role as a journalist and public speaker as contributions to a wider movement that she sought to further develop. As such, she was instrumental in the growth of the black women's club movement that would serve as the collective voice to move the agenda of empowerment forward.

The Black Women's Club Movement

As part of her commitment to group-centered leadership, Ida B. Wells began to search for a more defined base. In doing so, she found a collective of Black women leaders in the Black women's club movement. Black women began to organize themselves into "clubs" and "leagues" in the early nineteenth century. The earliest formal association documented is the Colored Women's League of Washington, established in 1829.[29] Understandably, Black women's clubs grew much more rapidly following Emancipation, with the exponential growth in the late 1800s necessitating the formation of umbrella organizations. In 1885, the National Federation of Colored Women's Clubs was founded; the Women's Loyal Union was also established. The two would merge in 1896 to form the National Association of Colored Women's Clubs.[30] While some scholars assert that Black women's clubs were apolitical social service organizations that simply fell in line with the model of the White women's clubs, I contend that the formation of Black women's clubs, while possessing elements of White gendered normalcy, is more clearly reflective of Black women's desire to establish a safe space where Black womanhood is centered and to form a vehicle through which a Black feminist approach to political action could be practiced.[31]

I maintain that the provision of social service is in itself often political. When we define political actions broadly—as the attempt to address and redistribute power in society—social service politicizes on two levels. First, it meets core needs of service recipients, enabling them to move beyond the realm of survival, freeing them to think and act politically. Second, the providers of the service are empowered themselves in that they become cognizant of their own ability to shape their communities. Volunteer work increasingly has been recognized as a form of political action, which stands alone as well as contributing to other, more mainstream forms, including the participation in electoral politics and the lobbying of public officials.[32] Thus, the opening of kindergartens, the development of homes for the elderly and displaced, the establishment of scholarship funds, the offering of employment training and placement programs, and the founding of childcare facilities for Black children by Black clubwomen were all political actions.

In addition to social service being a political action, the provision of service is also illustrative of a core tenet of Black feminist leadership. Through the provision of social service, Black clubwomen were engaged proactively, rather than taking a simply reactive posture. Social service for clubwomen meant assessing community needs and seeking to meet those needs, without the prompting of some catastrophe that forced their response. Through proactive leadership, communities become self-defining, outlining their own agendas rather than having their plan of action dictated to them by those in power. Such an approach not only affirms the provision of social service as a political action, but begins to carve out a leadership model that is both conceptually and actually specific to Black women.

Radical Activism among Black Club Women

The work of Black women's clubs was not limited to social service. Many clubs were established with a primary purpose of shaping public policy in ways that advanced the interests of Black women, the Black community, and women as a whole. Central to the agenda of Black women's clubs was the protection of Blacks against lynching. As political movements, club actions overlapped significantly with the anti-lynching movement. Rosalyn Terborg-Penn notes that at the height of the lynching era in the late nineteenth century (also the height of the formation of Black women's clubs), the primary goal of the clubs was the attainment of federal anti-lynching legislation. Black women's clubs lobbied the president and legislature and after many years were successful in getting a bill introduced by Congressman Leonides Dyer of Missouri in 1918.[33] While the legislation was not passed, consistent with the Black feminist model of leadership introduced here, Black women's clubs did not limit their actions to the realm of formal politics.

In addition to the push for anti-lynching legislation, Black women recognized the club movement as a vehicle through which they could organize and oppose lynching utilizing both traditional and nontraditional methods.[34] Nontraditional methods were carried out largely through the financial and moral support for Ida B. Wells in her appeal for international pressure to oppose lynching. It was the Women's Loyal Union, with Josephine St. Pierre Ruffin as president, that hosted Wells in her first public address in 1892 and awarded her a $500 honorarium.[35] Both Wells and the clubwomen recognized the strength that would come through the overlap of the anti-lynching and club movements and went on to continue their work together well into the twentieth century.[36]

The anti-lynching efforts of Black women's clubs were not so much about the personal protection of clubwomen themselves, or even that of their families, but the defense of the whole of the Black community. Black women's clubs initially were organized in Northern states, where lynching was not as frequent; furthermore, while women also were lynched, the more common victims of lynching were Black men. The support given by clubwomen to the anti-lynching movement demonstrates not only their radical ideological stance, but also radicalism in action through an embrace of a collectivist organizing model.[37]

The praxis of collective empowerment was not limited to the anti-lynching efforts of Black clubwomen, but formed the core of their approach to leadership. With a motto of "Lifting as We Climb," Black women's clubs were much more than social organizations for nineteenth-century middle-class Black women. Although Black women's clubs membership was comprised mainly of middle-class women, this was largely because such women had more time and resources to engage in club activities. This is not to say that clubs did not practice some degree of classism; in fact, even Ida B. Wells, who played a central role in the club movement, but whose background was not middle class, met with some resistance from women of higher economic status.[38] However, such divides are outweighed by the collective approach to empowerment advocated by clubwomen. The National Association of Colored Women's Clubs motto suggests an approach to Black empowerment that rejects the notion of individualism, instead embracing a more collectivist view. Where many of the writings of Black clubwomen indicate that there were some bourgeois tendencies among clubwomen, the overall approach to leadership and goals of activism affirm that members saw themselves as members of the whole of the Black community. Thus, uplift for them was dependent upon collective empowerment.

> [W]omen were guided out of their narrow spheres into a bigger and more progressive atmosphere learning that the world was not made for "me and my wife, my son John and his wife, us four and no more," but that they were living in an age where there were big things to be done for Humanity and the world.[39]

This collectivist approach also was carried into the organizing model of the Black women's club movement. While the individual contributions of members and non-members regularly received accolades from the whole of the membership, it was the collective body that engaged in actions to move club agendas forward.[40] In her work *Lifting as the Climb*, Elizabeth Lindsay Davis, a Black clubwoman herself, asserts that Black women's clubs were more than organizations, but were a movement that offered a way for Black women to organize and through which they could represent themselves, rather than being subject to the definitions imposed by White, male-dominated society. The means through which the goals envisioned by Black women would be achieved would be through collective engagement. Hence, while some women were named individually, more often Davis refers to "our" efforts, successes, and goals—including the organizing and hosting of forums against lynching, the building of homes for the elderly, and the establishment of scholarship funds for Black students.

Black women's clubs provided a space where Black women could come together to formulate ideologies and engage in actions that were developed proactively and self-defined, where methods would be both traditional and nontraditional, and where group-centered leadership allowed for an approach to political action that sought substantive change. While clubs consisted mainly of middle-class Black women, they were much less exclusive than they often were perceived to be, in that they saw themselves a part of the whole of the Black collective and viewed their interests and advance as intrinsically linked with the uplift of Blacks as a whole. As such, they sought to build coalitions with other progressive organizations and with individuals who were not necessarily Black women. The vision of the Black women's club movement is perhaps most clearly laid out by Josephine St. Pierre Ruffin in her 1895 address at the first National Conference of the Colored Women of America in Boston:

> Our woman's movement is a woman's movement in that it is led and directed by women for the good of women and men, for the benefit of all of humanity, which is more than any one branch or section of it. We want, we ask the active interest of our men, and, too, we are not drawing the color line; we are women, American women, as intensely interested in all that pertains to us as such as all other American women, we are not alienating or withdrawing, we are only coming to the front, willing to join any others in the same work and cordially inviting and welcoming others to join us.[41]

The Legacy of Black Feminist Leadership

This chapter argues that leadership among Black women is defined differently than leadership for other groups. The early work of Black women through the overlapping anti-lynching and club movements builds a leadership model that is rooted in traditional African gender roles, shaped by a history of American slavery, and draws from early abolitionist efforts. This model, at its core, is a Black feminist one, in that it seeks to encompass the simultaneous realities of race, gender, and class and to eradicate all forms of oppression that accompany multi-axis identities. The distinct leadership model developed here takes on a radical approach—favoring fundamental transformation over limited reform.

Under the Black feminist praxis, transformational goals require the adoption of group-centered leadership that incorporates a process of collective visioning and action. As such, the model shifts the paradigm of leadership away from the proffered asymmetrical relationship between the leader and his followers toward a structure that relies on the contributions made by all members of the movement. Similarly, rather than liberal reformist agendas that often bring benefit to the most privileged members of the group, gains are measured by collective vis-à-vis individual advance. Hence, Black feminist leadership models may present the best prospect for transformative change.

Notes

1. See Melina Abdullah, "Greater than the Sum of Her Parts: A Multi-Axis Analysis of Black Women and Political Representation" (Ph.D. dissertation, University of Southern California, 2002); Wendy Smooth, *Perceptions of Power and Influence: The Impact of Race and Gender on Legislative Influence* (forthcoming; also Ph.D. dissertation, University of Maryland, 2001); and Kimberly Springer, ed., *Still Lifting, Still Climbing: African American Women's Contemporary Activism* (New York: New York University Press, 1999).

2. See Ivan Van Sertima, *Black Women in Antiquity* (New York: Transaction Publishers, 1995); Nah Dove, "African Womanism: An Afrocentric Theory," *Journal of Black Studies* 28, no. 5 (1998).

3. See the narrative of Harriet Jacobs, first published in 1861, *Incidents in the Life of a Slave Girl* (New York: Dover Publications, 2001); and the reprint of Sojourner Truth and Oliver Gilbert's 1850 classic *The Narrative Life of Sojourner Truth* (New York: Dover Publications, 1997).

4. Robin Kelley discusses these everyday acts of resistance in his work *Race Rebels: Culture, Politics, and the Black Working Class* (New York: Free Press, 1994).

5. This concept is derived from Orlando Patterson *Slavery and Social Death: A Comparative Study* (Cambridge: Harvard University Press, 1982).

6. Mamie Locke, "From Three-Fifths to Zero: The Implications of the Constitution for African-American Women, 1787–1870," *Women and Politics Institute Journal* 10, no. 1 (1990): 378.

7. Ibid., 383.

8. See Rosalyn Terborg-Penn, "Black Male Perspectives on the Nineteenth Century Woman" and "Discrimination against Afro-American Women in the Woman's Movement," both in *The Afro-American Woman: Struggles and Images*, ed. Sharon Harley and Rosalyn Terborg-Penn (Baltimore: Black Classic Press, 1997).

9. See Terborg-Penn, "Discrimination against Afro-American Women in the Woman's Movement."

10. See James Cutler, *Lynch Law: An Investigation into the History of Lynching in the United States* (New York: Negro Universities Press, 1905/1969).

11. Shirley Wilson Logan, *We Are Coming: The Persuasive Discourse of Nineteenth-Century Black Women* (Carbondale: Southern Illinois University Press, 1999), 70.

12. The Ku Klux Klan (KKK) played a central role in the formation of lynch mobs, rallying public frenzy. Once lynchings were carried out, the KKK concealed the identities of both active and passive perpetrators. See *Lynch Law.*

See also Christopher Waldrep, *The Many Faces of Judge Lynch: Extralegal Violence and Punishment in America* (New York: Palgrave MacMillan, 2002).

13. Logan, *We Are Coming*, 70.

14. Ida B. Wells-Barnett discusses the lynching of Thomas Moss, Calvin McDowell, and Henry Stewart, People's Grocery Store owners in Memphis, Tennessee, as being motivated by the threat that their business success posed to a rival white grocery store in *Crusade for Justice: The Autobiography of Ida B. Wells* ed. Alfreda M. Duster (Chicago: University of Chicago Press, 1970). It was this atrocity that served as a catalyst for Wells's participation in the anti-lynching movement. Mob violence resulting from black economic gain continued well into the twentieth century, including the murders and destruction in Rosewood, Florida. See Michael D'Orso, *Like Judgment Day: The Ruin and Redemption of a Town Called Rosewood* (New York: Putnam, 1996). Additional examples, including the burning of Black Wall Street in Oklahoma, are discussed by Lee E. Williams in *Anatomy of Four Race Riots: Racial Conflict in Knoxville, Elaine, Tulsa and Chicago, 1919– 1921* (Hattiesburg: University and College Press of Mississippi, 1972).

15. The Civil Rights Act of 1875 came out of Reconstruction and reflected an ideology that the most viable means for dealing with the "Negro question" was to allow for their limited integration into society. "Be it enacted that all persons within the jurisdiction of the United States shall be entitled to the full and equal enjoyment of the accommodations, advantages, facilities, and privileges of inns, public conveyances on land or water, theaters, and other places of public amusement; subject only to the conditions and limitations established by law, and applicable alike to citizens of every race and color, regardless of any previous condition of servitude." (See the United States Civil Rights Act of 1875.) The Act barred legal segregation in both publicly and privately owned establishments and accommodations and required that the federal government protect the rights of blacks against private citizens and state and local governments who attempted to restrict access.

16. See Waldrep, *The Many Faces of Judge Lynch*; Wells-Barnett, *Crusade for Justice*.

17. See Joanne Grant, *Ella Baker: Freedom Bound* (Indianapolis: Wiley Publishers, 1999).

18. Logan, *We Are Coming*, 12.

19. See Gloria Wade-Gayles, "Black Women Journalists in the South, 1880– 1905: An Approach to the Study of Black Women's History," *Callaloo* no. 11/13 (February–October 1981): 138–52.

20. Wells was invited to be a contributor to *Living Way* and *Evening Star*.

21. Wells-Barnett, *Crusade for Justice*.

22. See Linda O. McMurry, *To Keep the Waters Troubled: The Life of Ida B. Wells* (New York: Oxford University Press, 1998).

23. Logan, *We Are Coming*, 15.

24. Wells-Barnett, *Crusade for Justice*, 231.

25. Ida B. Wells-Barnett, *Selected Works of Ida B. Wells Barnett*, ed. Trudier Harris (New York: Oxford University Press, 1991), 42.

26. Wells-Barnett, *Crusade for Justice*, 62.

27. There are some commonalities held by Wells and other Black women in her position, most notably Mary Church Terrell with whom she was acquainted. There are some overlaps among Black male, White female, and Black feminist leadership styles. Black men tend to depart from the strict asymmetric form advocated by the traditional White male model by using a core group of supporters to push agendas forward. The use of group action is also core to Black feminist leadership. However, what differentiated the group dynamic as employed by Black men as opposed to Black women is that Black male leadership stops short of engaging the group in the leadership process. Alternatively, Black feminists tend to be much more willing to engage in shared power and responsibility. Like Black women, White women tend to be more willing to share in power within the group. However, they are less likely to support radical agendas, instead favoring liberal reform.

28. Wells settled permanently in the North after receiving word that the *Memphis Free Speech* office had been burned and her partner threatened following the publication of a particularly scathing article that she wrote opposing lynching. In 1884, Wells was removed from a first-class railroad car because of her race. After a physical altercation with the conductor, she filed a lawsuit against the railroad that was won, then overturned on appeal by the Tennessee Supreme Court in 1887 (see Wells-Barnett, *Crusade for Justice*), 35–46. Wells unsuccessfully lobbied President McKinley to issue an Executive Order prohibiting lynching (See Logan, *We Are Coming*), 70–71.

29. See Elizabeth Lindsay Davis, *Lifting as They Climb*, (New York: GK Hall and Co., 1922; reprint New York: Macmillan, 1996).

30. See Elizabeth Lindsay Davis, *The Story of the Illinois Federation of Colored Women's Clubs*, ed. Sheila Smith McCoy (New York: GK Hall and Co., 1933, 1997).

31. See bell hooks, *Ain't I a Woman: Black Women and Feminism* (Boston: South End Press, 1981).

32. See Sidney Verba, Kay Lehman Schlozman, and Henry E. Brady, *Voice and Equality: Civic Voluntarism in American Politics* (Cambridge: Harvard University Press, 1995).

33. Rosalyn Terborg-Penn, "African-American Women's Networks in the Anti-Lynching Crusade," in *Gender, Class, Race and Reform in the Progressive Era*, ed. Noralee Frankel and Nancy Dye, (Lexington: University of Kentucky Press, 1991), 148–61.

34. This concept of a combined traditional and nontraditional approach to organizing is introduced by Patricia Hill Collins in *Black Feminist Thought: Knowledge, Consciousness and the Politics of Empowerment*, 2nd edition (New York: Routledge, 2000), 222–25. Collins asserts that the combined approach is necessary for the sort of institutional transformation that Black women seek to bring about. See also Paula Giddings, *When and Where I Enter: The Impact of Black Women on Race and Sex in America* (New York: William Morrow, 1984); and Gerda Lerner, ed., *Black Women in White America: A Documentary History* (New York: Vintage Books, 1972).

35. Wells-Barnett, *Selected Works*, 14.

36. Virtually all Black women's clubs established anti-lynching committees—some of the most active committees of the clubs. See Terborg-Penn, "African-American Women's Networks." Recognizing the central role that the black women's clubs played in the anti-lynching movement and the potential for transformative politics that the club movement carried, Ida B. Wells worked diligently to establish numerous clubs herself. See Davis, *The Story of the Illinois Federation.*

37. I am defining "radical" as an ideology that seeks fundamental transformation—one that moves beyond an approach of liberal reform. With lynching as an entrenched norm of the time, the anti-lynching movement sought substantive change in not only the act of lynching itself, but those political, social, and economic conditions that bred the view that Black lives were dispensable. Historically, the anti-lynching movement also was considered radical and viewed as a threat to the existing hierarchy of power.

38. Wells was born into slavery and the daughter of former slaves. See Wells-Barnett, *Crusade for Justice*, 3–6.

39. Davis, *The Story of the Illinois Federation*, 12.

40. Individuals were recognized regularly for contributions ranging from monetary donations to the preparation of food and the typing of minutes. Highest honors were given through the naming of clubs after those who were deemed worthy of such recognition, including Ida B. Wells, Frederick Douglass, and Phyllis Wheatley. See Davis, *The Story of the Illinois Federation* 1997; N.F. Mossell, *The Work of the Afro-American Woman* (New York: Oxford University Press, 1988).

41. Davis, *Lifting*, 19.

Chapter 16

Shadowboxing

Liberation Limbos—Ida B. Wells

JOY JAMES

> To justify their own barbarism they assume a chivalry which they do not possess.
> True chivalry respects all womanhood.
> —Ida B. Wells

The Memphis Diary of Ida B. Wells, edited by Miriam Decosta-Willis, reveals the private concerns of anti-lynching crusader Ida B. Wells (1862–1931).[1] Detailing Wells's life from age twenty-four to sixty-eight, the diaries recount the mundane distractions and preoccupations of a young, unmarried woman and, later, wife, mother, and matron. Scholar Mary Helen Washington writes in her foreword to *The Memphis Diary*: "Every woman who has ever kept a diary knows that women write in diaries because things are not going right." According to Washington, Wells recorded intimate details of her life as "a way of clarifying and affirming her own growth" and to express her feelings about being "stuck in an unfulfilling job, struggling to make ends meet as she tries to keep up with the Black bourgeoisie in Memphis, and desperately trying to find a satisfying romantic relationship with a man."[2] These concerns may sound depressingly or humorously familiar to those who can trace their postmodern frustrations to the post-bellum age.

The vulnerability expressed in *The Memphis Diary*—which Wells never intended for publication—proves to be its most striking feature because

of the strong contrast it offers to the public figure of Wells as the courageous and militant "race woman" of the turn-of-the century anti-lynching
crusades. With pistol at hand, she fearlessly castigated a society that upheld white supremacy through violence while masking white racist terror
as sexual protection. The private life revealed in the diary, unlike the public life documented in her memoir *Crusade for Justice,* presents an insecure
young woman who grows into a maturity as a fighter who, despite her
strength, seems to be weighed down by domestic concerns and the lack
of resources and public recognition that she rightly believed her due.

As a militant, Wells coupled speech with a courageous insurgency that
became noteworthy for her refusal or inability to compromise. Curiously,
a few contemporary feminists have depicted her as reluctant to speak
about, or "indifferent" to, sexual violence against white women. Such feminists have alleged that she blamed white rape victims for the lynchings of
their black assailants. These reductionist and conservative portraits of
Wells's iconoclasm inaccurately reflect both her sexual politics and the
historical record.[3]

Credible historical accounts depict Wells as a radical antiracist motivated by a public hostility toward lynchings rather than personal animos-
ity toward white women. Contempt for sexual violence in their lives likely
would have alienated her influential white women supporters. Wells never
categorically denied that black men assaulted white women. The body of
her writings and research, in which the word "many" is generally used to
describe false accusations of rape, makes no assertion of universal black
innocence. Her position is best revealed in a letter by Boston's Women's
Era Club leader Florida Ruffin Ridley, which is reprinted in her memoir:

> All that we ask for is justice—not mercy or palliation—simply justice.
> Surely that is not too much for loyal citizens of a free country to demand . . .
> We do not pretend to say there are no black villains. Baseness is not confined
> to race. We read with horror of two different colored girls who recently
> have been horribly assaulted by white men in the South. We should regret
> any lynchings of the offenders by black men but we shall not have occasion.
> Should these offenders receive any punishment at all, it will be a marvel.[4]

Similarly, Wells adhered to women's club leader Mary Church Terrell's
1904 rebuttal to an article in the *North American Review* that justified lynching by depicting black males as sexual predators of white females. Church
Terrell decried the belief that African Americans were insensitive to rape,
writing: "[I]t is a great mistake to suppose that rape is the real cause of

lynching in the South. Beginning with the Ku Klux Klan the negro has been constantly subjected to some form of organized violence ever since he became free . . . out of every 100 negroes who are lynched, from 75–85 are not even accused of this crime, and many who are accused of it are innocent."[5] The antilynching campaigns, as battles against racial-sexual terror, provided the model for twentieth-century militant antiracist feminism.

Although whites had been the majority of the lynching victims in the antebellum years, after the Civil War whites were rarely lynched. Rather, lynchings became a barbaric form of collective punishment meted out against black communities to ensure white dominance. Ritualized murders of black Americans were rationalized by the mythology of black rapists obsessed with white females. Sexual realities became convoluted by sexual politics, which inverted the interracial sexual violence of the era. The sexual politicians of lynching grossly exaggerated the likelihood of black male assaults on white females while ignoring the widespread prevalence of white male sexual assaults against black females. By draping lynching in the cloak of antisexual violence rhetoric, and thus by legitimizing (and therefore, logically, increasing) violence against them, the lives of millions of black females were destabilized. Feeding on the racist stereotypes of black bestiality, lynch mythology masked sexual violence against black females and justified racial violence against blacks.

Nineteenth-century African Americans recognized that lynchings were part of a terrorist campaign in an undeclared racial war to destroy the newly won independence of free black communities. Racialized, antiblack atrocities became routine rituals as whites sought to remove African Americans from economic and political power. After the aborted Reconstruction, through legislation and extra-legal violence as well as the rise of the convict prison lease system, most southern blacks were forced into economic subservience and dependency.[6]

Analyzing the "political economy of racism," historian Jack Bloom describes how white supremacy found its most violent expression in the Ku Klux Klan, which had widespread support among whites:

All classes in the South appear to have been involved in [the Ku Klux Klan] and to have used it for different purposes. In the predominantly white counties, which were usually located in the hills away from the fertile plantation areas, the Klan was used to drive blacks out so as to eliminate them as competitors with white laborers. In the black belt, the upper classes sometimes opposed the Klan because its violence was disruptive to labor and investment alike. Nonetheless, the upper class used the Klan to control black labor, even to the detriment of white labor. Blacks who tried to leave the area were threatened with murder, and some of them were killed. When they did leave, they were sometimes pursued and dragged back, even across state lines.[7]

At the turn of the century, within the climate of a low-intensity race war, black women led the antilynching campaigns as an antiviolence, antiracist feminist movement. They highlighted the racial inversion of sexual violence as propaganda to justify white supremacy and obscure sexual assaults. Waging the campaigns as resistance to both racial and sexual violence, antilynching crusaders such as Wells, Ruffin Ridley, and Church Terrell established a political language to critique U.S. racial-sexual politics and challenge the "moralism" of the white-dominated press, courts, and police.

Skeptical that media, court, or mob prosecution was motivated by the desire to end sexual violence, these women conducted and publicized investigative reporting to ascertain facts distorted or denied by mainstream institutions. Their demands for justice challenged the U.S. "red record," in Wells's words, of African Americans disproportionately sentenced, brutalized, imprisoned, and murdered at the whim of whites; the low visibility of sexual assaults against black women; and pervasive social and government indifference to sexual and racial violence.

Denouncing the lynchings of African Americans for alleged and real crimes against property and whites (which included social "crimes" such as talking back), the crusader Wells argued that the charge of rape, used in only a fraction of lynchings, became the general rationalization for racist violence in that era. With this accusation, even those who considered themselves above the mob mentality acquiesced to lynchings as a preventive measure to ensure the safety of white females. At the same time, these apologists turned a blind eye to the more prevalent problem of white male sexual violence against women, particularly black women.

To demystify the belief that white men enforced written or unwritten laws for the protection of white females, Wells engaged in a radical critique of lynching apologias, exploring their basis in psychosexual mythology. She proved relentless in her critique of the sexual politics of lynching. Her demystification of "rape," controversial a century ago and remaining so today, was the cornerstone of moral and political resistance to racist violence justified as the vindication or prevention of *sexual* violence.

In her memoir, she recalls her initial belief in European-American assertions that lynching was to protect white women's virtue and restrain the "sexual savagery" of African-American men. The 1892 Memphis lynchings of three friends and associates—Thomas Moss, Calvin McDowell, and Will Stewart—for competing with white businesses by opening the People's Grocery Company, taught her otherwise.[8] According to Wells, that was the year of the greatest number of reported lynchings, most of which were committed in Tennessee, Alabama, Arkansas, Georgia, and Mississippi.[9] Of the 241 murdered, 160 were African American, including 5 women or girls.[10]

As an editor and co-owner of Memphis's African-American paper, the *Free Speech*, Wells began, through her writings, to promote militant critiques and confrontations. In May 1892, after more lynchings followed the deaths of her friends, Wells wrote an editorial ridiculing the charge of "rape" as justification for racist killings. Her editorial reads in part: "Eight Negroes lynched since last issue of the *Free Speech*. Three were charged with killing white men and five with raping white women. Nobody in this section believes the old thread-bare lie that Negro men assault white women. If Southern white men are not careful they will overreach themselves and a conclusion will be reached which will be very damaging to the moral reputation of their women."[11] In response, the city's white citizens burned the paper's offices and threatened to lynch the writer. The bounty they placed on Wells's head exiled her from the South for decades. Yet, that year, African-American women convened in Brooklyn, the largest gathering of club women during that era, for a testimonial for Wells and raised $500 to publish an antilynching pamphlet, *Southern Horrors,* and to finance her first antilynching speaking tour.

Wells publicly exposed the fact that voluntary sexual relationships between European-American females and African-American males were defined by whites as "sexual assaults" in order that consensual relations could be reconstructed as rape.

> With the Southern white man, any mesalliance existing between a white woman and a colored man is a sufficient foundation for the charge of rape. The Southern white man says that it is impossible for a voluntary alliance to exist between a white woman and a colored man, and therefore, the fact of an alliance is a proof of force. In numerous instances where colored men have been lynched on the charge of rape, it was positively known at the time of lynching, and indisputably proven after the victim's

death, that the relationship sustained between the man and woman was voluntary and clandestine, and that in no court of law could even the charge of assault have been successfully maintained.[12]

Such voluntary interracial associations were punishable by the death of the African-American male involved. Although there were instances of white females being ostracized, institutionalized, and beaten for engaging in such alliances, a repudiation of the relationship through the rape accusation brought absolution. African-American males had no such escape clause. Consequently, Wells asserted that these liaisons were often "voluntary" only on the part of the white females involved.

African-American antilynching activists rejected the dominant culture's distortions concerning sex and violence. Although they had no control over how white males treated white females, black women organized, through the Negro Women's Club Movement, against their own sexual exploitation and against assault by men both white and black. These activist-writers did not separate the issues of gender and sexual violence from race politics. For decades, women such as Wells urged American white women to respond to the political use of the rape charge in lynchings. Black women recognized the connections between resistance to sexual violence and resistance to racial violence: Neither for white nor especially for black women was there prosecution of sexual assault under the lynch law, where prosecution of actual sexual violence was irrelevant. Resisting racial violence and protesting white supremacist terror and sexual violence against African-American women, children, and men, women in the antilynching campaigns could not realistically separate instances of racist and sexual violence, for race was "sexualized" and sex was "racialized." The dual realities of the assaults against African Americans did not permit prioritizing "race" before "sex." Consequently, black women built institutions and women's organizations that confronted sexual violence at the same time that they challenged the lynch law.

Wells methodically critiqued the white press and conducted painstaking research and investigative reporting to verify the accuracy of white newspaper articles and editorials vilifying African Americans.[13] Doing so was particularly important since the white press gave the imprimatur for society's racism. Expressing courageous commitments in political writing, Wells's exhortations in her *Free Speech* editorials led thousands of African Americans to leave Memphis for the western territories in a mass migration that caused a serious financial loss for the city's white merchants.

Her editorials also inspired hundreds of African Americans to boycott the electric trolley. The efficacy of her political writing is evident in the success of the boycott and the intense hatred many whites felt toward this young black woman. She had a keen organizational sense and understood the political economy of racism.

In 1893 and 1894, when there was no response from national religious, civic, or women's groups, or even the government, to counter lynching, Wells took the campaign and the story of the political economy of racism to England in speaking tours. Meeting there with prominent leaders, she worked with women's groups to help launch the first antilynching organization in the world, the London Antilynching Committee. Due to financial pressure from the English—England imported and processed southern cotton—lynchings were halted in Memphis for several decades. By coupling economic boycotts with black institution-building, Wells played a critical role in developing a number of significant political African-American institutions, such as the Club Movement, the National Association for the Advancement of Colored People (NAACP), and the Afro-American press.

Although economic competition was a major factor in white violence and lynchings, Wells also noted emotional or psychological motivations: "The more I studied the situation, the more I was convinced that the Southerner had never gotten over his resentment that the Negro was no longer his plaything, his servant, and his source of income."[14] Contemporary Church Terrell was blunter: "Lynching is the aftermath of slavery. The white men who shoot negroes to death and flay them alive, and the white women who apply flaming torches to their oil-soaked bodies today, are the sons and daughters of women who had but little, if any, compassion on the race when it was enslaved."[15]

Wells's ability to depict the society that condoned lynchings was an essential aspect of her public speaking and writings. She focused on the duplicity of the legal system in lynching and sexual violence, its double standards, and the cultural taboo surrounding interracial sex.[16] Her analysis of the politics of lynching appears in her news dispatches, where she identifies three supporting pillars: The

> machinery of law and politics is in the hands of those who commit the lynching . . . it is only wealthy white men whom the law fails to reach . . . hundreds of Negroes including women and children are lynched for trivial offenses on suspicion and in many cases when known to be guiltless of

any crime ... the law refused to punish the murderers because it is not considered a crime to kill a Negro ... Many of the cases of "Assault" are simply adulteries between white women and colored men.[17]

One of the first to publicly criticize state complicity in racial repression, Wells's critique led her to indict white American's "law and order" rationalizations for lynchings.[18] The first rationalization was that lynching existed to suppress African-American-led "race riots," which, as Wells observes, never materialized. The second reason for white terrorism was that it prevented "Negro domination" of whites through the vote; however, by the late 1800s, African Americans had already been so persecuted as to effectively prevent their serious participation in most elections.[19]

When this second reason became acknowledged as specious, a third rationalization for the unrelenting white mob violence and an acquiescent state emerged, according to Wells:

> Brutality still continued; Negroes were whipped, scourged, exiled, shot and hung whenever and wherever it pleased the white man so to treat them, and as the civilized world with increasing persistency held the white people of the South to account for its outlawry, the murderers invented the third excuse—that Negroes had to be killed to avenge their assaults upon women. There could be framed no possible excuse more harmful to the Negro and more unanswerable if true in its sufficiency for the white man.[20]

Wells's image on a 1990s U.S. postage stamp for Black History Month belies her confrontation with the state. She refers to but never fully addresses the state's complicity in lynching in *Mob Rule in New Orleans.* The government's failure to prosecute lynchers partly explains why some lynch mobs consisted of up to ten thousand whites. Although she carried a pistol, Wells never fully analyzed the "criminalization" of African-American self-defense, particularly in response to police brutality and killings. Aware of the role of the police and probably the presiding district judge in the 1892 Memphis lynchings, she never explicitly outlined the state's role in appropriating the function of the lynch mob. Historical dilemmas continue to confront African Americans today: sentence disparities, "legal lynchings" through racialized sentencing, the racist application of the death penalty, guard killings of black prisoners.[21] Despite evident abuses, Wells appealed to the state, and remained largely silent about the possibility of African-American resistance strategies to the government.[22]

The antilynching crusades were an early form of radical black feminism, and the crusaders' legacies and impact are felt today. Author Joanne Braxton writes that while reading autobiographies of women such as Ida B. Wells, she first met the "outraged mother" or ancestor mothers "in search of a tradition to claim them."[23] According to Braxton, a balance between the "confessional narrative and the historical memoir" allows Wells to relate both her public and private "duties" and contributions and "to demonstrate her development as a political activist and as an outraged mother." For Braxton, Wells's memoir "looks forward to the modern political autobiographies of Anne Moody, Shirley Chisholm, and Angela Davis. It represents an important link between the old and the new, part of the lost ground of Afro-American literary tradition."[24]

In spite of her remarkable achievements, Ida B. Wells had discernible flaws. She seems to have promoted self-serving mythology in her memoir when she writes, without fully crediting him for his influence on her development, that Frederick Douglass believed in African-American men's proclivity toward rape; there is no known record of this as Douglass's position.[25] Also, at times Wells's single-minded pursuit of justice limited her compassion for those caught in the political fray. For example, early in her career, when her *Free Speech* editorials exposed the sexual relationships of incompetent black women teachers with corrupt white male school board members, Wells showed little pity for the woman who committed suicide when her "mesalliance" was publicized. The white school board, angered at the exposure of its corruption, fired Wells, who subsequently became a journalist.

An organizer of the Alpha Suffrage Club, Illinois's first African-American Women's Suffrage Club, Wells merged gender, sexuality, and race. She also forged a link between racial and sexual violence useful to black males as well as antiracist whites and organizations such as the NAACP and the white Association of Southern Women for the Prevention of Lynching, which formed after the height of lynching and remained marginalized among white feminists. Organizing against lynching created a unique form of feminism shaped by race, sex, gender, and class as Wells merged two activist and powerful influences, black feminism and black nationalism. For Braxton,

> the result of this fusion was the development of a race-centered, self-conscious womanhood in the form of the black women's club movement. Whereas the white woman's movement reflected her commitment to temperance and suffrage, the black woman's movement was born in the

outrage of the slave mother and the struggle against lynching. Racial oppression, not sexism, was the primary issue. For an Ida B. Wells or a Frances E. W. Harper, a blow at lynching was a blow at racism and the brutally enforced sexual double standard that pervaded the South. It was a defense of the entire race.[26]

Black women, as iconoclast feminists organizing against racist violence, invariably worked for "the defense of the entire race." It does not necessarily follow that their politics served only male interests.

Varied responses to Ida B. Wells and the antilynching crusaders are found today. As noted earlier, although in previous centuries interracial rape against African-American females was common (the vast majority of sexual violence against females stemmed from white males), today, the greatest number of assaults against black females are by black males. In the United States, where nine out of ten reported sexual assaults occur within the same ethnic group according to FBI statistics—the 1983 Cambridge documentary film *Rape Culture* places the figures in reported interracial rapes at 8 percent for white male assaults of black females and 5 percent for black male sexual assaults against white females—the most "heinous" and sensationalized assaults are the less than 10 percent that are interracial. For many African Americans, the assault of black females by white males remains the most horrific manifestation of sexual violence, just as whites had mandated (and continue to perceive) black assaults of white females to be the most heinous form of sexual abuse.

Given racism's long history in the United States, a suspicion of state authority, particularly in interracial rape cases, is common place in African-American communities. Ida B. Wells wrote in *A Red Record*: "Think and act on independent lines . . . remembering that after all, it is the white man's civilization and the white man's government which are on trial."[27] Yet a singular focus on white malfeasance and sexual policing of blacks may obscure black sexual policing of black females. Logically, if a white female falsely accused a black male of rape in order to shield a white male (or herself) from retribution, a black female might choose or be coerced into the same strategy. In the perverse inversion of racial progress, blacks can now, without corroborating evidence, accuse whites of rape without the threat of death by lynching.

In contemporary organizing around interracial rape cases in which black females are victimized, black males who see themselves as the "natural" protectors of black females can appropriate the words of female anti-lynching crusaders. In patriarchal race crusades, male dominance of the discourse belies die protofeminist fiery oratory and fierce analyses of women such as Mary Church Terrell and Wells in their opposition to racial and sexual violence.[28] Some antiracists invoke Wells's militancy without her feminism in order to put the "white man's government" on trial. The judicial and social indifference to antiblack violence, police malfeasance, and racialized violence marauding as "protection" for the "law-abiding," or for whites, encourage acquiescence to this form of counter-feminism as well as to black female dependency on black males for "protection." As contemporary black rhetorical vigilantes stake a "protective" claim on the black female body, establishing their proprietorship, they displace black female agency and silence forms of feminist resistance.

In recent memory, the most controversial example of such a claim has been the 1987 Tawana Brawley case, where in November of that year a black teenager alleged that she had been abducted and gang-raped by a group of white men that included state officials. In the Brawley case, her advocates Al Sharpton, Alton Maddox, and Vernon Mason deployed Ida B. Wells's dissection of American racial-sexual politics, using historical narratives to mobilize contemporary black public outrage against white men by portraying Brawley as the personification of black female prey hunted by white male predators.[29] Their prosecutorial performances turned a family tale of private pain and assault into a public spectacle of racial rage. In the process, black females, as exploitable and expendable, became mere backdrops to unfolding racial dramas, produced and directed by men.[30]

Three years after and thousands of miles apart from the Brawley incident, the issue of protection was raised again by black women in Oxford, Ohio. In 1990, the Ku Klux Klan, based in its national headquarters in Indiana, decided to stage a march and rally in the local campus town of Oxford. The general negative responses to the Klan's march centered on individual expressions of intimidation and anger. Little collective, organized response existed until one night when, as part of a women's film festival, a small number of students viewed William Greaves's documentary, *Ida B. Wells: A Passion for Justice.* During the discussion session that followed the video screening, an African-American woman senior moderated as students shared their impressions of Wells's courage and influential activism, which began at such a young age—their own age. Later in their dorm rooms, women continued exploring their inspiration for the story of Wells's resistance in juxtaposition with their feelings of anger and fear about the upcoming Klan march. Discussions turned into strategy sessions. Within a day, young women decided to allow their admiration for Wells to lead them to organize a countereducational critique on the racism, homophobia, sexism, and anti-Semitism that was visibly increasing on campus prior to the Klan's display of power.

Leading the organizing, African-American female students formed a coalition with whites, Jews, gays, and lesbians. Some of the young black women leaders at that time experienced the most violent racial-sexual assaults on the campus during their student years. At an early organizing meeting, one senior spoke of being dragged off a catwalk into bushes as her white male assailant yelled "nigger bitch" while punching her repeatedly. As she struggled away, she noticed white student spectators who made no effort to assist or intervene. Later, she found the university's investigation and handling of the attack to be equally unresponsive. Unlike the model of militancy embodied by Wells, and the emergent antiracist feminism of the youths, faculty criticisms and complaints about white-dominated universities did not translate into support for the student-initiated organizing. Only a few faculty or administrators (two white female and one black female professor) publicly supported a student "speak-out" (an open-mike educational gathering, not a demonstration or rally) against racist, sexist, and homophobic violence prevalent at the university. University employees mirrored the divisions among African-American students; more cautious or conservative ones dismissed student organizers as "radical" and ridiculed them for "overreacting." Rather than pull blacks together, if only in a temporary formation, the KKK march exacerbated divisions among students, faculty, and administrators.

Loyalty to the university, along with homophobia, sexism, and caste elitism, as well as fear of confrontation, allowed faculty and more conservative African-American students to distance themselves from black female student activists and others who organized to counter the Klan. Faculty and administrators likely viewed their class and caste status as granting immunity from the most extreme forms of violence.[31] Youths face the greatest dangers from racial-sexual violence. Racist/anti-Semitic verbal abuse and physical violence increased on campus prior to the Klan demonstration. At the same time that most black and white faculty refused to actively support student organizing, the university administration refused to publicly and aggressively denounce and prosecute hate speech and hate crimes on campus.

The Klan marched in the university town on its designated weekend, undisrupted by the nonviolent black or multiethnic protesters who modeled the civil rights movement. However, white antiracist skinheads (a minority among skinheads), largely nonstudents and nonuniversity employees, carpooled or took buses in from Cincinnati and derailed the march, tossing Molotov cocktails at the Klan demonstrators, which forced local police to cancel the event. The following Sunday, a multiracial alliance of students held a speak-out against hatred in the campus chapel with a full-capacity gathering and an open mike, denouncing anti-Semitic, racist, and heterosexist bias and violence.

An iconoclast eventually marginalized by most of white America and the black middle class for her militancy, Wells conceivably could have recognized in such disparate responses by the youths (for some, she stood as icon) the mirrored images of her own politics. Her legacy—which included educational interventions, political writings, and unwavering advocacy for black self-defense against violent racist attacks—is met with ambivalence by contemporary Americans. For most Americans, Ida B. Wells resides in the shadows of political memory, but her legacy manifests itself in the contemporary activism of antiracists. It also resonates within the struggles of women and men in the civil rights movement of the 1930s through the 1960s. Within the praxis of Ella Baker, we see that under prolonged conditions of stress and struggle, Ida B. Wells's radical iconoclasm has become normative.

Notes

1. Miriam Decosta-Willis, ed., *The Memphis Diary of Ida B. Wells* (Boston: Beacon Press, 1997).

2. Ibid., ix.

3. For a critical review of black feminist revisionist accounts of Ida B. Wells, see Joy James, "Sexual Politics," in *Transcending the Talented Tenth: Black Leaders and American Intellectuals* (New York: Routledge, 1997), 61–82.

4. Reprinted in Ida B. Wells, *Crusade for Justice*, ed. Alfreda Duster (Chicago: University of Chicago Press, 1970).

5. Quoted in Gerder Lerner, ed., *Black Women in White America: A Documentary History* (New York: Vintage, 1974), 207.

6. Jack M. Bloom, *Class, Race and the Civil Rights Movement* (Bloomington: Indiana University Press, 1987).

7. Ibid., 32.

8. African-American men had fired on white unidentified plainclothes de-

tectives, armed with rifles, who were hiding at night in the alley behind the offices of the black-owned business. Wells was the godmother of Thomas and Bettye Moss's infant daughter, Maurine (Wells, *Crusade for Justice*, 47–52).

9. John D'Emilio and Estelle Freedman, *Intimate Matters: A History of Sexuality in America* (New York: Harper & Row, 1988), documents that between 1889 and 1940, at least 3,800 men and women were lynched in the South and the bordering states, with an average of 200 lynchings per year during the 1890s. In his preface to *On Lynchings*, a collection of Wells's three pamphlets—*Southern Horrors: Lynch Law in All Its Phases* (1892); *A Red Record: Lynchings in the U.S., 1892, 1893, 1894* (1895); and *Mob Rule in New Orleans* (1900), August Meier notes that the numbers of African Americans reported lynched averaged over 100 a year during the 1880s and the 1890s, with lynching "peaking" in 1892 when 161 women and men were murdered. Ida B. Wells-Barnett, *On Lynchings: Southern Horrors, A Red Record, Mob Rule in New Orleans* (New York: Arno Press, 1969). Meier refers only to African Americans lynched; D'Emilio and Freedman include whites as well. Lynching has become identified with African Americans, yet prior to the Civil War, the majority of lynching victims were white. Similarly, in the early eighteenth century, slavery came to represent the African condition, although Europeans and Native Americans had been enslaved along with Africans prior to and during that era.

10. Meticulous in her research, Wells used deaths reported in the white press; believing the reports to be an undercount, she nevertheless felt that whites could not argue that their own numbers were exaggerated.
Wells's citations of reasons given for the lynchings reported in 1892 reveal the source of her outrage: "Rape, 46; murder, 58; rioting, 3; race prejudice, 6; no cause given, 4; incendiarism, 6; robbery, 6; assault and battery, 1; attempted rape, 11; suspected robbery, 4; larceny, 1; self defense, 1; insulting women, 2; desperadoes, 6; fraud, 1; attempted murder, 2; no offense stated, boy and girl, 2 . . . In the case of the boy and girl . . . their father, named Hastings, was accused of the murder of a white man; his fourteen-year-old daughter and sixteen-year old son were hanged and their bodies filled with bullets, then the father also was lynched. This was in November 1892, at Jonesville, Louisiana" (Wells-Barnett, *A Red Record*, in *On Lynchings*, 20).

11. Wells, *Crusade for Justice*, 65–66.

12. Wells-Barnett, *A Red Record*, in *On Lynchings*, 11.

13. One of Wells's most impressive legacies is her principled journalism to determine and disseminate facts concerning racialized violence, despite the dangers of publicizing the truth. After her 1895 marriage to Ferdinand Barnett, she purchased and became editor of the Chicago-based *African American Conservator*, which her husband had founded.

14. Wells, *Crusade for Justice.* Quote reprinted in Paula Giddings, *When and Where I Enter: The Impact of Black Women on Race and Sex in America* (New York: Vintage, 1986), 26. Giddings notes the rising economic influence of the black community; the National Negro Business League reported that at one time, 187,000

African-American farmers owned farms in the South, some as large as 1,000 acres. This economic base meant political power during the Reconstruction era, where often in the "Black Belt" blacks outnumbered whites.

15. Quoted in Lerner, *Black Women in White America*, 209.

16. Wells rountinely contested antiblack racism in the white press such as that found in the *Memphis Daily Commercial* article of May 17, 1892, entitled "More Rapes, More Lynchings": In response to the article's statement that "The generation of Negroes which have grown up since the war have lost in large measure the traditional and wholesome awe of the white race which kept the Negroes in subjection ... There is no longer a restraint upon the brute passion of the Negro," Wells responds: "The thinking public will not easily believe freedom and education more brutalizing than slavery, and the world knows that the crime of rape was unknown during four years of Civil War, when the white women of the South were at the mercy of the race which is all at once charged with being a bestial one" (Wells-Barnett, *A Red Record*, in *On Lynchings*, 5).

Her claim that no rapes of white females by black males were reported during the Civil War is contested by Martha Hodes, "The Sexualization of Reconstruction Politics: White Women and Black Men in the South after the Civil War," in *American Sexual Politics: Sex, Gender, and Race since the Civil War* ed. John C. Fout and Maura Shaw Tantillo, (Chicago: University of Chicago Press, 1990), 19.

17. Wells, *Crusade for Justice*, 137. This passage appeared in a special correspondence from Liverpool for the *Inter-Ocean*, April 9, 1894, and is in part a response to lynching apologists Women's Christian Temperance Union leader Francis Willard, former *Christian Advocate* editor Oscar P. Fitzgerald, and former Emory University president Atticus Haygood; both men later became bishops (Wells, *Crusade for Justice*, 136).

18. Wells's critique of three rationalizations for terrorism against African Americans in the postbellum South is similar to that of Frederick Douglass. According to Douglass, the

Justification for the murder of Negroes was said to be Negro conspiracies, Negro insurrections, Negro schemes to murder all the white people, Negro plots to burn the town ... times have changed and the Negro's accusers have found it necessary to change with them ... Honest men no longer believe that there is any ground to apprehend Negro supremacy ... altered circumstances have made necessary a Sterner, stronger, and more effective justification of Southern barbarism, and hence we have ... to look into the face of a more shocking and blasting charge. (quoted in D'Emilio and Freedman, *Intimate Matters*, 218).

19. *A Red Record* asserts: "The white man's victory soon became complete by fraud, violence, intimidation and murder ... [with] the Negro actually eliminated from all participation in state and national elections, there could be no longer any excuse for killing Negroes to prevent "Negro Domination," 10.

20. Ibid.

21. According to Amnesty International, the General Assembly of the Organization of American States (OAS) discussed a treaty to abolish the death

penalty in 1987. That same year, the European Parliament condemned the continuing use of the death penalty in the United States, noting that although an increasing "number of countries are abolishing or no longer applying the death penalty, states in the U.S. are committed to it." In many states, persons under eighteen can be executed; the race of victim and defendant is a factor in death sentencing. Between 1977 and 1986, nearly 90 percent of prisoners executed had been convicted of killing whites, although the number of black victims was approximately equal to that of white victims. See Enid Harlow, David Matas, and Jane Rocamora, eds., *The Machinery of Death: A Shocking Indictment of Capital Punishment in the US* (New York: Amnesty International U.S.A., 1995).
For additional documentation of human rights abuses of the incarcerated, see Elihu Rosenblatt, ed., *Criminal Injustice* (Boston: South End Press, 1996).

22. Threats by the Secret Service to prosecute her for treason failed to stop Wells's educational organizing and protest on behalf of the "martyred" African-American soldiers of the 24th Infantry. In 1917, while stationed in Houston, Texas, one hundred armed black troops in the 24th Infantry marched on the town to defend themselves against racist assaults. In the aftermath of the confrontation, sixteen whites and four black soldiers died. The U.S. Army hanged nineteen soldiers and court-martialed and imprisoned fifty following the revolt.

23. See Joanne Braxton, *Black Women Writing Autobiography: A Tradition Within Tradition* (Philadelphia: Temple University Press, 1989), 2.

24. Ibid., 138.

25. Wells, *Crusade for Justice*, 72–73.

26. Braxton, *Black Women Writing Autobiography*, 122.

27. Wells-Barnett, *A Red Record*, in *On Lynching*.

28. According to Gerda Lerner, "The myth of the black rapist of white women is the twin of the myth of the bad black woman—both designed to apologize for and facilitate the continued exploitation of black men and women. Black women perceived this connection very clearly and were early in the forefront of the fight against lynching. Their approach was to prove the falseness of the accusation, the disproportion between punishment and crime, the absence of equality, and lastly, to point to the different scales of justice meted out to the white and the black rapist. An often neglected aspect of this problem is the judicial indifference to sexual crimes committed by black men upon black women." See Gerda Lerner, "Black Women Attack the Lynching System," in *Black Women in White America*, 193–94.

29. If Anita Hill's defense team had used the antebellum imagery of black female sexual victimization against the white male senators interrogating her, Hill might have had a stronger chance of convincing the American public of the veracity of her accusations; perhaps only the black female raped-by-slavemaster narrative could have countered Thomas's black-male-lynching narrative.

30. The Brawley case was "closed" in July 1998 when Steven Pagones was awarded a cash settlement against Brawley (who never attended the trial or had an attorney present), Sharpton, Maddox, and Mason for slander. Pagones, a white

former Wappingers Falls assistant district attorney, accused by Brawley's handlers of being her abductor and rapist, had asked for nearly $400 million but was awarded slightly less than $1 million. It was initially thought that the trial, which became known as the "Tawana Brawley Defamation Trial," would last one month; it began in November 1997 and ended in July 1998 with the reading of the verdict. Performance marked the trial throughout. Brawley never testified, neither before the 1988 grand jury that exonerated the accused or the later defamation trial. Appropriating her voice and body to fight their own battles with white men and institutional power, black men offered no evidence of an assault and "shielded" her from testimony that could have clarified the events surrounding her four-day disappearance. As Michael A. Hardy, attorney for Al Sharpton stated, equating Sharpton's actions with Martin Luther King Jr.'s civil rights advocacy (and martyrdom): "We have been here for a greater purpose . . . Reverend Sharpton's business, if you will, was the business of Civil Rights" (W. Glaberson, "Sharpton Lawyer Says Brawley Case Is Test of Civil Rights," *New York Times,* July 2, 1998).

31. Alongside community women and men, two white women and I were the only faculty to actively organize with students.

Part VI

Black Feminist Theory
From the Nineteenth Century
to the Twenty-First

Chapter 17

Some Core Themes of Nineteenth-Century Black Feminism

KRISTIN WATERS

The postmodern movement that wielded considerable influence in the 1980s and 1990s urged the development of situated, contingent frameworks as set against the grand narratives of modernism.[1] Scholars were asked to practice a "wariness toward generalizations which transcend boundaries of culture and region" and to engage in studies that are "pragmatic, *ad hoc*, contextual and local."[2] Yet the dominant metanarratives of the past provide powerful and pervasive frameworks for structuring politics and experience. These narratives, in the form of canonical teachings, still are held firmly in universities for the purposes of teaching and generating research. In practice, these frameworks influence the way that ordinary people think and speak, vote and create policy, about ethics, politics, and society.

Given these circumstances, without constructing alternative metanarratives—oppositional discourses—about the less well-rehearsed theories of Western thought, scholars, activists, and ordinary people will lack the most powerful and persuasive means of countering the existing tall tales. It makes sense, therefore, in all branches of theory, to create new narratives based on primary sources and new scholarship about old events and historical ideas. Of course, since we cannot be content to create universal and essentialized versions, we are confronted with the dual task of both constructing new metadiscourses that carry some power and weight against the canonical ones, and simultaneously maintaining the differences exemplified by the situated and contextual component parts. As critical race feminism proposes, we must "construct alternative social realities and protest against acquiescence to unfair arrangements designed for the benefit of others."[3]

This chapter explores some of the origins of black feminism. Writing in the spirit of work by Patricia Hill Collins, Darlene Clark Hine, Beverly Guy-Sheftall, Paula Giddings, Gerda Lerner, and many others, my aim is to shed light on some of the subtle and deep philosophical, social, and political thought of the time.[4] For those willing to recognize it, a continuity of ideas rightfully can be traced into the twentieth and twenty-first centuries, a legacy of black feminist theory that demonstrates a set of political traditions—an alternative discourse—that rivals the other grand narratives, primarily of white, conservative, mainstream, liberal, and even radical theories. As with other theories, black feminism not a single, uniform body of thought. Rather, there are multi-stranded and multi-faceted black feminisms, some more radical, some more mainstream, yet the *subjects* they address remain fairly consistent throughout. The central ideas are exemplified here by attending mainly to the work of three writers— Maria W. Stewart (*Writings and Addresses*, 1831–1833), Frederick Douglass (*Writings and Addresses*), and Anna Julia Cooper (*A Voice from the South*, 1892)— and to that of their current interpreters. In particular, I address the themes of a) religion and spirituality as sources of oppression and liberation, b) women's special role—a gendered conception of ethics, c) the multiple facets of the matrix of oppression and domination, d) control of sexuality and reproduction, and e) a gendered approach to knowledge.

Religion/Spirituality as Sources of Oppression/Liberation

The themes of ethics and virtue in nineteenth-century African-American literature bear strong ties to Christian religion. One pair of narrative threads concerns the struggle for moral superiority of white over black or black over white, depending on the racial identity or the racial politics of the speaker. Whites not only owned slaves but they also controlled the way that slaves were portrayed. All available means were used to characterize blacks as immoral and inhuman. The propaganda war was carried on in the newspapers, in the courts, in conversation, and from the pulpit.

Black Americans countered the barrage of white criticism with a twofold approach. One was to expose the hypocrisy and contradictory nature of white Christianity, while the other was to exhort blacks to exhibit moral purity and to gain strength from spirituality. These strategies were both intricate and dangerous, inviting backlash and retaliation. The first strategy of exposing the hypocrisy of white Christianity as a bulwark of slavery was dangerous because by inflaming listeners it risked violent response by white vigilantes. It was perceived as potentially fomenting rebellion and even treason since, after all, slavery was the law of the land, written into the U.S. Constitution. A very different approach sometimes used by black speakers was to exhort their audiences to exhibit greater spiritual and moral purity. This approach was problematic because it potentially fueled the contention that blacks were less moral than whites. But it was also a call to action.

The Hypocrisy of White Americans and the Contradictory Nature of White Christianity

Maria W. Stewart's first public speech, "Religion and the Pure Principles of Morality, the Sure Foundation on Which We Must Build," delivered in 1831, takes aim at the hypocrisy and moral culpability of white Americans: "I have been taking a survey of the [white] American people . . . their highest aim is to excel . . . How very few of them bestow a thought upon the sons of Africa."[5] According to Stewart, the moral failure of white Americans is apparent:

> Oh, America, America, foul and indelible is thy stain! Dark and dismal is the cloud that hangs over thee, for thy cruel wrongs and injuries to the fallen sons of Africa. Thou art almost become drunken with the blood of her slain; thou hast enriched thyself through her toils and labors; and now thou refuseth to make even a small return. (230)

In contrast, white Americans, especially in the South, used Christianity and scripture as foundational and authoritative sources for the enslavement of blacks. Frederick Douglass, one of the most important black feminists of his time, sums it up in the following way:

> Can these things [the cruelties/tortures of slavery] be possible in a land professing Christianity? Yes, they are so; and this is not the worst. No, a darker feature is yet to be presented than the mere existence of these facts. I have to inform you that the religion of the southern states, at this time, is the great supporter, the great sanctioner of the bloody atrocities to which I have referred. While America is printing tracts and Bibles; send-

ing missionaries abroad to convert the heathen; expending her money in various ways for the promotion of the gospel in foreign lands—the slave not only lies forgotten, uncared for, but is trampled under foot by the very churches of the land. What have we in America? Why, we have slavery made part of the religion of the land. Yes, the pulpit there stands up as the great defender of this cursed institution, as it is called. Ministers of religion come forward and torture the hallowed pages of inspired wisdom to sanction the bloody deed. They stand forth as the foremost, the strongest defenders of this "institution." (266)

Later in the century, even after emancipation, Anna Julia Cooper affirms Douglass's contention. Writing to inspire black women to high moral goals, she sharply criticized white Christianity's historical role in women's oppression, arguing: "And yet the Christian Church . . . would seem to have been doing even less to protect and elevate woman than the little done by secular society" (339). The argument made against white Christianity had much to recommend it. First, the hypocrisy, the contradictory nature of "Whiteanity," as it was sometimes called, was easy to grasp; it did not require formal education. The gospel professed an egalitarian ideology, yet Christianity was being used to shore up a slave society. Although literacy for slaves was outlawed for about fifty years mid-century, they could learn and memorize teachings from the gospel and theorize as well as experience their oppression in the name of religion. (A parallel might be drawn between early use by blacks of scriptural teachings to fight oppression and the late twentieth-century development of liberation theologies, for example in Latin America, to fight against oppressive hierarchies.) The argument also had an irresistible dual character. While African Americans often were forced into Christianity, the creative melding by blacks of African religious traditions and the religious traditions of their oppressors produced a syncretic religion that was less hypocritical, less contradictory, and at the same time allowed blacks to claim the moral high ground; some small spiritual solace in a dispiriting world.

Exhortation to Exhibit Moral Purity: A Coded Message?

Stewart, Douglass, and Cooper all make the complex claim that African Americans should be more diligent in exhibiting ethical behavior. The language of writers from oppressed groups, for whom forthrightness is a dangerous luxury, is rarely literal, and generally multi-layered. The call to morality serves at least four functions. First, and perplexingly, it seems to affirm the white argument that blacks were immoral (with all that follows about the nature and humanity of African Americans). The meanings and sincerity of this claim require careful scrutiny. Second, it functions to insist that the inspired practice of Christianity would provide spiritual strength for those who were in dire need of it. Third, and crucially, it provides a smoke screen for the hidden agenda of rebellion and opposition to all oppression. And finally, it provides a rally to the collective action needed to oppose white domination effectively.

Stewart's speech, "Religion and the Pure Principles of Morality," exemplifies all of these components. She shows herself to be a serious and severe moral critic, as when she says, "I see the greater part of our community following the vain bubbles of life with so much eagerness, which will only prove to them like a serpent's sting upon the bed of death" (216). Yet she also sees religion to be a source of spiritual strength: "Arm yourselves with the weapons of prayer. Put your trust in the living God. Persevere strictly in the paths of virtue. Let nothing be lacking on your part; and in God's own time, and his time is certainly the best, he will surely deliver you with a mighty hand and with an outstretched arm" (221). To what degree was the exhortation to improve morally a smoke screen for other arguments? No doubt religion and spirituality were vitally important in African-American culture. Religion provided one of the few available vehicles for covertly maintaining the remnants of African culture. The sanctuary of the church was important for a group that was scrutinized closely, and it provided some measure of privacy in which to conduct a wide range of activities—social, religious, even business and professional. It provided a space for the spirituality that was vital to survival. Thus, the religious connection formed the background of cultural practice.

Yet it is apparent that Stewart (and later, Douglass) also uses religious persuasion subversively to mask the language of rebellion. Her argument progresses, from the importance for African Americans of engaging in moral practices, to the exhortation to demonstrate and *live* their moral superiority to whites, to the clear contradictions of "whiteanity" and the ultimate doom of white slave culture, to the agency of African Americans in bringing this about. She writes: "AND WE CLAIM OUR RIGHTS. We will tell you that we are not afraid of them that kill the body, and after that can do no more; but we will tell you whom we do fear. We fear Him who is able, after He hath killed, to destroy both soul and body in hell together" (220). Stewart sympathized greatly with armed uprisings like the American Revolution. In "An Address Delivered at the African Masonic Hall" (*On African Rights and Liberty*, 1833), she forthrightly declares: "Many powerful sons and daughters of Africa will shortly arise, who will put down vice and immorality among us, and declare by Him that sitteth upon the throne that they will have their rights; and if refused, I am afraid they will spread horror and devastation around" (220). The liberal language of rights and freedom, radical in its day, permeates this text and fuses with the religious language, to make the case for ending the oppression of African Americans, men and women, free and enslaved.

Contemporary Themes

Religious influence on ethics and politics currently is discussed in popular media with regard to topics such as abortion, "family values," the teaching of evolutionary theory, and "faith-based initiatives." Yet scholars and activists seem reluctant to take up our society's saturation with religious beliefs that profoundly affect gendered and "raced" social issues. The underlying suppositions of particular religions promote particularized concepts of race and gender and of moral superiority and inferiority. These topics present a fertile field for contextualized study, over and against the narratives of black and white political theories. For example, how are the code words for race ("social programs," "welfare mothers," "urban crime," "affirmative action") used in political discourse, but also in church sermons and religious literature, to promote racial hatred? Nineteenth-century black political theorists closely studied the employment of Christianity in promoting racial oppression. Although the risk of repercussions is far less today, contemporary theorists shy away from providing a close analysis of religion's racist aspects. This reticence, especially on the part of scholars and political activists who otherwise might be expected to provide a critique of the racist forms of Christianity, is evidence of John Stuart Mill's insight that social pressure and practice are often more efficacious in suppressing free speech even than government regulation.[6] Such practices as the use of Christian prayers in the U.S. Congress, the holding of prayer meetings in government offices by high officials, and the widespread assumption, even in an ever-more-diverse nation that (white) Christianity should be the prevailing social norm create an exceedingly chilly climate for analysis and critique. In other words, most mainstream theorists and policy makers are failing persistently to address contemporary uses of Christianity in the service of racial hatred. (Remember, for example, that in the 1990s dozens of black churches were burned to the ground in attacks that pitted white, Christian-based ideologies against black loci of power and yet these attacks are not addressed as a major moral issue.)

The theme of Christianity as a source of both liberation and oppression persists in the reality of the lives of blacks and whites today. Among public intellectuals and activists, Cornel West, Michael Eric Dyson, and Jill Nelson are among the few who address these issues.[7] Some black feminists attend to how ideology functions to perpetuate racism and/or effect liberation. Among these, the theme of religion as both oppressive and liberatory is explored widely. For example, the theologian Jacqueline Grant, in addressing the invisibility of black women in black theology, writes that "Many black women are enraged as they listen to 'liberated' black men speak about the 'place of women' in words and phrases similar to those of the very white oppressors they condemn."[8] She argues for an authentic theology of liberation that arises from the experiences and intellect of black women.

In *A Singing Something: Womanist Reflections on Anna Julia Cooper*, Karen Baker-Fletcher develops a womanist theology based on the concept of vocality as an embodied ontological form shared by God and humanity. Baker-Fletcher examines "Cooper's argument for women's movement from silence and subjugation to a model of bold vocalization and independence to consider how her concept of woman's voice provides a resource for a contemporary theological concept of women's embodiment and prophetic message of freedom and equality."[9] Her argument connects epistemology, the notion of moving from silence to knowledge, with theology, the connections between vocality and spirituality. Her work provides one of the most comprehensive accounts to date of a single aspect of Cooper's writings.

Angela Y. Davis, in *Blues Legacies and Black Feminism: Gertrude "Ma" Rainey, Bessie Smith, and Billie Holiday*, provides a complex analysis of the relations among gender equality, female sexuality, the blues, spirituality, and religion.[10] She notes that the black church is "the most powerful institution" in black culture, underscoring that it is also the premier site of the ideology of male domination. She explores and challenges the necessity of a binary opposition between the blues, often associated with female sexuality and even with the devil, and spirituality identified with the black

Christian church. Davis identifies the ways in which the blues contribute to self-reflexivity and self-consciousness for black women. To see this as concomitant with the development of an alternative form of spirituality is also to identify a possible alternative to the polarization of oppression/ liberation that seems endemic to Christianity.

Black feminist treatments of religion issue from several different quarters of nineteenth-century black theory and lead in several different directions. Some develop into critiques of mainstream religion, others into critiques of black masculinist ideologies, and still others into new understandings of theology. Work such as Grant's, Davis's and Baker-Fletcher's reveals a continuity of thought over time that can be emulated in other areas as well.

Women's Special Role: A Gendered Conception of Ethics

Black Women's Role as Educators and Moral Guides

All of Maria W. Stewart's speeches provide some sort of gendered analysis. A second core theme of black feminism that she expresses is the notion that women have a special role in promoting morality: "O, ye daughters of Africa, awake! Awake! Arise! No longer sleep nor slumber, but distinguish yourselves. Show forth the world that ye are endowed with noble and exalted faculties" (215); and further,

> O woman, woman! Upon you I call; for upon your exertions almost entirely depends whether the rising generation shall be any thing more than we have been or not. O Woman, woman! Your example is powerful, your influence great; it extends over your husbands and your children and throughout the circle of your acquaintance. Then let me exhort you to cultivate among yourselves a spirit of Christian love and unity, having charity one for another, without which all our goodness is as sounding brass, and a tinkling cymbal. (224–25).

Stewart was among the earliest writers in this tradition to articulate the notion that women had a special moral role, a theme famously articulated by Anna Julia Cooper in later years when she wrote that "Only the BLACK WOMAN can say 'when and where I enter, in the quiet undisputed dignity of my womanhood, without violence and without suing or special patronage, then and there the whole *Negro race enters with me*'" (341). Stewart and Cooper develop the notion adopted by the clubwomen's movement that women are moral leaders, that tending to morality is part of their special role. Cooper grounds this role in the experiences and responsibilities of women:

> The position of woman in society determines the vital elements of its regeneration and progress. Now that this is so on *a priori* grounds all must admit. And this not because woman is better or stronger or wiser than man, but from the nature of the case, because it is she who must first form the man by directing the earliest impulses of his character. (340)

Cooper takes as axiomatic that women will be responsible for the care of young children. But although she calls this "a priori," it is not (as she makes clear) because of woman's *nature* but because Cooper cannot imagine men performing the tasks of caring for infants and young children. From our standpoint, it is easier to grasp the need not to essentialize women's role in childcare and education, but from her point of view, only slightly removed from slavery and immersed in nineteenth-century patriarchalism, it is difficult to imagine men performing these duties. Still, for Cooper, the concept of a special moral role for women is grounded not in childbearing; it comes about because women "direct the earliest impulses of . . . character."

Black literature is permeated (perhaps sufficiently to call it an additional core theme) with the idea of the critical importance of education. Douglass describes bribing and tricking white children into teaching him to read. Literacy for him was a prerequisite for freedom. Cooper dedicated herself and her life to promoting the idea of classical and elite education for blacks, over and against the Booker T. Washington model of training for vocational skills. Since moral education is part and parcel of early childhood training, Cooper argued that such training was the special moral responsibility of women. Women, therefore, had to be moral leaders and guides.

Feminist Concepts and Nonfeminists Ones

Understanding the theme of black women as moral leaders and guides is complicated by the corresponding but not analogical eighteenth- and nineteenth-century ideologies of "republican motherhood" and the "cult of true womanhood" that emerged from the creation of the nation. These white-created myths about the exalted position of women in society differ in important ways from black and feminist ideology. The dominant ideology served to constrain and maintain white women in the domestic sphere by glorifying the values of marriage, motherhood, and womanly virtue. In the revolutionary period, the notion of republican motherhood was one ostensibly of public virtue—creating new citizens for the republic, but the description of this as a public role (for white women) is deceptive. Historian Joan Hoff argues that

> a private female version of patriotic virtue came into vogue in the 1780s, which helped to ensure that [white] women's work would continue to be objectified and isolated in a separate sphere ... because as second-class citizens post-revolutionary women did not possess the constitutional rights capable of influencing the public sphere ... Privatization and patriotic feminisation of virtue came at the very moment when postrevolutionary leaders were getting on with the business of carving out political privileges and economic opportunities for themselves and for succeeding generations of white males.[11]

With the further entrenchment of liberalism, capitalism, and individualism in the nineteenth century, the cult of true womanhood emerged. Sociologist Alice Rossi identifies the qualities comprising this ideology as piety, purity, submissiveness, and domesticity.[12] The ideology was supported legally, through barriers to white women entering the public sphere, as well as through custom and religion. Cooper in fact critiques the cult in her identification of decadent white Southern culture with medieval chivalry, both of which she finds hypocritical: "Respect for woman, the much lauded chivalry of the Middle Ages, meant what I fear it still means to some men in our own day—respect for the elite few among whom they expect to consort" (339). "True womanhood" was reserved for a class of elite white woman who derived their elevation from the slavocracy that supported them. In both its classism and its racism, the cult of true womanhood differed from its African-American counterpart. The ideology of black female moral leadership may have modeled itself consciously on the white cult as a way of gaining credibility in a racist society, but in practice the differences could not be greater. First, in the cult of true womanhood, women engaged in only the most delicate domestic chores. In contrast, black women as moral leaders were industrious, performing domestic or field labor as well as educating children and maintaining the home. Second, the cult of true womanhood was a political ideology designed to restrain women; it was not generated primarily by women themselves for the purposes of liberation, but by a white South-

ern Christian sensibility for the purposes of oppression and control. In
contrast, Cooper describes her vision of the role of women:

> The [black] woman of today finds herself in the presence of responsibil-
> ities which ramify through the profoundest and most varied interests of
> her country and race. Not one of the issues of this plodding, toiling, sin-
> ning, repenting, falling, aspiring humanity can afford to shut her out, or
> can deny the reality of her influence. No plan for renovating society, no
> scheme for purifying politics, no reform in church or in state, no moral,
> social or economic question, no movement upward or downward in the
> human plane is lost on her. A man once said when told his house was afire:
> "Go tell my wife; I never meddle with household affairs." But no woman
> can possibly put herself or her sex outside any of the interests that affect
> humanity. All departments in the new era are to be hers, in the sense that
> her interests are in all and though all: and it is incumbent on her to keep
> intelligently and sympathetically *en rapport* with all the great movements of
> her time, that she may know on which side to throw the weight of her in-
> fluence. She stands now at the gateway of this new era of American civi-
> lization. In her hands must be moulded the strength, the wit, the states-
> manship, the morality, all the psychic force, the social and economic
> intercourse of that era. To be alive at such an epoch is a privilege, to be a
> woman then is sublime. (142–43)

This is hardly the submissive, domesticated "true woman." It is a concept
of genuine, proactive "public virtue," of women engaged in every part of
public life. The idea of black women as social and moral leaders is a self-
generated, self-reflexive arm of a liberation movement designed to help
bring women to consciousness about social conditions in modern society and about the kinds of activities, education, and organizing required
to bring about change. In contrast to submissiveness, struggle against oppression is a key feature of black women's leadership.

Contemporary Themes

More recently, it has become difficult for black women to promote a gendered conception of ethics because of its ties to the ideological constructions of black womanhood. For black women, the concept of womanhood
is complicated seriously by the prevailing ideologies of masculinity and
femininity, of what it means to be a woman, a mother, a wife, a sister, a
daughter, a friend.

For example, the image of black women as mothers/educators is tied
to the troublesome portrayal of black women as mammies that writers

such as Collins, Adrienne Rich, and many others warn against. Of course, black women long have been responsible for the early care and education of both black and white children, and often for white children at the expense of their own. Rich's "Disloyal to Civilization" warns about sentimentalizing this relationship and valorizes cultures of resistance that defy it.[13] Collins theorizes about the use of the stereotype "mammy," to offset the stereotyped image of the "Jezebel," the first portraying the kindly, controlled, black mother-educator, the second portraying the sexually charged and out-of-control animalistic black seductress. The power of the second image to outrage white sensibility plays off of the power of the first to soothe it. Both are distortions and serve specific political functions. For example, the first is tied to acceptable roles for black women such as domestic worker or service worker and the second is tied to unacceptable (but equally controlled) roles such as sex worker.

But the mammy is a black woman who is the surrogate mother to *white* children. Black women as moral leaders are seen in relation not to white but to *black* children, families, and communities. Angela Davis has a different take on the role of the black woman as mother, homemaker, and educator. She notes that:

> With the black slave woman, there is a strange twist of affairs: in the infinite anguish of ministering to the needs of men and children around her (who were not necessarily members of her immediate family), she was performing the *only* labor of the slave community that could not be directly and immediately claimed by the oppressor.[14]

Providing the seed of autonomy for both black women and men, they become "the custodian of the house of resistance," a central insight tied to Stewart's and Cooper's notion of women as moral leaders. As much as any theme in black feminist literature, the notion of a special moral role for black women is complicated almost impossibly by the definitions of women found in dominant ideologies. Stewart and Cooper are clear about the gendering of moral education. Through the twentieth century it becomes much less clear.

The concept of women as moral leaders reached its zenith during the club women's movement in the late nineteenth and well into the twentieth centuries with the work of Josephine St. Pierre Ruffin, Mary Church Terrell, Mary McCloud Bethune, and the thousands of women who worked in and through the clubs. But in the mid- to late twentieth century, several factors emerged, one might say conspired, to drive black women's leadership underground. While the stereotype of the dangerous black matriarch has its seeds in slavery, the image did not gain full expression until the publication of the 1965 federal government study *The Negro Family: The Case for National Action,* by the late Senator Daniel Patrick Moynihan that lay the blame for what is termed the "defective black family" at the feet of the black women who had, in Davis's terms, struggled in "the infinite anguish of ministering to the needs of men and children around her."[15] The impact of this cruel and misleading "social scientific study" was quite successfully to undercut black women's already-tenuous leadership roles by blaming black women for their successes as well as shortcomings, and by shoring up anti-black sexism in both the black and white communities. For example, sexism in the Civil Rights movement prevented women organizers such as Ella Baker from achieving the recognition they deserved, and the emerging women's liberation movement often made matters worse rather than better for black women.

The flawed and often racist liberal model of white feminism promoted an individualist approach to women's advancement and devalued the collectivist social networks common to black women's community organizing and self-help. While white women were fleeing the dull bourgeois lives articulated by Betty Friedan and others in search of "fulfilling" professional careers, many black women were longing to leave behind the drudgery of forced employment mainly in the service sector, in order to spend more time on their children, their families and themselves. They sought more latitude for leadership and educational roles in their families and communities, instead of servicing the needs of whites. For the most part, black women and the issues that compelled them were invisible to mainstream feminism. Does this mean that the nineteenth-century tradition of black women's activism and leadership has faded in the last decades?

While it seems as though much has conspired against a continuum of black women's leadership of the kind that existed from the nineteenth through the early twentieth centuries, many writers challenge us to look beyond the campaign to make black women's activism seem either pathological or invisible. In *Still Lifting, Still Climbing: African American Women's Contemporary Activism,* Kimberly Springer focuses on actual movements protesting intra-racial rape and the new slavery in the prison industrial complex, lobbying for better employment and organizing, critiquing the media, and promoting the arts.[16]

In the same volume, Aaronette White asserts that,

> The Black feminist movement does not mobilize through an institution-
> alized formal social movement organization. In fact, historically, most
> Black feminists fought (and many still fight) for gender equality through
> African American organizations. Most recently, however, black feminist
> collectives have operated through local communities in decentralized, often
> segmented ways referred to in the literature as "submerged networks.[17]

Still, we must ask why black women's leadership, so successful at the turn
of the last century, has been driven underground. Cooper contends that
"all departments in the new era are to be [the Black woman's]...She
stands now at the gateway of this new era of American civilization. In her
hands must be moulded the strength, the wit, the statesmanship, the
morality, all the psychic force, the social and economic intercourse of
that era. To be alive at such an epoch is a privilege, to be a woman then is
sublime," and yet the campaign against African Americans and black
women has been so successful that as we enter the twenty-first century,
the only moderately safe leadership for black women is activism that is
largely segregated, hidden, and submerged. With so many forces working
against it, Sheila Radford-Hill argues that "it will require time and a concerted strategy to strengthen and extend the sisterhood."[18]

Matrices of Oppression

A central way in which black feminism has differed from white since the
nineteenth century is the unmediated recognition of a matrix of race, gender, and class oppression/domination. This idea, which is as much a
methodology as a theme of black feminism, provides a mode of analysis
for particular social and political problems and different individual and
group identities. It insists on an analysis that gives a multidimensional
perspective on oppression based on the notion that different forms of
oppression operate fluidly, sometimes simultaneously and sometimes se-
quentially. Forms of oppression such as racism, classism, or sexism are
not viewed competitively, or additively, but as multiple dimensions of the
same phenomenon—oppression—often having different historical origins, different forms and manifestations, and different results.

Stewart brings the matrix to bear on many of the analyses she provides.
She underscores the impediments of class distinction when she asks, "How
long shall the fair daughters of Africa be compelled to bury their minds

and talents beneath a load of iron pots and kettles?" (219). Race, gender, and class are all responsible for the labor conditions that prevent women from saving to build the educational institution that Stewart envisions: "How long shall a mean set of men flatter us with smiles, and enrich themselves with our hard earnings?" (219). She provides an astute gender analysis, which is again joined with an analysis of race and class: it is black *women* who enrich "a mean set of *men*," it is *black* women, not white, who are slaves to domestic service; it is black women as a *class* of domestic workers who "bury their minds and talents beneath a load of pots and pans" (italics mine).

Later in the century, Frederick Douglass attended to the matrix of oppression in some startling ways. When he attended the 1848 Seneca Falls convention as a reporter for his newspaper, the *North Star,* he became engaged in the discussion that took place about the content of the *Declaration of Sentiments* that was being composed and he argued vociferously that women should be admitted to the elective franchise. Better than some of the [white] women attendees, he understood the link between race and gender oppression and the importance of the vote for breaking those chains. Curiously, the banner motto of his abolitionist newspaper was "Right Knows No Sex," drawing attention to gender rather than race oppression. For Douglass, the confluence of race and gender oppression was obvious, but for many white abolitionists it was not. He notes:

> Many who have at last made the discovery that the Negroes have some rights as well as other members of the human family, have yet to be convinced that women are entitled to any. Eight years ago a number of persons of this description actually abandoned the anti-slavery cause, lest by giving their influence in that direction they might possibly be giving countenance to the dangerous heresy that woman, in respect to rights, stands on an equal footing with man. (271)

In his early years of political activism, Douglass readily understood the importance of drawing connections between different kinds of oppression: "Standing ... upon the watch-tower of human freedom, we cannot be deterred from an expression of our approbation of any movement, however humble, to improve and elevate the character of members of the human family" (271). Still, the steady influence of and pressure from abolitionists blind or hostile to gender oppression led Douglass in the 1860s to declare for "the Negroes' Hour" in support of the Fourteenth and Fifteenth Amendments to the United States Constitution, which gave due process, equal protection, and the vote to black men, but not to black or white women. This example serves as but one of many object lessons in adopting a uni-dimensional mode of analysis and eschewing the matrices of oppression, or one that unilaterally ranks one form of oppression as more severe and more deserving of remedy than another without exploring the meanings and the material conditions created by different forms of oppression. Black women were resoundingly oppressed under slavery, yet they were erased from the equation in the support of the male "Negroes' Hour."

Late-twentieth-century literature by black women addresses the persistent and ongoing erasure of black women in literature. An early example is Gloria Hull, Patricia Bell Scott, and Barbara Smith's groundbreaking collection, *Some of Us are Brave*, the title of which indicates the perception that, "all the blacks are men, all the women are white," but some—the black women who suffer from the erasure of social analysis—are brave.[19]

For African-American women, the operant oppression could change with dizzying rapidity, or multiple oppressions could occur simultaneously. Writing from the perspective of one subjected to multiple oppressions, Cooper makes clear the links between different kinds of oppressions: "And when farther on . . . our train stops at a dilapidated station . . . I see two dingy little rooms with "FOR LADIES" swinging over one and "FOR COLORED PEOPLE" over the other [I wonder] under which head I come" (348). In this brief anecdote Cooper encapsulates both the identity problems that some postmodern writing investigates and the ways that oppression can operate along different but intersecting planes.

Contemporary Themes

These insights underscore the need for a dynamic approach to oppression and domination as examined in social and political theory. The complexities of social location for black women speak to epistemological issues and the importance of standpoint in generating ethical claims from a particular subject position. One way in which we learn how the failure of the dominant cultures—even feminist ones—to understand the oppositional discourses of the subordinate ones is to see that attention to the dynamic character of oppression might have precluded the kinds of disputes about primacy that dominated the white feminist literature of the 1970s and 1980s. During this time, radical and socialist feminists heatedly debated which type of oppression was more fundamental: gender or class.

Yet, the feminist literature and disputes from the 1980s about "the unhappy marriage of marxism and feminism" seemed oblivious to the dynamic character of multiple oppressions.[20] Why was the marriage unhappy? Using the white metanarratives of radicalism and marxism, feminists searched for a state-of-nature account in which the original oppression could be located and designated, for example, rape as the source of gender domination, or class power-struggle as the source of class domination. The universalized and essentialized narratives failed to take account of the fluidity of oppression based upon particular historical conditions and social locations. In this marriage, as Gloria Joseph pointed out, race oppression was an unwelcome third party.[21] Yet Cooper and Stewart both understood, a century earlier, that race, class, gender, and other oppressions could be simultaneous or sequential, single or multiple or accumulative. No ahistorical ordering would capture the dynamism of oppression.

Among current writers who draw on historical black feminism, Joy James and Angela Davis both take class into careful account, and resist eliding race and class oppression. Davis investigates the ways in which the black feminism that issues from the blues challenges the emerging class distinctions developed during the Harlem Renaissance. Drawing on, and to some degree mimicking, a European cultural hierarchy that valorized "high culture," many of the artists and admirers of the Harlem Renaissance looked down upon the blues as a raw, lower-class art form. The exceptions were Zora Neale Hurston and Langston Hughes, both of whom understood the subtle and multi-textural consciousness of blues music and lyrics. Davis says of Hughes that "more than anyone else, he attempted to incorporate the social realities of the masses of black people into his art . . . and was least influenced by the intelligensia's bourgeois, anti-working class attitudes."[22] Bessie Smith's music is not raw, but smooth and subtle. Nonetheless, the more homogenized music of Ethel Waters was more palatable for the newly developing class consciousness of 1920s Harlem because it provided an urban sophistication that contrasted with Smith's music. But Bessie Smith, according to Davis, "more accurately represented the socio-historical patterns of black people's lives." So in the blues tradition there is a feminist articulation of the lives and oppressions faced by black Americans in and beyond the slavocracy, in other words, a critical consciousness of race, class, and gender.

Useful conceptions are articulated by many writers, beginning with

Gloria Hull, Patricia Bell Scott, and Barbara Smith, and moving through the work of Deborah K. King ("multiple jeopardy, multiple consciousness"), Patricia Hill Collins ("the matrix of oppression"), Rosa M. Brewer ("the simultaneity of oppressions"), and others. Sensitive analyses will both employ the theoretical mechanisms and problematize the potentially essentializing elements of the matrix. Stewart and Cooper both succeed in "fracturing" the conceptions of race and gender while at the same time calling on the power of group identities, obliquely addressing concerns about essentializing that were not even to be raised officially until a century later.

The rise of global feminisms has intensified the need for fluid models for understanding oppression and domination. In this spirit, critical legal theorist Adrien Katherine Wing issues a "call for a deeper understanding of the lives of women of color based on the multiple nature of their identities."[23] Wing provides examples of the insidious denial of multiple oppression, recent legal cases in which the "court stated that [five black women challenging a seniority system] were entitled to bring suit for 'race discrimination, sex discrimination, or alternatively either, but not a combination of both.'"[24] Yet she asserts "affirmatively . . . that we black women are more than 'multiply burdened' entities subject to a multiplicity of oppression, discrimination, pain and depression. Our essence is also characterized by a multiplicity of *strength, love, joy* (with a spin/leap/alive we're alive), and *transcendence* that flourishes despite adversity."[25] True to the historical traditions of black women intellectuals, Wing intertwines hope with struggle as a way of providing a clear-eyed vision that resists the "murder of the spirit."[26]

Control of Sexuality/Reproduction

Another core theme of nineteenth-century black feminism foreshadows contemporary concerns. At a time when it was difficult to speak openly about sexuality, African Americans were acutely aware, because it was so pervasive, that their sexuality and reproduction were controlled by the dominant white culture. Stewart's first speech about morality addresses the special degradation that black women suffered in slavery and in a racist society. Given the difficulties of addressing this directly, Stewart does a remarkably good job: "Oh, America, America, . . . thou hast caused the daughters of Africa to commit whoredoms and fornications; but upon thee be thy curse" (19–20). The "whoredoms and fornications" refer in part to the ones compelled of female slaves by plantation owners through rape and other forms of sexual exploitation.

In the same vein, Anna Julia Cooper writes: "My mother was a slave and the finest woman I have ever known . . . Presumably my father was her master, if so I owe him not a sou and she was always too modest and shamefaced ever to mention him" (320). Scholars agree with her assessment of her paternity, since plantation owners frequently practiced the systematic sexual assault of women slaves, serving the multiple purposes of ready sexual gratification, the structured exercise of power and terror designed to maintain a docile slave-class, and the eugenic production of a crop of light-skinned offspring thought to be more suitable for house service. Thus, the circumstances of Anna Julia Cooper's birth exemplify the problematic confluence of race and gender oppression and control over black women's sexuality.

Douglass repeatedly addresses these issues of control and lack of autonomy in his speeches and writings when he refers to the fact that slaves could not enter into marriage:

> The marriage institution cannot exist among slaves, and one-sixth of the population of democratic American is denied its privileges by the law of the land. What is to be thought of a nation boasting of its liberty, boasting of its humanity, boasting of its Christianity, boasting of its love of justice and purity, and yet having within its own borders three million persons denied by law the right of marriage?—what must be the condition of that people? (262)

Douglass provides a few anecdotes about the results of these barriers, for example, a slave whose common-law wife was sold to another master. When he attempted to say goodbye to her, he was bludgeoned and died, partly from the blow and partly from a broken spirit. Douglass says, "such scenes are the every-day fruit of American slavery" (265). The denial of marriage meant that *any* sexual relations were necessarily outside the sanction of law and religion. Personal avowals of love or fidelity could be rendered meaningless or worthless at the Master's whim. Children were necessarily born out of wedlock. Autonomy or choice about personal relationships, sexuality, and reproduction were extremely constrained and tenuous at best.

Among the white community, issues of control of sexuality and reproduction, addressed by outcasts such as Margaret Sanger in the early twentieth century, were not a central theme of feminism until the last third of the twentieth century. Among blacks, the conditions of slavery and oppression made control of sexuality and reproduction absolutely central to what it meant to be a black woman, to have a family, to live free from or subjected to violence or sexual violence. The first black political theorist to address these issues extensively was Ida B. Wells in the late nineteenth and well into the twentieth century. Wells commanded public attention through her campaigns against the widespread lynching of black men. Joy James sketches the important links that Wells made between racism and control of sexuality. According to James, Wells understood and lectured about how:

> [r]itualized murders of black Americans were rationalized by the mythology of black rapists obsessed with white females. Sexual realities became convoluted by sexual politics, which inverted the interracial sexual violence of the era. The sexual politicians of lynching grossly exaggerated the likelihood of black male assaults on white females while ignoring the widespread prevalence of white male sexual assaults against black females. By draping lynching in the cloak of antisexual violence rhetoric, and thus by legitimizing (and, therefore, logically, increasing) violence against them, the lives of millions of black females were destabilized. Feeding on the racist stereotypes of black bestiality, lynch mythology masked sexual violence against black females and justified racial violence against blacks.[27]

Notice how the use of the matrix of oppression allows James *and* Wells to provide a complex analysis. Rather than flattening the critique to address only sexual violence against women or racial violence against blacks, the practice of lynching is seen vis à vis the mythologizing theories and brutal practices regarding, separately, black men, black women, white men, and white women. Yet none of the findings are universalized. White women were made to seem the victims, and therefore in need of protection (control), even when they engaged in consensual relations with black men (something that this ideology deemed to be impossible). White men were seen to be chivalrous—a theme adopted by both Cooper and Wells—as a mask for barbarous acts of sexual violence against black and white women and of murderous violence against black men. Black men were characterized as the major perpetrators of crime, a forceful mythology that continues to function today as reflected by the vastly disproportionate number of black males in our criminal justice system. (A frequently used metaphor is that the nation's prisons are the slave ships of today.)

And black women, as usual, remained the invisible victims of the real but disguised crime—rape by white men. Wells's campaigns made this reality visible and exemplify the black women's struggle for social justice.

Wells's political theory provides the link between Stewart's and Douglass's antebellum recognition of control of sexuality and reproduction and the explicitly theorized analysis of this control found in contemporary black feminist literature. As James says, Wells's "demystification of 'rape,' controversial a century ago and remaining so today, was the cornerstone of moral and political resistance to racist violence justified as the vindication or prevention of *sexual* violence."[28] As is to be expected of someone who uses a multiple-oppression approach, Wells notes the class-based, economic analysis that forms a third element of the practice of lynching, namely that men often were lynched for economic reasons. Black businesses that successfully competed with white ones often had their owners designated for lynching, an efficient way of eliminating competition. Indeed, Wells knew similar tactics firsthand because her own business, the newspaper *Free Speech*, was burned down after she wrote her first editorial exposing the mythological underpinnings of lynching.

James designates the anti-lynching campaigns as "an early form of radical black feminism" and notes that, "expanding on the traditions with which Maria Stewart struggled, ancestors Ida B. Wells and Ella Baker challenged racial-sexual violence and exploitation."[29] Insofar as these and other connections can be made to the political theory of Maria W. Stewart and Frederick Douglass, we can establish a direct link between the early articulations of this theme and its contemporary manifestations.

Contemporary Themes

Many contemporary black feminist theorists have addressed at some length the issues of control of sexuality and reproduction, among them Angela Davis, Audre Lorde, Hazel Carby, Toni Morrison, Patricia Hill Collins, bell hooks, and Joy James.[30]

James also uses historical themes in black feminism to create contemporary understandings. She describes the various forms of black feminist theory as "shadows" because of the unlikelihood in a white-dominant culture that the varieties of black feminism ever will be differentiated sufficiently. Yet she develops a black socialist-feminist viewpoint that challenges the liberal individualized and privatized accounts of violence. In her consideration of the work of Wells and Ella Baker, she draws attention to the fact that "Baker and Wells re-focus theoretical attention on the state and capital as the primary agents of women's suffering."[31] Here, again, race, class, and gender converge. A historicized black feminist theory developed from a range of sources will consider carefully sexuality as a core theme: the stereotyped portrayals, the almost impossible complexities, the dominations and submissions, and the multiple areas of other-control versus self-determination.

A comprehensive analysis of this issue comes, not surprisingly, from Patricia Hill Collins' *Black Sexual Politics: African Americans, Gender and the New Racism*. A finely nuanced investigation, this work explores politics, economics, and popular culture to reveal gender ideology as the single most powerful mechanism for creating new forms of racism in the United States. Collins writes that:

> Pandering to misogyny in the African American communities, new versions of black gender ideology evolve into one of perpetrator and victim in which African American men are "too weak" *because* African American women are "too strong" . . . helping to deflect attention away from the major structural changes of the new racism, African American men and women are encouraged to blame one another for economic, political and social problems within African American communities.[32]

Gender ideologies tied to notions of sexuality and reproduction are possibly the most influential means of maintaining racism and sexism. Popular culture provides fluid and mutable concepts of race and sex that can be transformed by the dominant culture to adapt for new conditions and new forms of racist expression. Understanding issues such as violence (both in personal relationships and in the wider society), the rape culture, and hypersexuality as portrayed in the media, particularly in film, music, and on the internet, requires an understanding of the origins of these ideologies in order to address their woeful legacies.

Gendered Knowledge

Control of the Canon—Oppression, Silencing, and Erasure

Feminism has taken as a central theme the idea that canonical knowledge is typically gendered as male. This is done in part by authorizing only knowledge produced from certain locations, such as historically male-only universities, governments, or research institutions. Further, women's knowledge is excluded by silencing women's speech and erasing the historical accomplishments and ideas of women. Maria W. Stewart was one of the first feminists to note the systematic erasure of women as a way of controlling knowledge. In her "Farewell Address," Stewart developed a refined set of arguments, based on the historical achievements of women, to demonstrate, *contra* St. Paul, that women are as worthy as men:

> In the 15th century . . . [we find] women occupying the chairs of Philosophy and Justice; women writing in Greek, and studying Hebrew. Nuns were poetesses, and women of quality Divines; and young girls who had studied Eloquence . . . The religious spirit which has animated women in all ages, showed itself at this time. It has made them by turns, martyrs, apostles, warriors, and concluded in making them divines and scholars. (231)

The movement has chronicled the multiple ways in which women's achievements are made to disappear. Early feminists such as Mary Wollstonecraft and Stewart faced serious structural barriers to being heard, including a lack of formal education, a social stricture against women entering professions, including writing and speaking, and the public's strong predisposition to consider women writers or orators as sexually promiscuous and unworthy. Stewart's role is especially important, as she is considered one of the first women, black or white, to speak publicly in the United States. Discrediting tactics were and are worse for black women. Minority opinions have been subjected to ridicule, denied a forum, and ignored by the press. They have been misrepresented and belittled, portrayed as dangerous, or worse, as trivial.

Violence and the threat of violence are among the most effective ways of silencing non-dominant views; whether it is battering in the home or violence in slavery and domestic service, sanctions threatened through the legal system, or as part of a system of publicly condoned crime such as lynching, they provide a most effective means of censorship. Speaking out against slavery had a treasonous flavor, and a fairly well-established, if loose-knit code prevailed for murdering those who threatened the system of slavery. Stewart was well aware of this ultimate threat to speech, for her mentor, David Walker, most likely was murdered for promoting political and civil rights for blacks.

Those obstacles facing most women were and are considerably multiplied for black women in the United States. Consider, for example, the work of Frances E. W. Harper. Although she wrote more than a dozen books and was the one of the most popular woman poets of her time, she is largely unknown today, and her first book of published poetry is completely lost to us. In fact, little is known about many black women writers, and the authority of their speech is often questioned.

Knowledge and Education

Education was a lifelong theme for Stewart and represents one of the primary ways in which racism has been extended into the twenty-first century, through the deprivation of educational opportunities for many blacks. The lack of access to equal education and the roadblocks for those who have managed to gain an education have led some to abandon hope for equal education, and others to champion a new separatism as the hope for integrated access becomes more distant.

Stewart's own education, gained unsystematically and perhaps at some peril, led her to the startlingly contemporary belief that "knowledge is power." She most likely was aware of laws such as the North Carolina Act of 1831 prohibiting teaching slaves to read, which was typical of many laws enacted at the time. The institution of slavery and the oppression of free blacks depended on the systematic imposition of illiteracy, for the nascent black abolitionist movement would use pamphlets smuggled from North to South to spread the word of rebellion. Throughout her life, Stewart believed education to be the enabling condition of freedom.

Contemporary Themes: The Black Feminist Standpoint

Contemporary feminism has identified the importance of situated knowledges in which social locations are identified, something Anna Julia Cooper takes as primary. According to Cooper, "It is not the intelligent woman vs. the ignorant woman; not the white woman vs. the black, the brown, and the red,—it is not even the cause of woman vs. man. Nay, 'tis woman's strongest vindication for speaking that *the world needs to hear her voice*" (319). Cooper's essays provide a cornerstone of systematic black feminist thought, revealing a continuity of black women's experiences and ideas from the nineteenth century to the present. The very title of her book resonates with contemporary themes: *A Voice from the South* emphasizes the importance of vocality in the women's movements—the theme of oppressive silencing and the effort to be heard. By subtitling the book "By a Black Woman of the South," Cooper goes on to locate herself, racially, geographically, and in terms of gender. In so positioning herself, she authorizes her social location not as an individual, as one in the classical liberal tradition would, but as a representative of a group whose locus, whose positionality, previously has not had epistemological standing. She foreshadows Patricia Hill Collins's more comprehensive articulation of a black feminist standpoint "that reconceptualizes the social relations of dominance and resistance" and "addresses ongoing epistemological debates": "Offering subordinate groups new knowledge about their own experiences can be empowering. But revealing new ways of knowing that allow subordinate groups to define their own reality has far greater implications."[33] In asking for an audience to listen to "a voice from the South by a woman of the South," Cooper articulates Collins's thesis that "Black women intellectuals have a distinctive standpoint of self, community and society," that constitutes a subjugated knowledge not widely known or understood. Cooper offers a black feminist theory that does not essentialize the role of black women, but valorizes the influence of the traditional women's role as early childhood educators and thus as holding the key to moral as well as scholarly and practical education. Writers such as Stewart and Cooper lay the groundwork for black women's standpoint epistemologies. In contemporary work, Collins, Patricia J. Williams, and others fully articulate this vision.

Conclusion

The metadiscourses of white feminism are beginning to be widely known; in particular, the suffrage movement of nineteenth-century feminism is slipping into mainstream culture and knowledge, yet there is little recognition of the two-centuries-old tradition of black feminist thought, a tradition that transcends simple historical interest and provides the foundation for transformative political action. There is a level of sophistication to nineteenth-century black feminist analysis that has much to teach us about social theory and practice in the twenty-first century. Current black feminists in and out of the academy have worked hard to address these issues. Mainstream sociologists, historians, political scientists, and philosophers have done much less well at admitting alternative constructions, to everyone's detriment. The history of ideas about oppositional discourses can significantly improve all knowledge projects, in politics, ethics, and in crucial practical arenas as well. The oppression of African-American women and men is and continues to be one of the most cen-

tral stories of American history, and our ideas about ethics and social justice can be framed, either from the standpoint of the dominant racist and
sexist society, or from the standpoint of oppressions that bring a clearer
eye to justice and injustice. By exploring themes of black feminism, we
find specific categories of analysis to aid in this project.

Notes

1. The phrases "black feminism" and "African-American feminism" carry
political meanings that are too numerous to cover fully here. Some hold that
"African American" may convey connotations of patriarchal Afrocentricity or
that most black Americans have scant connection with Africa. Some writers,
such as Alice Walker, have held that the term "feminist" connotes *white* women
and that "womanist" should be substituted (*In Search of Our Mothers' Garden: Womanist Prose* [New York: Harcourt Brace Jovanovich, 1983]). Karen Baker-Fletcher
also adopts this term (*A Singing Something: Womanist Reflections on Anna Julia Cooper*
[New York: Crossroad Press, 1994]). Angela Y. Davis argues that the notion of
an African-American ideology is derived from a "masculinist past situated in an
African imaginary," and that "this imagined masculinist past erases the relative
equality of women characteristic of the slave community" (*Blues Legacies and Black
Feminism: Gertrude "Ma" Rainey, Bessie Smith, and Billie Holiday* [New York: Pantheon
Books, 1998], 122). Others, such as Lewis R. Gordon, hold that using the term
"black," without specifying U.S. or North American, represents a colonial carry-
over that privileges blacks in the United States over and above blacks worldwide.
For example, see Gordon's *Her Majesty's Other Children: Sketches of Racism from a Neocolonial Age* (New York: Roman and Littlefield, 1997). In this essay, I use both
terms, often in accordance with the preference of the authors under discussion.

2. Linda J. Nicholson and Nancy Fraser, "Social Criticism without Philosophy: An Encounter between Feminism and Postmodernism," in *Feminism/
Postmodernism*, ed. Linda J. Nicholson (New York: Routledge, 1990), 5, 21.

3. Adrien Katherine Wing, ed., *Critical Race Feminism: A Reader* (New York:
New York University Press, 1997), 3.

4. Patricia Hill Collins has produced an unparalleled body of work that articulates themes from current black feminism, occasionally reaching into the
past as well. See *Black Feminist Thought: Knowledge, Consciousness, and the Politics of Empowerment* (New York: Routledge, 1991 and 2000); *Fighting Words: Black Women and
the Search for Justice* (Minneapolis: University of Minnesota Press, 1998); *Black Sexual Politics: African Americans, Gender and the New Racism* (New York: Routledge,
2004); and *From Black Power to Hip Hop: Racism, Nationalism, and Feminism* (Philadelphia: Temple University Press, 2006). Many others have contributed to this effort,
for example Paula Giddings, *When and Where I Enter: The Impact of Black Women on
Race and Sex in America* (New York: William Morrow, 1984); Deborah Gray White,

Ar'n't I a Woman? Female Slaves in the Plantation South (New York: W.W. Norton, 1985); Darlene Clark Hine, Elsa Barkley Brown, and Rosalyn Terborg-Penn, eds., *Black Women in America: A Historical Encyclopedia* (New York: Carlson, 1993). For a more complete listing, see the Selected Bibliography to this volume.

5. Kristin Waters, ed., *Women and Men Political Theorists: Enlightened Conversations* (Oxford: Blackwell Publishers, 2000). All parenthetical page numbers in the text refer to this volume.

6. John Stuart Mill, *On Liberty* (London: Longman, Roberts and Green, 1869).

7. See, for example, Cornel West, *Keeping Faith: Philosophy and Race in America* (New York: Routledge, 1993); Michael Eric Dyson, *Between God and Gangsta Rap: Bearing Witness to Black Culture* (Oxford: Oxford University Press, 1996); and Jill Nelson, *Straight, No Chaser: How I Became a Grown-up Black Woman* (New York: Penguin, 1997).

8. Jacqueline Grant, "Black Theology and the Black Women," *Words of Fire: An Anthology of African-American Feminist Thought*, ed. Beverly Guy-Sheftall, (New York: New Press, 1995), 323.

9. Karen Baker-Fletcher, *A Singing Something: Womanist Reflections on Anna Julia Cooper* (New York: Crossroad Press, 1994), 15.

10. Davis, *Blues Legacies*.

11. Joan Hoff, *Law, Gender, and Injustice: A Legal History of U.S. Women* (New York: New York University Press,1991), 40.

12. Alice Rossi, *The Feminist Papers: From Adams to Beauvoir* (New York: Columbia University Press, 1973).

13. Adrienne Rich, "Disloyal to Civilization," in *On Lies, Secrets and Silence: Selected Prose 1966–1978* (New York: W.W. Norton, Co., 1979).

14. Angela Davis, "Reflections on the Black Woman's Role in the Community of Slaves," in *Words of Fire*, 205.

15. Daniel Patrick Moynihan, *The Negro Family: The Case for National Action* (Washington, D.C.: U.S. Government Printing Office, 1965).

16. Kimberly Springer, ed., *Still Lifting, Still Climbing: African American Women's Contemporary Activism* (New York: New York University Press, 1999).

17. Aaronette White, "Talking Black, Talking Feminist: Gendered Micro-mobilization Processes in a Collective Protest against Rape," in *Still Lifting*, 189–218.

18. Sheila Radford-Hill, "Keepin' It Real: A Generational Commentary on Kimberly Springer's 'Third Wave Black Feminism,'" in *Signs: Journal of Women in Culture and Society* 27 no. 4 (2002), 1989.

19. Gloria T. Hull, Patricia Bell Scott, and Barbara Smith, eds., *But Some of Us Are Brave: Black Women's Studies* (New York: Feminist Press, 1986).

20. Lydia Sargent, ed., *Women and Revolution: A Discussion of the Unhappy Marriage of Marxism and Feminism* (Boston: South End Press, 1981).

21. Gloria Joseph, "The Incompatible Menage A Trois: Marxism, Feminism and Racism," in *Women and Revolution*, 93.

22. Davis, *Blue Legacies*, 151–52.

23. Wing, *Critical Race Feminism*, 4.

24. Ibid., 30.

25. Ibid., 31. The phrase "with a spin/leap/alive we're alive" is quoted by Wing from a poem by e. e. cummings.

26. Patricia J. Williams, *The Alchemy of Race and Rights: Diary of a Law Professor* (Cambridge, Mass.: Harvard University Press, 1993).

27. Joy James, *Shadowboxing: Representations of Black Feminist Politics* (New York: St. Martin's Press, 1999), 48.

28. Ibid., 49.

29. Ibid., 54 and 70.

30. Hazel V. Carby, *Reconstructing Womanhood: The Emergence of the Afro-American Woman Novelist* (New York: Oxford University Press, 1987); Angela Y. Davis, *Women, Race and Class*, (New York: Vintage, 1983); bell hooks, *Feminist Theory: From Margin to Center*, 2nd ed. (Cambridge, Mass.: South End Press, 2000); James, *Shadowboxing*; Audre Lorde, *Sister/Outsider: Essays and Speeches* (Freedom, Calif.: The Crossing Press, 1984); Toni Morrison, *Playing in the Dark: Whiteness and the Literary Imagination* (New York: Vintage Books, 1993); Patricia Hill Collins, *Black Feminist Thought: Knowledge, Consciousness, and the Politics of Empowerment*, 2nd ed. (New York: Routledge, 2000).

31. James, *Shadowboxing*, 70.

32. Collins, *Black Sexual Politics: African Americans, Gender and the New Racism* (New York: Routledge, 2004), 184.

33. Collins, *Black Feminist Thought*, 222.

Chapter 18

The Politics of Black Feminist Thought

PATRICIA HILL COLLINS

In 1831, Maria W. Stewart asked, "How long shall the fair daughters of Africa be compelled to bury their minds and talents beneath a load of iron pots and kettles?" Orphaned at age five, bound out to a clergyman's family as a domestic servant, Stewart struggled to gather isolated fragments of an education when and where she could. As the first American woman to lecture in public on political issues and to leave copies of her texts, this early U.S. Black woman intellectual foreshadowed a variety of themes taken up by her Black feminist successors.[1]

Maria Stewart challenged African-American women to reject the negative images of Black womanhood so prominent in her times, pointing out that race, gender, and class oppression were the fundamental causes of Black women's poverty. In an 1833 speech she proclaimed, "Like King Solomon, who put neither nail nor hammer to the temple, yet received the praise; so also have the white Americans gained themselves a name . . . while in reality we have been their principal foundation and support." Stewart objected to the injustice of this situation: "We have pursued the shadow, they have obtained the substance; we have performed the labor, they have received the profits; we have planted the vines, they have eaten the fruits of them" (59).

Maria Stewart was not content to point out the source of Black women's oppression. She urged Black women to forge self-definitions of self-reliance and independence. "It is useless for us any longer to sit with our hands folded, reproaching the whites; for that will never elevate us," she exhorted. "Possess the spirit of independence . . . Possess the spirit of men, bold and enterprising, fearless and undaunted" (53). To Stewart, the power of self-definition was essential, for Black women's survival was at stake. "Sue for your rights and privileges. Know the reason you cannot attain them. Weary them with your importunities. You can but die if you make the attempt; and we shall certainly die if you do not" (38).

Stewart also challenged Black women to use their special roles as mothers to forge powerful mechanisms of political action. "O, ye mothers, what a responsibility rests on you!" Stewart preached. "You have souls committed to your charge . . . It is you that must create in the minds of your little girls and boys a thirst for knowledge, the love of virtue, . . . and the cultivation of a pure heart." Stewart recognized the magnitude of the task at hand. "Do not say you cannot make any thing of your children; but say . . . we will try" (35).

Maria Stewart was one of the first U.S. Black feminists to champion the utility of Black women's relationships with one another in providing a community for Black women's activism and self-determination. "Shall it any longer be said of the daughters of Africa, they have no ambition, they have no force?" she questioned. "By no means. Let every female heart become united, and let us raise a fund ourselves; and at the end of one year and a half we might be able to lay the corner stone for the building of a High School, that the higher branches of knowledge might be enjoyed by us" (37). Stewart saw the potential for Black women's activism as educators. She advised, "Turn your attention to knowledge and improvement; for knowledge is power" (41).

Though she said little in her speeches about the sexual politics of her time, her advice to African-American women suggests that she was painfully aware of the sexual abuse visited upon Black women. She continued to "plead the cause of virtue and the pure principles of morality" for black women (31). And to those Whites who thought that Black women were inherently inferior, Stewart offered a biting response: "Our souls are fired with the same love of liberty and independence with which your souls are fired . . . [T]oo much of your blood flows in our veins, too much of your color in our skins, for us not to possess your spirits" (40).

Despite Maria Stewart's intellectual prowess, the ideas of this extraordinary woman come to us only in scattered fragments that not only suggest her brilliance but speak tellingly of the fate of countless Black women intellectuals. Many Maria Stewarts exist, African-American women whose minds and talents have been suppressed by the pots and kettles symbolic of Black women's subordination.[2] Far too many African-American women intellectuals have labored in isolation and obscurity and, like Zora Neale Hurston, lie buried in unmarked graves.

Some have been more fortunate, for they have become known to us, largely through the efforts of contemporary Black women scholars.[3] Like Alice Walker, these scholars sense that "a people do not throw their geniuses away" and that "if they are thrown away, it is our duty as artists, scholars, and witnesses for the future to collect them again for the sake of our children, . . . if necessary, bone by bone."[4]

This painstaking process of collecting the ideas and actions of "thrown away" Black women like Maria Stewart has revealed one important discovery. Black women intellectuals have laid a vital analytical foundation for a distinctive standpoint on self, community, and society and, in doing so, created a multifaceted, African-American women's intellectual tradition. While clear discontinuities in this tradition exist—times when Black women's voices were strong, and others when assuming a more muted tone was essential—one striking dimension of the ideas of Maria W. Stewart and her successors is the thematic consistency of their work.

If such a rich intellectual tradition exists, why has it remained virtually invisible until now? In 1905, Fannie Barrier Williams lamented, "The colored girl . . . is not known and hence not believed in; she belongs to a race that is best designated by the term 'problem,' and she lives beneath the shadow of that problem which envelops and obscures her."[5] Why are African-American women and our ideas not known and not believed in?

The shadow obscuring this complex Black women's intellectual tradition is neither accidental nor benign. Suppressing the knowledge produced by any oppressed group makes it easier for dominant groups to rule because the seeming absence of dissent suggests that subordinate groups willingly collaborate in their own victimization.[6] Maintaining the invisibility of Black women and our ideas not only in the United States, but in Africa, the Caribbean, South America, Europe, and other places where Black women now live, has been critical in maintaining social inequalities. Black women engaged in reclaiming and constructing Black women's knowledges often point to the politics of suppression that affect their projects. For example, several authors in Heidi Mirza's edited volume on Black British feminism identify their invisibility and silencing in the contemporary United Kingdom.[7] Similarly, South African businesswoman Danisa Baloyi describes her astonishment at the invisibility of African women in U.S. scholarship: "As a student doing research in the United States, I was amazed by the [small] amount of information on Black South African women, and shocked that only a minuscule amount was actually written by Black women themselves."[8]

Despite this suppression, U.S. Black women have managed to do intellectual work, and to have our ideas matter. Sojourner Truth, Anna Julia Cooper, Ida B. Wells-Barnett, Mary McLeod Bethune, Toni Morrison, Barbara Smith, and countless others have consistently struggled to make themselves heard. African women writers such as Ama Ata Aidoo, Buchi Emecheta, and Ellen Kuzwayo have used their voices to raise important issues that affect Black African women.[9] Like the work of Maria W. Stewart and that of Black women transnationally, African-American women's intellectual work has aimed to foster Black women's activism.

This dialectic of oppression and activism, the tension between the suppression of African-American women's ideas and our intellectual activism in the face of that suppression, constitutes the politics of U.S. Black feminist thought. More important, understanding this dialectical relationship is critical in assessing how U.S. Black feminist thought—its core themes, epistemological significance, and connections to domestic and transnational Black feminist practice—is embedded fundamentally in a political context that has challenged its very right to exist.

The Suppression of Black Feminist Thought

The vast majority of African-American women were brought to the United States to work as slaves in a situation of oppression. Oppression describes any unjust situation where, systematically and over a long period of time, one group denies another group access to the resources of society. Race, class, gender, sexuality, nation, age, and ethnicity among others constitute major forms of oppression in the United States. However, the convergence of race, class, and gender oppression characteristic of U.S. slavery shaped all subsequent relationships that women of African descent had within Black American families and communities, with employers, and among one another. It also created the political context for Black women's intellectual work.

African-American women's oppression has encompassed three interdependent dimensions. First, the exploitation of Black women's labor essential to U.S. capitalism—the "iron pots and kettles" symbolizing Black women's long-standing ghettoization in service occupations—represents the economic dimension of oppression.[10] Survival for most African-American women has been such an all-consuming activity that most have had few opportunities to do intellectual work as it has been traditionally defined. The drudgery of enslaved African-American women's work and the grinding poverty of "free" wage labor in the rural South tellingly illustrate the high costs Black women have paid for survival. The millions of impoverished African-American women ghettoized in Philadelphia, Birmingham, Oakland, Detroit, and other U.S. inner cities demonstrate the continuation of these earlier forms of Black women's economic exploitation.[11]

Second, the political dimension of oppression has denied African-American women the rights and privileges routinely extended to White male citizens.[12] Forbidding Black women to vote, excluding African-Americans and women from public office, and withholding equitable treatment in the criminal justice system all substantiate the political subordination of Black women. Educational institutions have also fostered this pattern of disenfranchisement. Past practices such as denying literacy to slaves and relegating Black women to underfunded, segregated Southern schools worked to ensure that a quality education for Black women remained the exception rather than the rule.[13] The large numbers of young Black women in inner cities and impoverished rural areas who continue to leave school before attaining full literacy represent the continued efficacy of the political dimension of Black women's oppression.

Finally, controlling images applied to Black women that originated during the slave era attest to the ideological dimension of U.S. Black women's oppression.[14] Ideology refers to the body of ideas reflecting the interests of a group of people. Within U.S. culture, racist and sexist ideologies permeate the social structure to such a degree that they become hegemonic, namely, seen as natural, normal, and inevitable. In this context, certain assumed qualities that are attached to Black women are used to justify oppression. From the mammies, Jezebels, and breeder women of slavery to the smiling Aunt Jemimas on pancake-mix boxes, ubiquitous Black prostitutes, and ever-present welfare mothers of contemporary popular culture, negative stereotypes applied to African-American women have been fundamental to Black women's oppression.

Taken together, the supposedly seamless web of economy, polity, and ideology function as a highly effective system of social control designed to keep African-American women in an assigned, subordinate place. This larger system of oppression works to suppress the ideas of Black women intellectuals and to protect elite White male interests and worldviews. Denying African-American women the credentials to become literate certainly excluded most African-American women from positions as scholars, teachers, authors, poets, and critics. Moreover, while Black women historians, writers, and social scientists have long existed, until recently these women have not held leadership positions in universities, professional associations, publishing concerns, broadcast media, and other social institutions of knowledge validation. Black women's exclusion from positions of power within mainstream institutions has led to the elevation of elite White male ideas and interests and the corresponding suppression of Black women's ideas and interests in traditional scholarship.[15] Moreover, this historical exclusion means that stereotypical images of Black women permeate popular culture and public policy.[16]

U.S. and European women's studies have challenged the seemingly hegemonic ideas of elite White men. Ironically, Western feminisms have also suppressed Black women's ideas.[17] Even though Black women intellectuals have long expressed a distinctive African-influenced and feminist sensibility about how race and class intersect in structuring gender, historically we have not been full participants in White feminist organizations.[18] As a result, African-American, Latino, Native American, and Asian-American women have criticized Western feminisms for being racist and overly concerned with White, middle-class women's issues.[19]

Traditionally, many U.S. White feminist scholars have resisted having Black women as full colleagues. Moreover, this historical suppression of Black women's ideas has had a pronounced influence on feminist theory. One pattern of suppression is that of omission. Theories advanced as being universally applicable to women as a group upon closer examination appear greatly limited by the White, middle-class, and Western origins of their proponents. For example, Nancy Chodorow's work on sex role socialization and Carol Gilligan's study of the moral development of women both rely heavily on White, middle-class samples.[20] While these two classics made key contributions to feminist theory, they simultaneously promoted the notion of a generic woman who is White and middle class. The absence of Black feminist ideas from these and other studies placed them in a much more tenuous position to challenge the hegemony of mainstream scholarship on behalf of all women.

Another pattern of suppression lies in paying lip service to the need for diversity, but changing little about one's own practice. Currently, some U.S. White women who possess great competence in researching a range of issues acknowledge the need for diversity, yet omit women of color from their work. These women claim that they are unqualified to understand or even speak of "Black women's experiences" because they themselves are not Black. Others include a few safe, "hand-picked" Black women's voices to avoid criticisms that they are racist. Both examples reflect a basic unwillingness by many U.S. White feminists to alter the paradigms that guide their work.

A more recent pattern of suppression involves incorporating, changing, and thereby depoliticizing Black feminist ideas. The growing popularity of postmodernism in U.S. higher education in the 1990s, especially within literary criticism and cultural studies, fosters a climate where symbolic inclusion often substitutes for bona fide substantive changes. Because interest in Black women's work has reached occult status, suggests Anne duCille, it "increasingly marginalizes both the black women critics and scholars who excavated the fields in question and their black feminist 'daughters' who would further develop those fields."[21] Black feminist critic Barbara Christian, a pioneer in creating Black women's studies in the U.S. academy, queries whether Black feminism can survive the pernicious politics of resegregation.[22] In discussing the politics of a new multiculturalism, Black feminist critic Hazel Carby expresses dismay at the growing situation of symbolic inclusion, in which the texts of Black women writers are welcome in the multicultural classroom while actual Black women are not.[23]

Not all White Western feminists participate in these diverse patterns of suppression. Some do try to build coalitions across racial and other markers of difference, often with noteworthy results. Works by Elizabeth Spelman, Sandra Harding, Margaret Andersen, Peggy McIntosh, Mab Segrest, Anne Fausto-Sterling, and other individual U.S. White feminist thinkers reflect sincere efforts to develop a multi-racial, diverse feminism. However, despite their efforts, these concerns linger on.[24]

Like feminist scholarship, the diverse strands of African-American social and political thought have also challenged mainstream scholarship. However, Black social and political thought has been limited by both the reformist postures toward change assumed by many U.S. Black intellectuals and the secondary status afforded the ideas and experiences of African-American women.[25] Adhering to a male-defined ethos that far too often equates racial progress with the acquisition of an ill-defined manhood has left much U.S. Black thought with a prominent masculinist bias.

In this case, the patterns of suppressing Black women's ideas have been similar yet different. Though Black women have played little or no part in dominant academic discourse and White feminist arenas, we have long been included in the organizational structures of Black civil society. U.S. Black women's acceptance of subordinate roles in Black organizations does not mean that we wield little authority or that we experience patriarchy in the same way as do White women in White organizations.[26] But with the exception of Black women's organizations, male-run organizations have historically either not stressed Black women's issues, or have done so under duress.[27] For example, Black feminist activist Pauli Murray found that from its founding in 1916 to 1970, the *Journal of Negro History* published only five articles devoted exclusively to Black women.[28] Evelyn Brooks Higginbotham's historical monograph on Black women in Black Baptist churches records African-American women's struggles to raise issues that concerned women.[29] Even progressive Black organizations have not been immune from gender discrimination. Civil rights activist Ella Baker's experiences in the Southern Christian Leadership Conference illustrate one form that suppressing Black women's ideas and talents can take. Ms. Baker virtually ran the entire organization, yet had to defer to the decision-making authority of the exclusively male leadership group.[30] Civil rights activist Septima Clark describes similar experiences: "I found all over the South that whatever the man said had to be right. They had the whole say. The woman couldn't say a thing."[31] Radical African-American women also can find themselves deferring to male authority. In her autobiography, Elaine Brown, a participant and subsequent leader of the 1960s radical organization the Black Panther Party for Self-Defense, discusses the sexism expressed by Panther men.[32] Overall, even though Black women intellectuals have asserted their right to speak both as African-Americans and as women, historically these women have not held top leadership positions in Black organizations and have frequently struggled within them to express Black feminist ideas.[33]

Much contemporary U.S. Black feminist thought reflects Black women's increasing willingness to oppose gender inequality within Black civil society. Septima Clark describes this transformation:

> I used to feel that women couldn't speak up, because when district meetings were being held at my home . . . I didn't feel as if I could tell them what I had in mind . . . But later on, I found out that women had a lot to say, and what they had to say was really worthwhile . . . So we started talking, and have been talking quite a bit since that time.[34]

African-American women intellectuals have been "talking quite a bit" since 1970 and have insisted that the masculinist bias in Black social and political thought, the racist bias in feminist theory, and the heterosexist bias in both be corrected.[35]

Within Black civil society, the increasing visibility of Black women's ideas did not go unopposed. The virulent reaction to earlier Black women's writings by some Black men, such as Robert Staples's analysis of Ntozake Shange's choreopoem, *For Colored Girls Who Have Considered Suicide,* and Michele Wallace's controversial volume, *Black Macho and the Myth of the Superwoman,* illustrates the difficulty of challenging the masculinist bias in Black social and political thought.[36] Alice Walker encountered similarly hostile reactions to her publication of *The Color Purple.* In describing the response of African-American men to the outpouring of publications by Black women writers in the 1970s and 1980s, Calvin Hernton offers an incisive criticism of the seeming tenacity of a masculinist bias:

> The telling thing about the hostile attitude of black men toward black women writers is that they interpret the new thrust of the women as being "counter-productive" to the historical goal of the Black struggle. Revealingly, while black men have achieved outstanding recognition throughout the history of black writing, black women have not accused the men of collaborating with the enemy and setting back the progress of the race.[37]

Not all Black male reaction during this period was hostile. For example, Manning Marable devotes an entire chapter in *How Capitalism Underdeveloped Black America* to how sexism has been a primary deterrent to Black community development.[38] Following Marable's lead, work by Haki Madhubuti, Cornel West, Michael Awkward, Michael Dyson, and others suggests that some U.S. Black male thinkers have taken Black feminist thought seriously.[39] Despite the diverse ideological perspectives expressed by these writers, each seemingly recognizes the importance of Black women's ideas.

Black Feminist Thought as Critical Social Theory

Even if they appear to be otherwise, situations such as the suppression of Black women's ideas within traditional scholarship and the struggles within the critiques of that established knowledge are inherently unstable. Conditions in the wider political economy simultaneously shape Black women's subordination and foster activism. On some level, people who are oppressed usually know it. For African-American women, the knowledge gained at intersecting oppressions of race, class, and gender provides the stimulus for crafting and passing on the subjugated knowledge of Black women's critical social theory.[40]

As an historically oppressed group, U.S. Black women have produced social thought designed to oppose oppression. Not only does the form assumed by this thought diverge from standard academic theory—it can take the form of poetry, music, essays, and the like—but the purpose of Black women's collective thought is distinctly different. Social theories emerging from and/or on behalf of U.S. Black women and other historically oppressed groups aim to find ways to escape from, survive in, and/or oppose prevailing social and economic injustice. In the United States, for example, African-American social and political thought analyzes institutionalized racism, not to help it work more efficiently, but to resist it. Feminism advocates women's emancipation and empowerment, Marxist social thought aims for a more equitable society, while queer theory opposes heterosexism. Beyond U.S. borders, many women from oppressed groups also struggle to understand new forms of injustice. In a transnational, postcolonial context, women within new and often Black-run nation-states in the Caribbean, Africa, and Asia struggle with new meanings attached to ethnicity, citizenship status, and religion. In increasingly multicultural European nation-states, women migrants from former colonies encounter new forms of subjugation. Social theories expressed by women emerging from these diverse groups typically do not arise from the rarefied atmosphere of their imaginations. Instead, social theories reflect women's efforts to come to terms with lived experiences within intersecting oppressions of race, class, gender, sexuality, ethnicity, nation, and religion.[41]

Black feminist thought, U.S. Black women's critical social theory, reflects similar power relationships. For African-American women, critical social theory encompasses bodies of knowledge and sets of institutional practices that actively grapple with the central questions facing U.S. Black women as a collectivity. The need for such thought arises because African-American women as a group remain oppressed within a U.S. context characterized by injustice. This neither means that all African-American women within that group are oppressed in the same way, nor that some U.S. Black women do not suppress others. Black feminist thought's identity as a "critical" social theory lies in its commitment to justice, both for U.S. Black women as a collectivity and for that of other similarly oppressed groups.

Historically, two factors stimulated U.S. Black women's critical social theory. For one, prior to World War II, racial segregation in urban housing became so entrenched that the majority of African-American women lived in self-contained Black neighborhoods where their children attended overwhelmingly Black schools, and where they themselves belonged to all-Black churches and similar community organizations. Despite the fact that ghettoization was designed to foster the political control and economic exploitation of Black Americans, these all-Black neighborhoods simultaneously provided a separate space where African-American women and men could use African-derived ideas to craft distinctive oppositional knowledges designed to resist racial oppression.[42]

Every social group has a constantly evolving worldview that it uses to order and evaluate its own experiences.[43] For African-Americans this worldview originated in the cosmologies of diverse West African ethnic groups.[44] By retaining and reworking significant elements of these West African cultures, communities of enslaved Africans offered their members explanations for slavery alternative to those advanced by slave owners.[45] These African-derived ideas also laid the foundation for the rules of a distinctive Black American civil society. Later on, confining African-Americans to all-Black areas in the rural South and Northern urban ghettos fostered the solidification of a distinctive ethos in Black civil society regarding language, religion, family structure, and community politics.[46] While essential to the survival of U.S. Blacks as a group and expressed differently by individual African-Americans, these knowledges remained simultaneously hidden from and suppressed by Whites. Black oppositional knowledges existed to resist injustice, but they also remained subjugated.

As mothers, othermothers, teachers, and churchwomen in essentially all-Black rural communities and urban neighborhoods, U.S. Black women participated in constructing and reconstructing these oppositional knowledges. Through the lived experiences gained within their extended families and communities, individual African-American women fashioned their own ideas about the meaning of Black womanhood. When these ideas found collective expression, Black women's self-definitions enabled them to refashion African-influenced conceptions of self and community. These self-definitions of Black womanhood were designed to resist the negative controlling images of Black womanhood advanced by Whites as well as the discriminatory social practices that these controlling images supported. In all, Black women's participation in crafting a constantly changing African-American culture fostered distinctively Black and women-centered worldviews.

Another factor that stimulated U.S. Black women's critical social theory lay in the common experiences they gained from their jobs. Prior to World War II, U.S. Black women worked primarily in two occupations—agriculture and domestic work. Their ghettoization in domestic work sparked an important contradiction. Domestic work fostered U.S. Black women's economic exploitation, yet it simultaneously created the conditions for distinctively Black and female forms of resistance. Domestic work allowed African-American women to see White elites, both actual and aspiring, from perspectives largely obscured from Black men and from these groups themselves. In their White "families," Black women not only performed domestic duties but frequently formed strong ties with the children they nurtured, and with the employers themselves. On one level this insider relationship was satisfying to all concerned. Accounts of Black domestic workers stress the sense of self-affirmation the women experienced at seeing racist ideology demystified. But on another level these Black women knew that they could never belong to their White "families." They were economically exploited workers and thus would remain outsiders. The result was being placed in a curious outsider-within social location, a peculiar marginality that stimulated a distinctive Black women's perspective on a variety of themes.[47]

Taken together, Black women's participation in constructing African-American culture in all-Black settings and the distinctive perspectives gained from their outsider-within placement in domestic work provide the material backdrop for a unique Black women's standpoint. When armed with cultural beliefs honed in Black civil society, many Black women who found themselves doing domestic work often developed distinct views of the contradictions between the dominant group's actions and ideologies.

Moreover, they often shared their ideas with other African-American women. Nancy White, a Black inner-city resident, explores the connection between experience and beliefs:

> Now, I understand all these things from living. But you can't lay up on these flowery beds of ease and think that you are running your life, too. Some women, white women, can run their husband's lives for a while, but most of them have to ... see what he tells them there is to see. If he tells them that they ain't seeing what they know they are seeing, then they have to just go on like it wasn't there![48]

Not only does this passage speak to the power of the dominant group to suppress the knowledge produced by subordinate groups, but it illustrates how being in outsider-within locations can foster new angles of vision on oppression. Ms. White's Blackness makes her a perpetual outsider. She could never be a White middle-class woman lying on a "flowery bed of ease." But her work of caring for White women allowed her an insider's view of some of the contradictions between White women's thinking that they are running their lives and the patriarchal power and authority in their households.

Practices such as these, whether experienced oneself or learned by listening to African-American women who have had them, have encouraged many U.S. Black women to question the contradictions between dominant ideologies of American womanhood and U.S. Black women's devalued status. If women are allegedly passive and fragile, then why are Black women treated as "mules" and assigned heavy cleaning chores? If good mothers are supposed to stay at home with their children, then why are U.S. Black women on public assistance forced to find jobs and leave their children in day care? If women's highest calling is to become mothers, then why are Black teen mothers pressured to use Norplant and Depo Provera? In the absence of a viable Black feminism that investigates how intersecting oppressions of race, gender, and class foster these contradictions, the angle of vision created by being deemed devalued workers and failed mothers could easily be turned inward, leading to internalized oppression. But the legacy of struggle among U.S. Black women suggests that a collectively shared, Black women's oppositional knowledge has long existed. This collective wisdom in turn has spurred U.S. Black women to generate a more specialized knowledge, namely, Black feminist thought as critical social theory. Just as fighting injustice lay at the heart of U.S. Black women's experiences, so did analyzing and creating imaginative responses to injustice characterize the core of Black feminist thought.

Historically, while they often disagreed on its expression—some U.S. Black women were profoundly reformist while more radical thinkers bordered on the revolutionary—African-American women intellectuals who were nurtured in social conditions of racial segregation strove to develop Black feminist thought as critical social theory. Regardless of social class and other differences among U.S. Black women, all were in some way affected by intersecting oppressions of race, gender, and class. The economic, political, and ideological dimensions of U.S. Black women's oppression suppressed the intellectual production of individual Black feminist thinkers. At the same time, these same social conditions simultaneously stimulated distinctive patterns of U.S. Black women's activism that also influenced and was influenced by individual Black women thinkers. Thus, the dialectic of oppression and activism characterizing U.S. Black women's experiences with intersecting oppressions also influenced the ideas and actions of Black women intellectuals.

The exclusion of Black women's ideas from mainstream academic discourse and the curious placement of African-American women intellectuals in feminist thinking, Black social and political theories, and in other important thought such as U.S. labor studies has meant that U.S. Black women intellectuals have found themselves in outsider-within positions in many academic endeavors.[49] The assumptions on which full group membership are based—Whiteness for feminist thought, maleness for Black social and political thought, and the combination for mainstream scholarship—all negate Black women's realities. Prevented from becoming full insiders in any of these areas of inquiry, Black women remained in outsider-within locations, individuals whose marginality provided a distinctive angle of vision on these intellectual and political entities.

Alice Walker's work exemplifies these fundamental influences within Black women's intellectual traditions. Walker describes how her outsider-within location influenced her thinking: "I believe . . . that it was from this period—from my solitary, lonely position, the position of an outcast—that I began really to see people and things, really to notice relationships."[50] Walker realizes that "the gift of loneliness is sometimes a radical vision of society or one's people that has not previously been taken into account."[51] And yet marginality is not the only influence on her work. By reclaiming the works of Zora Neale Hurston and in other ways placing Black women's experiences and culture at the center of her work, she draws on alternative Black feminist worldviews.

Developing Black Feminist Thought

Starting from the assumption that African-American women have created independent, oppositional yet subjugated knowledges concerning our own subordination, contemporary U.S. Black women intellectuals are engaged in the struggle to reconceptualize all dimensions of the dialectic of oppression and activism as it applies to African-American women. Central to this enterprise is reclaiming Black feminist intellectual traditions.[52]

For many U.S. Black women intellectuals, this task of reclaiming Black women's subjugated knowledge takes on special meaning. Knowing that the minds and talents of our grandmothers, mothers, and sisters have been suppressed stimulates many contributions to the growing field of Black women's studies.[53] Alice Walker describes how this sense of purpose affects her work: "In my own work I write not only what I want to read—understanding fully and indelibly that if I don't do it no one else is so vitally interested, or capable of doing it to my satisfaction—I write all the things *I should have been able to read.*"[54]

Reclaiming Black women's ideas involves discovering, reinterpreting, and, in many cases, analyzing for the first time the works of individual U.S. Black women thinkers who were so extraordinary that they did manage to have their ideas preserved. In some cases this process involves locating unrecognized and unheralded works, scattered and long out of print. Marilyn Richardson's painstaking editing of the writings and speeches of Maria Stewart, and Mary Helen Washington's collections of Black women's writings typify this process.[55] Similarly, Alice Walker's efforts to have Zora Neale Hurston's unmarked grave recognized parallel her intellectual quest to honor Hurston's important contributions to Black feminist literary traditions.[56]

Reclaiming Black women's ideas also involves discovering, reinterpreting, and analyzing the ideas of subgroups within the larger collectivity of U.S. Black women who have been silenced. For example, burgeoning scholarship by and about Black lesbians reveals a diverse and complex history. Gloria Hull's careful compilation of the journals of Black feminist intellectual Alice Dunbar-Nelson illustrates the difficulties of being closeted yet still making major contributions to African-American social and political thought.[57] Audre Lorde's autobiography, *Zami*, provides a book-length treatment of Black lesbian communities in New York.[58] Similarly, Kennedy and Davis's history of the formation of lesbian communities in 1940s and 1950s Buffalo, New York, strives to understand how racial segregation influenced constructions of lesbian identities.

Reinterpreting existing works through new theoretical frameworks is another dimension of developing Black feminist thought. In Black feminist literary criticism, this process is exemplified by Barbara Christian's landmark volume on Black women writers, Mary Helen Washington's reassessment of anger and voice in *Maud Martha*,—a much-neglected work by novelist and poet Gwendolyn Brooks—and Hazel Carby's use of the lens of race, class, and gender to reinterpret the works of nineteenth-century Black women novelists.[59] Within Black feminist historiography the tremendous strides that have been made in U.S. Black women's history are evident in Evelyn Brooks Higginbotham's analysis of the emerging concepts and paradigms in Black women's history, her study of women in the Black Baptist Church, Stephanie Shaw's study of Black professional women workers during the Jim Crow era, and the landmark volume *Black Women in America: A Historical Encyclopedia*.[60]

Developing Black feminist thought also involves searching for its expression in alternative institutional locations and among women who are not commonly perceived as intellectuals. As defined in this volume, Black women intellectuals are neither all academics nor found primarily in the Black middle class. Instead, all U.S. Black women who somehow contribute to Black feminist thought as critical social theory are deemed to be "intellectuals." They may be highly educated. Many are not. For example, nineteenth-century Black feminist activist Sojourner Truth is not typically seen as an intellectual.[61] Because she could neither read nor write, much of what we know about her has been recorded by other people. One of her most famous speeches, that delivered at the 1851 women's rights convention in Akron, Ohio, comes to us in a report written by a feminist abolitionist some time after the event itself.[62] We do not know what Truth actually said, only what the recorder claims that she said. Despite this limitation, in that speech Truth reportedly provides an incisive analysis of the definition of the term woman forwarded in the mid-1800s:

> That man over there says women need to be helped into carriages, and lifted over ditches, and to have the best place everywhere. Nobody ever

helps me into carriages, or over mud puddles, or gives me any best place! And ain't I a woman? Look at me! Look at my arm! I have ploughed, and planted, and gathered into barns, and no man could head me! And ain't I a woman? I could work as much and eat as much as a man—when I could get it—and bear the lash as well! And ain't I a woman? I have borne thirteen children, and seen them most all sold off to slavery, and when I cried out with my mother's grief, none but Jesus heard me! And ain't I a woman?[63]

By using the contradictions between her life as an African-American woman and the qualities ascribed to women, Sojourner Truth exposes the concept of woman as being culturally constructed. Her life as a second-class citizen has been filled with hard physical labor, with no assistance from men. Her question, "and ain't I a woman?" points to the contradictions inherent in blanket use of the term "woman." For those who question Truth's femininity, she invokes her status as a mother of thirteen children, all sold off into slavery, and asks again, "and ain't I a woman?" Rather than accepting the existing assumptions about what a woman is and then trying to prove that she fit the standards, Truth challenged the very standards themselves. Her actions demonstrate the process of deconstruction—namely, exposing a concept as ideological or culturally constructed rather than as natural or a simple reflection of reality.[64] By deconstructing the concept "woman," Truth proved herself to be a formidable intellectual. And yet Truth was a former slave who never learned to read or write.

Examining the contributions of women like Sojourner Truth suggests that the concept of "intellectual" must itself be deconstructed. Not all Black women intellectuals are educated. Not all Black women intellectuals work in academia. Furthermore, not all highly educated Black women, especially those who are employed in U.S. colleges and universities, are *automatically* intellectuals. U.S. Black women intellectuals are not a female segment of William E. B. DuBois's notion of the "talented tenth." One is neither born an intellectual nor does one become one by earning a degree. Rather, doing intellectual work of the sort envisioned within Black feminism requires a process of self-conscious struggle on behalf of Black women, regardless of the actual social location where that work occurs.

These are not idle concerns within new power relations that have greatly altered the fabric of U.S. and Black civil society. Race, class, and gender still constitute intersecting oppressions, but the ways in which they are now organized to produce social injustice differ from prior eras. Just as theories, epistemologies, and facts produced by any group of individuals represent the standpoints and interests of their creators, the very definition of who is legitimated to do intellectual work is not only politically contested, but is changing.[65] Reclaiming Black feminist intellectual traditions involves much more than developing Black feminist analyses using standard epistemological criteria. It also involves challenging the very terms of intellectual discourse itself.

Assuming new angles of vision on which U.S. Black women are, in fact, intellectuals, and on their seeming dedication to contributing to Black feminist thought raises new questions about the production of this oppositional knowledge. Historically, much of the Black women's intellectual tradition occurred in institutional locations other than the academy. For example, the music of working-class Black women blues singers of the 1920 and 1930s is often seen as one important site outside academia for this intellectual tradition.[66] Whereas Anne duCille quite rightly warns us about viewing Black women's blues through rose-colored glasses, the fact remains that far more Black women listened to Bessie Smith and Ma Rainey than were able to read Nella Larsen or Jessie Fauset.[67] Despite impressive educational achievements that have allowed many U.S. Black women to procure jobs in higher education and the media, this may continue to be the case. For example, Imani Perry suggests that the music of Black women hip-hop artists serves as a new site of Black women's intellectual production.[68] Again, despite the fact that hip-hop contains diverse and contradictory components and that popularity alone is insufficient to confer the title "intellectual," many more Black women listen to Queen Latifah and Salt 'N' Pepa than read literature by Alice Walker and Toni Morrison.[69]

Because clarifying Black women's experiences and ideas lies at the core of Black feminist thought, interpreting them requires collaborative leadership among those who participate in the diverse forms that Black women's communities now take. This requires acknowledging not only how African-American women outside of academia have long functioned as intellectuals by representing the interests of Black women as a group, but how this continues to be the case. For example, rap singer Sister Souljah's music as well as her autobiography *No Disrespect* certainly can be seen as contributing to Black feminist thought as critical social theory.[70] Despite her uncritical acceptance of a masculinist Black nationalist ideology, Souljah is deeply concerned with issues of Black women's oppression, and offers an important perspective on contemporary urban culture. Yet while young Black women listened to Souljah's music and thought about her ideas, Souljah's work has been dismissed within feminist classrooms in academia as being "nonfeminist." Without tapping these nontraditional sources, much of the Black women's intellectual tradition would remain "not known and hence not believed in."[71]

At the same time, many Black women academics struggle to find ways to do intellectual work that challenges injustice. They know that being an academic and an intellectual are not necessarily the same thing. Since the 1960s, U.S. Black women have entered faculty positions in higher education in small but unprecedented numbers. These women confront a peculiar dilemma. On the one hand, acquiring the prestige enjoyed by their colleagues often required unquestioned acceptance of academic norms. On the other hand, many of these same norms remain wedded to notions of Black and female inferiority. Finding ways to temper critical responses to academia without unduly jeopardizing their careers constitutes a new challenge for Black women who aim to be intellectuals within academia, especially intellectuals engaged in developing Black feminist thought.[72]

Surviving these challenges requires new ways of doing Black feminist intellectual work. Developing Black feminist thought as critical social theory involves including the ideas of Black women not previously considered intellectuals—many of whom may be working-class women with jobs outside academia—as well as those ideas emanating from more formal, legitimate scholarship. The ideas we share with one another as mothers in extended families, as othermothers in Black communities, as members of Black churches, and as teachers to the Black community's children have formed one pivotal area where African-American women have hammered out a multifaceted Black women's standpoint. Musicians, vocalists, poets, writers, and other artists constitute another group from which Black women intellectuals have emerged. Building on African-influenced oral traditions, musicians in particular have enjoyed close association with the larger community of African-American women constituting their audience. Through their words and actions, grassroots political activists also contribute to Black women's intellectual traditions. Producing intellectual work is generally not attributed to Black women artists and political activists. Especially in elite institutions of higher education, such women are typically viewed as objects of study, a classification that creates a false dichotomy between scholarship and activism, between thinking and doing. In contrast, examining the ideas and actions of these excluded groups in a way that views them as subjects reveals a world in which behavior is a statement of philosophy and in which a vibrant, both/and, scholar/ activist tradition remains intact.

Notes

1. Marilyn Richardson, ed., *Maria W. Stewart: America's First Black Woman Political Writer* (Bloomington: Indiana University Press, 1987). All further references to Richardson's edition appear in the text, in parentheses, after the quotations.

2. Beverly Guy-Sheftall, "Remembering Sojourner Truth: On Black Feminism," *Catalyst* (Fall 1986): 54 –57. Numerous Black women intellectuals have explored the core themes first articulated by Maria W. Stewart. See Gloria T. Hull, Patricia Bell Scott, and Barbara Smith, eds., *But Some of Us Are Brave: Black Women's Studies* (Old Westbury, N.Y.: Feminist Press, 1982). Sharon Harley and Rosalyn Terborg-Penn's groundbreaking collection of essays on Black women's history, *The Afro-American Woman: Struggles and Images* (Port Washington, N.Y.: Kennikat Press, 1978) foreshadowed volumes on black women's history such as Paula Giddings, *When and Where I Enter: The Impact of Black Women on Race and Sex in America* (New York: William Morrow, 1984), and Deborah Gray White, *Ar'n't I a Woman? Female Slaves in the Plantation South* (New York: W.W. Norton, 1985), and the important historical encyclopedia by Darlene Clark Hine, Elsa Barkley Brown, and Rosalyn Terborg-Penn, eds., *Black Women in America: A Historical Encyclopedia* (New York: Carlson, 1993). A similar explosion in Black women's literary criticism has occurred, as evidenced by the publication of book-length studies of Black women writers such as those by Barbara Christian (*Black Feminist Criticism: Perspectives on Black Women Writers* [New York: Pergamon Press, 1985], Hazel V. Carby (*Reconstructing Womanhood: The Emergence of the Afro-American Woman Novelist* [New York: Oxford University Press, 1987]), and Anne duCille (*Skin Trade* ([Cambridge, Mass.: Harvard University Press, 1996]).

3. Hine, Brown, and Terborg-Penn, *Black Women in America*; Beverly Guy-Sheftall, ed., *Words of Fire: An Anthology of African-American Feminist Thought* (New York: New Press, 1995).

4. Alice Walker, *In Search of Our Mothers' Gardens: Womanist Prose* (New York: Harcourt Brace Jovanovich, 1983), 92

5. Fannie Barrier Williams, "The Colored Girl," in *Invented Lives: Narratives of Black Women 1860–1960*, ed. Mary Helen Washington (Garden City, N.Y.: Anchor, 1987), 150.

6. James C. Scott, *Weapons of the Weak: Everyday Forms of Peasant Resistance* (New Haven, Conn.: Yale University Press, 1985).

7. Heidi Safia Mirza, ed., *Black British Feminism: A Reader* (New York: Routledge, 1997).

8. Danisa E. Baloyi, "Apartheid and Identity: Black Women in South Africa," in *Connecting across Cultures and Continents: Black Women Speak Out on Identity, Race, and Development*, ed. Achola O. Pala (New York: United Nations Development Fund for Women, 1995), 41.

9. Adeola James, *In Their Own Voices: African Women Writers Talk* (Portsmouth, N.H.: Heinemann, 1990).

10. Angela Y. Davis, *Women, Race, and Class* (New York: Random House, 1981); Manning Marable, "Grounding with My Sisters: Patriarchy and the Exploitation of Black Women," in *How Capitalism Underdeveloped Black America* (Boston: South End Press, 1983), 69–104; Jacqueline Jones, *Labor of Love, Labor of Sorrow: Black Women, Work, and the Family from Slavery to the Present* (New York: Basic Books, 1985); Teresa L. Amott and Julie Matthaei, *Race, Gender, and Work: A Multi-Cultural Economic History of Women in the United States* (Boston: South End Press, 1991).

11. Rose Brewer, "Theorizing Race, Class and Gender: The New Scholarship of Black Feminist Intellectuals and Black Women's Labor," in *Theorizing Black Feminisms: The Visionary Pragmatism of Black Women*, ed. Stanlie M. James and Abena P. A. Busia (New York: Routledge, 1993); Barbara Omolade, *The Rising Song of African American Women* (New York: Routledge, 1994).

12. Margaret A. Burnharn, "An Impossible Marriage: Slave Law and Family Law," *Law and Inequality* 5 (1987): 187–225; Judy Scales-Trent, "Black Women and the Constitution: Finding or Place, Asserting Our Rights," *Harvard Civil Rights–Civil Liberties Law Review* 24 (Winter 1989): 9–43; Mary Frances Berry, *Black Resistence, White Law: A History of Constitutional Racism in America* (New York: Penguin, 1994).

13. Leith Mullings, *On Our Own Terms: Race, Class, and Gender in the Lives of African American Women* (New York: Routledge, 1997).

14. Mae King, "The Politics of Sexual Stereotypes," *Black Scholar* 4, nos. 6–7 (1973): 12–23; White, *Ar'n't I a Woman?*; Carby, *Reconstructing Womanhood*; Patricia Morton, *Disfigured Images: The Historical Assault on Afro-American Women* (New York: Prager, 1991).

15. Evelyn Brooks Higginbotham, "Beyond the Sound of Silence: Afro-American Women in History," *Gender and History* 1, no. 1 (1989): 50–67; Morton, *Disfigured Images*; Patricia Hill Collins, *Fighting Words: Black Women and the Search for Justice* (Minneapolis: University of Minnesota Press, 1998), 95–123.

16. Michele Wallace, *Invisibility Blues: From Pop to Theory* (New York: Verso, 1990); Wahneema Lubiano, "Black Ladies, Welfare Queens, and State Minstrels: Ideological War by Narrative Means," in *Race-ing Justice, En-Gendering Power*, ed. Toni Morrison (New York: Pantheon, 1992), 323–63; K. Sue Jewell, *From Mammy to Miss America and Beyond: Cultural Images and the Shaping of U.S. Social Policy* (New York: Routledge, 1993).

17. DuCille, *Skin Trade*.

18. Giddings, *When and Where I Enter*; Maxine Baca Zinn, Lynn Weber Cannon, Elizabeth Higginbotham, and Bonnie Thornton Dill, "The Costs of Exclusionary Practices in Women's Studies," *Signs* 11, no. 2 (1986); Nancie Caraway,

Segregated Sisterhood: Racism and the Politics of American Feminism (Knoxville: University of Tennessee Press, 1991).

19. Cherrie Moraga and Gloria Anzaldua, eds., *This Bridge Called My Back: Writings of Radical Women of Color* (Watertown, Mass.: Persephone Press, 1981); Barbara Smith, "Racism and Women's Studies," in *But Some of Us Are Brave;* Bonnie Thornton Dill, "Race, Class and Gender: Prospects for an All-Inclusive Sisterhood," *Feminist Studies* 9, no. 1 (1983): 131–50; Angela Y. Davis, *Women, Culture, and Politics* (New York: Random House, 1989).

20. Nancy Chodorow, *The Reproduction of Mothering* (Berkeley: University of California Press, 1978; Carol Gilligan, *In a Different Voice* (Cambridge, Mass.: Harvard University Press, 1982).

21. DuCille, *Skin Trade,* 87

22. Barbara Christian, "Diminishing Returns: Can Black Feminism(s) Survive the Academy?" in *Multiculturalism: A Critical Reader,* ed. David Theo Goldberg (Cambridge: Basil Blackwell, 1994).

23. Hazel Carby, "The Multicultural Wars," in *Black Popular Culture,* ed. Michele Wallace and Gina Dent (Seattle: Bay Press, 1992), 187–99.

24. Elizabeth V. Spelman, *Inessential Woman: Problems of Exclusion in Feminist Thought* (Boston: Beacon, 1988); Sandra Harding, *The Science Question in Feminism* (Ithaca, N.Y.: Cornell University Press, 1986); Sandra Harding, *Is Science Multicultural? Postcolonialisms, Feminisms, and Epistemologies* (Bloomington: Indiana University Press, 1998); Margaret L. Andersen, "Feminism and the American Family Ideal," *Journal of Comparative Family Studies* 22, no. 2 (Summer 1991): 235–46; Peggy McIntosh, *White Privilege and Male Privilege: A Personal Account of Coming to See Correspondences through Work in Women's Studies,* Working Paper No. 189 (Wellesley, Mass.: Center for Research on Women, Wellesley College, 1988); Mab Segrest, *Memoir of a Race Traitor* (Boston: South End Press, 1994); Anne Fausto-Sterling, "Gender, Race and Nation: The Comparative Anatomy of 'Hottentot' Women in Europe, 1815–1817," in *Deviant Bodies: Critical Perspectives on Difference in Science and Popular Culture,* ed. Jennifer Terry and Jacqueline Urla (Bloomington: Indiana University Press, 1995), 19–48.

25. Harold Cruse, *The Crisis of the Negro Intellectual* (New York: William Morrow, 1967); Cornel West, "Philosophy and the Afro-American Experience," *Philosophical Forum* 9, nos. 2–3 (1977–1978): 117–48.

26. Sara Evans, *Personal Politics* (New York: Vintage, 1979); Cheryl Townsend Gilkes, "'Together and in Harness': Women's Traditions in the Sanctified Church," *Signs* 10, no. 4 (1985): 678–79.

27. Frances Beale, "Double Jeopardy: To be Black and Female," in *The Black Woman: An Anthology,* ed. Toni Cade Bambara (New York: Signet, 1970), 90–100; Manning Marable, "Grounding with My Sisters: Patriarchy and the Exploitation of Black Women," in *How Capitalism Underdeveloped Black America* (Boston: South End Press, 1983), 69–104.

28. Pauli Murray, "The Liberation of Black Women," in *Voices of the New Feminism,* ed. Mary Lou Thompson (Boston: Beacon, 1970), 87–102.

29. Evelyn Brooks Higginbotham, *Righteous Discontent: The Women's Movement in the Black Baptist Church, 1880–1920* (Cambridge, Mass.: Harvard University Press, 1993).

30. Ellen Cantarow, *Moving the Mountain: Women Working for Social Change* (Old Westbury, N.Y.: Feminist Press, 1980).

31. Cynthia Stokes-Brown, ed., *Ready from Within: Septima Clark and the Civil Rights Movement* (Navarro, Calif.: Wild Trees Press, 1986), 79.

32. Elaine Brown, *A Taste of Power: A Black Women's Story* (New York: Pantheon, 1992).

33. Giddings, *When and Where I Enter.*

34. Stokes-Brown, *Ready from Within*, 82.

35. Toni Cade Bambara, ed. *The Black Woman: An Anthology* (New York: Signet, 1970); Bonnie Thornton Dill, "The Dialectics of Black Womanhood," *Signs* 4, no. 3 (1979): 543–55; June Jordan, *Civil Wars* (Boston: Beacon, 1981); The Combahee River Collective, "A Black Feminist Statement," in *But Some of Us Are Brave*, 13–22; Audre Lorde, *Sister/Outsider: Essays and Speeches* (Trumansberg, N.Y.: Crossing Press, 1984).

36. Robert Staples, "The Myth of Black Macho: A Response to Angry Black Feminists," *Black Scholar* 10, no. 6 (1979): 24–33; Ntozake Shange, *For Colored Girls Who Have Considered Suicide/When the Rainbow Is Enuf* (New York: Macmillan, 1975); Michele Wallace, *Black Macho and the Myth of the Superwoman* (New York: Dial Press, 1978).

37. Calvin Hernton, "The Sexual Mountain and Black Women Writers," *Black Scholar* 16, no. 4 (1985): 5.

38. Marable, "Grounding with My Sisters."

39. Haki R. Madhubuti, ed., *Confusion by Any Other Name: Essays Exploring the Negative Impact of the Blackman's Guide to Understanding the Blackwoman* (Chicago: Third World Press, 1990); Cornel West, *Race Matters* (Boston: Beacon, 1993); Michael Awkward, "A Black Man's Place(s) in Black Feminist Criticism," in *Representing Black Men*, ed. Marcellus Blount and George P. Cunningham (New York: Routledge, 1996), 3–26; Michael Eric Dyson, *Race Rules: Navigating the Color Line* (New York: Vintage, 1996).

40. My use of the term "subjugated knowledge" differs somewhat from Michel Foucault's definition (*Power/Knowledge: Selected Interviews and Other Writings 1972–1977*, ed. Colin Gordon [New York: Pantheon, 1980]). According to Foucault, subjugated knowledges are "those blocs of historical knowledge which were present but disguised," namely, "a whole set of knowledges that have been disqualified as inadequate to their task or insufficiently elaborated: naïve knowledges, located down on the hierarchy, beneath the required level of cognition or scientificity" (82). I suggest that Black feminist thought is not a "naïve knowledge" but has been made to appear so by those controlling knowledge validation procedures. Moreover, Foucault argues that subjugated knowledge is "a particular, local, regional knowledge, a differential knowledge incapable of unanimity and which owes its force only to the harshness with it is opposed by

everything surrounding it" (82). The component of Black feminist thought that analyzes Black women's oppression partially fits this definition, but the long-standing, independent, African-derived influences within Black women's thought are omitted from Foucault's analysis. Collins, *Fighting Words*, 3–10.

41. Jacqui M. Alexander and Chandra Talpade Mohanty, *Feminist Genealogies, Colonial Legacies, Democratic Futures* (New York: Routledge, 1997); Mirza, *Black British Feminism*.

42. Gregory D. Squires, *Capital and Communities in Black and White: The Intersections of Race, Class, and Uneven Development* (Albany: State University of New York Press, 1994).

43. Mechal Sobel, *Trabelin' On: The Slave Journey to an Afro-Baptist Faith* (Princeton, N.J.: Princeton University Press, 1979).

44. Cheikh Diop, *The African Origin of Civilization: Myth or Reality?* (New York: L. Hill, 1974).

45. Herbert Gutman, *The Black Family in Slavery and Freedom, 1750–1925* (New York: Random House, 1976); Thomas L. Webber, *Deep Like the Rivers* (New York: W.W. Norton, 1978); Sobel, *Trabelin' On*.

46. Geneva Smitherman, *Talkin and Testifyin: The Language of Black America* (Boston: Houghton Mifflin, 1977); Sobel, *Trabelin' On*; Peter J. Paris, *The Spirituality of African Peoples: The Search for a Common Moral Discourse* (Minneapolis: Fortress, 1995); Niara Sudarkasa, "Interpreting the African Heritage in Afro-American Family Organization," in *Black Families*, ed. Harriette Pipes McAdoo (Beverly Hills, Calif.: Sage, 1981), 37–53; Elsa Barkley Brown, "Negotiating and Transforming the Public Sphere: African American Political Life in the Transition from Slavery to Freedom," *Public Culture* 7, no. 1 (1986): 107–46.

47. Patricia Hill Collins, "Learning from the Outsider Within: The Sociological Significance of Black Feminist Thought," *Social Problems* 33, no. 6 (1986): 14–32; Alice Childress, *Like One of the Family: Conversations from a Domestic's Life* (1956; Boston: Beacon, 1986).

48. John Langston Gwaltney, *Drylongso, A Self-Portrait of Black America* (New York: Vintage, 1980), 148.

49. Hull, Scott, and Smith, *But Some of Us Are Brave*; Barbara Christian, "But Who Do You Really Belong to—Black Studies or Women's Studies?" *Women's Studies* 17, no. 1–2 (1989): 17–23.

50. Walker, *In Search of Our Mothers' Gardens*, 244.

51. Ibid., 264.

52. Harley and Terborg-Penn, *Afro-American Woman*; Hull, Scott, and Smith, *But Some of Us Are Brave*; James and Busia, *Theorizing Black Feminisms*; Beverly Guy-Sheftall, "The Evolution of Feminist Consciousness among African-American Women," in *Words of Fire*, 1–22.

53. Hull, Scott, and Smith, *But Some of Us Are Brave*.

54. Walker, *In Search of Our Mothers' Gardens*, 13.

55. Richardson, *Maria W. Stewart*; Mary Helen Washington, ed., *Black-eyed Susans: Classic Stories by and about Black Women* (Garden City, N.Y.: Anchor, 1975; Mary

Helen Washington, ed., *Midnight Birds* (Garden City, N.Y.: Anchor, 1980); Mary Helen Washington, ed., *Invented Lives: Narratives of Black Women 1860–1960* (Garden City, N.Y.: Anchor, 1987).

56. Alice Walker, ed., *I Love Myself When I Am Laughing, and Then Again when I Am Looking Mean and Impressive: A Zora Neale Hurston Reader* (Old Westbury, N.Y.: Feminist Press, 1979).

57. Gloria T. Hull, ed., *Give Us Each Day: The Diary of Alice Dunbar-Nelson* (New York: W.W.Norton, 1984).

58. Audre Lorde, *Zami, A New Spelling of My Name* (Trumansberg, N.Y.: Crossing Press, 1982).

59. Christian, *Black Feminist Criticism*; Washington, *Invented Lives*; Carby, *Reconstructing Womanhood.*

60. Higginbotham, *Righteous Discontent*; Stephanie J. Shaw, *What a Woman Ought to Be and to Do: Black Professional Woman Workers During the Jim Crow Era* (Chicago: University of Chicago, 1996); Hine, Brown, and Terborg-Penn, *Black Women in America.*

61. Collins, "Learning from the Outsider Within." Sojourner Truth's actions exemplify Antonio Gramsci's contention in *Selection from the Prison Notebooks* (London: Laurence and Wishhort, 1971) that every social group creates one or more "strata of intellectuals which give it homogeneity and an awareness of its own function not only in the economic but also in the political and social fields" (Collins 5). Academics are the intellectuals trained to represent the interests of the groups in power. In contrast, "organic" intellectuals depend on common sense and represent the interests of their own group. Sojourner Truth typifies an "organic" or everyday intellectual, but she may not be certified as such by the dominant group because her intellectual activity threatens the prevailing social order. The outsider-within position of Black women academics encourages us to draw on the traditions of both our discipline of training and our experiences as Black women but to participate fully in neither.

62. Nell Painter, "Sojourner Truth," in *Black Women in the America*, 1172–76.

63. Bert James Loewenberg and Ruth Bogin, eds., *Black Women in Nineteenth-Century American Life: Their Words, Their Thoughts, Their Feelings* (University Park: Pennsylvania State University Press, 1976), 235.

64. Collins, *Fighting Words*, 137–45.

65. Karl Mannheim, *Idealogy and Utopia* (New York: Harcourt, Brace and World, 1936); Antonio Gramsci, *Selections from the Prison Notebooks* (London: Lawrence and Wishart, 1971).

66. Angela Y. Davis, *Blues Legacies and Black Feminism* (New York: Vintage, 1998).

67. Anne duCille, "Blue Notes on Black Sexuality: Sex and the Texts of the Twenties and Thirties," in *American Sexual Politics: Sex, Gender, and Race Since the Civil War*, ed. John C. Fout and Maura Shaw Tantillo (Chicago: University of Chicago Press, 1993), 193–219.

68. Imani Perry, "It's My Thang and I'll Swing It the Way That I Feel!" in *Gender, Race and Class in Media*, ed. Gail Dines and Jean Humez (Thousand Oaks, Calif.: Sage, 1995), 524–30.

69. Tricia Rose, *Black Noise: Rap Music and Black Culture in Contemporary America* (Hanover, N.H.: Wesleyan University Press, 1994).

70. Sister Souljah, *No Disrespect* (New York: Random House, 1994).

71. Williams, "The Colored Girl," 150.

72. Collins, *Fighting Words*, 95–123.

Chapter 19

Black Feminist Theory

Charting a Course for Black Women's Studies in Political Science

EVELYN M. SIMIEN

Only the black woman can say, when and where I enter . . . then and
there the whole race enters with me.
—Anna Julia Cooper, *A Voice from the South*, 1892

Despite the emergence of the study of women and politics within the
discipline of political science, efforts to transform the curriculum
and integrate perspectives of African-American women have met with
limited success. Few scholarly books or journal articles have been written
about African-American women as political actors—candidates for elective office, grassroots organizers, party activists, voters, and partisan, ideologically engaged citizens—although African-American women have a long
history of active participation in politics. Overcoming racism and sexism
has had a profound impact on African-American women's political activism, inspiring them to participate actively in anti-slavery networks, civil
rights organizations, and black feminist collectives. Yet, they remain con-
spicuously absent from the canon in political science.

African-American women, such as Harriet Tubman, Mary Church Terrell, Anna Julia Cooper, Ida B. Wells-Barnett, Rosa Parks, Ella Baker, Daisy
Bates, Diane Nash, and Fannie Lou Hamer, mobilized others in their

struggle against slavery, lynching, and segregation. In more contemporary times, Maxine Waters, Lani Guinier, Anita Hill, Shelia Jackson-Lee, Elaine Jones, Dorothy Height, and Eleanor Holmes Norton have led the fight to ensure civil rights compliance, equitable treatment under the law, and the right to vote. But, how many of these important African-American women would be recognized by students enrolled in colleges and universities across this country? How many political science majors and doctoral candidates would be aware of these women who have made vast contributions to American society, yet have gone unnoticed?

This chapter charts a course for black women's studies in political science, drawing on black feminist theory to critique dominant approaches used by empirically trained political scientists to measure the simultaneous effects of race and gender. It does not profess to be a comprehensive survey of black feminist scholarship; rather, it demonstrates ways in which black feminist theory can inform quantitative analyses of black attitudes toward gender equality and feminist priorities. By drawing this material link between black feminist theory and quantitative methods, I contribute to our practical and theoretical understanding of black feminism in both the social sciences and humanities. The upshot is that black feminist theory paves the way for a compelling research agenda in political science, putting the perspectives and experiences of African-American women at the center rather than in their historically marginal position. For once, black feminist perspectives might transform our knowledge and understanding of the ways in which scholars, primarily in the field of American politics, have ignored, conceptualized, measured, and modeled the intersection (or interaction) of race and gender in the political realm. Organized around the most salient themes that delineate the contours of black feminist thought, this chapter directs critical attention to the study of African-American women in politics.

Frankly, I pull together so much of what has been a murky mire of assumptions and clear away a lot of the underbrush of popular discourse so prevalent around issues of black feminist sentiments, cross-pressures, and womanist ideals. Building upon prior research, I posit that black feminist consciousness arises from an understanding of intersecting patterns of discrimination. Because the totality of black female experiences cannot be treated as the sum of separate parts, they must be analyzed together. If race and gender are studied as separate categories, one cannot explain how attitudes might change as a result of cross-pressures to subordinate the interests of black women so as to protect black men. In view of this, I start with a discussion of black feminist consciousness, providing an overview of its origins, offering a definition, and emphasizing themes that delineate its contours. To underscore the importance of studying black feminist voices in politics, I discuss the limitations of available data and quantitative approaches used hitherto by political scientists.

Out of Sight, Out of Mind: Black Feminist Intellectual—Anna Julia Cooper

The earliest and most visible manifestations of black feminist consciousness appeared in the written scholarship of Anna Julia Cooper. Her seminal work, *A Voice from the South,* is considered the first black feminist text. Writing in 1892, prior to W. E. B. DuBois' declaration that the problem of the twentieth century was the color line, Cooper asserted that women of African descent were "confronted by a woman question and a race problem" and remarked that "while our men seem thoroughly abreast of the times on every other subject, when they strike the woman question, they drop back into sixteenth century logic."[1] Given her status as a member of the black intelligentsia, these comments call attention to the male-dominated character of black leadership and raise questions about conventional notions of respectable manhood and true womanhood at the turn of the century. Taken together, these statements also capture the essence of black feminist thought as interlocking systems of oppression that circumscribe the lives of African-American women.

A consummate teacher, intellectual mind, and much sought after lecturer, Anna Julia Cooper was critical of educational systems that failed to consider the needs of African-American women. With an academic career that lasted longer than that of DuBois, her political philosophy on a variety of issues ranging from women's rights to black liberation, from segregation to literary criticism, has been virtually ignored and conveniently forgotten. While she advocated liberal arts education, she subscribed to bourgeois notions of respectability and genteel femininity for black female elites that prevented her from recognizing the intellectual and leadership abilities of black women laborers.[2] In her own words, Cooper opined, "We can't all be professional people. We must have a backbone to the race" and attributed agency to black women college graduates.[3] Her condemnation of the women's movement and its leaders, Susan B. Anthony and Anna B. Shaw, for their unwillingness to oppose racism in women's clubs was accepted and applauded by black male authority until she expressed disapproval of those conservative black male leaders who marginalized the plight and potential of black women in their discussions of the race problem.[4] Cooper, whose political philosophy was ahead of her contemporaries, has not garnered nearly as much scholarly attention as her black male counterparts when her scholarship and political activism compel juxtaposition with fellow black leaders, specifically DuBois, whom she found an ally.

While DuBois long has been viewed as an intellectual giant, Cooper has been largely ignored—unexamined. The mother of black feminism, Cooper deserves special recognition for her intellectual prowess. She was a well-respected figure during an intense period of civil rights activism, marking the rise of black female-led institutions and organizations.[5] Mirroring the reality of this black woman intellectual, as she effectively has been written out of history, black feminist theory has not garnered much scholarly attention in political science. That is to say, in spite of the progress that has been made in recent years, too few political scientists deem African-American women and black feminist theory worthy of intellectual inquiry. I am optimistic, however, that this essay will stimulate more theoretical and empirically based work on the subject.

In Defense of Ourselves: Black Feminist Theorists

Since slavery's abolition and women's suffrage, the character of black women has been attacked and impugned repeatedly, stereotypes of black women have been promoted for political ends (e.g., the matriarch, the jezebel, and the welfare queen), and black women have been blamed for numerous social and political ills.[6] Feeling called upon to defend black womanhood and reject a plethora of cultural images that support stereotypes about intelligence and innate ability, black feminists from Anna Julia Cooper and Ida B. Wells-Barnett through bell hooks and Patricia J. Williams have explored the related ideas of "dual consciousness," of writing "from the borders," of theorizing as an "outsider" making creative use of their marginal status as "seventh sons" or "outsiders" with unreconciled strivings and warring ideals.[7] Black feminist theorizing then constitutes a pragmatic response to those circumstances that impinge the lives of black women.[8] For black female intellectuals who produce such independent, specialized knowledge, the "outsider status is a kind of unresolved wound," whereby the burden of race and gender discrimination almost ensures the rejection of their intellectual work on epistemological grounds by a more powerful insider community.[9] This sort of rejection is due to their lack of control over the apparatuses of society that sustain ideological hegemony and make the articulation of a self-defined standpoint difficult.[10]

Ostensibly, this essay can be added to a relatively short list of scholarly work that poses a fundamental challenge to the paradigmatic thought of a more powerful insider community. By demonstrating that the dominant conceptualization of group consciousness has been ineffective in articulating the politicized group consciousness of black women, this work urges public opinion scholars and survey researchers to reconsider the ways in which social scientists traditionally measure specific strands of group consciousness. It is argued here that black female intellectuals in particular, and black women in general, readily recognize disadvantage and discrimination due to their "dual identity" and their "politicized group consciousness" stemming from day-to-day encounters with race and gender oppression. The idea is that interlocking systems of oppression (racism and sexism) predispose black women to double consciousness. This notion of double consciousness connotes an acute sense of awareness.

Black women begin to see themselves through the eyes of others and measure their self-worth by the tape of a hegemonic society that expresses support for cultural images that promote negative stereotypes of black women for political ends.[11] Given that black women face discrimination on the basis of race and gender, it is likely that many black women possess a sense of group consciousness derived from their unique disadvantaged status in the United States. Similarly, it is quite possible that many black men are cognizant of and sympathetic toward the particular predicament of black women because they too suffer from race oppression and class exploitation in the occupationally segregated labor market.[12] Thus, black women and men share a common experience that makes their individual fate inextricably tied to the race as a whole.[13]

Talking Black, Talking Feminist: Defining Black Feminist Consciousness

Any discussion of black feminist consciousness must begin with some sort of definition, based on the literature derived from the ideas and experiences of black women. Simply defined, black feminist consciousness is the recognition that African-American women are *status deprived* because they face discrimination on the basis of race and gender. Having to bear the burdens of prejudice that challenge people of color, in addition to the various forms of subjugation that hinder women, African-American women are doubly disadvantaged in the social, economic, and political structure of the United States. African-American women occupy the lower stratum of the social hierarchy, are predominately found in clerical and service jobs, and are most likely to be single heads of households.[14] African-American women also lag behind every other race-sex group on practically every measure of socio-economic well-being—income, employment, and education. As a result, they are subject to multiple burdens—joblessness and domestic violence; teen pregnancy and illiteracy; poverty and malnutrition—which define their cumulative experience with race and gender oppression in the United States.

Much of the important work on black feminism comes from a small cadre of black female intellectuals outside of political science. The work of Audre Lorde, bell hooks, Barbara Smith, and Patricia Hill Collins, among others, is both theoretical and qualitative. While these scholars provide a range of perspectives, several recurring themes that delineate the contours of black feminist thought appear in their work. I discuss the most salient themes in the following section.

First, black feminist scholars have focused on the concept of intersectionality. It is the notion that "race, class, gender, and sexuality are co-dependent variables that cannot be separated or ranked in scholarship, political practice, or in lived experience" when classism and heterosexism constitute twin barriers linked with racism and sexism that uphold and sustain each other.[15] For this reason, Tamara Jones reminds us that African-American women "don't have the luxury of choosing to fight only one battle" because they contend with multiple burdens.[16] Similarly, Adrien Wing argues that the actuality of layered experiences cannot be treated as separate or distinct parts.[17]

Second, black feminist scholars have addressed the issue of gender inequality within the black community.[18] During the civil rights movement, black women were not recognized for their numerous political activities, such as behind-the-scenes organizing, mobilizing, and fundraising. Positions of leadership were reserved for black males. Smooth and Tucker, who cite the Million Man March as yet another classic example, argue that in more recent years black women's activism has been ignored and black men have been given credit.[19] Other scholars charge that the black church has validated the patriarchal nature of black male-female relationships through its biblical teachings and exclusion of black women from the clergy, key decision-making processes, and financial governing boards.[20] Thus, black feminists recognize that gender inequality exists within the black community and point to the patriarchal nature of black male-female relationships within the context of the civil rights movement, the Million Man March, and the black church whereby leadership roles were reserved for black men.

Third, black feminists have maintained that feminism benefits the black community by challenging patriarchy as an institutionalized oppressive structure and advocating the building of coalitions. Black feminists have made conscious efforts to avoid attacking individual black men in order to work with them to further their cause of equality and justice for women. Collins maintains that black feminism is a social justice project and building coalitions is central to advancing that project.[21] Deborah Robinson avers that the "black community must move from the position of singular activism for the good of the movement" because progressive black women are committed to struggle against both racism and sexism.[22] In short, black feminism benefits the struggle for black liberation rather than divides members into factions because the fight against economic exploitation, gender subordination, racial discrimination, and heterosexism are related intimately to the pursuit of social justice.[23]

Fourth, black feminists insist that a sense of belonging or conscious loyalty to the group in question (i.e., black women) arises from everyday experiences with race, class, and gender oppression. Shared experiences with interlocking systems of domination then drive black women and sympathizers to political activism.[24] The individual who comes to realize that she shares a common fate with other black women, and that her individual life chances are inextricably tied to the group, begins to view collective action as a necessary form of resistance. Since the mid-1970s, black feminists and sympathizers have come to accept rallies, marches, and press releases as necessary acts of resistance to Clarence Thomas's nomination to the Supreme Court, the exaltation of Mike Tyson upon his release from prison, and the Million Man March. This stage of group identification, whereby individuals see themselves as sharing a common fate with other black women, is referred to here as linked fate with black women.

Thus far, scholars have emphasized several themes underlying black feminist consciousness: intersectionality, gender inequality, black feminism benefits the black community, and linked fate with black women. From a theoretical perspective, the concept of black feminist consciousness is rich and well-developed. Unfortunately, empirical assessments of black feminist consciousness have been more limited.

Empirical Approaches

Political scientists have taken two main approaches to studying support for gender equality and feminist priorities among black women, both of which fail to problematize the group consciousness of African-American women. As debates about intersecting patterns of race and gender discrimination evolve outside of the discipline, most political science scholarship has focused on either race *or* feminist consciousness—not black feminist consciousness. A compelling body of literature asserts that black women experience racism in ways different from black men and that black women have different experiences with sexism than white women in this country. Despite this, political scientists have used inappropriate measures for African-American women and relied on survey data that reinforce sex-role stereotypes.

More specifically, scholars have used survey items for black women that were designed to tap feminist consciousness among white women. For example, the homemaker item specifically asks whether the respondent thinks of herself as a homemaker most of the time, some the time, occasionally, or never. The traditional housewife model has never fit most African-American women. They are more likely to be single heads of households, their labor participation rate historically has exceeded that of white women, and they usually possess more decision-making authority in their parental and conjugal roles.[25] A measure of attitude in social scientific study, the "feeling thermometer" for the women's movement is just as problematic. During its history, the women's movement experienced problems recruiting and mobilizing black women because the movement was driven by the aims and objectives of white, middle-class women who treated the interests of black women as secondary to their own. Many black women formed their own groups, choosing not to participate in the white-dominated mainstream women's liberation movement.[26] Still, social scientists have used problematic approaches to measure feminist consciousness among women.[27] Both assume that white feminism and black feminism are comparable. This is, in fact, an empirical question. Thus, I argue that using survey items designed for white women results in a measurement of support for white feminism among black women—not black feminist consciousness.

Alternatively, political scientists have measured gender identification and race identification and then used the interaction of these two variables to create a measure of the politicized group identification of black women. Robinson empirically tested two competing hypotheses about the effects of multiple group identity on race consciousness by constructing an interaction term that was the product of women's linked fate and black linked fate to measure multiple group identity.[28] Similarly, Gay and Tate empirically tested two competing hypotheses about the simultaneous effects of gender and race on liberal policy positions by creating the same interaction term that was the product of women's linked fate and black linked fate.[29] This measurement strategy is faulty because it assumes that race and gender identification are separate constructs. It has several problems, especially when considering that the hierarchy of interests within the black community prioritizes race over gender. For example, race identification became equated with an assertion of black masculinity during the black power movement with the rise of such nationalist organizations as the Nation of Islam and the Black Panther Party.[30] By prioritizing the lived experience of African-American men and equating it with the black political agenda, the black power movement treated the struggle of black women against patriarchy as antithetical to the larger community narrative of racial discrimination. In light of this example, interaction terms composed of one measure of race identification and one measure of gender identification are far too simplistic. Ostensibly, this measurement approach fails to assess the simultaneity of oppression along with the hierarchy of interests within the black community. In both instances, political scientists fail to consider the complexity of historical circumstances—racial formation, labor exploitation, and gender subordination—that define the lives of African-American women as they are affected simultaneously by their race and gender identities.

Another limitation of the empirical research is that while all these studies have been driven by empirical concerns, their findings appear to be somewhat mixed and contradictory. Fulenwider, who documented

African-American women's lack of support for the women's movement and its tactics, found that African-American women opposed the need to organize and work together along-side white women to combat discrimination.[31] African-American women were less supportive of abortion than white women, but they were more likely to reject traditional sex-role stereotyping and sex discrimination in the workplace. Ransford and Miller found that African-American women were no more feminist in their sex-role outlook than white women.[32] In fact, African-American women were more traditional rather than more feminist in their sex-role outlook than white women when they identified themselves as middle class. Like Fulenwider, Wilcox examined the attitudes of African-American women on sex discrimination, feminist priorities, and collective action strategies.[33] He found that most black feminists favored collective action that was inclusive of white women and that those black feminists who did not trust whites, lived outside the South, and possessed higher levels of education were more likely to favor separatist feminist action that is exclusively black. Wilcox concluded that race consciousness acted as a catalyst for feminist consciousness because African-American women who identify strongly with their race were more likely to hold feminist views.[34] Mansbridge and Tate have since argued that African-American women will support their interests as women, but their support can be muted and even overwhelmed when those interests collide with race.[35] Using the Anita Hill/Clarence Thomas episode as an illustrative example, they contend that this high-stakes dispute between a black female law professor and a black male Supreme Court Justice nominee called into question race loyalty for African-Americans in general and African-American women in particular. The overwhelming majority of African-American men and women expressed disbelief in Anita Hill's charges of sexual harassment against Clarence Thomas. Mansbridge and Tate suggest that the media's image of an African-American woman attacking an African-American man worked in Thomas's favor because African-American women often are asked to choose between their commitments to anti-sexist and anti-racist struggles, feeling they must choose the latter. Otherwise, they might be viewed as a traitor to the race.[36]

Another limitation of the empirical research is its tendency to focus on feminist support among women without assessing the level of support for these same principles among men. Given the emphasis of many black feminists on building coalitions with black men and the rise of the men's movement to end patriarchy, it seems most appropriate to examine the extent to which black men endorse black feminist ideals. Arguably, the best measurement approach is one that captures the simultaneity of oppression with multiple items for various themes at the core of black feminist thought. This approach requires a model true to its theoretical origins, embracing several interrelated attitudes and beliefs derived from the ideas and experiences of African-American women. The specification of basic models and the analysis strategies employed must capture the core themes that define this unique angle of vision, arising from an understanding of interlocking systems of oppression. By presenting and evaluating a scale of black feminist thought, which is both reliable and internally coherent, public opinion scholars might wed black feminist theory with numbers. To date, only two empirically trained political scientists have examined black feminist consciousness in this manner, using data from the 1993 National Black Politics Study (NBPS)—Michael C. Dawson and myself.[37]

Only the 1993 NBPS contained items needed to develop an adequate measure of this construct. However, only six items were available in the 1993 NBPS that measured various dimensions of black feminist consciousness. All six items are at the core of how scholars and activists define black feminism, but the use of single-item measures for various dimensions should be avoided because they are most susceptible to measurement error. Besides this, the scale yielded a clearly different structure for black women and men when estimated separately using factor analysis.[38] In an effort to improve the measure, it is necessary to include multiple items for each dimension. Once validated, this scale might determine black attitudes toward such important feminist concerns as paid maternity leave, federally subsidized childcare, sexual harassment, abortion, affirmative action, welfare reform, and equal pay. These issues constitute those in which white feminist organizations as well as black feminist organizations have lobbied and, as a result, received a good deal of media attention.

Conclusion

This chapter started with a discussion of black feminist consciousness, providing a brief overview of its origins, offering a definition, and emphasizing the most salient themes that delineate its contours. Along the way, I exposed the deficiencies and limitations of dominant approaches that fail to consider the complexity of black female experiences—dual identity, cross-cutting versus consensus issues, and the hierarchy of interests. Unmasking problems inherent to research design and question wording, I suggest that the choice of data to be analyzed and the interpretation of that data rest upon a narrow and exclusive definition of group consciousness. Unfortunately, most national surveys of Americans do not include a large enough sample of African-American respondents and most national surveys of African Americans lack the necessary components to construct a full measure of black feminist consciousness (e.g., the 1984, 1988, and 1996 National Black Election Studies). In light of this, no prior analysis has gone on to ask why, if this should be so, and clarify the findings when public opinion scholars and survey researchers traditionally measure race *or* feminist consciousness—not black feminist consciousness.

In closing, I urge political scientists to design survey items that capture the simultaneity of oppression, privileging the lived experience of African-American women so not to silence black feminist voices in politics. Otherwise, the study of public opinion and political behavior will remain largely limited with little prescriptive utility for individuals and groups that confront interlocking systems of oppression. Of course, the move toward a more inclusive discipline with prescriptive relevance to marginalized groups can only be undertaken by those genuinely committed to social justice. My broadest goal is then to assist others in developing a framework within which to evaluate critically the American political system, disputing taken-for-granted views and considering black feminist perspectives that counter the mainstream.

Notes

1. Bert James Loewenberg and Ruth Bogin, eds. *Black Women in Nineteenth-Century American Life: Their Words, Their Thoughts, Their Feelings* (University Park: Pennsylvania State University Press, 1976), 244; Anna Julia Cooper, "The Status of Woman in America," in *Words of Fire: An Anthology of African-American Feminist Thought* ed. Beverly Guy-Sheftall (New York: New Press, 1995), 45.

2. Paula Giddings, *When and Where I Enter: The Impact of Black Women on Race and Sex in America* (New York: Quill William Morrow, 1984); Guy-Sheftall, *Words of Fire;* Kevin K. Gaines, *Uplifting the Race* (Chapel Hill: University of North Carolina Press, 1996); Joy James, *Transcending the Talented Tenth* (New York: Routledge, 1997).

3. Giddings, *When and Where I Enter*, 103.

4. Ibid.; *Words of Fire*; Gaines, *Uplifting the Race*; James, *Transcending the Talented Tenth.*

5. Gaines, *Uplifting the Race*; James, *Transcending the Talented Tenth.*

6. Angela Y. Davis, *Women, Race, and Class* (New York: Vintage, 1981); Sue K. Jewell, *From Mammy to Miss America and Beyond: Cultural Images and the Shaping of U.S. Social Policy* (New York: Routledge, 1993); Dorothy Roberts, *Killing the Black Body* (New York: Vintage, 1997).

7. W. E. B. DuBois, *The Souls of Black Folk* (New York: Dover, 1994), 2.

8. Stanlie M. James and Abena P. A. Busia, eds., *Theorizing Black Feminisms: The Visionary Pragmatism of Black Women* (New York: Routledge, 1993); Patricia Hill Collins, *Fighting Words* (Minneapolis: University of Minnesota Press, 1998); Patricia Hill Collins, *Black Feminist Thought: Knowledge, Consciousness, and the Politics of Empowerment* (New York: Routledge, 2000).

9. Patricia J. Williams, *The Alchemy of Race and Rights: Diary of a Law Professor* (Cambridge: Harvard University Press, 1991), 89.

10. Collins, *Fighting Words* and *Black Feminist Thought.*

11. DuBois, *Souls of Black Folk*, 2.

12. Mae King, "Oppression and Power: The Unique Status of Black Women in the American Political System," *Social Science Quarterly* 56 (1975): 117–28; Pauline Stone, "Feminist Consciousness and Black Women," in *Women: A Feminist Perspective*, ed. Jo Freeman (Paolo Alto, Calif.: Mayflower Publishing Co., 1979) 1979; Deborah King, "Multiple Jeopardy, Multiple Consciousness: The Context of Black Feminist Ideology," *Signs* 14 (1988): 42–72.

13. Davis, *Women, Race, and Class*; David Jaynes and Robin Williams, *A Common Destiny: Blacks and American Society* (Washington, D.C.: National Academy Press, 1989); Michael C. Dawson, *Behind the Mule: Race and Class in African-American Politics* (Chicago: University of Chicago Press, 1992); Katherine Tate, *From Protest to Politics* (Cambridge, Mass.: Harvard University Press, 1993).

14. Julianne Malveaux, "Gender Differences and Beyond: An Economic Perspective on Diversity and Commonality among Women," in *Theoretical Perspectives on Sexual Difference*, ed. Deborah L. Rhode (New Haven, Conn.: Yale University Press, 1990); Paula S. Rothenberg, *Race, Class, and Gender in the United States: An Integrated Study* (New York: St. Martin's Press, 1995); Audrey Rowe and John M. Jeffries, *The State of Black America* (New York: National Urban League, 1996); Jessie Carney Smith and Carrell P. Horton, *Statistical Record of Black America*, 1997); Irene Browne, ed., *Latinas and African American Women at Work: Race, Gender, and Economic Inequality* (New York: Russell Sage, 1999).

15. Barbara Ransby, "Black Feminism at Twenty-One: Reflections on the Evolution of a National Community," *Signs* 25 (2000): 1218.

16. Tamara Jones, "Building Effective Black Feminist Organizations," *Souls* 2 (2000): 56.

17. Adrien Katherine Wing, ed., *Critical Race Feminism: A Reader* (New York: New York University Press, 1997).

18. Collins, *Black Feminist Thought*; Frederick C. Harris, *Something Within: Religion*

in African American Political Activism (New York: Oxford Press, 1999); bell hooks, *Feminist Theory: From Margin to Center* (Boston: South End Press, 1984); bell hooks, *Talking Back* (Boston: South End Press, 1989); Barbara Smith, "Some Home Truths about the Contemporary Feminist Movement," in *Words of Fire;* Wendy Smooth and Tamelyn Tucker, "Behind But Not Forgotten: Women and the Behind the Scenes Organizing of the Million Man March," in *Still Lifting, Still Climbing: African American Women's Contemporary Activism,* ed. Kimberly Springer (New York: New York University Press, 1999).

19. Smooth and Tucker, "Behind But Not Forgotten."

20. Harris, *Something Within.*

21. Collins, *Black Feminist Thought.*

22. Deborah Robinson, "The Effect of Multiple Group Identity on Race Consciousness" (Ph.D. dissertation, University of Michigan, 1987), 83.

23. Ransby, "Black Feminism at Twenty-One."

24. Robinson, "The Effect of Multiple Group Identity"; Clyde Wilcox, "Black Women and Feminism," *Women and Politics* 10 (1990): 65–84.

25. Elizabeth Almquist, "Untangling the Effects of Race and Sex: The Disadvantaged Status of Black Women," *Social Science Quarterly* 56 (1975): 129–42; King, "Oppression and Power"; Browne, *Latinas and African American Women at Work.*

26. Almquist, "Untangling the Effects," hooks, *Feminist Theory* and *Talking Back;* Guy-Sheftall, *Words of Fire.*

27. Pamela Conover, "Feminists and the Gender Gap," *The Journal of Politics* 50 (1988): 985–1010; Elizabeth Adell Cook, "Measuring Feminist Consciousness," *Women and Politics* 9 (1989): 71–88.

28. Robinson, "The Effect of Multiple Group Identity."

29. Claudine Gay and Katherine Tate, "Doubly Bound: The Impact of Gender and Race on the Politics of Black Women," *Political Psychology* 19 (1998): 169–84.

30. Tate, *From Protest to Politics.*

31. Claire Knoche Fulenwider, *Feminism in American Politics* (New York: Praeger, 1980).

32. Edward Ransford and Jon Miller, "Race, Sex, and Feminist Outlooks," *American Sociological Review* 48 (1983): 46–59.

33. Wilcox, "Black Women and Feminism."

34. Ibid.

35. Jane Mansbridge and Katherine Tate, "Race Trumps Gender: Black Opinion on the Thomas Nomination," *PS: Political Science and Politics* 25 (1992): 488–92.

36. Ibid.

37. Michael C. Dawson, *Black Visions* (Chicago: University of Chicago Press, 2001); Evelyn M. Simien, "Gender Differences in Attitudes Toward Black Feminism Among African Americans," *Political Science Quarterly* 119 (2004): 315–38.

38. Dawson, *Black Visions;* Simien, "Gender Differences."

SELECTED BIBLIOGRAPHY

Andolsen, Barbara. 1986. *"Daughters of Jefferson, Daughters of Bootblacks": Racism and American Feminism.* Macon, Ga.: Mercer University Press.

Andrews, William L. 1986. *Sisters of the Spirit: Three Black Women's Autobiographies of the Nineteenth Century.* Bloomington: Indiana University Press.

Asante, Molefi Kete. 1987. *The Afrocentric Idea.* Philadelphia: Temple University Press.

Baker, Houston. 1972. *Long Black Song.* Charlottesville: University of Virginia Press.

Baker-Fletcher, Karen. 1994. *A Singing Something: Womanist Reflections on Anna Julia Cooper.* New York: Crossroad Press.

Bambara, Toni Cade, ed. 1970. *The Black Woman: An Anthology.* New York: Signet.

Berry, Mary Frances. 1994. *Black Resistance, White Law: A History of Constitutional Racism in America.* New York: Penguin.

Cannon, Katie G. 1988. *Black Womanist Ethics.* Atlanta: Scholars Press.

Carby, Hazel V. 1987. *Reconstructing Womanhood: The Emergence of the Afro-American Woman Novelist.* New York: Oxford University Press.

Cary, Mary Ann Shadd. *Provincial Freeman. 1853–1859.* "Nineteenth Century African-American Newspapers." Accessible Archives, Inc., http://www.accessible.com/search/prdcls.asp.

Christian, Barbara. 1990. "The Race for Theory." In *Making Face, Making Soul: Haciendo Caras,* ed. Gloria Anzaldua. San Francisco: Aunt Lute Books.

———, ed. 1985. *Black Feminist Criticism: Perspectives on Black Women Writers.* New York: Pergamon Press.

Clark Hine, Darlene, Wilma King, and Linda Reed, eds. 1995. *"We Specialize in the Wholly Impossible": A Reader in Black Women's History.* Brooklyn: Carlson Publishing.

Collins, Patricia Hill. 1991, 2000. *Black Feminist Thought: Knowledge, Consciousness, and the Politics of Empowerment.* New York: Routledge.

———. 1998. *Fighting Words: Black Women and the Search for Justice.* Minneapolis: University of Minnesota Press

———. 2006. *From Black Power to Hip Hop: Racism, Nationalism, and Feminism.* Philadelphia: Temple University Press.

Cooper, Anna Julia. 1988 (1892). *A Voice From the South.* Introduction by Mary Helen Washington. Oxford: Oxford University Press.

Davis, Angela Y. 1983. *Women, Race and Class.* New York: Vintage.

———. 1990. *Women, Culture and Politics.* New York: Vintage.

———. 1998. *Blues Legacies and Black Feminism: Gertrude "Ma" Rainey, Bessie Smith, and Billie Holiday.* New York: Pantheon Books.

Delany, Martin R. 1993. *The Condition, Elevation, Emigration, and Destiny of the Colored People of the United States, Politically Considered.* Baltimore: Black Classic Press.

Douglass, Frederick. 1993. *Narrative of the Life of Frederick Douglass, an American Slave, Written by Himself,* ed. David W. Blight. Boston: Bedford Books.

duCille, Ann. 1993. *The Coupling Convention: Sex, Text, and Tradition in Black Women's Fiction.* New York: Oxford University Press.

Foster, Frances Smith. 1993. *Written By Herself: Literary Production by African-American Women, 1746–1892.* Bloomington: Indiana University Press.

Fulenwider, Claire Knoche. 1980. *Feminism in American Politics.* New York: Praeger.

Gere, Anne Ruggles. 1997. *Intimate Practices: Literacy and Cultural Work in U.S. Women's Clubs, 1880–1920.* Urbana: University of Illinois Press.

Giddings, Paula. 1999. *When and Where I Enter: The Impact of Black Women on Race and Sex in America.* New York: Bantam Books.

Gilroy, Paul. 2000. *Against Race: Imagining Political Culture Beyond the Color Line.* Cambridge, Mass.: Harvard University Press.

Gordon, Dexter B. 2003. *Black Identity: Rhetoric, Ideology, and Nineteenth-Century Black Nationalism.* Carbondale: Southern Illinois University Press.

Gordon, Lewis R. 1997. *Her Majesty's Other Children: Sketches of Racism from a Neocolonial Age.* New York: Roman and Littlefield, 1997.

Grant, Jacquelyn. 1989. *White Women's Christ and Black Women's Jesus: Feminist Christiology and Womanist Response.* Atlanta: Scholars Press.

Guy-Sheftall, Beverly, ed. 1995. *Words of Fire: An Anthology of African-American Feminist Thought.* New York: New Press.

Harley, Sharon, and Rosalyn Terborg-Penn, eds. 1978. *The Afro-American Woman: Struggles and Images.* Port Washington, N.Y.: Kennikat Press.

Harper, Frances E. W. 1992 (1892). *Iola Leroy, or Shadows Uplifted.* In *The African-American Novel in the Age of Reaction.* New York: Mentor.

Higginbotham, Evelyn Brooks. 1993. *Righteous Discontent: The Women's Movement in the Black Baptist Church, 1880–1920.* Cambridge, Mass.: Harvard University Press.

Hine, Darlene Clark, Elsa Barkley Brown, and Rosalyn Terborg-Penn, eds. 1993. *Black Women in America: A Historical Encyclopedia.* New York: Carlson.

hooks, bell. 1981. *Ain't I a Woman: Black Women and Feminism.* Boston: South End Press.

———. 1984, 2000. *Feminist Theory: From Margin to Center.* Cambridge: South End Press.

———. 1990. *Yearning: Race, Gender, and Cultural Politics.* Boston: South End Press.

Hopkins, Pauline E. 1988 (1900). *Contending Forces: A Romance Illustrative of Negro Life North and South.* New York: Oxford University Press.

Hull, Gloria T., Patricia Bell Scott, and Barbara Smith, eds. 1986. *But Some of Us Are Brave: Black Women's Studies.* New York: Feminist Press.

Hutton, Frankie. 1993. *The Early Black Press in America, 1827 to 1860.* Westport, Conn.: Greenwood Press.

Jacobs, Harriet [Linda Brent]. 1861. *Incidents in the Life of a Slave Girl, Written by Herself,* ed. L. Maria Child. Boston: for the author. Reprint, New York: Harcourt

Brace Jovanovich, 1973; Cambridge, Mass.: Harvard University Press, 1987; New York: Dover Publications 2001.

James, Joy. 1997. *Transcending the Talented Tenth*. New York: Routledge.

―――. 1999. *Shadowboxing: Representations of Black Feminist Politics*. New York: St. Martin's Press.

James, Stanlie M., and Abena P. A. Busia, eds. 1993. *Theorizing Black Feminisms: The Visionary Pragmatism of Black Women*. New York: Routledge.

Johnson, James Weldon. 1976. *God's Trombones*. New York: Penguin Books.

Jones, Jacqueline. 1985. *Labor of Love, Labor of Sorrow: Black Women, Work, and the Family from Slavery to the Present*. New York: Basic Books.

Lerner, Gerda, ed. 1992. *Black Women in White America: A Documentary History*. New York: Vintage Books.

Lincoln, C. Eric, and Lawrence H. Mamiya. 1990. *The Black Church in the African American Experience*. Durham: Duke University Press.

Loewenberg, Bert James, and Ruth Bogin, eds. 1976. *Black Women in Nineteenth-Century American Life: Their Words, Their Thoughts, Their Feelings*. University Park: Pennsylvania State University Press.

Logan, Shirley Wilson. 1999. *We Are Coming: The Persuasive Discourse of Nineteenth-Century Black Women*. Carbondale: Southern Illinois University Press.

―――. 1995. *With Pen and Voice: A Critical Anthology of Nineteenth-Century African-American Women*. Carbondale: Southern Illinois University Press.

Lorde, Audre. 1984. *Sister/Outsider: Essays and Speeches*. Freedom, Calif.: The Crossing Press.

Morrison, Toni. 1987. *Beloved*. New York: Random House.

―――. ed. 1992. *Rac-ing Justice, En-gendering Power: Essays on Anita Hill, Clarence Thomas, and the Construction of Social Reality*. New York: Pantheon Books.

―――. 1993. *Playing in the Dark: Whiteness and the Literary Imagination*. New York: Vintage Books.

Omolade, Barbara. 1994. *The Rising Song of African American Women*. New York: Routledge.

Painter, Nell Irvin. 1996. *Sojourner Truth: A Life, A Symbol*. New York: W.W. Norton.

Peterson, Carla. 1995. *"Doers of the Word:" African-American Women Speakers and Writers in the North (1830–1880)*. New York: Oxford University Press.

Pough, Gwendolyn D. 2004. *Check It While I Wreck It: Black Womanhood, Hip Hop Culture and the Public Sphere*. Boston: Northeastern University Press.

Prince, Nancy. 1850. *A Narrative of the Life and Travels of Mrs. Nancy Prince. Written by Herself*. Boston: by the author.

Rael, Patrick. 2002. *Black Identity and Black Protest in the Antebellum North*. Chapel Hill: University of North Carolina Press.

Reed, Adolph, Jr. 1999. *Stirrings in the Jug: Black Politics in the Post-Segregation Era*. Minneapolis: University of Minnesota Press.

Rhodes, Jane. 1998. *Mary Ann Shadd Cary: The Black Press and Protest in the Nineteenth Century*. Bloomington: Indiana University Press.

Richardson, Marilyn, ed. 1987. *Maria W. Stewart, America's First Black Woman Political Writer: Essays and Speeches.* Bloomington: Indiana University Press.

Shelby, Tommie. 2005. *We Who Are Dark: The Philosophical Foundations of Black Solidarity.* Cambridge, Mass.: Belknap Press of Harvard University Press.

Smith, Jessie Carney, and Carrell P. Horton. 1997. *Statistical Record of Black America.* Detroit: Gale Research.

Sterling, Dorothy, ed. 1984. *We Are Your Sisters: Black Women in the Nineteenth Century.* New York: W. W. Norton.

Stuckey, Sterling. 1987. *Slave Culture: Nationalist Theory and the Foundations of Black America.* New York: Oxford University Press.

Terborg-Penn, Rosalyn. 1998. *African American Women in the Struggle for the Vote, 1850–1920.* Bloomington: Indiana University Press.

Townsend Gilkes, Cheryl. 2001. *If It Wasn't for the Women: Black Women's Experience and Womanist Culture in Church and Community.* Maryknoll: Orbis Books.

Truth, Sojourner. 1995. "Speech Delivered to the Woman's Rights Convention, Akron, Ohio." In *With Pen and Voice: A Critical Anthology of Nineteenth-Century African-American Women,* ed. Shirley Wilson Logan, 24–27. Carbondale: Southern Illinois University Press.

Walker, Alice. 1983. *In Search of Our Mothers' Gardens: Womanist Prose.* New York: Harcourt Brace Jovanovich.

Walker, David. 2000. *David Walker's APPEAL to the Coloured Citizens of the World,* edited and introduction by Peter P. Hinks. University Park, Penn.: Pennsylvania State University Press.

Waters, Kristin, ed. 2000. *Women and Men Political Theorists: Enlightened Conversations.* Oxford: Blackwell Publishers.

Wells, Ida B. 1997. *Southern Horrors and other Writings: the Anti-Lynching Campaign of Ida B. Wells, 1892–1900,* edited by Jacqueline Jones Royster. Boston: Bedford Books.

Welter, Barbara. 1977. *Dimity Convictions: the American Woman in the Nineteenth Century.* Athens: Ohio University Press.

West, Cornel. 1993. *Race Matters.* Boston, Beacon.

White, Deborah Gray. 1985. *Ar'n't I a Woman? Female Slaves in the Plantation South.* New York: W. W. Norton.

Williams, Patricia J. 1991. *The Alchemy of Race and Rights: Diary of a Law Professor.* Cambridge, Mass.: Harvard University Press.

Wing, Adrien Katherine, ed. 1997. *Critical Race Feminism: A Reader.* New York: New York University Press.

Yellin, Jean Fagin. 1989. *Women and Sisters: The Antislavery Feminists in American Culture.* New Haven, Conn.: Yale University Press.

Yellin, Jean Fagin, and John C. Van Horne, eds. 1997. *The Abolitionist Sisterhood: Women's Political Culture in Antebellum America.* Ithaca, N.Y.: Cornell University Press.

Melina Abdullah teaches Pan-African Studies at California State University, Los Angeles. Her areas of research include black feminism/womanism, political activism and Hip Hop. She earned her Ph.D. and M.A. in Political Science from the University of Southern California and her B.A. in African-American Studies from Howard University. As a scholar-activist, she seeks to engage in work that contributes to the body of scholarly literature, and believes that such scholarship must be linked with tangible work that empowers oppressed communities and leads to substantive change in societal power allocation.

Lena Ampadu is Vice-Chair of and Associate Professor in the English Department at Towson University, where she teaches African American literature, African women writers, and composition and rhetoric. She has scholarly work published in *Callaloo, Composition Studies, African American Rhetoric(s): Interdisciplinary Perspectives*, and *Journal of the Association for Research on Mothering*. Her current research interests include the rhetoric of nineteenth-century African-American women, and oral traditions in the literature of women of African descent.

Karen Baker-Fletcher is Associate Professor of Theology at Perkins School of Theology, Southern Methodist University in Dallas, Texas. An eco-womanist, she is the author of *A Singing Something: Womanist Reflections on Anna Julia Cooper* and *Sisters of Dust, Sisters of Spirit: Womanist Wordings on God and Creation* (Fortress Press, 1998). She has a new book at press with Chalice Press entitled *Dancing with God: Womanist Reflections on the Trinity*, which examines crucifixion, lynching, and hate crime from a Trinitarian perspective.

R. Dianne Bartlow is an Assistant Professor in the Department of Women's Studies at California State University, Northridge. She is a feminist scholar interested in representations of African-American women in popular music, culture, and media, early black feminist thought, and violence against women. Her published work includes co-authoring "Exploring New Frontiers: Women of Color in Academia," in *Women in Mass Communication* (Second Edition), edited by Pamela Creedon, and several creative scholarship projects. Bartlow also has worked extensively in television production and is a multiple Emmy Award winning director/writer/producer.

Hazel V. Carby is the Charles C. and Dorothea S. Dilley Professor of African American Studies and Professor of American Studies and Director of the Initiative on Race, Gender and Globalization at Yale University. Her publications include *Reconstructing Womanhood* (OUP, 1987); *Race Men* (Harvard, 1998); *Cultures in Babylon* (Verso, 1999); "A Strange and Bitter Crop: The Spectacle of Torture," *Open Democracy;* "The New Auction Block: Blackness and the Marketplace," in *Companion to African American Literature,* ed. Lewis Gordon, and "Postcolonial Translations" for Ethnic and Racial Studies. Her current work in progress is Child of Empire: Racializing Subjects in Post WWII Britain. Hazel Carby is a dual citizen of the United Kingdom and the United States.

Patricia Hill Collins, Professor of Sociology at the University of Maryland, is a social theorist whose research and scholarship have dealt primarily with issues of race, gender, social class, sexuality, and/or nation. Her first book, *Black Feminist Thought: Knowledge, Consciousness, and the Politics of Empowerment,* published in 1990, with a revised tenth-year-anniversary edition published in 2000, won the Jessie Bernard Award of the American Sociological Association for significant scholarship in gender and the C. Wright Mills Award of the Society for the Study of Social Problems. She also published *Fighting Words: Black Women and the Search for Justice* (University of Minnesota Press, 1998); *Black Sexual Politics: African Americans, Gender, and the New Racism* (Routledge, 2004); and *From Black Power to Hip Hop: Racism, Nationalism, and Feminism* (Temple University Press, 2005). Professor Collins is also Charles Phelps Taft Emeritus Professor of Sociology within the Department of African American Studies at the University of Cincinnati.

Carol B. Conaway is Joint Assistant Professor of the Department of Communication and the Women's Studies Program at the University of New Hampshire in Durham. Her research is on the intersection of race, ethnicity, gender, and class in the press. Some of her publications include *Framing Identity: The Press and Crown Heights, Crown Heights: The Race War that Wasn't,* and *The Rhetoric of Territory and Peoplehood in Rabbinic Midrashim.* Her current work is on black-Jewish relations and the press. She was a Ford Foundation Fellow, and a Post-Doctoral Fellow of the Shorenstein Center on Press, Politics, and Public Policy at the Kennedy School of Government at Harvard University. A graduate of Bryn Mawr College in philosophy, she received her Ph.D. from MIT in political science.

Olga Idriss Davis is Associate Professor of Communication at the Hugh Downs School of Human Communication at Arizona State University in Tempe. Her work in critical performance studies, Black feminist theory, and womanist theory examines the politics of the Black body, identity, race, gender, sexuality, and class from the discursive construction of power. Her critical work on the Tulsa Race Riot of 1921 points to narrative discourse as a foundational tenet in the search for identity in African-American culture.

Vanessa Holford Diana is Professor of English and Coordinator of the Women's Studies Program at Westfield State College in Westfield, Massachusetts, where she teaches courses in multicultural American literature and women's studies. Her research focuses on fiction by nineteenth- and twentieth-century women writers of color in the United States.

Janice W. Fernheimer is Assistant Professor at Rensselaer Polytechnic Institute, where she teaches interdisciplinary courses in the Language, Literature, and Communication Department. She completed her Ph.D. in English at the University of Texas at Austin. Her doctoral work focused on black Jewish identity construction in the United States and Israel, and the practical application of Kenneth Burke's, Chaim Perelman and Lucie Olbrechts-Tyeca's, and Wayne Booth's rhetorical theories. The project built on primary research conducted in Dimona, Israel, and archival materials housed in the Schomburg Center for Research in Black Culture in New York.

Michelle N. Garfield is Associate Dean in the Franklin College of Arts and Sciences at the University of Georgia. She earned her Bachelor's degree in history from Princeton University. She then attended Yale University, where she earned a Master's degree in African-American Studies. Her Ph.D. in history is from Duke University. She teaches in history and African-American studies. Her research interest is in nineteenth-century African-American history. Dr. Garfield is currently working on a history of a local African-American community in rural Georgia.

Joy James is the John B. and John T. McCoy Presidential Professor of Africana Studies at Williams College. Her publications include *Resisting State Violence: Gender, Race, and Radicalism in US Culture* (Minnesota, 1996); *Transcending the Talented Tenth: Black Leaders and American Intellectuals* (Routledge, 1997); and *Shadowboxing: Representations of Black Feminist Politics* (St. Martin's, 1999). Edited works include the co-edited volume *Spirit, Space and Survival: African American Women in (White) Academe* (Routledge, 1993), which received the 1994 Gustavus Myers Outstanding Book on Human Rights Award. Other edited volumes include *The Angela Y. Davis Reader* (Blackwell, 1998); and *The Black Feminist Reader*, co-edited with T. Denean Sharpley Whiting (Blackwell, 2000).

Valerie Palmer-Mehta is an Assistant Professor of Communication at Oakland University in Rochester, Michigan. Her research examines how power and identities are communicated and negotiated in U.S. public culture. Her work can be found in Elwood Watson's *The Oprah Anthology*, David Lavery's *Reading the Sopranos*, *Journal of American Culture*, and *Text and Performance Quarterly*.

Carla L. Peterson is a Professor in the Department of English at the University of Maryland, and affiliate faculty of the departments of Women's Studies, American Studies, and African-American Studies. She is the author of *"Doers of the Word": African-American Women Speakers and Writers in the North (1830–1880)*. She has published numerous essays on nineteenth-century African-American literature and culture. Her current project is a social and cultural history of African

Americans in nineteenth-century New York City as seen through the lens of family history, tentatively titled *Black Gotham: Family History and African American Community in Nineteenth-Century New York.*

Marilyn Richardson is a former Fellow of Harvard's Radcliffe Institute and the DuBois Institute. Her publications include *Black Women and Religion,* (G.K. Hall) and *Maria W. Stewart: America's First Black Woman Political Writer* (Indiana University Press), along with numerous essays, articles, and reviews. She has taught at Harvard University, Boston University, and the Massachusetts Institute of Technology. She is a former curator of Boston's Museum of Afro-American History and the African Meeting House on Beacon Hill. Richardson is the principal of African-Americana Consultants, providing programming, exhibitions, and research resources to a range of clients including schools, libraries, museums, and historical societies. She currently is completing a book on the nineteenth-century sculptor Edmonia Lewis.

Evelyn M. Simien is an Assistant Professor in the Department of Political Science at the University of Connecticut. Her research has appeared in such peer-reviewed journals as *Frontiers: A Journal of Women's Studies, Social Science Quarterly, the Journal of Black Studies, Women and Politics,* and *Political Science Quarterly.* She is the author of *Black Feminist Voices in Politics.*

Ebony A. Utley is an Assistant Professor of Communication Studies at California State University, Long Beach. Her specializations are rhetorical criticism and rhetorical theory. She was an Arnold L. Mitchem Fellow in the Department of Social and Cultural Sciences at Marquette University. She received her Ph.D. in Communication Studies at Northwestern University. Her dissertation considers how figures of God function as audiences in rap lyrics.

Mary Helen Washington is a Professor of English at the University of Maryland at College Park. She is the editor of *Black-Eyed Susans/Midnight Birds: Stories By and About Black Women* (1980); *Invented Lives: Narratives of Black Women 1860–1960* (1987); and *Memory of Kin: Stories About Family by Black Writers* (1990).

Kristin Waters writes about gender, race, epistemology, and social and political theory. Her publications include an edited collection, *Women and Men Political Theorists: Enlightened Conversations* (Blackwell, 2000); "(Re)turning to the Modern: Radical Feminism and The Postmodern Turn," in *Radically Speaking: Reclaiming Feminism,* ed. Bell and Klein (Spinifex, 1996); and "Women in Kantian Ethics: A Failure in Universality," in *Modern Engendering: Critical Feminist Readings in Modern Western Philosophy,* ed. Bat Ami Bar On (SUNY, 1994). Currently Professor of Philosophy at Worcester State College in Massachusetts, she is also a Visiting Research Associate at the Brandeis University Women's Studies Research Center.

INDEX

Abdullah, Melina, 8

Abjection, black resistance to, 156

Abolitionism: black, 14–15, 18, 59, 218; criticism of white, 94, 95; and literary societies, 5, 118–19, 125; publications, 4, 14–15, 18–20, 31, 58–59, 113–14, 160, 163, 218; and public voice for slaves, 110; vs. racial equality, 218; Stewart's role in, 19, 33; Truth's role in, 160–67; and women's rights movement, 78

Academics and intellectuals, 411–12, 417n61

Academic vs. vocational education for blacks, 254, 373

Activism: collective focus of, 425–26; David Walker's, 15–16, 17; and egalitarian marriage ideal, 187–88; fictional resistance literature as, 4, 173–89; journalistic, 140, 219–20, 333–34; literary societies' role in, 116–27; and oppression, 396, 406; resistance narratives as, 173–89, 329; Wells's, 313–14, 318; and women's role in black community, 394. *See also* Black press; Militant activism; Resistance theory; White press

Adams, John, 30

"Address Before the Afric-American Female Intelligence Society" (Stewart), 32, 42, 47–48, 51, 65–66

"Address Delivered at the African Masonic Hall" (Stewart), 66–67, 370

Adelphic Union, 124

Africa and African culture: and black Christianity, 44, 368, 369; and black women's oppositional knowledges, 403; collectivist perspective in, 132, 154; emigration to, 24, 59, 225–26,

229; as source of cultural pride, 25; and Truth, 6, 131, 154–60, 166; and Wells's storytelling style, 315

Afric-American Female Intelligence Society, 28, 32, 42, 47–48, 51, 65–66, 124

African American, connotational issues, 390n1. *See also entries beginning with "Black"*; Race theory; Racism

African-American oral culture and Truth's rhetoric, 154–61, 165–66

Africana womanism, 41, 42, 52n16

African Baptist Church, 14

African Literary Society, 124

African Masonic Hall, Stewart's speech at, 66–67, 370

African Meeting House, 14, 40

African Methodist Church Review, 206

African Methodist Episcopal (AME) Church, 39, 44

African Methodist Episcopal Zion (AMEZ) Church, 39, 132

Afro-American Jeremiad, The (Howard-Pitney), 57

"Ain't I a Woman?" (Truth), 41, 162–66

Allen, Richard, 50

Alpha Suffrage, 354

Alternative meta-narratives. *See* Oppositional discourses/knowledges

Ambiguity, gender, black women's, 82, 143–44, 156–57, 162–66, 330, 374

Ambiguity of Truth's social position, 135, 136, 149–54, 155–56

AME (African Methodist Episcopal) Church, 39, 44

American Colonization Society, 59, 229

American Equal Rights Association, The, 194

American Moral Reform Society, 121

tional womanhood, 105–8, 156–57, 174–75; and ghettoization, 403; Harper's, 176–81; to Ku Klux Klan march, 357–58; narrative as social activism, 4, 6, 173–89; rhetorical methods, 291–92, 297–98, 309, 316; and Stewart's mission, 5, 17–18, 25; and subtle leadership styles, 8; subversive expression, 6, 32, 98, 108–11, 156, 161–62, 369–70; Truth's, 139, 153, 156; unique forms of black women's, 404; Wells's, 309, 312–19, 323, 325, 334–35, 352. *See also* Abolitionism; Oppositional discourses/knowledges

Restoration theme in black jeremiads, 56, 57

Rhetoric: Cooper's, 288–89, 290, 291, 292–303; definitions, 38–39; fiction as reform, 175; Harper's, 193–212; Prince's, 93; Stewart's, 4, 21–25, 38–51; Truth's, 155–56, 157–60, 160–61, 162, 163; Wells's, 309–25

Rhetorical questioning style, 22, 45, 48–49, 63, 164, 301

Rhodes, Jane, 219, 224, 239–40

Rhythms of discourse, 22, 39, 45–46, 158

Rich, Adrienne, 376

Richardson, Marilyn, 4, 407

Ridley, Florida Ruffin

Right to vote. *See* Suffrage movement

Robinson, Deborah, 425, 427

Root, Maria P. P., 173

Rossi, Alice, 374

Ruffin, Josephine St. Pierre, 339

Running style in Stewart's rhetoric, 46

Rush Education Society, 124

Russwurm, John B., 18, 114, 218

Schiller, Dan, 148

Scholarship, black women's challenges to, 396, 399–400

Schools, independent black, 14. *See also* Education

Scott, Patricia Bell, 380, 382

Second Great Awakening, 134, 135

Second vs. first wave feminism, 201, 203, 208, 210, 279–83, 331

Secular heroines from ancient times, 67–68, 81, 387

Segregation: in antebellum North, 21, 58; of black women's ideas, 399; and black women's labor, 404; and community solidarity, 403, 406; and incarceration of blacks, 8, 377; as perversion of American family tree, 185; Wells's resistance to, 313–14, 334; and white feminist racism, 206

Self-determination for black community, 48

Self-improvement and literary societies, 113–27. *See also* Uplift, racial

Self-reliance ideology: and black press, 217–18; for black women, 40, 72, 91–92, 94, 99–100, 107–8; and emigration solutions, 223, 225–26, 231, 234, 236, 245n40; Haiti as example of, 48; and literary societies, 126; and responsibility for racial uplift, 62; for women, 64, 393–94

Self-representation, 130, 136, 147–54, 174, 179

Sentence shaping, 22, 40, 46–47, 302

Sentimental novel form: and evil master character, 177–78; Jacobs's subversion of, 98, 108–9; as political argumentation, 6, 175; vs. Truth's ethnobiographies, 140; Wilson's use of, 94, 95

Separatism, educational, 388

Separatist-emigrationist perspective, 216, 217, 219, 225–26, 229, 238, 245n40

Sermonic tradition, black, 4–5, 38–47, 51, 133

Sexism: in black activist organizations, 400–401, 421, 422, 424–25; by black men, 220, 221, 222, 224, 227–28, 250–51, 258, 265, 330–31, 355–56, 362n30, 429; and black women's private/public roles, 27, 28; black women's unique experience of, 176–79, 252, 426; Christian, 39–40, 233–34, 252, 368, 371; and Cooper's dismissal as principal, 253–54, 255; in journalism, 19, 221; and Stewart, 26–27, 51. *See also* Private sphere; True womanhood, cult of